Greater Philadelphia and the Nation

A NEW HISTORY FOR THE TWENTY-FIRST CENTURY

VOLUME 2

Greater Philadelphia and the NATION

Edited by

Charlene Mires and Jean R. Soderlund

PENN

University of Pennsylvania Press

Philadelphia

The University of Pennsylvania Press gratefully acknowledges funding support for the print version of *The Encyclopedia of Greater Philadelphia* from the Philadelphia Funder Collaborative for the Semiquincentennial, a philanthropic partnership of the Connelly Foundation, the William Penn Foundation, the Neubauer Family Foundation, the Pew Charitable Trusts, the Hamilton Family Charitable Trust, and Comcast; and from the members of the External Board of Advisors of the University of Pennsylvania Press.

Published by
University of Pennsylvania Press
Philadelphia, Pennsylvania 19104-4112, USA

www.pennpress.org

EU Authorized Representative: Easy Access System Europe
Mustamäe tee 50, 10621 Tallinn, Estonia, gpsr.requests@easproject.com

Printed in the United States of America on acid-free paper

10 9 8 7 6 5 4 3 2 1

Hardcover ISBN: 978-1-5128-2663-0

A catalogue record for this book is available from the Library of Congress.

Cover and Book Design by Shubhani Sarkar, sarkardesignstudio.com

Front cover—*Top: Cecil B. Moore Philadelphia Freedom Fighters* © 2021 City of Philadelphia Mural Arts Program / Felix St. Fort & Gabe Tiberino, 2201 College Avenue. Photo by Steve Weinik. Reprinted by permission. *Bottom:* Chestnut Street banks, 1856, Chromolithograph by Edward Collins and Charles M. Autenrieth, Library Company of Philadelphia.

Back cover—*Top: Signing of the Constitution*, by Howard Chandler Christy, 1940, Architect of the Capitol. *Middle:* Super Bowl celebration, 2018, Photograph by J. Fusco for Visit Philadelphia. *Bottom:* Host Dick Clark (*center*) on the set of *American Bandstand*, 1957, Special Collections Research Center, Temple University Libraries.

Published in association with
The Encyclopedia of Greater Philadelphia

EDITOR-IN-CHIEF
Charlene Mires

Mid-Atlantic Regional Center for the Humanities
(MARCH)
at Rutgers University—Camden

The Greater Philadelphia Region
EDITED BY
Howard Gillette, Jr. AND Carolyn Adams

Greater Philadelphia and the Nation
EDITED BY
Charlene Mires AND Jean R. Soderlund

Greater Philadelphia and the World
EDITED BY
Andrew Heath

Contents

Chapter 5

REVOLUTION REMEMBERED

Chapter 6

CONTRADICTIONS OF ENSLAVEMENT AND SERVITUDE

Chapter 7

CAPITAL OF BLACK AMERICA

Chapter 8

CONTESTING AND EXPANDING THE NATION

Chapter 9

DEFENDING THE NATION

Chapter 10

THE REGION'S REACH TO THE NATION

CHAPTER 11

PHILADELPHIA IN AMERICAN POPULAR CULTURE

Preface

We all exist in place and time. Place may seem easy enough to visualize, starting with the room where you are reading this book, your home, street, and neighborhood. Beyond that immediate view, though, you might need a map to see your town, county, or the route you travel to and from work—and a more extensive map or even a satellite view to find your place within a wider region, the nation, and the world. While existing in those many dimensions, you also inhabit a place in time, marked by a date within the narrative of your personal experience. But this, too, extends and entwines with multiple layers of time, from family lineage and cultural heritage to flows of social, political, and economic history. Compounding matters, none of us stands still. We constantly move in place and time, interacting with multiple communities as visible as a stadium filled with fans or as virtual as a network of users of a data stream.

How are we to fathom this complex web of existence and history, to see not only ourselves but also our neighbors and common interests? How can we know what has gone before and prepare for what may come next? How can we sort through and assess the avalanche of information produced moment by moment in a digital age? These are some of the needs that the editors seek to address with this book, one of a set of three published simultaneously by the University of Pennsylvania Press: *The Greater Philadelphia Region*; *Greater Philadelphia and the Nation*; and *Greater Philadelphia and the World*. This book and its companions derive from more than a decade of collaboration among hundreds of writers, editors, research assistants, and civic partners who took up the challenge of advancing knowledge of Philadelphia and the surrounding region. Their findings first appeared digitally, one topic at a time, in *The Encyclopedia of Greater Philadelphia*. However, these books are not a print replica of the *Encyclopedia*, which at the time of the books' publication exists online at https://philadelphiaencyclopedia.org/ as a project of the Mid-Atlantic Regional Center for the Humanities (MARCH) at Rutgers University—Camden. The books are, instead, curated and updated collections of selected topics. They are arranged thematically, highlighting connections that may not become apparent from casual Internet searching, and framed with new essays that illuminate the rich patterns of the region's experience. The goal is to draw insights from the encyclopedia's many parts, to create a different reading experience and deeper understanding of the region's reach and history.

By happy coincidence, the digital *Encyclopedia of Greater Philadelphia* grew at a pace that enabled publication of these thematic books for 2026, the nation's 250th anniversary. It is a fitting time to reflect on Philadelphia's impact and reach across the region, the nation, and the world. Drawing upon recent generations of scholarship, and often advancing new knowledge, these books convey to the general reading public an up-to-date, diverse history of Philadelphia in its many dimensions. They are milestones that offer starting points for the next generations who take up the challenge of understanding this dynamic region, whether they are pursuing personal knowledge, insights for news reporting or tourism, local information for teaching, foundations for new research, or background for developing public policy.

Philadelphians have not often paused to assess the deep history of their city and the surrounding region. The first attempt came in the 1820s, while memories of the colonial and Revolutionary eras remained. To preserve those memories, John Fanning Watson, a banker, collected oral histories for his *Annals of Philadelphia*, published in multiple editions beginning in 1830. Decades passed before the three-volume *History of Philadelphia, 1690–1884*, appeared as one of many such massive histories published in the years following the nation's centennial. Its lead author, J. Thomas Scharf, a Baltimore-based author of similar histories of his home city and St. Louis, teamed with Philadelphia journalist Thompson Westcott to produce the work. A generation later, in 1912, the prolific biographer and history writer Ellis Paxson Oberholtzer published *Philadelphia: A History of the City and Its People, a Record of 225 Years.* Journalist Joseph Jackson compiled a four-volume *Encyclopedia of Greater Philadelphia* during the 1930s, but the next deep dive into the city's history did not come until the multiple-authored *Philadelphia: A 300-Year History*, which finally appeared in 1982 after many years of effort shepherded to conclusion by historian Russell F. Weigley.

In contrast to these earlier works, this book and its companions encompass not only the city but also a "Greater Philadelphia" extending across eastern Pennsylvania, southern New Jersey, and northern Delaware. "Greater Philadelphia" is a phrase with resonance for Philadelphia dating at least to the 1890s, an era of growth, annexation, and aspiration for cities in the United States. Philadelphia accomplished its greatest leap of annexation earlier, in 1854, when the city's limits extended to the boundaries of Philadelphia County. But in the last decade of the nineteenth century, as electric streetcars brought outlying towns into urban orbits, Philadelphia joined other cities in imagining a "greater" region of cities and suburbs. The phrase "Greater Philadelphia" (or uncapitalized "greater Philadelphia") became common during the period bookended by Chicago's 1889 vote to annex 126 square miles, which allowed it to surpass Philadelphia in population, and the consolidation of five boroughs into "The City of Greater New York" in 1898. During the 1890s, the reach of the streetcar lines also inspired boosters of "Greater Camden" and "Greater Wilmington" to imagine orbits of influence centered on their cities and converging with more populous Philadelphia. As the Wilmington *Evening Journal* editorialized in 1895, "In a few years the great metropoli of Pennsylvania and Delaware will be connected by a chain of residences, and then may come a greater Philadelphia."

More than a geographic term, "Greater Philadelphia" at the turn of the twentieth century signaled superiority and aspiration. Philadelphia politicians invoked the phrase as early as 1894, when Samuel H. Ashbridge campaigned for mayor on the platform "A Greater Philadelphia." By this he meant that an already "great" city could be made greater through improvements such as better port facilities on the Delaware River. Subsequent mayoral candidates, both Democrats and Republicans championed Greater Philadelphia as a shorthand for their commitment to progress. By the time John E. Reyburn served as mayor, between 1907 and 1911, the Greater Philadelphia envisioned by his comprehensive planning committees included projects such as the diagonal parkway between city hall and Fairmount Park, a convention hall, and modern subways.

Philadelphia businesses also adopted and propelled "Greater Philadelphia" into common usage. In the wake of the economic panic of 1893, for example, the Wanamaker & Brown and William H. Wanamaker stores celebrated their survival in business with ads published in three states proclaiming, "Greater Philadelphia recognized our courage and sound judgment by flocking into our stores." Newspaper ads for the larger Wanamaker's department store regularly described its scope of business as "Greater Philadelphia," and Gimbel Brothers ran "Greater Philadelphia Sales." Reaching out to the wider region, the J.B. Van Sciver Company of Camden proclaimed itself "The Furniture Center of Greater Philadelphia." During the First World War, shipbuilding on the Delaware River helped to define a "Greater Philadelphia" industrial region uniting the three states of Pennsylvania, New Jersey, and Delaware.

By the 1920s, organizations and businesses ranging from sports clubs to real estate firms adopted names starting with "Greater Philadelphia" to associate their activities not only with the city but also its suburbs. The phrase reached greatest prominence in the middle of the twentieth century, when business leaders formed a Greater Philadelphia Movement to reform the city's corrupt politics and redevelop Center City, but it echoed through organizational names into the twenty-first century. While indicating scopes of interest connecting the city and its suburbs, the phrase continued to infer aspirations to greatness.

This book adopts "Greater Philadelphia" in its geographic sense to indicate a regional scope. Like earlier uses, the term as used here is not limited by a fixed geographic boundary but rather refers to the interdependence between the city and its periphery across parts of three states: southeastern Pennsylvania, southern New Jersey, and northern Delaware. Embedded in this region are flows of people, cultures, ideas, and products that connect the Philadelphia area with the nation and the world. Each topic developed for *The Encyclopedia of Greater Philadelphia*, the source for many of the essays in this book, represents a focused investigation into the region's scope and impact. The extent of the region emerges differently by topic and across time, but patterns are evident and revealing.

To highlight connections among topics, section introductions and conclusions in this book were written by the volume co-editors, Jean R. Soderlund (chapters 3, 4, 6, and 7) and Charlene Mires (chapters 5, 9, 10, and 11). The co-editors collaborated on chapter 8 and acknowledge the inspiration of the essay "Cradle of Liberty," by Gary B. Nash, in the online *Encyclopedia of Greater Philadelphia*. Numerous editors of *The Encyclopedia of Greater Philadelphia* had a hand in developing the selected essays, and they are listed in the acknowledgments that follow the text. Also important to production of this manuscript were managing editor Hillary S. Kativa, who coordinated the illustrations; copy editor (and website managing editor) Donald D. Groff; copy editor Tamara Gaskell; editorial assistants Joshua DiPrima, Luke Hoheisel, and Elizabeth Eimer; and our editor Robert Lockhart of the University of Pennsylvania Press. In keeping with the goals of *The Encyclopedia of Greater Philadelphia*, we hope that the collective effort to create this book serves to connect the past with the present, to build community, and to create a legacy that benefits the Philadelphia region.

CHARLENE MIRES

Editor-in-Chief,
The Encyclopedia of Greater Philadelphia

Chapter 1

CHALLENGING THE NATION'S PARADOX

FREEDOM SEEKERS AND ENTREPRENEURS

Jean R. Soderlund

In 1774, the First Continental Congress met in Carpenters' Hall, Philadelphia, to organize resistance to Great Britain's actions against the North American colonies. Two years later, on July 4, 1776, the Second Continental Congress issued the Declaration of Independence, forming a new nation, the United States. Signed in the Pennsylvania State House (later Independence Hall), the declaration proclaimed that "all men are created equal, that they are endowed by their Creator with certain unalienable Rights, that among these are Life, Liberty and the pursuit of Happiness."

Even as these words were written, and throughout the Revolutionary War, Constitutional Convention, and 250 years since 1776, fulfilling the promise of freedom and equality remained contested and complex. The nation's fundamental paradox was insistent and clear as enslavement, racial violence, and injustice existed side-by-side with the declaration's promises. The Philadelphia region, like the nation, prospered as people fled oppression, expanded definitions of freedom, and followed entrepreneurial dreams. Yet the nation's paradox persisted, as many sought liberty and opportunity for themselves while denying these rights to others.

The declaration's words held special resonance in the Delaware Valley, where a century earlier William Penn and other founders of Pennsylvania, West New Jersey, and Delaware built on the mutual goals of personal liberty and peace developed between Lenape people and Swedish and Finnish colonists in the seventeenth century. The Quaker founders sought economic opportunity and freedom from religious persecution in their homelands, but at the same time refrained from offering liberty to all. While welcoming people of many religions and creating governments that empowered a broad electorate of free white men, they enslaved people imported from Africa and the Caribbean and denied economic and political rights to women. Amid the eighteenth-century surge of people arriving from Great Britain, Europe, and Africa, Benjamin Franklin fled to Philadelphia from an apprenticeship in Boston to build a successful career in printing. An entrepreneur as well as freedom seeker, he created civic and cultural organizations and served as postmaster general, diplomat, and statesman. He too enslaved Black people, joining the antislavery campaign only in his later years when he became president of the Pennsylvania Abolition Society.[1]

When Philadelphia served as the nation's capital during the American Revolution and the 1790s, Franklin was one of many regional entrepreneurs and freedom seekers who influenced national policy and debates. Political, moral, religious, and economic leaders and their followers—many born in the Delaware Valley and new arrivals—sought practical fulfillment of the founding ideals of the region and United States. The immigrants Thomas Paine, Charles Thomson, and Esther DeBerdt Reed settled in the Delaware Valley, then made key contributions during the Revolution. Paine aroused Patriot support with the stirring pamphlet *Common Sense*, while Thomson served as secretary of the Continental

Congresses and Reed led an effort among Philadelphia women to raise funds for the Continental army. Delaware's Caesar Rodney rode through the night to cast a pivotal vote for independence. One of many enslavers among the declaration's signers, Rodney exemplified the paradox of the nation's birth. Before and during the Revolution, enslaved and free Black people, with Quaker allies, worked to abolish enslavement. In 1780, Pennsylvania's radical unicameral assembly took the first legislative antislavery action in the nation. The Gradual Abolition Act of 1780 was significantly flawed but served as a foundation to undermine enslavement in the North.

The battle against enslavement and racism influenced the culture and politics of the Philadelphia region throughout its history. African American entrepreneurs, moral and religious leaders, and freedom seekers made Philadelphia the capital of Black America in the late eighteenth and early nineteenth centuries, a period of national economic growth and increasing conflict between the North and South. Among Black abolitionists and entrepreneurs in Philadelphia, James Forten served on an American privateer during the Revolution, then owned and expanded a sailmaking business on the city's waterfront. Richard Allen and Absalom Jones, who were born enslaved, founded churches and antislavery organizations that anchored Black communities. Allen's church, Mother Bethel African Methodist Episcopal Church at Sixth and Lombard Streets in Philadelphia, grew into a national and international denomination. Black activists petitioned the U.S. Congress against enslavement, opposed laws to restrict freedom seekers from settling in Pennsylvania, and fought for suffrage and equal rights. Beginning in the 1830s, Black abolitionists Robert Purvis, Margaretta Forten, William Still, and others pushed the region to the center of national debates over fugitive slave laws and kidnapping of free Black people by southerners. Heroes such as Harriet Tubman operated the Underground Railroad through Delaware, Pennsylvania, and New Jersey, expanding its scope after passage of the national Fugitive Slave Act of 1850, which jeopardized the freedom of Black people throughout the North. Seeking liberty and opportunity was fraught with danger, whether on rural roads or city streets. In the 1830s and 1840s, Black residents in Philadelphia faced assaults by Irish immigrants and other white people. Irish Catholics then became targets of native-born Protestants who attacked their neighborhoods and churches.

The Philadelphia region, as the nation's first major banking center and early shipbuilding hub, shaped U.S. economic and military development. To solve the nation's financial crisis during the Revolutionary War, Philadelphia financier Robert Morris, who was an enslaver and participated in the Atlantic slave trade, in 1781 obtained a charter for the Bank of North America, the first commercial bank to conduct business with and for the U.S. government. The bank stabilized the nation's currency, protected the Confederation Congress from bankruptcy, and served as a precedent for the first Bank of the United States, founded in 1791 while Philadelphia was the nation's capital. When the Bank of the United States charter expired in 1811, Stephen Girard, an immigrant from France, purchased the stock of the Philadelphia branch, creating a private business, Girard Bank. He provided much of the funding for the War of 1812. The owner of a Louisiana plantation worked by enslaved people, Girard in 1831 bequeathed a large part of his immense fortune to establish a boarding school for poor white orphaned boys in Philadelphia, which in 1848 became Girard College. In 1968, civil rights activists won desegregation of the school after a long legal battle and protests led by the militant lawyer and politician Cecil B. Moore.

Entrepreneurs in the Philadelphia area similarly developed industries that promoted commercial aspirations beyond the nation's borders. Based on shipbuilding that had existed on the Delaware River since the seventeenth century, shipyards and affiliated crafts constructed vessels during the Revolution and again after Congress passed the Naval Act of 1794 establishing the U.S. Navy. In 1798, during the Quasi-War with France, Philadelphia residents raised funds to build the warship *Philadelphia*, commissioned in 1800 to protect American ships from the French and against Mediterranean pirates during the First Barbary War. In 1801, Congress designated Southwark as the site of the Philadelphia Navy Yard (later moved to League Island), which built, repaired, overhauled, and provisioned ships during the War of 1812, Civil War, World Wars I and II, and other conflicts until its closure in 1996.

The Civil War brought economic opportunity and the national abolition of enslavement along with

FIGURE 1. *Preparation for War to defend Commerce. The Swedish Church Southwark with the building of the Frigate* Philadelphia, by William Birch, 1800. LIBRARY OF CONGRESS.

unprecedented destruction of lives and property in the United States. After the Confederate assault on Fort Sumter in 1861, Delaware Valley men signed up quickly to fill Union ranks. In 1863, General George G. Meade of Philadelphia assumed command of the Union Army of the Potomac, which defeated General Robert E. Lee's Confederate army at the Battle of Gettysburg. Black men from the Philadelphia area joined the Fifty-Fourth and Fifty-Fifth Massachusetts Voluntary Infantry Regiments after federal approval of enlistment of African Americans in 1863. Black leaders Octavius V. Catto and Jacob C. White then helped to raise eleven U.S. Colored Troops regiments that trained just north of Philadelphia at Camp William Penn. The region's industry, railroads, and wharves played a major role in the Union effort as Frankford Arsenal produced munitions and Delaware's DuPont Company supplied approximately 40 percent of the army's black powder. Philadelphia financier Jay Cooke, who had arrived in Philadelphia in 1838, assisted President Abraham Lincoln's administration in funding the Union military by selling more than $500 million in bonds throughout the nation, earning a handsome commission for himself.

The Delaware Valley, like the nation, faced a mix of challenges and opportunities after the Civil War. Octavius Catto, Caroline LeCount, William

FIGURE 2. Congress of Racial Equality activists sat at the base of the Liberty Bell, while others demonstrated outside Independence Hall, September 21, 1963. SPECIAL COLLECTIONS RESEARCH CENTER, TEMPLE UNIVERSITY LIBRARIES.

Still, members of the Philadelphia Female Anti-Slavery Society, and others fought segregation on Philadelphia streetcars when Black soldiers were denied transportation to Camp William Penn. The Pennsylvania legislature responded in 1867, outlawing segregation on public transit. With a history of education for Black people in the region since the colonial period, Philadelphia-area residents, particularly women, traveled to teach at freedmen's schools in the South. Among educators and activists in the Delaware Valley, Fanny Jackson Coppin, who was born enslaved in Washington, D.C., in 1865 graduated from Oberlin College and began teaching Greek, Latin, and mathematics at Philadelphia's Institute for Colored Youth (later Cheyney University). In 1869, she became principal, expanding the curriculum and working with employers to hire her students in jobs appropriate for their education. Coppin was also active in national organizations and, in 1902, became an African Methodist Episcopal missionary to Cape Town, South Africa.

In the twentieth century, during the period of two world wars, large numbers of Black Americans fled violence, segregation, and poverty in the South to find freedom and opportunity in northern cities. In Philadelphia, Camden, and other parts of the Delaware Valley, they sought work in companies such as the Cramp and Sun shipyards, Baldwin Locomotive, Pennsylvania and Reading Railroads, Campbell Soup, and Philadelphia Transportation Company. As in the 1830s and 1840s, they encountered hostility, including deadly riots in Chester in 1917 and Philadelphia in 1918 and, during World War II, the hate strike by white workers at the Philadelphia Transportation Company in reaction to the company's decision to employ Black drivers and conductors. Among those who relocated from Georgia was Richard R. Wright Sr., who was born enslaved, became a teacher and college president in Savannah, and then moved to Philadelphia in 1921. He founded National Freedom Day in 1942 to commemorate approval of the Thirteenth Amendment to the U.S. Constitution and the ongoing contest for equal rights.

With migration from the South, African American organizations in New Jersey and Pennsylvania took advantage of increased voting strength to gain civil rights protections, for example the successful effort by the National Association for the Advancement of Colored People (NAACP) to gain protection against discrimination in the 1947 New Jersey Constitution. When New Jersey voters approved the new constitution by a three-to-one majority, the NAACP called them "torchbearers for justice." Progress was slow in the Delaware Valley, however, as fair employment programs remained gradual, dependent upon white employers, unions, and workers to adopt nondiscrimination.[2]

The Reverend Leon Sullivan of Philadelphia's Zion Baptist Church fused economic, political, and moral strategies to target unfair labor practices while highlighting the contradictions embedded in the Declaration of Independence. His campaign built on civil rights tactics used in the Depression, "Don't Buy Where You Can't Work" protests, and economic boycotts like those of the American Revolution. Sullivan used the power of Black churches throughout the region, in 1959 calling together "the 400 Ministers" to boycott thirty companies, including Tasty Baking Company,

Breyer Ice Cream Company, Sunoco, Pepsi-Cola, and Gulf Oil. Sullivan gained national prominence with the success of his selective patronage program, which Martin Luther King Jr.'s Southern Christian Leadership Conference adopted in 1962 as Operation Breadbasket. Chapters of the Congress of Racial Equality and Maggie Kuhn's Gray Panthers used similar tactics in their civil rights campaigns.[3]

The struggle for rights extended beyond the region's African American organizations. In the late nineteenth and twentieth centuries, industrialization in the Delaware Valley, as in the United States, encouraged migration of Chinese and Puerto Rican people who organized collectively to establish strong communities and defend individual rights. During the 1870s and 1880s, Chinese migrants settled at Ninth and Race Streets in Philadelphia after being forced out of the American West by racist violence. They established laundries, shops, restaurants, and homes in the neighborhood known as Chinatown, which continues—despite periodic threats of displacement by eminent domain and developers—to serve as a social and cultural hub for Asian Americans from throughout the Philadelphia region. By 1900, small numbers of people migrated from Puerto Rico to Philadelphia where they worked in Baldwin Locomotive Works, cigar factories, and on the wharves. During and after World War I, many arrived from the island as the Campbell Soup Company, for example, attracted workers to its Camden plant and as local farms sought agricultural laborers. Families settled in Philadelphia, Camden, and rural South Jersey, forming community organizations, businesses, and church congregations.[4]

In the twenty-first century, battles continued for equality and freedom in education, employment, women's and LGBT rights, voting rights, and health care—indeed they continued for life itself as the murders of George Floyd in Minneapolis, Minnesota, and men and women in other cities and towns made clear. One response to these murders by activist groups such as Black Lives Matter was to reassess who should be memorialized as national and regional heroes. Recent memorials to Richard Allen, Octavius V. Catto, Fanny Jackson Coppin, and Leon Sullivan highlight the importance of recognizing their contributions and stature in a region that has for years prominently honored William Penn, Benjamin Franklin, Walt Whitman, and Commodore John Barry.

Freedom seekers and entrepreneurs of the Greater Philadelphia region have animated the words of the Declaration of Independence, expanding their meaning to construct a more inclusive community. Paradoxically, some of these same people have erected barriers for others to achieve their dreams. Champions of freedom continue the region's legacy and inspire emulation and innovation. More than tourist attractions and memorials to the Revolutionary War, the Liberty Bell, Independence Hall, and the President's House symbolize the centuries-long struggles of individuals and groups over who may share in the nation's promise of equal rights to life, liberty, and the pursuit of happiness.

NOTES

1. More detail and sources for most of this essay can be found in this volume. For more information and sources on the Lenape people and colonists in the Delaware Valley, see Howard Gillette Jr. and Carolyn T. Adams, eds., *The Greater Philadelphia Region: A New History for the Twenty-First Century*, vol. 1 (University of Pennsylvania Press, 2026).
2. Thomas J. Sugrue, *Sweet Land of Liberty: The Forgotten Struggle for Civil Rights in the North* (Random House, 2008), 116–21.
3. Sugrue, *Sweet Land of Liberty*, 126–29.
4. On immigration and industrialization, see Andrew Heath, ed., *Greater Philadelphia and the World: A New History for the Twenty-First Century*, vol. 3 (University of Pennsylvania Press, 2026).

Chesnut hill
Swedes Ford
Reading 22 Miles
GERMAN TOWN
actual Survey
made by
SCULL
of the Province
ylvania
MAP
Engraved by
JACKSON
Falls
Germantown
Old Road
New Road
Road to Reading
Cohoksink Rivulet
a Ferry
Governor Penns House
Barracks
Kinsington
Lancaster 66 Miles
a Ferry
Road
Ferry
Coopers Ferry
PHILADELPHIA
SCHUYLKILL
RIVER
PENNSYLVANIA
Old Barracks
Chester and Derby Road
Road
Stream

Chapter 2

A Nation's Past, the Region's Legacy

Charlene Mires

The Philadelphia region's deep history, reaching back to the eras of Lenape sovereignty, colonization, and the emergence of a new nation, has bestowed multiple legacies tied to the past. Some of these legacies suggest timelessness, like the Lenape people's designation for their homeland, "Lenapehoking." Others are hopeful and visionary, yet difficult to uphold. From William Penn, Philadelphia inherited aspirations for a "City of Brotherly Love," the "Holy Experiment," and the "greene Country Towne." Echoing from the past, "The Quaker City" persisted as a Philadelphia reputation, joined by "Cradle of Liberty" as a memory of the American Revolution and "Athens of America" as a reference to prominence in fine arts—identities also claimed by Boston.[1]

Legacies such as these have defined and elevated Greater Philadelphia's place in American history. They do not, however, mark the end of the region's role in the life of a growing and changing nation. With historic legacies in tow, Philadelphians and their neighbors forged into the future. The city and nearby counties in southeastern Pennsylvania, South Jersey, and northern Delaware often embraced their distinctive pasts to create pride of place, to honor ancestral ties, and to yield economic benefits. Because milestone events in the nation's founding occurred in Philadelphia, the city and iconic regional places like Valley Forge appeared in every child's history textbook. But at the same time, the region sought to be economically competitive, contemporary, and impactful as the nation expanded across the continent. Greater Philadelphia grappled with the persistent challenges of being simultaneously historic and modern; people of the region acted locally not only to honor the past but also to challenge the nation to live up to its founding ideals.

The question of how the region would embrace or shake loose from its historic past can be traced to at least the early nineteenth century. During the 1820s and 1830s the new phenomenon of leisure tourism, made possible by expanding transportation networks, suggested that the Philadelphia region's greatest appeal might lie not only in its historic places but even more so with contemporary innovations, cultural institutions, and sites of scenic beauty. Tourists of this era sought out the Fairmount Water Works, Eastern State Penitentiary, and the monumental Laurel Hill Cemetery. They took in exhibitions at the Pennsylvania Academy of the Fine Arts or Charles Willson Peale's Museum, attended theatrical performances, and explored nature in public gardens and along the Wissahickon Valley. Some also pursued places with historic associations, but the old Pennsylvania State House, where Americans declared independence from Great Britain in 1776, remained in use for courts and other purposes. Philadelphians had rescued the building from demolition in part for its historic value but also because the work of democracy literally continued to take place there when ballots were collected and counted on election days.

Gradually over the nineteenth century, the old State House became fully presented to the public as a historic site and known as Independence Hall. Regard for the

FIGURE 3. Philadelphia City Hall's William Penn statue in the foreground of One Liberty Place, 2010. History prevailed over the Philadelphia skyline until late in the twentieth century. PHOTOGRAPH BY G. WIDMAN FOR VISIT PHILADELPHIA.

eighteenth-century landmark paralleled the emergence of local historical societies, founded mostly by white elites devoted to the colonial and Revolutionary past. During the tumultuous first half of the nineteenth century, Philadelphia and its historic associations also served as touchstones for defending and contesting the scope of the nation's founding ideals. Native-born, white Americans invoked the legacy of the founders to the point of violence against immigrants and their communities. African Americans, women, and laborers deployed the language of the American Revolution to assert their rights as citizens.[2]

The pull between past and present resonated in Philadelphia through the late 1860s and early 1870s during the debate over where to build a new city hall. In a nation expanding westward and spawning newer interior competitors like Cincinnati, St. Louis, and Chicago, Philadelphia's municipal government continued to occupy eighteenth-century buildings on Independence Square. Some argued that a new city hall should be placed in that traditional location, surrounding Independence Hall, but others regarded the square as hallowed ground. Another proposed site, Washington Square, also carried associations with the American Revolution as a burial ground later named for the first president of the United States. The debate over memory of the Revolution mixed with the legacies of William Penn and his surveyor, Thomas Holme, who had designated a center square for future public buildings. Ultimately, the choice of the center square followed the westward growth of the city while also honoring Philadelphia's mix of historical legacies—sparing Independence Square from being obliterated by a massive municipal building fit for the nineteenth century (dwarfing Independence Hall), eliminating Washington Square as an option, and placing city hall at the site Penn intended. The resulting building by John McArthur Jr., the world's tallest occupied structure and the nation's largest municipal building when completed in 1901, announced Philadelphia as a modern city capable of great things (although by the time of its completion, its Second Empire style of architecture had fallen out of fashion). Alexander Milne Calder's statue of William Penn atop the tower signaled a city that retained pride in its past, although the decades-long period of construction also reflected another emerging reputation of Philadelphia, which journalist Lincoln Steffens labeled "the most corrupt and the most contented" of American cities.[3]

The region's desire to move forward while also capitalizing on the past resonated through the grandest of national commemorations, the centennial of the Declaration of Independence in 1876. Philadelphia and surrounding counties had historic sites of the American Revolution in abundance, and their appeal could not be denied. However, Philadelphia also was a booming industrial city seeking to highlight modern progress in a nation that spanned from coast to coast. In 1876, Independence Hall attracted visitors with new exhibits styled as the "National Museum" and took center stage for the Fourth of July, but the modern marvels of the Centennial Exhibition in Fairmount Park—the first full-scale world's fair in the United States—drew greater attention. There, more than ten million visitors (including local people and repeat visits) could witness the spectacle of the massive Corliss steam engine powering the exhibits of Machinery Hall and admire the latest arts and manufactures from around the world. Alexander Graham Bell demonstrated his new invention, the telephone. History served as a baseline for measuring how far the nation, and Philadelphia, had come. While celebrating progress, however, exhibits at the Centennial rendered Native Americans as primitive people of the past. Women, African Americans, Irish Catholics, and Jewish Americans acted on their own initiative to create monuments or exhibits to commemorate their contributions to the nation. In the wake of the Civil War, few southerners contributed to the exhibits or attended.

Despite the elevation of William Penn to the top of Philadelphia City Hall, where he remained the highest point of the skyline for most of the twentieth century, visions for the future of Philadelphia and the region during the late nineteenth and early twentieth century emphasized growth, progress, and modern improvements. Civic leaders promoted a "Greater Philadelphia" (as well as "Greater Camden" and "Greater Wilmington"), a "City of Homes," the "Workshop of the World," and the "City of Firsts." Other American cities claimed similar (and in some instances, identical) mantles in their competition for economic advancement. For example, the newer city of Chicago, which surpassed Philadelphia in population to become the nation's second-largest city by 1890, also became known as a "City of Homes."

This era of great waves of industrialization, urbanization, immigration, and internal migration also provoked initiatives to embrace and preserve the past. In and around Philadelphia, a fundraising campaign during the 1890s saved the Betsy Ross House from demolition, Pennsylvania appointed the Valley Forge Park Commission in 1893, and New Jersey made the Indian King Tavern (built ca. 1750) in Haddonfield its first government-owned historic site in 1903. The first preservation organization in Delaware, the Friends of Old Drawyers, formed in 1895 to save the Presbyterian church by that name (built ca. 1773) in New Castle County. Such projects often emanated from Americans who could trace their lineage to European colonial and Revolutionary ancestors. Notably, however, local initiatives also assured that African American contributions to American history would be documented. As migration from the South brought new Black residents to the region, Philadelphia African Americans with deeper roots formed the American Negro Historical Society in 1897. A narrative of local Black history spanning enslavement, freedom, and the impact of migration on the city also appeared in W. E. B. Du Bois's landmark sociological study, *The Philadelphia Negro* (1899). In 1913, Black leaders organized the Pennsylvania Emancipation Exposition to mark the fiftieth anniversary of freedom with demonstrations of African American economic, political, and social progress.

Philadelphia had another chance for national attention in 1926, the 150th anniversary of the Declaration of Independence. In keeping with the times, the 1926 Sesquicentennial International Exposition in

South Philadelphia turned the city's historic assets into modern spectacles. It was not enough that Philadelphia had the Liberty Bell, which had reached celebrity status while touring the nation by rail on seven occasions between 1885 and 1915. At the Sesquicentennial, visitors encountered an eighty-foot-tall, electrified Liberty Bell studded with twenty-six thousand light bulbs straddling Broad Street. It was not enough that the oldest sections of the city retained original buildings from the eighteenth century. Visitors could avoid venturing into slum conditions in the shadow of Independence Hall because a faux-colonial "High Street" of replica eighteenth-century buildings had been created on the Sesquicentennial grounds, simultaneously old and new, "historic" yet cleaned up for convenient consumption.

Forces of past and present combined to reshape the landscape of Philadelphia in the first half of the twentieth century. City planners and architects, seeking to counteract deteriorating urban conditions, carried out projects such as the Benjamin Franklin Parkway (built 1917–26) and joined with patriotic citizens to support creation of Independence National Historical Park (authorized by Congress in 1948). These projects, requiring demolition of many blocks of eighteenth- and nineteenth-century structures and displacing businesses and people who occupied them, created new, attractive cultural districts and settings for the large-scale events that became a hallmark of Philadelphia later in the century.

Historic sites associated with bedrock American ideals escalated in appeal in the years following World War II, when the Cold War between the United States and the Soviet Union placed a high value on the "American way of life." Long lines formed at Independence Hall as families sought to instill civic values in their children during vacation trips made possible by new interstate highways. Philadelphia boosters recognized the economic benefits of this historical tourism, which contributed to regional prominence even as the nation's population began to shift toward Sun Belt cities like Los Angeles and Houston. But local promoters also sought to modernize the city's appeal. In 1960 the Convention and Visitors Bureau opened a new headquarters and visitor center resembling a space-age flying saucer near the foot of the Benjamin Franklin Parkway, a mile west of the "historic district." After a 1967 study found that visitors considered Philadelphia an above-average place to visit historic sites, but not especially exciting, tourism promoters countered with slogans inviting visitors to have a "Philadelphia Fling" and promising that "Summer Time is Fun Time in Philadelphia." Philadelphians themselves seemed to need convincing of the city's charms, as evidenced by a billboard and slogan for a Chamber of Commerce event in 1972: "Philadelphia isn't as bad as Philadelphians say it is."

The approaching 1976 bicentennial of the Declaration of Independence offered a new opportunity to capitalize on the region's claims to historical fame, but in a new national context. Civil rights movements of the 1950s and 1960s had awakened demands for a more inclusive, complex history of the United States. Locally, Philadelphia gained increased attention to ethnic and immigrant experiences with the founding of the Balch Institute for Ethnic Studies in 1971. For the Bicentennial—a decentralized, nationwide celebration—Philadelphia created attractions that reached beyond the largely Eurocentric, elite narratives of the nation's founding that had dominated earlier commemorations. Bicentennial initiatives included the Afro-American Historical and Cultural Museum (later renamed the African American Museum in Philadelphia), the National Museum of Jewish American History, a Living History Center, and the Mummers Museum. The traditional center of historical attention, Independence National Historical Park, added modern amenities. History literally moved forward in space and time when the Liberty Bell was relocated from Independence Hall to its own new, modern pavilion. The Bicentennial year showed Philadelphians embracing history but adapting it for twentieth-century expectations and purposes.

The region's historic attributes became increasingly important as economic assets during the 1980s and 1990s, as globalization made place marketing a key strategy for localities seeking to differentiate themselves and attract investment. During this period, Philadelphia literally reached new heights by allowing glass-clad skyscrapers to reach higher than the statue of William Penn atop city hall. Yet the region's painful transition from industrial powerhouse to the postindustrial economy (including its slip in 1990 to fifth-ranking city in population behind New York, Los Angeles, Chicago, and Houston) also raised the stakes for heritage tourism as a sector of the regional economy. Success depended on reaching new audiences and marketing both the old and the new—for example, promising that gay and lesbian travelers could "Get Your History Straight and Your Night Life Gay." Ironically, places that had appealed to nineteenth-century tourists because they were new and innovative, such as Eastern State Penitentiary and the Fairmount Water Works, gained new purposes as historic places and education centers. At these sites and many more, complexities of the nation's history rooted in race and social justice moved more to the forefront of the region's historic identity, often as a result of persistent local activism. Tourists encountered a broader, more complex presentation of Philadelphia's place in the nation's history, including enslavement in George Washington's presidential residence and fugitive slave hearings in Independence Hall itself. The modern appeal of the city and the region also built upon the arts, on museums and sites focusing on science and medicine, on sports and recreation, on activities for children, on a surge of innovative restaurants, and on depictions of Philadelphia in popular culture.

It is too soon to know what the commemoration of the nation's 250th anniversary in 2026 will reveal about the region's dual characters as local and national, historic and modern. Local people and places have demonstrated the capacity to protect and celebrate historical legacies with national significance, even while desiring to complicate those legacies and move forward with changing times. Amid skyscrapers, highways, and suburban sprawl, the past remains embedded in the lived experience of Philadelphia and the surrounding region. History continues to be made, building on the past and creating new legacies for the future.

NOTES

1. These and other aspects of Philadelphia's reputation are explored further in the digital *Encyclopedia of Greater Philadelphia*, https://philadelphiaencyclopedia.org/themes/.

2. See Gary B. Nash, *First City: Philadelphia and the Forging of Historical Memory* (Philadelphia: University of Pennsylvania Press, 2002); Charlene Mires, *Independence Hall in American Memory* (Philadelphia: University of Pennsylvania Press, 2002).

3. Howard Gillette Jr., "Philadelphia City Hall: Monument to a New Political Machine," *Pennsylvania Magazine of History and Biography* 97, no. 2 (April 1973): 233–49.

Chapter 3

Nation Founded

Introduction

From 1764 to 1789, the Delaware Valley became the birthplace of American independence and the new nation, conceived through debate within Philadelphia's halls and accomplished through bloodshed in streets, roads, and fields. During the Revolutionary War, the fledgling nation's survival and growth depended significantly on the city and the larger Philadelphia region as troops attacked and stripped provisions from homes. The transition from the imperial monarchy to a republican government, achieved through crowd actions, major battles and skirmishes, two Continental Congresses, the Confederation Congress, and the Constitutional Convention, transformed Philadelphia from a growing provincial seaport to the first capital of the United States.

The Philadelphia region quickly became involved in the Revolutionary crisis that began in the British North American colonies soon after the Seven Years' War (1756–63). Crowds protested and merchants boycotted British goods in Philadelphia and other ports when the British government attempted to force the colonists to help pay for the war and ongoing military and administrative costs. In 1764, Parliament passed the Sugar and Currency Acts that enlarged the power of vice-admiralty courts, which lacked juries; expanded the use of search warrants; and prohibited legislatures from issuing paper money. While colonists disputed these laws, the Stamp Act (1765) caused a storm of opposition because Parliament rather than the representative provincial assemblies imposed an internal tax on newspapers and documents such as deeds, liquor licenses, and playing cards. Activists denounced this as a blatant case of taxation without representation. Though Parliament repealed the Stamp Act in 1766, after British manufacturers petitioned for relief from colonial boycotts, the British government continued to claim it could enact laws for the colonies "in all cases whatsoever." Passage of the Townshend Revenue Act (1767), which placed import duties on tea, glass, paper, lead, and paint, elicited further resistance when Philadelphia lawyer John Dickinson published essays highlighting the renewed effort to undermine colonial rights. While many Philadelphia merchants, concerned about economic losses, resisted nonimportation until March 1769, opposition to the Townshend Act catalyzed the political alliance of artisans and mechanics with Philadelphia radicals. Parliament then repealed most of the Townshend duties, retaining the duty on tea.

The crisis abated for several years until Parliament approved the Tea Act (1773) and responded to the Boston Tea Party with the Coercive Acts (1774), attempting to isolate Boston by closing its port and taking direct control of the Massachusetts government. In response, delegations from twelve of the thirteen provinces convened, on September 5, 1774, the First Continental Congress at Carpenters' Hall in Philadelphia. The Congress was unprepared to declare independence but advised colonists to learn "the art of war," banned British trade, and formed the Association, a network of local committees to enforce the boycotts. The committees assumed governmental functions, thus vesting sovereignty in the people rather than Parliament.

The Second Continental Congress met at the Pennsylvania State House (later Independence Hall) in Philadelphia on May 10, 1775, appointing George Washington as commander-in-chief of the Continental army. Sentiment grew for independence after King George III declared the thirteen colonies in "an open and avowed rebellion" and Thomas Paine, an English-born pamphleteer recently arrived in Philadelphia, published *Common Sense* in 1776, rousing public sentiment that "'TIS TIME TO PART." As British warships and troops advanced on New York, Congress debated the Declaration of Independence, approving it unanimously on July 2, 1776. The delegates then drafted the Articles of Confederation, which upheld the sovereignty of the individual states but also empowered the Congress to fight a war of independence, treat with foreign powers and Native peoples, and settle common lands held by the government. While Congress operated under the Articles during the war, despite delay in ratification until 1781, its lack of authority to tax directly severely hampered its ability to supply the Continental army.

The Revolutionary War descended on the Philadelphia region in late 1776 when, after losses in New York to the British army commanded by General William Howe, the Continental army escaped across New Jersey to eastern Pennsylvania. The British followed, plundering New Jersey towns and farms. Washington's army pulled off a stunning victory on Christmas night, crossing the Delaware River to surprise 1,400 Hessians at Trenton, then in January 1777 defeated the British at Princeton. Washington set up his winter encampment at Morristown, in northern New Jersey, where Continental troops could reconnoiter the British in New Brunswick and New York and maintain communications between New England through Philadelphia to the South. New Jersey earned the name of "Crossroads of the Revolution" as more than six hundred battles and skirmishes took place within its boundaries and on adjacent waterways.

In summer 1777, with Washington blocking Howe's route across New Jersey, the British forces sailed around the Delmarva Peninsula to occupy Philadelphia from September 1777 to June 1778. To seize the city, Howe's army defeated Washington's forces at the battles of Brandywine and Germantown. Howe gained little by invading Philadelphia as his soldiers occupied homes and stole supplies from residents who stayed because they were Loyalists, neutral, or could not afford to escape. Washington's army, headquartered at Valley Forge, used its time in winter encampment to train as a more modern army and curbed British plundering in rural Pennsylvania. Patriot troops defended Fort Mercer and Fort Mifflin, which initially blocked British supply from the Delaware River, but evacuated in mid-November after weeks of continuous bombardment of Fort Mifflin. The Royal and Patriot armies clashed in several small engagements near Philadelphia during the British occupation. Severe conflict between Patriots and Loyalists continued in New Jersey and Pennsylvania after British troops departed the region to invade the South.

The Patriot victory at Yorktown in 1781 and Treaty of Paris (1783) brought independence and expanded boundaries, yet prospects for the United States seemed uncertain. In the mid-1780s, with economic turmoil and protests in Pennsylvania, Massachusetts, and other states, sentiment grew for a stronger national government. The Constitutional Convention met in Philadelphia in summer 1787, designing a new federal framework of three branches—a bicameral legislature, strong executive, and independent judiciary—in which states continued to hold substantial powers. Delaware, Pennsylvania, and New Jersey became the first states to join the new government, as Delaware and New Jersey ratified the Constitution unanimously and Pennsylvania by a 46–23 vote. Philadelphia celebrated ratification on July 4, 1788, with the Grand Federal Procession to the Bush Hill estate of William Hamilton. After the first Congress met and President George Washington was inaugurated in New York City in 1789, the national government returned to Philadelphia from 1790 to 1800, a decade in which the Greater Philadelphia region served as the capital of politics, arts, and finance in the new republic.

Revolutionary Crisis

Shannon E. Duffy

The Stamp Act of 1765, the first direct tax ever imposed by the British government on colonial Americans, inadvertently provoked a ten-year clash of wills between Great Britain and the colonies that led to the American Revolutionary War. During this Revolutionary crisis period (1765–75), colonists resisted imperial taxes and other parliamentary innovations with protests and with boycotts of British goods, called nonimportation agreements. Many Philadelphians initially proved more reluctant to join the protests than colonists to the north and south. However, with much of the trade of Pennsylvania, New Jersey, Delaware, and parts of New York flowing through the city's port, Philadelphia became a central focus for enforcing nonimportation. Ultimately, popular anger over British "encroachments" forced a realignment of power in the town and province and brought Philadelphia-area merchants and consumers into greater support for the resistance movement.

Britain's Parliament passed the Stamp Act on March 22, 1765, to offset the huge debt amassed during the recent Seven Years' War (1754–63). The British government intended the Stamp Act to defray the cost of "defending, protecting, and securing" the "British colonies and plantations in America." The terms of the act required colonials to purchase special paper from designated commissioners for a wide variety of legal and business transactions, varying from court pleadings and wills to newspapers and gaming cards. Contracts written on other than stamped paper were null and void, and counterfeiting the stamps was deemed a capital offense.

The British government seriously underestimated the anger this law would provoke. Colonial "Patriots" argued that cooperation with the law, which imposed taxation without American representation in Parliament, was akin to accepting economic slavery. Major riots occurred in Boston and New York City. Colonial legislatures and newspapers issued strongly worded protests. A German-language press in Germantown encouraged readers to resist the *unerträglichen* ("unbearable") Stamp Act. Everywhere, angry mobs targeted royal officials; the *Constitutional Courant* (Woodbridge, New Jersey) called American-born men who would cooperate with such an act the "vipers of human kind" and the "worst of parricides." In October 1765, nine of the thirteen colonies sent representatives to a Stamp Act Congress in New York City to draft a unified protest.

In comparison with other colonial cities, Philadelphia's initial response to the crisis was mild. While other colonial assemblies took a leading role in organizing the resistance, Pennsylvania's assembly, dominated by the Quaker Party of Benjamin Franklin and Joseph Galloway, remained caught up in its struggle to end the Penn family's proprietorship, supported by the Proprietary Party. Franklin, serving in London at the time as colonial agent, so misjudged colonial response that he recommended a trusted colleague, John Hughes, for the post of Pennsylvania stamp act distributor.

Franklin's popularity among the mechanics and artisans muted Philadelphia's protests, but both he and Hughes were castigated for their apparent support of the unpopular measure. On the night of September 16, 1765, a large mob gathered at the State House to target individuals associated with the act, including Franklin, Hughes, and Galloway. Franklin's wife, Deborah Read Franklin, reported to her husband that the crowd was dissuaded from attacking the Franklin home by an association of over eight hundred men formed "for the Preservation of the Peace of the City," who convinced the protesters to disperse. Once the stamps themselves arrived on October 5, another huge crowd corralled stamp distributor Hughes and made him swear not to execute the act or permit the stamps to be unloaded.

Amid the riots, congresses, petitions, and threats, the most potent form of protest was a new type of resistance action: colonial boycotts of British goods. Called "nonimportation agreements" (when merchants signed them) and "nonconsumption agreements" (when citizens signed them), these agreements were the first large-scale boycotts in history. Made possible by colonial Americans' growing importance as British consumers, they were promoted through colonial newspapers and broadsides that encouraged readers to show patriotic resistance to the unjust acts.

Philadelphia's merchants pledged cooperation with nonimportation, albeit somewhat reluctantly. Philadelphia docks tried to unload all ships by

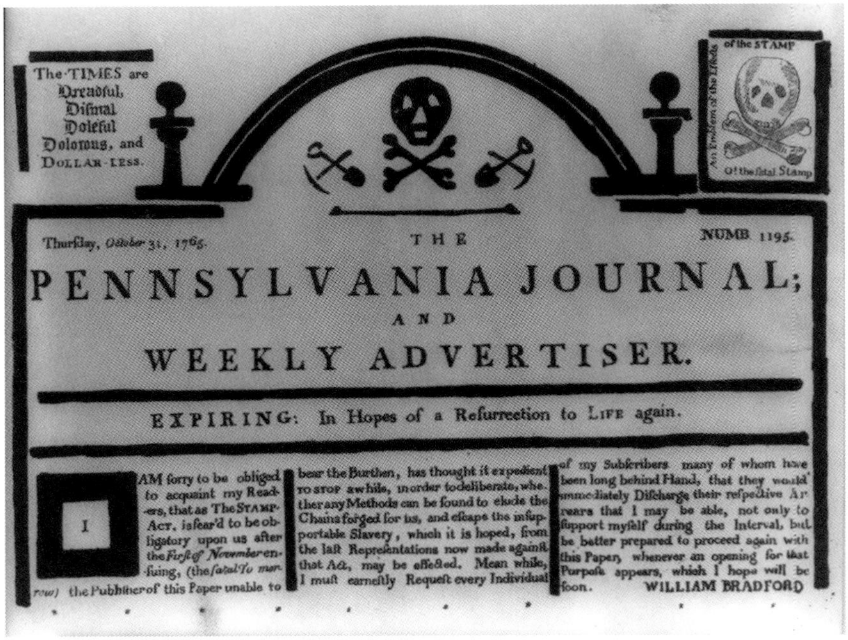

The TIMES are Dreadful, Dismal Doleful Dolorous, and DOLLAR-LESS.

An Emblem of the Effects of the STAMP O! the fatal Stamp

Thursday, October 31, 1765. THE NUMB. 1195.

PENNSYLVANIA JOURNAL; AND WEEKLY ADVERTISER.

EXPIRING: In Hopes of a Resurrection to LIFE again.

I AM sorry to be obliged to acquaint my Readers, that as The STAMP-ACT, is fear'd to be obligatory upon us after the First of November ensuing, (the fatal To-morrow) the Publisher of this Paper unable to bear the Burthen, has thought it expedient TO STOP awhile, in order to deliberate, whether any Methods can be found to elude the Chains forged for us, and escape the insupportable Slavery, which it is hoped, from the last Representations now made against that Act, may be effected. Mean while, I must earnestly Request every Individual of my Subscribers many of whom have been long behind Hand, that they would immediately Discharge their respective Arrears that I may be able, not only to support myself during the Interval, but be better prepared to proceed again with this Paper, whenever an opening for that Purpose appears, which I hope will be soon. WILLIAM BRADFORD

FIGURE 4. *Pennsylvania Journal and Weekly Advertiser,* published by William Bradford with a protest against the Stamp Act, October 31, 1765. LIBRARY OF CONGRESS.

November 1, 1765, the date when the Stamp Act would go into effect, accordingly preserving "October 31" on their forms as an unloading date for several weeks—if a ship had begun to be unloaded by the end of October, it was "grandfathered" under the pre-act terms. As late as December, ship owners still received port authorities' go-ahead to clear ships, under the fiction that the stamps were somehow inaccessible. Even Philadelphia's vermin reportedly assisted the resistance effort, as one newspaper gleefully reported: "a Quantity of the Stamp Paper, on board the *Sardoine* Man of War, has been gnawed to pieces by the Rats!"

The 1765 Stamp Act proved an abysmal failure. Mobs ultimately forced all the stamp distributors to resign. Not one of the thirteen colonies collected a shilling from the tax, and the boycott worsened England's already-depressed economy. The act was repealed within a year. When news of the repeal reached Philadelphia on May 19, 1766, large crowds drank to the health of King George III.

In May 1767, the British Parliament again tried to tax the American colonies, prompting a second round of protests and nonimportation agreements. Chancellor of the Exchequer Charles Townshend proposed duties to exploit what he perceived to be an apparent flaw in the Patriots' argument. While the Patriots denied Parliament's right to tax, they acknowledged Parliament's right to regulate colonial trade. Accordingly, the Townshend Acts placed import duties on five categories of imported items: paper, glass, paint, lead, and tea.

While response to the Stamp Act had been immediate and spontaneous, resistance to the Townshend duties was not. Philadelphia's merchant community remained divided, both because many of the wealthier merchants sought to obtain repeal of the duties quietly, through their contacts with English merchant houses, and also because merchants trading primarily in manufactured British goods stood to be much more heavily affected by the terms of the boycott than those houses trading primarily with the West Indies.

As segments of the Philadelphia merchants' community resisted calls for an intercolonial nonimportation agreement, political power in Philadelphia began to shift to the mechanic and artisan community, which was more heavily in favor of the ban. By the summer of 1770, Philadelphia radicals, working with the artisans and mechanics, were a new force in Philadelphia politics. Nonimportation appealed to Philadelphia mechanics from the start, as they also had an economic motive to support the boycott, which reduced competition from imported British manufactured goods and hence aided domestic manufactures.

The protest movement also found a powerful advocate in John Dickinson, a Philadelphia lawyer connected to Pennsylvania's Proprietary Party. Dickinson's *Letters from a Farmer in Pennsylvania*, which ran in the *Pennsylvania Chronicle* from December 1767 to February 1768, attacked the taxes on both constitutional and economic grounds. Dickinson argued that if such taxes were accepted meekly, worse would follow, endangering the very notion of private property.

By May 1768, Boston and New York had agreed upon an intercolonial nonimportation agreement. Anti-British sentiment grew with the garrisoning of troops in Boston and the dissolving of the Massachusetts legislature. A majority of Philadelphia merchants finally adopted nonimportation on March 10, 1769. However, Patriot enforcement methods (including threats of violence to persons or establishments) alienated many of the Quaker elite, and the Philadelphia Yearly Meeting discouraged Quakers from supporting nonimportation, dividing the city's leadership.

On April 12, 1770, Parliament repealed all of the Townshend duties save the one on tea, which was retained to make a point about Parliament's right to tax the colonies. By the fall of 1770, Philadelphia's radical leaders tried frantically to hold nonimportation together. In late September, the Philadelphia merchants ended the boycott for all products other than tea, and by December, the intercolonial boycott was defunct.

Anglo-American relations calmed somewhat in the next few years, until May 1773, when Parliament renewed the taxation controversy by passing the Tea Act. This law lowered the existing tax on tea in an effort to convince Americans to switch from smuggled foreign tea and also granted agents of the East India Company exclusive rights to sell tea in the colonies. Patriots reacted strongly both to this perceived effort to trick Americans into paying a hidden tax and to the precedent established by granting such a monopoly to a small group of merchants. One broadside called on the "industrious and respectable Body of TRADESMEN and MECHANICS of Pennsylvania" to fight to defend the "dear-earned Fruits of our Labour" from a "Set of luxurious, abandoned and piratical Hirelings" who would ruin not only colonial merchants, but also the mechanics and artisans, if such monopolistic grants spread to other items of trade.

As tension over the Tea Act grew, colonial protests increasingly stressed moral arguments as well as economic concerns, presenting British imported goods as dangerous luxury items that were corrupting American morals and health. One writer in Chester, Pennsylvania, noted the manifest virtue that American merchants were showing in resisting the "Pandora's box" of danger that the tea ships represented, despite the profits that they could have made from the trade. "A Sermon on Tea," printed in Lancaster, went so far as to depict tea as an evil in itself, blaming "the tea-table" for encouraging female gossip and malevolent rumors, extravagance, sexual promiscuity, and physical infirmities. A mass town meeting on October 16 determined that anyone helping tea ships unload their goods into Philadelphia was "an enemy to his country" and demanded the resignation of the tea consignees. Once the tea itself showed up in late November aboard the *Polly*, the ship's captain was quickly persuaded by threats of fire, tar, and feathering to sail back to London without attempting to unload the cargo.

After the colonies received word of the Coercive Acts, passed by Parliament in response to the Boston Tea Party of December 16, 1773, nonimportation and nonconsumption agreements became truly continental. A large meeting of the "freeholders and freemen of the city and county of Philadelphia" declared the Boston Port Act unconstitutional and resolved to support Bostonians "as suffering in the common cause of America." Berks County, Pennsylvania, was one of many communities across America to begin collecting relief supplies to aid the people of Boston. The First Continental Congress, meeting in Philadelphia in September 1774 with twelve of the thirteen colonies represented, set up an association to oversee boycott of all British products. A total prohibition on imports began in December, and an export embargo was to start in September 1775 if necessary. The Association called for every community to set up elected committees in order to enforce its terms, giving them sweeping authority to inspect commercial records and properties and to publicize violators. Nonimportation and nonconsumption remained major strategies for the American protest movement until the outbreak of war in April 1775 moved the quarrel to a different level.

FIGURE 5. *Reading the Declaration of Independence by John Nixon, from the steps of Independence Hall, Philadelphia, July 8, 1776*, drawn by E. A. Abbey, published in *Harper's Weekly*, July 15, 1876. LIBRARY OF CONGRESS.

Crowds (Colonial and Revolutionary Eras)

Toni Pitock

Ordinary people, often those who were ineligible to vote, helped to shape political culture in colonial and Revolutionary Pennsylvania, Delaware, and New Jersey despite domination of formal politics by social and economic elites. Crowds of inhabitants periodically engaged in public celebrations, civil disorder, and, occasionally, collective violence to support or oppose economic conditions and policies imposed by imperial, provincial, and local officials.

Unrest arose during periods of unemployment and economic stress. In Pennsylvania in the 1720s, hundreds of urban and rural commoners successfully demanded that the assembly approve paper currency, meant to pull the colony out of a steep recession. They assailed merchants and political authorities who sought to block the policy and threatened to raze the house of James Logan, prominent ally of the Penn family. Economic difficulties intensified another political conflict during the 1742 election as the dominant Quaker Party and the opposition Proprietary Party vied for control of the assembly. On October 1, 1742, a crowd of sailors angry about restrictions on wartime privateering rushed the courthouse, threatened to level the building, shouted abuses at the Quakers, and attacked their German supporters who responded forcefully.

Inhabitants made their voices heard when they believed that authorities undermined their interests. In 1756, during the Seven Years' War, Philadelphia tradesmen rioted when the British army began enlisting runaway servants, invalidating the terms of indentures. During Pontiac's War, settlers known as the Paxton Boys attacked peaceful Conestogas in Lancaster County, then headed toward Philadelphia where a crowd of three thousand gathered at the State House to demand protection against the marchers. Governor John Penn urged them to defend the city while Benjamin Franklin averted a confrontation by meeting the marchers at Germantown to hear their grievances.

Following the Seven Years' War, while the Pennsylvania legislature debated British taxes within the State House, the public created a vibrant informal political culture "out of doors." Ordinary people defended their "liberty" in newspaper articles and pamphlets and responded to each new act of Parliament and the Pennsylvania Provincial Assembly's response. Crowds aired grievances at mass meetings and protests that sometimes culminated in vandalism and violence. Most crowd actions in New Jersey took place in the northern part of the colony.

When news of the Stamp Act drew a crowd to the courthouse at Second and Market Streets on September 16, 1765, remonstrators threatened to attack the homes of Crown supporters, most notably Benjamin Franklin and Joseph Galloway, both members of the Provincial Assembly, and John Hughes, the official appointed to oversee compliance. A more moderate group of eight hundred men who formed an association "for the Preservation of Peace" persuaded protesters to disperse. The arrival of the official stamps on October 5 renewed opponents' indignation. Several thousand Philadelphians gathered to demand Hughes's resignation. A month later, a crowd hanged Hughes in effigy while Quaker Party supporters raised their voices in support of Hughes and Parliament.

Opposition mounted with the Townshend Revenue Act (1767) and the Tea Act (1773). Leaders such as John Dickinson and Charles Thomson organized nonimportation agreements while artisans and mechanics pressured hesitant members of the community, especially merchants, to participate in boycotts. In an effort to enforce compliance, they assembled on wharves to prevent merchants from unloading ships carrying British imports. Sailors, who opposed boycotts and embargoes, acted against supporters of nonimportation. In October 1769, a mob of seamen tarred and feathered a man who informed about illegally imported goods. In December 1773, eight thousand people gathered outside the State House to voice their opposition to the Tea Act.

In 1774, the First Continental Congress's boycott of trade and ban on consumption of British goods further mobilized the public. Committees of Safety stirred supporters to punish merchants who raised prices or hoarded goods and to chastise elites who flouted regulations. In 1775, the Second Continental Congress was forced to cancel a ball honoring Martha Washington when locals threatened to raze the City Tavern, where the event was to be held. The ball contravened Congress's proscription on entertainment, and the City Tavern, a gathering place for Philadelphia's leading citizens, was a symbol of their immoderation. As the Revolutionary crisis intensified, hostility to Britain increased. In 1776, when the Pennsylvania Provincial Assembly instructed its delegates to Congress not to sign the Declaration of Independence, a crowd of four thousand to five thousand people outside the State House denounced the assembly. Supporters of radical leaders Thomas Young, James Cannon, Thomas Paine, Timothy Matlack, and Daniel Roberdeau forced new assembly elections, in effect overturning elected representatives.

Once the colonies declared independence, crowds expressed their views through festivities and street theater as well as protests. Cheering crowds gathered in the State House yard to hear the Declaration of Independence and celebrated with bonfires and bell ringing. In New Castle, Delaware, the Declaration of Independence was read publicly on July 24 to a cheering crowd that promptly burned the king's arms that had formerly hung in the courthouse. In 1778, following the British evacuation of Philadelphia, dissatisfaction with the mood of the official Fourth of July parade led the "people out of doors" to coordinate a second procession. The boisterous crowd parodied the Loyalist women who delighted in the entertainments of the British during the occupation. Two years later, news of the treason of Benedict Arnold in September 1780 brought crowds into the streets on two consecutive days. They showed their loathing for the profligate former military governor and traitor by hanging and burning effigies of Arnold and, at the same time, cautioned others against collaborating with the British.

Members of the middling and lower classes suffered hardships during the Revolution and resented the Patriot elites who manipulated food prices and avoided military service. Sailors rioted in January 1779, demanding higher pay. In May, at a public meeting organized to appoint committees to investigate rising prices, leaders tacitly approved crowd action when they resolved that the public had a right to prevent abuses through price controls or some other means. Following the meeting, thousands were reported to have rioted, and crowds escorted a merchant, a butcher, and a speculator to the city jail. On October 4, two hundred militia members planned to make examples of the worst culprits by parading them through the streets. Their march culminated in a clash with merchant elites at the home of James Wilson, an event known as the Fort Wilson incident. In June 1783, a crowd of Pennsylvania troops gathered outside the State House to demand back pay, forcing the Confederation Congress to flee to Princeton, New Jersey.

Colonial and Revolutionary crowds acted of their own accord, protesting legislative measures and punishing people they considered enemies of the common good. Their legacy was preserved in the Pennsylvania Constitution of 1776 and in subsequent versions, which protected the right of the people to assemble, to express their grievances, and to demand redress.

Continental Congresses

Michael Karpyn

At the conclusion of the Seven Years' War in 1763, independence from Great Britain was an outlandish thought in the minds of most American colonists. Many enjoyed the protections and rights of one of the world's most powerful empires. Little more than a decade later, delegates from the thirteen colonies assembled in Philadelphia, risking their lives, fortunes, and sacred honor as they signed the Declaration of Independence. The First and Second Continental Congresses, meeting in Philadelphia in 1774 and for most of the period from 1775 to 1781, engaged in the complex politics surrounding independence and heightened the city's role in the emerging nation.

Tensions escalated between the British government and the American colonies in 1774 when the British Parliament passed the Coercive Acts to punish the city of Boston for the Boston Tea Party, putting the Massachusetts government under direct British control, closing the port of Boston, and quartering British troops in local buildings. Though focused on Massachusetts, the Coercive Acts drew concern from throughout the colonies. Many outside of Massachusetts viewed the acts as a violation of their rights under the English constitution; the outrage demanded a unified response.

But what response? Only the most radical among the colonists advocated for independence. Many others, including Pennsylvania political leaders John Dickinson and Joseph Galloway, acknowledged the need for political unity but also encouraged caution, nonviolent action, and a desire to reconcile their differences with the British government.

In September 1774, representatives of twelve colonies assembled in Philadelphia at Carpenters' Hall, then and since the meeting place for the Carpenters' Company of the City and County of Philadelphia. (Georgia did not send a delegation because of its need for help from British regulars for defense against the Creeks.) As the commercial center of the growing Delaware Valley economy, Philadelphia was well situated to host the First and Second Continental Congresses. The city's public buildings—including the Pennsylvania State House (later Independence Hall), British barracks in Northern Liberties, Pennsylvania Hospital, and Walnut Street Jail—helped to accommodate many of the government's needs. Philadelphia also contained more than enough diversions to entertain its distinguished visitors. Massachusetts's John Adams and Connecticut's Silas Deane noted the nearly unparalleled luxury in the Second Street home of John Cadwalader, with whom they both dined. Delegates also found entertainment in the exclusive clubs of Philadelphia's elite, including the Schuylkill Fishing Company, which was established in 1732.

Representatives only gradually moved toward a consensus for independence as they debated responses to the Coercive Acts and military escalation. At the First Continental Congress, when Galloway proposed a "plan of union" with Great Britain, the delegates voted it down, but narrowly. After seven weeks of debate, the Congress ended with the delegates agreeing only to form an association to boycott British goods and

FIGURE 6. Carpenters' Hall, Philadelphia, photographed by Carol M. Highsmith, 2013. The first Continental Congress met here in 1774. LIBRARY OF CONGRESS.

to meet again in May 1775. By the time the Second Continental Congress assembled, this time in the State House, events had moved forward rapidly. The delegates were dealing not solely with philosophical and political questions related to their rights as Englishmen but were responding to the hostilities that began between British regulars and Massachusetts militia at the Battles of Lexington and Concord on April 19, 1775. This Congress, now joined by Benjamin Franklin and Thomas Jefferson and presided over by John Hancock, appointed George Washington as commander of the Continental forces, managed the loosely organized colonial war effort, and debated whether to declare independence.

Initially, many of the delegates favored Dickinson's long-held position—reconciliation with Great Britain. In July 1775, delegates approved the Olive Branch Petition, drafted primarily by Dickinson, that affirmed the colonists' loyalty to King George III in an attempt to avoid further bloodshed. When the king rejected the petition because he considered the Second Continental Congress an illegal assembly and insincere in its intentions, support for independence grew. In 1776, the pamphlet *Common Sense* by Thomas Paine garnered enthusiastic public response. Amid news that the British sent a large army and ships to New York, Congress appointed a committee to draft the Declaration of Independence.

After formally declaring independence on July 2, 1776, the Second Continental Congress became the government of the United States, and Philadelphia became the nation's capital city. Congress was forced to relocate several times during the Revolution: to Baltimore, Maryland, when the British threatened Philadelphia in December 1776 and to York, Pennsylvania, during the British occupation of 1777–78. Regardless of its location, the weak powers of this first national government severely hindered the war effort. In 1777, the Second Continental Congress approved the Articles of Confederation, in which Congress lacked the crucial powers to tax and raise troops. Despite the delay in ratification until 1781, Congress governed under its framework, funding the Revolution to a large extent through printed money and loans.

Common Sense

John Saillant

Published in Philadelphia in its first edition in January 1776, Thomas Paine's *Common Sense* became one of the most widely disseminated and most often read political treatises in history. It looked forward to democratic politics and universal human rights, yet it also reflected local circumstances in Philadelphia. *Common Sense* was thus an overture to democracy and human rights as well as part of Philadelphia print culture and local politics.

Born in England, Paine adopted Philadelphia as a temporary home in November 1774, when he arrived with a letter of introduction from Benjamin Franklin, whom he had met in London. Franklin recognized Paine's skills as a writer and polemicist, and his letter helped Paine secure a position as the first editor of the

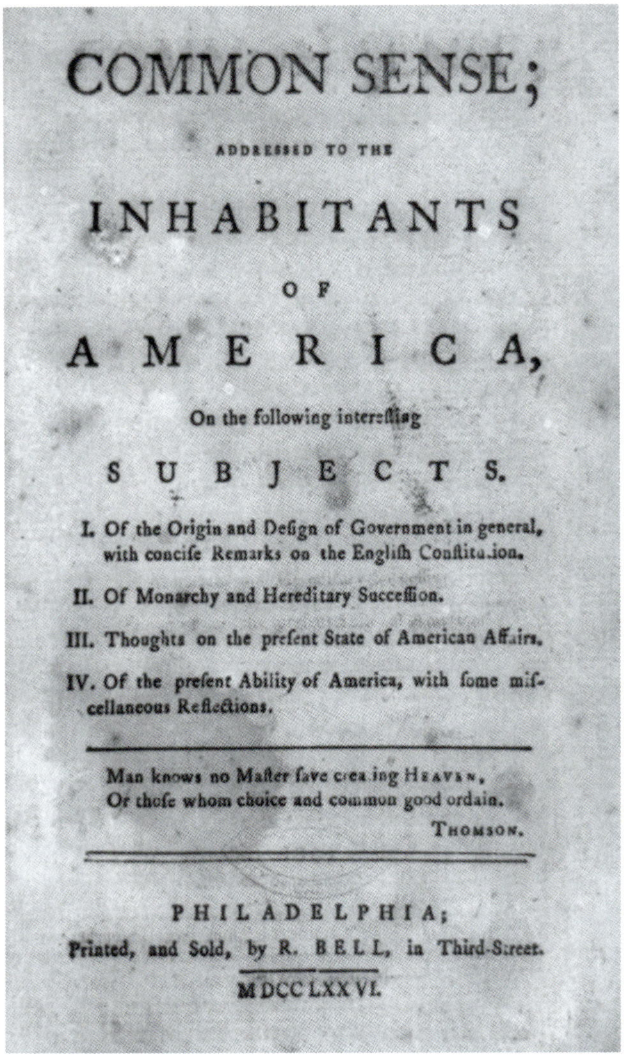

COMMON SENSE;

ADDRESSED TO THE

INHABITANTS

OF

AMERICA,

On the following interesting

SUBJECTS.

I. Of the Origin and Design of Government in general, with concise Remarks on the English Constitution.

II. Of Monarchy and Hereditary Succession.

III. Thoughts on the present State of American Affairs.

IV. Of the present Ability of America, with some miscellaneous Reflections.

Man knows no Master save creating HEAVEN,
Or those whom choice and common good ordain.
THOMSON.

PHILADELPHIA;
Printed, and Sold, by R. BELL, in Third-Street.
MDCCLXXVI.

FIGURE 7. *Common Sense; Addressed to the Inhabitants of America, On the following interesting Subjects*, by Thomas Paine, 1776. LIBRARY OF CONGRESS.

Pennsylvania Magazine. In eight months as editor, Paine increased subscriptions and popularized colonial essays and poetry (as opposed to reprints of British material). Upon leaving the *Pennsylvania Magazine*, Paine received encouragement from Franklin and Benjamin Rush to write *Common Sense*.

Already a leading mercantile city, Philadelphia became the political center of the thirteen colonies in 1774. The First Continental Congress met at Carpenters' Hall in September and October 1774, while the Second Continental Congress convened at the Pennsylvania State House in May 1775, declaring independence in July 1776. Throughout the period, colonists feared invasion by water as well as by land. Appearing in the midst of this heightened political state, *Common Sense* found an audience in Philadelphia and elsewhere.

Paine's renown in his own time and in later eras rested on his attack on traditional political authority and his defense of a radical form of democratic political participation. Paine had little inkling that politics dominated by white men would be, beginning in the nineteenth century, challenged by women and racial, ethnic, and sexual minorities. But he did define political participation and representation in ways that were in theory open to all. Much of American political thought after the War of Independence has entailed accepting or rejecting the notion of full political participation that Paine enunciated in *Common Sense*.

Paine's arguments against traditional political authority dissected notions like the divine right of kings, the legitimacy of custom, the social value of aristocrats, and the ability of monarchs to ensure peace and prosperity for their subjects. Often Paine used familial metaphors such as King George III as a father who had turned against his children. The implication was that ordinary people, who had experienced familial relations, could make informed judgments about weighty political matters. He cast the situation in the Anglo-American colonies in 1776 as historic and universal. "The cause of America is in a great measure the cause of all mankind," he wrote. "Many circumstances hath, and will arise, which are not local, but universal, and through which the principles of all Lovers of Mankind are affected."

Accordingly, in *Common Sense*, Paine cast himself as "under no sort of Influence public or private, but the influence of reason and principle." His arguments for democratic politics rested on a broad suffrage, annual elections, and a large unicameral body of legislators. He aimed for representative government close to voters and responsive to their interests, a revolutionary alternative to the English Parliament, the British Crown, and the colonial royal governors and councils. Paine's conclusion was therefore obvious. Reconciliation between Americans and the British government was impossible, and separation, independence, and unification of the colonies into a new nation should proceed.

The form of government *Common Sense* recommended—a unicameral legislature with annual elections—was indeed crafted in 1776 by a Pennsylvania convention charged with writing a constitution for the new state. Most of the former colonies wrote new constitutions at this time as replacements for their colonial charters.

The first edition of *Common Sense* was published anonymously by Scottish-born Philadelphia printer Robert Bell, who risked a charge of treason for disseminating the work. After arguing with Bell about profits and copyright, Paine appealed to Bell's competitors, the Bradford brothers, who published several enlarged editions, including the one most known to posterity, a third edition with new front and end matter and, for the first time, with Paine's name on the title page. The wrangling over the work simply added to its notoriety. Moreover, Paine castigated Pennsylvania Quakers for mixing religion and politics in their appeals for peace. The book was quickly republished in a number of American and European cities.

In the mid-1770s many Americans as well as many Philadelphians were torn between loyalty to the British Empire and anger over the incursions of imperial power into the colonies in the late 1760s and early 1770s. Paine's contemporaries (like modern scholars) perceived *Common Sense* as the decisive text that propelled colonial sentiment into independence. George Washington, for instance, praised its "sound Doctrine, and unanswerable reasoning." Edmund Randolph wrote that after the dissemination of *Common Sense*, "public sentiment which a few weeks before had shuddered at the tremendous obstacles, with which independence was environed, overleaped every barrier." Still, *Common Sense* also had critics, for example James Chalmers in *Plain Truth* (1776, printed by Bell).

Paine continued to exhort for the Patriot cause in a series of essays, *American Crisis*. Some of the language that Americans associate with the Revolution—for example, "These are the times that try men's souls"—flowed from Paine's pen in these years. But in 1790 Pennsylvanians dismantled and modified their radically democratic government. A new constitution enacted mixed government, balancing a lower house with an upper house and a governor. By then Paine had moved to England (where he wrote *Rights of Man*) and then France (where he wrote *The Age of Reason*).

In sum, *Common Sense* was one of the most significant catalysts of the War of Independence as well as a bellwether of democratic thought. Although the radical structure of government that Paine recommended proved short-lived in Pennsylvania, Americans at large have since the Revolution grappled with some of the central concerns of *Common Sense*. Americans still contest the balance between popularly elected governments (both state and federal) and individual rights. Moreover, Paine, often called "a citizen of the world," wrote in the *American Crisis*, "My attachment is to all the world, and not to any particular part." His sense of world citizenship remains pertinent in the twenty-first century, an era of energetic human migration, instantaneous electronic communication, and global ecological interdependence.

Declaration of Independence

Michael Karpyn

When the Second Continental Congress assembled in the Pennsylvania State House in Philadelphia in May 1775, the shooting war between British and colonial forces was underway and the delegates faced the task of funding and arming a Continental army, appointing its leadership, and managing a war against its powerful foe. Though the war had begun with the Battles of Lexington and Concord in Massachusetts a month before, on April 19, 1775, a formal political separation from the British Crown was not a foregone conclusion. Not until July 1776 did the delegates work through deep political divisions to create the Declaration of Independence, which gave birth to a new nation and cemented Philadelphia's reputation as a cradle of liberty.

Even in January 1776, a scant six months before independence was declared, many of the delegates thought that reconciliation with the Crown was the most prudent course of action. On January 9, 1776, Pennsylvania delegate James Wilson proposed that Congress reject any talk of independence. That same day, the printing shop of Robert Bell near Third and Walnut Streets issued a pamphlet written by Thomas Paine that magnified the desire for independence. Paine's *Common Sense*, with its rejection of monarchy as a form of government and its impassioned pleas for independence from Great Britain, electrified not only Philadelphia but also the thirteen colonies as a whole.

Between April and July 1776, a groundswell toward independence also emerged with more than ninety local declarations of independence adopted around the colonies. These included resolutions by militia companies in Philadelphia, Chester County, and Lancaster County, Pennsylvania.

The colonial governments of Delaware, New Jersey, and Pennsylvania did not initially share in the growing enthusiasm for independence. On May 1, 1776, voters in Pennsylvania elected a new provincial assembly that favored reconciliation. Delaware instructed its representatives to the Continental Congress to "concur" with other delegations but avoided the word "independence." After the Continental Congress urged colonies to form new governments on May 15, 1776, the New Jersey Provincial Congress changed positions, placing the royal governor, William Franklin, son of Benjamin Franklin, under arrest and sending a new delegation to Philadelphia with instructions to declare independence.

In the Continental Congress, Virginia delegate Richard Henry Lee on June 7, 1776, formally presented a plan for the colonies to declare independence, create a national government, and enlist the aid of foreign nations in the war effort. The motion was seconded by John Adams, but political resistance to independence was still deep among some delegates. In Pennsylvania's case, the Provincial Assembly meeting upstairs in the State House remained committed to reconciliation. With passage uncertain, the Continental Congress voted only to resume debate on Lee's resolution on July 1, 1776.

While those in favor of independence worked behind the scenes to win the votes needed for passage, a committee of five delegates—Adams, Benjamin Franklin, Roger Sherman of Connecticut, Robert R. Livingston of New York, and Thomas Jefferson of Virginia—set to work on the declaration itself. To complete this important task, Jefferson moved away from the activity surrounding the State House to the quieter outskirts of the city, at Seventh and Market Streets. Working in rented space on the second floor of the home of bricklayer Jacob Graff, Jefferson completed his draft in roughly two weeks.

After some minor editing and suggestions from Franklin and Adams, the document was presented to the Congress on June 28, 1776, for further editing and debate. The Congress made more than ninety modifications to Jefferson's draft, from changes in vocabulary and sentence structure to the elimination of some of Jefferson's listed grievances against King George III. These changes included removing the charge that the king had delivered the "un-Christian" practice of slavery to American colonies.

On July 1, after a long day of debate, the Congress voted. Each colony had one vote, requiring the delegations to decide among themselves how to cast their single vote. Pennsylvania and South Carolina voted no; New York—whose provincial government was then fleeing the invading British army—abstained. Delaware's two delegates present were split. Although a majority of the delegations at this moment voted in favor of the resolution, proponents of independence sought unanimous support.

On July 2, the remaining pieces fell into place. South Carolina reversed course and voted in favor of Lee's resolution. Delaware's Caesar Rodney, in an act memorialized in 1999 on Delaware's commemorative state quarter, rode through the night to arrive at the State House to break his delegation's tie in favor of independence. Within the Pennsylvania delegation, John Dickinson and Robert Morris, both opponents of independence, abstained, leaving Pennsylvania's delegation then 3–2 in favor of independence. Though against declaring independence, Dickinson recognized the symbolic importance of a unanimous decision. He then left Congress and volunteered for the Pennsylvania militia.

As Congress voted unanimously for the declaration, some of the delegates—Adams most famously—considered July 2 as the day of American independence. It was July 4, however, when final editing and wording of the document was approved and sent to Philadelphia printer John Dunlap at his shop at Second and Market Streets for publication. Philadelphians first heard the Declaration of Independence on July 8, when John

FIGURE 8. Declaration of Independence (1776), copperplate engraving produced by William J. Stone in 1823 when the original document was becoming worn with age. NATIONAL ARCHIVES.

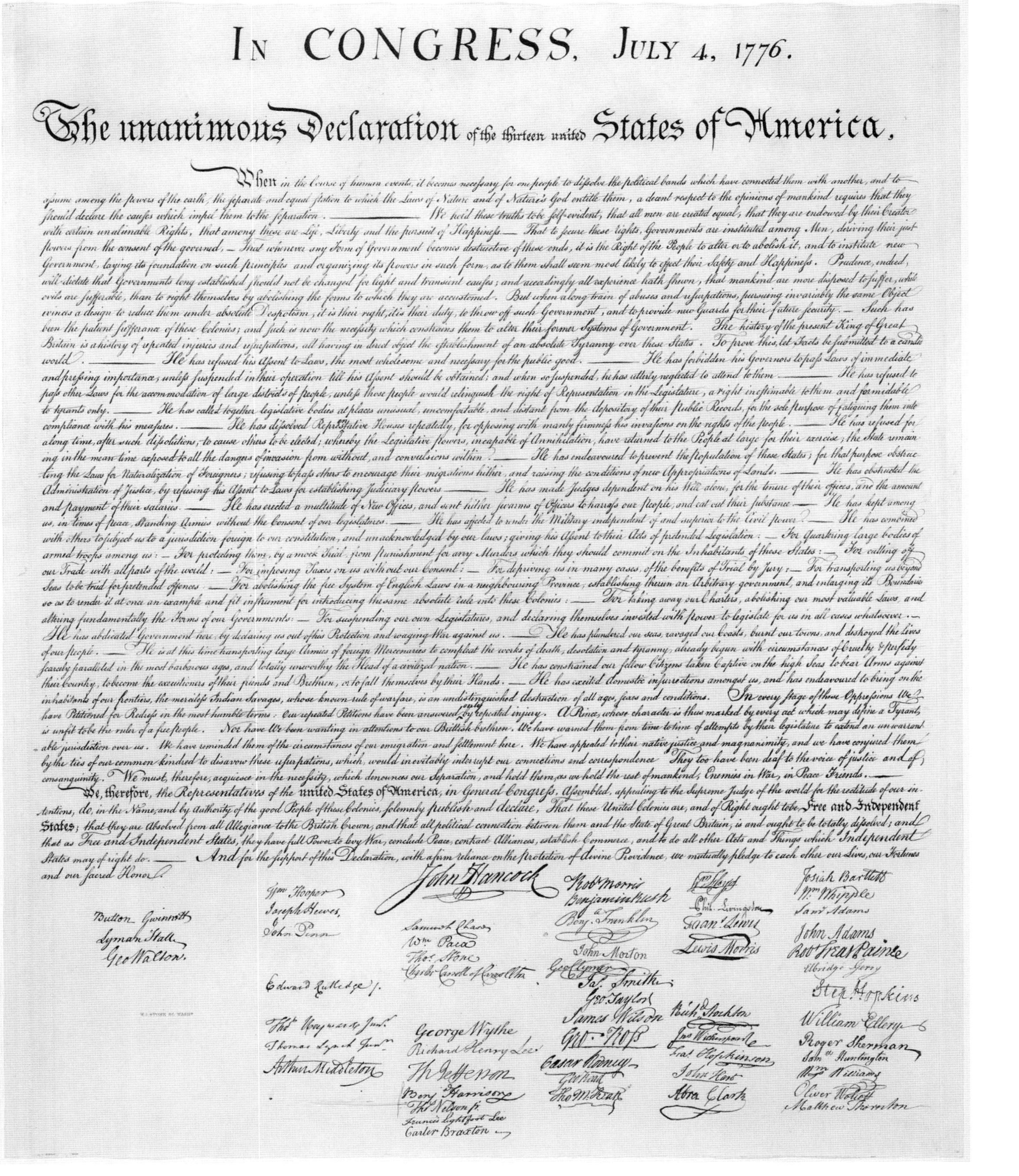

IN CONGRESS, JULY 4, 1776.

The unanimous Declaration of the thirteen united States of America,

When in the Course of human events, it becomes necessary for one people to dissolve the political bands which have connected them with another, and to assume among the powers of the earth, the separate and equal station to which the Laws of Nature and of Nature's God entitle them, a decent respect to the opinions of mankind requires that they should declare the causes which impel them to the separation. —— We hold these truths to be self-evident, that all men are created equal, that they are endowed by their Creator with certain unalienable Rights, that among these are Life, Liberty and the pursuit of Happiness. — That to secure these rights, Governments are instituted among Men, deriving their just powers from the consent of the governed, — That whenever any Form of Government becomes destructive of these ends, it is the Right of the People to alter or to abolish it, and to institute new Government, laying its foundation on such principles and organizing its powers in such form, as to them shall seem most likely to effect their Safety and Happiness. Prudence, indeed, will dictate that Governments long established should not be changed for light and transient causes; and accordingly all experience hath shewn, that mankind are more disposed to suffer, while evils are sufferable, than to right themselves by abolishing the forms to which they are accustomed. But when a long train of abuses and usurpations, pursuing invariably the same Object evinces a design to reduce them under absolute Despotism, it is their right, it is their duty, to throw off such Government, and to provide new Guards for their future security. — Such has been the patient sufferance of these Colonies; and such is now the necessity which constrains them to alter their former Systems of Government. The history of the present King of Great Britain is a history of repeated injuries and usurpations, all having in direct object the establishment of an absolute Tyranny over these States. To prove this, let Facts be submitted to a candid world. —— He has refused his Assent to Laws, the most wholesome and necessary for the public good. —— He has forbidden his Governors to pass Laws of immediate and pressing importance, unless suspended in their operation till his Assent should be obtained; and when so suspended, he has utterly neglected to attend to them. —— He has refused to pass other Laws for the accommodation of large districts of people, unless those people would relinquish the right of Representation in the Legislature, a right inestimable to them and formidable to tyrants only. —— He has called together legislative bodies at places unusual, uncomfortable, and distant from the depository of their Public Records, for the sole purpose of fatiguing them into compliance with his measures. —— He has dissolved Representative Houses repeatedly, for opposing with manly firmness his invasions on the rights of the people. —— He has refused for a long time, after such dissolutions, to cause others to be elected; whereby the Legislative powers, incapable of Annihilation, have returned to the People at large for their exercise; the State remaining in the mean time exposed to all the dangers of invasion from without, and convulsions within. —— He has endeavoured to prevent the population of these States; for that purpose obstructing the Laws for Naturalization of Foreigners; refusing to pass others to encourage their migrations hither, and raising the conditions of new Appropriations of Lands. —— He has obstructed the Administration of Justice, by refusing his Assent to Laws for establishing Judiciary powers. —— He has made Judges dependent on his Will alone, for the tenure of their offices, and the amount and payment of their salaries. —— He has erected a multitude of New Offices, and sent hither swarms of Officers to harrass our people, and eat out their substance. —— He has kept among us, in times of peace, Standing Armies without the Consent of our legislatures. —— He has affected to render the Military independent of and superior to the Civil power. —— He has combined with others to subject us to a jurisdiction foreign to our constitution, and unacknowledged by our laws; giving his Assent to their Acts of pretended Legislation: — For Quartering large bodies of armed troops among us: — For protecting them, by a mock Trial, from punishment for any Murders which they should commit on the Inhabitants of these States: — For cutting off our Trade with all parts of the world: — For imposing Taxes on us without our Consent: — For depriving us in many cases, of the benefits of Trial by Jury: — For transporting us beyond Seas to be tried for pretended offences — For abolishing the free System of English Laws in a neighbouring Province, establishing therein an Arbitrary government, and enlarging its Boundaries so as to render it at once an example and fit instrument for introducing the same absolute rule into these Colonies: — For taking away our Charters, abolishing our most valuable Laws, and altering fundamentally the Forms of our Governments: — For suspending our own Legislatures, and declaring themselves invested with power to legislate for us in all cases whatsoever. — He has abdicated Government here, by declaring us out of his Protection and waging War against us. — He has plundered our seas, ravaged our Coasts, burnt our towns, and destroyed the lives of our people. — He is at this time transporting large Armies of foreign Mercenaries to compleat the works of death, desolation and tyranny, already begun with circumstances of Cruelty & perfidy scarcely paralleled in the most barbarous ages, and totally unworthy the Head of a civilized nation. — He has constrained our fellow Citizens taken Captive on the high Seas to bear Arms against their Country, to become the executioners of their friends and Brethren, or to fall themselves by their Hands. — He has excited domestic insurrections amongst us, and has endeavoured to bring on the inhabitants of our frontiers, the merciless Indian Savages, whose known rule of warfare, is an undistinguished destruction of all ages, sexes and conditions. In every stage of these Oppressions We have Petitioned for Redress in the most humble terms: Our repeated Petitions have been answered only by repeated injury. A Prince, whose character is thus marked by every act which may define a Tyrant, is unfit to be the ruler of a free people. Nor have We been wanting in attentions to our Brittish brethren. We have warned them from time to time of attempts by their legislature to extend an unwarrantable jurisdiction over us. We have reminded them of the circumstances of our emigration and settlement here. We have appealed to their native justice and magnanimity, and we have conjured them by the ties of our common kindred to disavow these usurpations, which, would inevitably interrupt our connections and correspondence. They too have been deaf to the voice of justice and of consanguinity. We must, therefore, acquiesce in the necessity, which denounces our Separation, and hold them, as we hold the rest of mankind, Enemies in War, in Peace Friends.

We, therefore, the Representatives of the united States of America, in General Congress, Assembled, appealing to the Supreme Judge of the world for the rectitude of our intentions, do, in the Name, and by Authority of the good People of these Colonies, solemnly publish and declare, That these United Colonies are, and of Right ought to be Free and Independent States; that they are Absolved from all Allegiance to the British Crown, and that all political connection between them and the State of Great Britain, is and ought to be totally dissolved; and that as Free and Independent States, they have full Power to levy War, conclude Peace, contract Alliances, establish Commerce, and to do all other Acts and Things which Independent States may of right do. —— And for the support of this Declaration, with a firm reliance on the protection of divine Providence, we mutually pledge to each other our Lives, our Fortunes and our sacred Honor.

John Hancock

Button Gwinnett
Lyman Hall
Geo Walton.

Wm Hooper
Joseph Hewes,
John Penn

Edward Rutledge.

Thos Heyward Junr.
Thomas Lynch Junr.
Arthur Middleton

Samuel Chase
Wm. Paca
Thos. Stone
Charles Carroll of Carrollton

George Wythe
Richard Henry Lee
Th Jefferson
Benja Harrison
Thos Nelson jr.
Francis Lightfoot Lee
Carter Braxton

Robt Morris
Benjamin Rush
Benja. Franklin
John Morton
Geo Clymer
Jas. Smith
Geo. Taylor
James Wilson
Geo. Ross
Caesar Rodney
Geo Read
Tho M:Kean

Wm Floyd
Phil. Livingston
Frans. Lewis
Lewis Morris
Richd. Stockton
Jno Witherspoon
Fras. Hopkinson
John Hart
Abra Clark

Josiah Bartlett
Wm. Whipple
Saml. Adams
John Adams
Robt Treat Paine
Elbridge Gerry
Step. Hopkins
William Ellery
Roger Sherman
Saml. Huntington
Wm. Williams
Oliver Wolcott
Matthew Thornton

W. J. STONE SC. WASHN

Nixon, a lieutenant colonel in the Philadelphia militia, read the document aloud in the State House yard. The public reaction was passionate and widespread. According to historian William Hogeland, the crowd shouted "God bless the free states of North America!" three times. In the ultimate act of defiance, Pennsylvania militiamen removed the king's coat of arms from the State House and threw it into a large bonfire.

Thousands of visitors each year visit the Pennsylvania State House, situated on Chestnut Street between Fifth and Sixth Streets. They may not be aware of its history as a state house or that the Georgian style of its architecture expresses deep ties between Pennsylvania and British culture. These visitors are drawn by the significance of this building in the early history of this nation and know it better by the name it gained from the events of 1776—Independence Hall.

Loyalists

Shannon E. Duffy

During the American Revolution, Loyalists, or "Tories" as Patriots called them, included prominent political and religious leaders as well as many less affluent individuals from the Philadelphia region's Quaker and German pacifist communities. A large number of "neutrals" also struggled with increasing difficulty to remain uninvolved in the conflict. Religion, ethnicity, economic status, and local concerns influenced decisions to back the rebellion, remain loyal to Great Britain, or stay neutral. Many initially supported Patriot resistance against parliamentary taxation but gradually shifted their allegiance after protests turned into war and formal independence.

Historians estimate that 15 to 20 percent of white colonial men actively aided the British in their attempts to suppress the Revolution. Over the course of the war, about thirty thousand colonials bore arms for Britain. Many prominent Pennsylvania leaders ultimately sided with the Crown, including former Philadelphia mayor William Allen, Pennsylvania assembly speaker Joseph Galloway, and the Anglican rector of Christ Church Jacob Duché, who had given the blessing for the First Continental Congress. Former New Jersey assembly speaker Cortlandt Skinner became a British brigadier general, commanding the Loyalist "New Jersey Volunteers." New Jersey governor William Franklin, son of Benjamin Franklin, helped establish a Board of Associated Loyalists, coordinating Loyalist guerilla attacks throughout the mid-Atlantic region. Three thousand Philadelphia Loyalists left the city with the British army at the end of its occupation in 1778. Continentwide, by the war's end, sixty thousand to eighty thousand colonials chose exile rather than remain under the new American governments.

Many enslaved African Americans gave their support to the Loyalist side, while others fought for the Patriots. When offered freedom in exchange for war service, around twenty thousand enslaved people escaped to the British lines, mostly from the southern colonies, though at least sixty-seven came from the Philadelphia area. They took the opportunity to escape primarily for personal liberty, but evidence exists that some actively cheered for a British victory. The December 14, 1775, *Evening Post* alleged that an enslaved person in

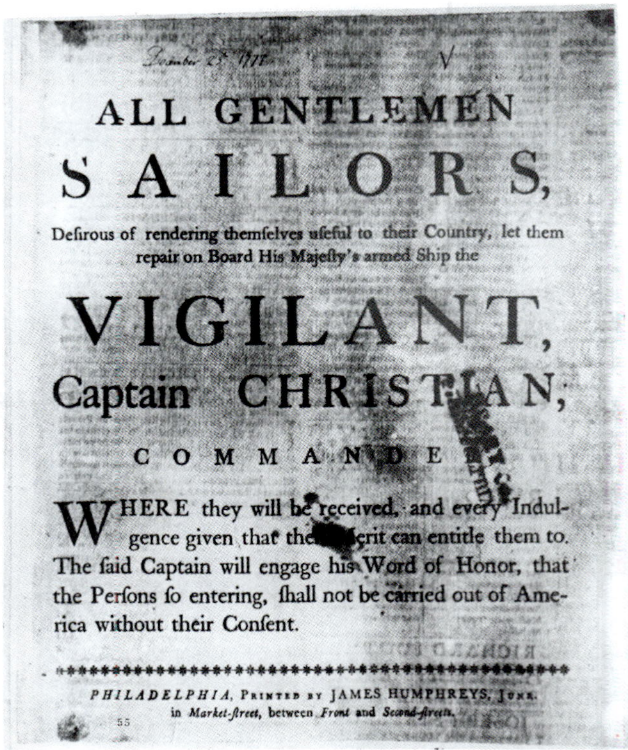

ALL GENTLEMEN

SAILORS,

Defirous of rendering themfelves ufeful to their Country, let them repair on Board His Majefty's armed Ship the

VIGILANT,

Captain CHRISTIAN,

COMMANDE[illegible]

WHERE they will be received, and every Indulgence given that th[illegible]erit can entitle them to. The faid Captain will engage his Word of Honor, that the Perfons fo entering, fhall not be carried out of America without their Confent.

PHILADELPHIA, Printed by JAMES HUMPHREYS, Junr. in Market-ftreet, between Front and Second-ftreets.

FIGURE 9. Recruitment broadside for Loyalist sailors to join the Royal Navy ship *Vigilant*, published in Philadelphia, 1777. LIBRARY OF CONGRESS.

Philadelphia threatened a white woman, "Stay you d—d white bitch 'till Lord Dunmore and his black regiment come, and then we will see who is to take the wall."

Ethnicity and religion often guided citizens' political allegiance in the Philadelphia region. Many Quaker and German pacifists tended toward neutrality or loyalism (as did the Anglicans), while Baptists and Presbyterians were more likely to lean Patriot. The Society of Friends (Quakers) forbade military service and any aid to violent rebellion; while many Friends had initially supported the resistance movement, they pulled away as colonial protests grew more violent. Many Quakers believed that to keep their faith they must not pay war taxes, pay fines in lieu of military service, swear oaths of allegiance, or aid military efforts in any manner. By 1775, monthly meetings throughout Pennsylvania, New Jersey, and Delaware removed members from their rolls for overt support of the rebellion. After the Declaration of Independence, when the new state governments demanded loyalty oaths and tax payments, the Quakers' situation became worse. A small group, the "Free Quakers" who supported the rebellion, splintered from the Philadelphia Yearly Meeting to form their own congregation, gathering in private homes before they built a meetinghouse in 1783.

Members of Amish, Brethren (Dunker), Mennonite, Moravian, and Schwenkfelder congregations had similar problems. On the eve of the Revolution, about ten thousand members of these German pacifist sects called Pennsylvania home. These "Peace Germans" believed that God alone possessed the right to overthrow a legal government, which rendered them unable to swear loyalty to any Revolutionary government—until final victory proved God's will. Like the Quakers, the Peace Germans were disappointed because the state's new government abandoned the policy of religious toleration that had drawn them to Pennsylvania. The Schwenkfelder Petition to the Pennsylvania Assembly (October 1777), signed by approximately 1,500 people from various German pacifist denominations, reminded the assembly that "the only reason for our journey" to America was to "become partakers of the benefits of the just and well-known religious freedom as well as civil rights in Pennsylvania." As far as can be determined, most of the Peace Germans were truly neutral, as opposed to politically committed to a British victory.

The shift in allegiance toward the British side was often gradual. Many future Loyalists, including prominent Pennsylvania leaders, supported some aspects of the Patriot resistance until escalating turbulence and the Patriots' path toward independence led them to withdraw their support. As royal governor of New Jersey, William Franklin refused to let the *Royal Charlotte* unload stamped paper in 1765, on the premise that he could not guarantee the cargo's safety; he later joined celebrations when the Stamp Act was repealed. One of two Quakers later hanged for treason, John Roberts, signed a resolution condemning the 1774 Boston Port Act as "unconstitutional; oppressive to the inhabitants of that town; dangerous to the liberties of the British Colonies." Joseph Galloway took a seat in 1774 at the First Continental Congress but later led the civilian government during the British occupation of Philadelphia.

For many Philadelphians, the outbreak of warfare forced their decision; for others, the Declaration of Independence was a step they could not take. After July 4, 1776, many Loyalists pointed to the declaration as proof that Patriot leaders had been deceptive in their true aims. Galloway said the document confirmed his longstanding suspicions: the radicals "had deceived the people from the beginning . . . and that notwithstanding all their solemn professions to the contrary, they ever had independence in their view."

For those who sought to remain aloof from the struggle, neutrality and noninvolvement became more difficult after 1776. Military losses of the Continental army in New York resulted in substantial recruits for the British that increased Patriot paranoia, leading to harsh anti-Loyalist laws. On the eve of the Battle of Trenton, the British reported that 4,836 New Jersey inhabitants had taken oaths of allegiance. George Washington wrote: "The conduct of the Jerseys has been most infamous; instead of turning out to defend their country and affording aid to our Army, they are making their submissions as fast as they can" (December 18, 1776). In response, state legislatures (including Pennsylvania's) passed laws that required oaths of allegiance, or "test oaths," to the new governments. Those who refused to swear (whether from political or religious scruples) were deemed nonjurors, subject to substantial fines and deprived of the right to vote, hold office, serve on juries, sue for debts, transfer real estate, or even hold some occupations. While few pacifists were imprisoned, the confiscations and fines ruined many families financially.

Patriot reprisals in Pennsylvania were harshest immediately before and after Philadelphia's nine-month occupation in 1777–78. On the eve of the British attack on the Revolutionary capital, fear that spies and collaborators would aid the British led Pennsylvania's legislature, on the advice of Congress, to arrest forty-one Philadelphians judged "disaffected to the American cause." Of these, twenty Quakers were banished to the frontier town of Winchester, Virginia, where they remained without trials for eight months until repeated petitions and complaints brought about their release. Two died before their discharge in April 1778.

After General William Howe's forces occupied Philadelphia on September 23, 1777, many formerly neutral and apolitical Philadelphia residents socialized openly with British officers, while area farmers supplied provisions to British and Hessian armies. Patriot anger reached a crescendo after the British staged the "Meschianza," an elaborate pageant to honor General Howe before his departure for London. The combination regatta, jousting tournament, and formal dinner cost over £3,000 and feted the elite women of Philadelphia, some from known Loyalist families and others who had previously claimed neutrality.

The end of the British occupation unleashed another wave of popular fury at such "Tory" collaborators, as the Pennsylvania government arrested at least 638 Philadelphians on suspicion of treason. More than one hundred people lost their property. Two of the arrested, Quakers John Roberts and Abraham Carlisle, faced trial for collaborating with the British. Carlisle had been a British gatekeeper, issuing passes out of the city; Roberts allegedly acted as a guide for the British raiding parties in the nearby countryside. Despite numerous appeals for clemency, both men were executed on November 4, 1778. More than four thousand Philadelphians attended the burial march.

Following the British loss at Saratoga in 1777 and the evacuation of Philadelphia, many mid-Atlantic Loyalists castigated the British for their mild prosecution of the war and advocated a much harsher line. Loyalist guerilla fighters wreaked havoc in Pennsylvania and New Jersey, conducting nighttime raids, burning farms and houses, and kidnapping Patriot leaders. William Franklin's Associated Loyalists worked as an autonomous military organization with the design of "annoying the sea coasts of the revolted provinces and distressing their trade." In some areas, the collapse of civil society led to banditry by militias of both sides, especially in the Pine Barrens of South Jersey and along the New York–New Jersey border.

The end of the war and terms of peace stunned many Loyalists, as the 1783 Treaty of Paris made few provisions to protect Loyalists or return their property. Its Article 5 promised only that "Congress shall earnestly recommend" the restitution of confiscated properties. State governments (not Congress) had conducted most confiscations, and the Articles of Confederation granted the national government little power to compel state compliance. Legal proscriptions against the Loyalists took years to repeal. The Test Laws were first challenged in the Pennsylvania General Assembly in 1784 and finally repealed two years later. In many places, Loyalists attempting to return to their communities experienced popular animosity. A mass meeting of Easton, Pennsylvania, residents protested the return of Loyalists who had fought with Native Americans, accusing them of having wet "their hands in the blood of our unprotected countrymen." In New Jersey, returning Loyalists were attacked with tar and feathers. Some German pacifists continued to feel unwelcome years after the war's conclusion. During the 1780s and 1790s, several Bucks County Mennonite congregations left to establish new communities in Ontario, Canada. While most states (including Pennsylvania) repealed anti-Loyalist laws before 1788, Pennsylvania's blacklist of individuals subject to arrest or confiscation was still in circulation as late as 1802. Such signs of continuing resentment toward both Loyalists and neutrals indicate that the divisions created by the Revolution persisted long after the peace.

Native Americans in the Revolutionary Era

Jean R. Soderlund

During the Revolutionary period, Native Americans in the Delaware Valley and western Pennsylvania pursued various strategies to preserve their families, communities, and culture. In the Philadelphia area, Lenape people retained the Brotherton reservation and

FIGURE 10. Members of the Oneida Indian Nation discussing the role of Native Americans at the Valley Forge Encampment during the Revolutionary War, 2009. NATIONAL PARK SERVICE.

independent towns despite greatly diminished lands and population loss from disease. Many Lenape families migrated to the Susquehanna and Ohio Valleys where, beginning in the 1750s, they united with Munsees, Shawnees, Haudenosaunee (Iroquois), and other Native people to fight colonization by European settlers. Some Delawares (Lenapes and Munsees) joined pacifist Moravian missions that moved westward from eastern Pennsylvania to the Ohio Country. At the Revolution's end in 1783, most Native towns in Pennsylvania had been destroyed regardless of whether they supported the Patriots or the British/Loyalists, or attempted to remain neutral.

Indigenous people lived near the Delaware River for more than ten thousand years before Dutch, Swedish, and English traders and settlers arrived in the seventeenth century. The Unami-speaking Lenape people controlled their homeland in what became southern New Jersey, eastern Pennsylvania, and Delaware, allying with neighboring Munsees in northern New Jersey and southern New York and the Nanticokes of Delaware and Maryland's Eastern Shore. The Lenape people and Pennsylvania's proprietors maintained mostly amicable relations until the fraudulent 1737 Walking Purchase in which proprietary agent James Logan guided the Penn family in seizing more than one million acres from central Bucks County to the Poconos. Land sales to European colonists pushed many Lenape families to central and western Pennsylvania where they joined the Conestogas (Susquehannocks), Shawnees, Senecas, and Natives from Maryland, Virginia, and North Carolina.

The Seven Years' War (1754–63) opened a series of conflicts lasting through the Revolution in which Native people battled European colonists for control of western Pennsylvania, the Ohio Country, and Great Lakes. After French and Indigenous forces, in July 1755, overwhelmed the army of British General Edward Braddock, Delawares and Shawnees attacked European settlements from western Pennsylvania to northwestern New Jersey.

Despite opposition by pacifist Quaker legislators, the Pennsylvania government funded the war and unleashed violence against Native people by offering scalp bounties. New Jersey required Lenape people to wear a red ribbon and carry identification. The New Jersey government also appointed five commissioners who instructed Lenape leaders to identify their land within the colony. When they submitted their list in 1758, the commissioners responded that colonists had settled on much of the territory. After protest, the Lenape negotiators yielded most of their lands in return for a three-thousand-acre reservation called Brotherton in southern Burlington County and rights to hunt and fish in the colony.

War continued after the 1763 British victory over the French. The British government attempted unsuccessfully with the Proclamation Line of 1763 to stop white settlement west of the crest of the Appalachian Mountains. In Pontiac's War (1763–65), many Delawares, Shawnees, Haudenosaunee, and other Indigenous people attacked forts and resisted colonization. During the conflict, vigilante Paxton Boys, mostly Scots Irish of Lancaster County, murdered their noncombatant Conestoga neighbors and then marched against pacifist Moravian Delawares who had taken refuge in Philadelphia. Though the Paxton Boys retreated after negotiating with Benjamin Franklin, hatred and conflict persisted as colonists pushed west.

With the Fort Stanwix Treaty of 1768, the Haudenosaunee signed away Delaware and Shawnee lands in the Susquehanna Valley without their permission, setting the stage for the removal of most Native people from Pennsylvania by the end of the Revolution. Like white Americans, Indigenous people took divergent stances in the war, and many changed their positions over time in response to Patriot and British actions. Native people engaged in localized fighting with settlers in the Juniata Valley, while conflict between Connecticut and Pennsylvania colonists in the Wyoming Valley engulfed Indigenous people as well. The Continental military campaigns led by General John Sullivan and Colonel Daniel Brodhead targeted Delaware and Haudenosaunee towns in northern and western Pennsylvania, Ohio, and New York, intensifying their antipathy toward the United States. While the majority of Native people sided with the British, members of the Oneida and Tuscarora nations of the Haudenosaunee and some Delaware and Shawnee communities allied with the Patriots. In 1778, Oneida fighters provided pivotal aid to the Continental army at Valley Forge. Native families often faced the same outcomes, however, regardless of their support for the Patriots, British, or neutrality. In 1782, for example, western Pennsylvania militia killed more than ninety Native men, women, and children from the Ohio Moravian missions of Gnadenhütten and Salem. By the Treaty of Paris (1783), most Indigenous communities in Pennsylvania had been ravaged or forced to migrate to New York, Ohio, or the Great Lakes region where they continued to struggle against land speculators, settlers, and the United States government into the nineteenth century.

Lenape people remained in the Delaware Valley during and after the Revolution, though the Brotherton reservation failed to attract more than fifty to sixty residents. Many more Lenapes lived in New Jersey at Coaxen, Crossweeksung, Cranbury, Cohanzick, in the Pine Barrens, and near the Atlantic shore. Lenape families also continued to reside in Delaware and eastern Pennsylvania. After declining earlier invitations to consolidate with the Delawares in Ohio, the Lenapes at Brotherton in 1802 sold the reservation and moved to New Stockbridge, New York, retaining rights to hunt and fish in New Jersey until 1832. Cohanzicks stayed in Cumberland County where they were joined by Lenapes and Nanticokes of the Delmarva Peninsula. Facing severe persecution, they shielded their families and identities through their religious communities during the nineteenth and twentieth centuries. The Oneida Nation in 2012 donated $10 million to the Museum of the American Revolution in Philadelphia to commemorate and preserve knowledge of its contributions to the American War of Independence.

Trenton and Princeton Campaign (Washington's Crossing)

Stuart Leibiger

One of the most significant events in the Revolutionary War was the Continental army's December 25, 1776, crossing of the Delaware River, led by General George Washington, which preceded three crucial American victories—two at Trenton and one at Princeton, New Jersey—that reignited the virtually extinguished Patriot cause. Immortalized in the famous 1851 painting by Emanuel Leutze, the crossing has become one of the most commemorated scenes in American iconography. The campaign enabled the rebel militia to reclaim most of New Jersey from the British and their Loyalist allies, helped the Continental Congress to recruit new fighting forces, and boosted public confidence in the commander in chief.

During the fall of 1776, British troops under General William Howe forced the Continental army to evacuate Manhattan and to retreat southwest across New Jersey. Numbering about three thousand men, Washington's shattered army escaped across the Delaware River into Pennsylvania on December 7, with the British in pursuit. The Continental Congress, fearing an enemy occupation of Philadelphia, fled to Baltimore. Howe, hoping to pacify New Jersey, spread his forces into seventeen outposts across the state.

After first making his headquarters at Summerseat, the home of Thomas Barclay in Falls Township across the Delaware from Trenton, Washington a week later relocated ten miles upriver to the Keith House near McConkey's Ferry in Upper Makefield Township. Washington deployed his men to guard the crossing points above and below Trenton as best they could and ordered Continental forces still in New Jersey under generals Charles Lee and Horatio Gates to reinforce him. Since the previous August, Washington had suffered a string of devastating defeats, had lost 90 percent of his men to battle casualties, desertion, and sickness, and lacked clothing and supplies for the few who remained. Nevertheless, he resolved to strike before expiring enlistments completely dissolved his army—and ended the Revolution—at the end of the year. Recognizing an opportunity to achieve numerical superiority over the Hessian garrison of Colonel Johann Rall in Trenton, Washington decided to recross the river and attack. Meanwhile, New Jersey militia under General Philemon Dickinson waged hit-and-run attacks that left the Hessians nervous and weary.

Washington planned a three-pronged crossing of the river for the night of December 25, to be followed by an attack on Trenton before sunrise. Contrary to myth, he did not strike on the day after Christmas because he expected the Hessians to be drunk from holiday revelry. Instead, he moved as soon as possible. Washington's forces would cross the river at McConkey's Ferry and hit Trenton from the north, while General James Ewing of the Pennsylvania militia would cross with seven hundred men from Falls Township to the Assunpink Creek south of Trenton, to prevent the Hessians from escaping. The third prong, consisting of Philadelphia militia known as the "Associators" commanded by Colonel John Cadwalader, would cross from Bristol, Pennsylvania, to Burlington, New Jersey, to stop Hessians under Colonel Carl von Donop from aiding Rall.

On the night of December 25, an ice-clogged river and a violent nor'easter featuring rain, hail, and snow delayed Washington's crossing of the Delaware by four hours. Marblehead, Massachusetts, fishermen under Colonel John Glover ferried the army across using large Durham boats designed for carrying iron ore down the river. So severe were the conditions that neither Ewing nor Cadwalader could cross the river. Having been warned to expect a midnight attack, the enemy lowered its guard at dawn, shortly before 2,500 Continentals launched a weather-delayed assault. Although taken by surprise, the Hessians might have withstood the offensive had Rall not been mortally wounded. The Continentals killed or wounded 106 Hessians and captured 916 more without suffering a fatality. The victorious army and its prisoners recrossed the river back to Pennsylvania at McConkey's Ferry.

Unaware of these developments, on December 27 the Associators crossed into New Jersey, where Cadwalader urged Washington to join him to renew the offensive. Persuading about half of his men to reenlist with a cash bounty of ten dollars, Washington on December 31 reoccupied Trenton, where he was joined by Cadwalader and Ewing. On the evening of January 2, the Continentals resisted probing attacks waged by Redcoats under General Charles Cornwallis in the Second Battle of Trenton. Rather than risk annihilation when the fighting resumed in the morning, Washington instead slipped south out of town during the night. Turning east and then north, the Continentals marched through Quaker Bridge toward Princeton to attack another British outpost under General Alexander Leslie. Instead they intercepted and routed an enemy regiment under Lieutenant Colonel Charles Mawhood headed for Trenton, as well as two additional regiments coming out of Princeton. After flirting with the idea of attacking yet

FIGURE 11. *Washington Crossing the Delaware*, by Emanuel Leutze, 1851. METROPOLITAN MUSEUM OF ART.

another British outpost at New Brunswick, Washington took his weary men into winter quarters at Morristown, New Jersey.

In ten days, Washington's three victories—two at Trenton and one at Princeton—turned the 1776–77 campaign around. To prevent further attacks against his vulnerable outposts, General Howe consolidated his forces in New Jersey, allowing Patriots to reassert themselves and leaving his pacification campaign in ruins. The victories lifted American spirits sufficiently to recruit additional forces to carry on the war. During the campaign, Washington, along with his officers, demonstrated charismatic leadership and moral courage. The commander in chief also gained confidence in himself, won newfound respect from his men, and shattered the belief in British invincibility. With the British threat no longer imminent, Congress returned to Philadelphia in March 1777 and remained there until Howe captured the city in September of that year.

Philadelphia Campaign

Jennifer Lawrence Janofsky

During the War of Independence, in 1777, the British moved to seize Philadelphia in a series of battles that contributed to a turning point in the war. While the Philadelphia campaign strained British resources and exposed serious leadership issues with General William Howe, the effectiveness of American forces led by General George Washington helped to bring France into the war as an American ally.

The summer of 1777 saw the British deeply entrenched in New York City with plans to seize Philadelphia, the Revolutionary capital, and destroy Washington's army. In a stalemate in New Jersey with Washington's forces, Howe received approval to begin a campaign against Philadelphia as long as his forces remained available to assist an invasion from Canada of General John Burgoyne. Howe sailed up the

Chesapeake Bay in August 1777 with a force of thirteen thousand troops, disembarking at the Head of Elk, Maryland. As Howe began his march to Philadelphia, Washington scrambled to respond. On September 11, 1777, British forces engaged with the Americans at the Battle of Brandywine, an engagement that saw strategic reconnaissance errors by the Americans. Washington hoped to force an attack on the high ground of Chadds Ford but a heavy fog provided protection for the British as they moved to outflank the Americans. With Washington's right flank completely exposed, the American troops could do little more than fight for time as they retreated to Chester.

Washington, alarmed at Howe's pace, sent the division of Brigadier General "Mad" Anthony Wayne to harass the British as they continued toward Philadelphia. Wayne set up camp in Paoli close to the British, who learned of Wayne's presence and launched a surprise attack on the night of September 20, 1777. The battle was considered a complete disaster for the Patriots with fifty-three men killed and seventy-one taken prisoner. Outraged at charges of misconduct, Wayne demanded a full court martial and investigation, which determined that he had made tactical mistakes but had not engaged in misconduct. The battle became a rallying cry for American soldiers who labeled the event the "Paoli Massacre."

Howe's army continued toward Philadelphia as the Continental Congress abandoned the city and evacuated briefly to Lancaster and then York, Pennsylvania. The British entered the city unopposed on September 26, positioning some troops in the outlying community of Germantown. Washington, seeing a divided force and hoping to retake the capital, attacked the British at Germantown on October 4, 1777. A heavy fog complicated communication during his four-pronged assault. Cliveden, home to the prominent lawyer Benjamin Chew, became the site of intense fighting as entrenched British troops fired heavily upon the advancing American army. Ultimately, confusion and a lack of organization contributed to Washington's defeat.

Nevertheless, the bold attack impressed European observers who began to believe a disciplined army could pose a serious threat to the British government. The American army continued to improve and demonstrate its proficiency on the battlefield. In addition, the dramatic American victory at Saratoga, New York, in October 1777, suggested the Patriots could win the war. Howe's inability or refusal to support Burgoyne's troops at Saratoga further compromised the Crown's ability to subdue the colonies and encouraged the French to ally with the American cause.

As Howe settled into Philadelphia, he faced the pressing problem of supplying his troops. Food and other provisions were scarce. Washington's army largely prevented the British from seeking supplies outside the city, and the main point of entry into the city—the Delaware River—remained closed through strategic fortifications constructed the previous spring. Fort Billingsport, Fort Mercer, and Fort Mifflin buttressed both sides of the river. A complicated system of weighted spears known as "chevaux de frise" lined the bottom of the river ready to pierce the hulls of unsuspecting British ships approaching the city. With the fort system and chevaux blocking supplies, Howe recognized, with winter looming, that effective action was needed.

In late October, Howe turned his attention to Fort Mercer, located at Red Bank on the New Jersey side of the Delaware. Situated on a high bluff overlooking the river, Mercer provided a strategic defensive location opposite Fort Mifflin on Mud Island, south of Philadelphia. On October 22, 1777, Hessian forces under the leadership of Colonel Carl von Donop left Haddonfield, New Jersey, with orders to take Fort Mercer. Von Donop, defeated at Trenton by Washington's forces, eagerly seized the opportunity to avenge his name. He commanded a Hessian force of approximately twelve hundred men who arrived at Red Bank late in the afternoon. Mercer's high walls as well as a series of sharpened logs known as abatis made the fort extremely difficult to scale. Complicating the Hessian assault was the arrival of the Pennsylvania navy under the leadership of John Hazelwood, who began a series of barrages from the river. Unable to scale the walls and without artillery pieces to breach the fort, many Hessians died and were buried in a mass grave near the fort. The following day, either by British design or the result of enemy fire, the British ships *Augusta* and *Merlin* took fire and exploded, an event so loud it was heard miles away.

Failing to take Mercer, the British turned their attention to Fort Mifflin, which had been constructed in

Between the two lines that crofs Philadelphia was the firft Plan of that City

1771 under the direction of British officer and engineer Captain John Montresor who, ironically, was now charged with destroying the fort. Lieutenant Colonel Samuel Smith of the Fourth Maryland Regiment commanded the fort with a force of two hundred men. Fort Mifflin saw the heaviest bombardment of the Revolutionary War. Beginning November 10, British forces shelled Mifflin by land and by water, inflicting heavy casualties. By November 15, the fort had been virtually destroyed with few men left to defend it. The Americans evacuated the fort and headed across the river to Fort Mercer. Within days of Mifflin's fall, the Americans abandoned Fort Mercer, restoring British access to the river.

The river cleared, Howe's troops received necessary provisions and settled in for winter. With the British now deeply established in Philadelphia, Washington's forces set up camp for the long winter at Valley Forge. In October 1777, however, Howe had submitted his resignation complaining he had not received the support he needed to perform his position effectively. The British relieved Howe of his duty in spring 1778, replacing him with General Henry Clinton. Howe's exit from Philadelphia is remembered for the elaborate party known as the "Meschianza," which included over four hundred guests and fireworks.

Along with the American victory at Saratoga, the Philadelphia campaign convinced France that the Americans were worthy allies. After the French entered the war on the side of the Americans in February 1778, the British abandoned Philadelphia in June and returned to New York for fear of an imminent French attack. Howe's missteps in the campaign exposed the weakness in British military leadership and allowed Washington's troops time to rest, train, and reorganize.

FIGURE 12. *A Map of that part of Pensylvania now the Principle [sic] seat of War in America wherein may be seen the Situation of Philadelphia, Red Bank, Mud Island, & Germantown,* surveyed by Nicholas Scull, engraved by L. Jackson, 1777. LIBRARY OF CONGRESS.

British Occupation of Philadelphia

Martha K. Robinson

On September 26, 1777, the British army marched into Philadelphia, beginning an occupation that lasted until the following spring. Its arrival led Patriots to flee and Loyalists to rejoice, although wartime shortages soon led to suffering for those who remained in the city. For the British, the occupation led to no concrete gains, as they abandoned the city the following June.

The occupation of Philadelphia deviated from a British plan, after two years of inconclusive war, to conquer New England in 1777 by sending two armies into New York State. The first, headed by General John Burgoyne, proceeded south from Canada. At the same time, forces led by General William Howe would have headed north from New York City along the Hudson River. These two armies would have divided New England from the other colonies, allowing the British to invade and conquer.

Howe, to the surprise of his superiors, did not follow through on this plan. Whether from personal dislike of Burgoyne, fear of allowing General George Washington time to rebuild his army, or doubts about his own ability to prosecute the Hudson River campaign, he rejected the plan. Instead, Howe set his sights on Philadelphia, sailing south along the Atlantic coast, heading up the Chesapeake Bay in August 1777 and landing at Head of Elk. The British general prioritized conquest of the American capital, but he also apparently hoped to draw Washington into a battle that might crush the Continental army once and for all. Furthermore, prominent Loyalists, including Joseph Galloway, had claimed that more than 75 percent of Americans in Philadelphia and the surrounding region were loyal to the Crown and would aid the British.

Howe defeated Washington at the Battle of Brandywine in September 1777 yet failed to destroy the Continental army. As the British approached Philadelphia, thousands of Patriot citizens fled, including the delegates to the Continental Congress. Sarah Logan Fisher, the wife of a prominent Philadelphia merchant, described "wagons rattling, horses galloping, women running, children crying, delegates flying, & altogether the greatest consternation, fright & terror that can be imagined." One estimate suggests that more than 10 percent of Philadelphia's homes were abandoned by their owners before the British arrived, and reports of looting and theft grew. When Howe entered Philadelphia on September 26, Loyalists lined the streets to welcome the return of British authority. On October 4, Washington tried but failed to dislodge the British at the Battle of Germantown.

Once in control of Philadelphia, Howe faced serious problems in supplying his troops and the city's inhabitants. Howe needed to take control the Delaware River from American forces at Fort Mifflin on Mud Island and Fort Mercer on the New Jersey side of the river to ensure an adequate supply of provisions. As the Americans successfully defended both forts until November, suffering followed in Philadelphia, with food and other provisions in short supply. British officers quartered with local citizens, churches became hospitals for sick and wounded soldiers, and Philadelphians described British and German soldiers stealing horses, cattle, wood, food, and clothing. The suffering of American prisoners in the Walnut Street Jail was especially severe, as prisoners endured hunger, cold, and abuse from their jailers. In October 1777, the Quaker diarist Elizabeth Drinker described the suffering of the city, writing "if things dont change 'eer long, we shall be in poor plight, everything scarce and dear, and nothing suffer'd to be brought in to us." Even after the forts fell, prices in the city remained high and citizens continued to complain of theft and other crimes committed by soldiers. Howe tried, without much success, to deter such behavior, offering monetary rewards for information about crimes. Frequent courts-martial sentenced men to up to a thousand lashes for plundering and other crimes.

During the long fall and winter months, the British built up the city's defenses, kept an eye on the American army at Valley Forge, and sent foragers into the countryside to search for wood and hay. But such tasks could not occupy the thousands of men in the army, and the British also turned to a wide variety of leisure activities. Some occupied themselves by arranging dinner parties, playing cards, drinking, gambling, and visiting prostitutes. British officers put on plays at the Southwark Theatre on Monday nights from January to May, performing at least fourteen different plays.

Following Howe's resignation, his officers planned a grand celebration to honor him before his departure. This "Meschianza" (in Italian, "medley"), held on May 18, 1778, began with elaborately decorated flatboats and galleys carrying officers and hundreds of guests down the river. This procession was followed by a tournament in which British officers dressed as medieval knights jousted in honor of the "Ladies of the Blended Rose" and the "Ladies of the Burning Mountain." The tournament was followed by a feast, fireworks, and dancing. Participants judged the event a stunning success, but not all Philadelphia citizens agreed. The Meschianza cost more than £3,000, a stunning amount of money in an occupied city where citizens complained regularly of shortages and high prices. The diarist Drinker criticized the officers' extravagance, writing, "How insensible do these people appear, while our Land is so greatly desolated, and Death and sore destruction has overtaken and impends over so many."

While Howe and his army spent the winter in Philadelphia, the fortunes of war were turning. On October 17, 1777, Burgoyne (lacking support from Howe) surrendered at Saratoga. This American victory encouraged the French to make an alliance with the Americans. With British plans in America threatened by the French fleet, the British could no longer afford to occupy Philadelphia, especially as they had gained nothing from being there. General Henry Clinton was ordered to abandon Philadelphia and retreat to New York. The British army left Philadelphia in June 1778, accompanied by some three thousand Loyalists.

The British occupation and abandonment of Philadelphia also led to difficult choices for Black residents of the city, both free and enslaved. In 1777 and 1778, it was unclear whether an American or a British victory would be more likely to lead to freedom and greater rights. On the one hand, Quaker and abolitionist sentiment in the Philadelphia region had been growing in the decade before the war. As individuals released enslaved people, the free Black population grew. Enslaved people in the region might have hoped that an American victory would lead to yet more manumissions or abolition. During the war, thirty-five Black men served in the Second Pennsylvania Brigade of the Continental army, and others served on American privateers. On the other hand, Black men and women in Philadelphia learned within a week of the November 7, 1775, proclamation of Lord Dunmore, governor

FIGURE 13. Hancock House at Hancock's Bridge, Salem County, New Jersey, photograph by George Neuschafer, 1941. The house was the site of a massacre of local militia by British soldiers in March 1778, during the British occupation.
LIBRARY OF CONGRESS.

of Virginia, that the British were offering freedom to enslaved people held by Patriots in return for supporting the British. During the occupation, many Black people seem to have decided that the British offered better prospects than the Americans and served among them as soldiers, guides, and laborers. When the British evacuated, dozens of enslaved people fled with them.

The occupation of Philadelphia accomplished little for the British war effort. The American government survived, since the Continental Congress fled the city. Washington's army survived the harsh winter at Valley Forge. Relations between the British and Loyalists in the Delaware Valley deteriorated. Worse, Howe had lost a vital opportunity. By failing to meet Burgoyne in New York, he had thrown away the best chance the British had to conquer New England.

Fort Wilson

David Reader

On October 4, 1779, the home of noted Pennsylvania lawyer and statesman James Wilson on the southwest corner of Third and Walnut Streets in Philadelphia became a flash point for Philadelphians divided by politics and class. The militia attack on "Fort Wilson" occurred in the wake of conflict over the Pennsylvania Constitution of 1776, rising inflation, and the recent departure of the British army. Wilson had come to symbolize the complicated politics of Philadelphia during the American Revolution.

The Pennsylvania Constitution of 1776 created two factions, Constitutionalists and Republicans. The Constitutionalists favored the Constitution of 1776, which established a unicameral legislature, a weak executive branch, and a broadened suffrage to include any free male age twenty-one or older who paid even the smallest tax. The Republicans favored a two-house legislature, a suffrage restricted to adult male property owners, and a strong executive branch with legislative veto power. Wilson, a Republican, shared in his party's disapproval of the radically democratic Constitution of 1776.

In January 1779, increasing prices of flour, wood, and grain renewed the demands by the Constitutionalists and working-class Philadelphians to impose price controls to stem inflation. But Wilson, Robert Morris, and the merchant class of Philadelphia benefited financially from free trade and inflationary prices on such necessities. Throughout the spring and summer of 1779, the working-class and militia families who bore the financial and military burdens of the war looked on the merchant class with disdain for their lack of service and control of the economy. The rising tension between the classes led the working-class men in the Pennsylvania

General Assembly to favor price controls. The Philadelphia Committee of Privates, an organization of representatives from local militias and the working class created in 1775, reemerged to secure price regulations and remedy other perceived acts of injustice by profiteers and Loyalists.

On Monday, October 4, 1779, a large number of militiamen gathered at Burns Tavern on Tenth Street between Race and Vine Streets to take action against any man associated with profiteering and sympathetic to the British. Headed by Captain Ephraim Faulkner, the militia called on Charles Willson Peale to lead their march through the city to arrest and detain their enemies. As some cried out "Get Wilson," Peale tried but failed to persuade the militia to abandon the plan. The militia captured four prominent merchants and forcefully marched them through the streets of Philadelphia in a display of public humiliation.

To avoid being captured by the militia, Wilson and other members of the Republican Society barricaded themselves inside Wilson's house. The militia stopped near Wilson's house when Captain Robert Campbell, who was inside, opened a window and either shouted to them to continue marching or shouted and fired his pistol at the militiamen. Storming the doors, the militiamen set fire to the first floor and killed Campbell before being turned away by the men inside. The arrival of Joseph Reed, president of the Pennsylvania Supreme Executive Council, and the City Troop of Light Horse ended the attack on Fort Wilson. At least four militiamen, one free Black youth (who joined the militia's march), and Captain Campbell were killed, and at least fourteen militiamen and three men from inside the house were wounded.

The arrest of several militiamen increased the tension throughout the city and surrounding areas. Wilson fled the city to Morris's country estate until October 19, 1779, when he returned to the city at night. The Pennsylvania assembly acted quickly to quell the tension between the classes through legislation that provided flour to the families of the militia and reemphasized the enforcement of the laws pertaining to military service. In March 1780 the Supreme Executive Council passed an act pardoning all involved in the attack on Fort Wilson.

Ladies Association of Philadelphia

Jacqueline Beatty

Philadelphia was a center of patriotic fervor and activity during the American Revolution. Many of its residents, including women, provided material and moral support for the Patriot cause. On June 12, 1780, one such Philadelphian, Esther DeBerdt Reed, penned a broadside entitled "The Sentiments of an American Woman," rousing dozens of women to form the Ladies Association of Philadelphia (LAP). This group of upper-class white women led a door-to-door campaign raising money for the Continental army commanded by George Washington. Through their efforts, the association's "ladies" came to recognize their essential role in winning American independence.

Reed and other LAP organizers affirmed women's partnership in the Revolution despite the Continental Congress's refusal to expand women's economic and political rights. During and after the war, American women continued to lose independent property rights when they married and lacked the right to vote (except for propertied women in New Jersey from 1776 to 1807).

In "The Sentiments of an American Woman," Reed summoned her female peers to fulfill the promise they made at the outset of the war, asserting that women were both "animated by the purest patriotism" and "born for liberty." She authoritatively dismissed the notion that women were not patriotic or political beings, maintaining that "the offering of the Ladies" was nothing new. Recalling women of the past who had proven the merit of their patriotic contributions, Reed reminded Philadelphia's women how they, along with women across the colonies, had participated in boycotts and spinning bees, working as exemplars of female patriotism.

Just three days after the *Pennsylvania Gazette* published Reed's broadside, more than thirty women gathered to discuss the best way to aid the Revolutionary troops. After a productive meeting, the newly formed LAP published its notes, which appeared in newspapers across the British colonies. Members similarly wrote letters to their acquaintances in neighboring colonies suggesting that they imitate these efforts. Sarah Franklin Bache wrote letters to her female friends

FIGURE 14. Esther DeBerdt Reed, by Charles Kennedy Burt, [1848?]. LIBRARY COMPANY OF PHILADELPHIA.

soliciting their assistance, and women in New Jersey and Maryland copied the LAP model in their own fundraising efforts. Working independently and without the assistance of men, the association collected more than $300,000 in Continental currency. Though the group originally thought that the sum should be distributed directly to the soldiers as remuneration for their patriotism, Washington desired that the funds be used to manufacture desperately needed clothing for the Continental army. These women obliged, many cutting linen they purchased and sewing shirts for the soldiers themselves. Washington thanked the LAP for its contribution to the cause of liberty, and one soldier composed a poem in the women's honor, recognizing "the patriot females who their country save." The work of the LAP became a model of political activity for women during the early republic. Most importantly, these Philadelphia women proved their mettle, took the initiative to participate in the American cause, and recognized their essential contribution to the colonies' ultimate victory.

Articles of Confederation

Michael DiCamillo

The Articles of Confederation provided a political framework for conducting the Revolution and established the Confederation Congress that governed the United States from 1781 to 1789. The Second Continental Congress, meeting at the Pennsylvania State House, in 1776 appointed a committee to draft the document and continued to debate its provisions until 1777, when the Continental Congress had relocated in York, Pennsylvania, during the British occupation of Philadelphia. The states formally ratified the Articles in 1781, furnishing a compact for the thirteen states until the United States Constitution became the nation's governing document.

The Continental Congress initiated the long process of creating a government for the United States by appointing a committee to draft the Articles in June 1776. Philadelphia's John Dickinson led the committee that expanded and retooled the ideas for colonial unification that Benjamin Franklin had proposed to the Congress nearly a year earlier, on July 21, 1775. Congress finally adopted the committee's work on November 15, 1777, and two days later submitted the document to the states for ratification. During the years before complete ratification, Congress worked within the framework of the Articles to advance the Revolutionary War.

Several small states including New Jersey, Delaware, and Maryland initially refused to ratify the document. New Jersey, echoing the sentiments of other holdouts, wanted Congress to control foreign trade and to take possession of any lands that the United States might acquire from Great Britain. New Jersey representatives argued that such powers would give Congress a means to generate revenue and pay its war debts. These powers would also prevent larger states—particularly those with large port cities and access to western lands—from dominating smaller, coastal states that lacked a major port. The pressing need for unity ultimately led the holdout states to capitulate with the hope that in time Congress would address their concerns. Complete state ratification of the Articles of Confederation occurred on March 1, 1781, when Maryland ratified the document.

The Articles of Confederation established a loose

FIGURE 15. John Dickinson, engraving by J. B. Forrest from a portrait by C. W. Peale painted in 1770. Dickinson led the committee that drafted the Articles of Confederation. LIBRARY OF CONGRESS.

compact among the states. It allowed each state to retain its sovereignty, including the power to tax its citizens, rather than share this legislative power with a national government as the United States Constitution later required. As a result of the problems experienced under British rule, few Americans wanted a strong national government. Instead, the Articles of Confederation created a single-branch, unicameral institution possessing the power to declare war, to establish foreign and Native American alliances, and to negotiate and approve treaties. After ratification, the Confederation Congress met in Philadelphia until mid-1783, moving successively to Princeton, New Jersey; Annapolis, Maryland; and Trenton, New Jersey, before settling in New York City from 1785 to 1789.

Under the Articles, the individual state legislatures held significant governing authority, including control of tariffs on foreign and interstate trade. Pennsylvania's state government profited from this power because tariffs on goods moving through Philadelphia created a sizable revenue stream. The situation disadvantaged New Jersey residents who paid more for essential goods imported from Philadelphia and New York because of state-imposed tariffs. Tariff wars frequently erupted between states as each attempted to create its own optimal trade markets, and the Articles of Confederation provided Congress no power to resolve these conflicts.

The Confederation Congress also lacked the ability to levy direct taxes, including those needed to repay staggering debts from the Revolutionary War. While Congress could raise revenue through requisitions sent to the states, no state paid its share in full, and Georgia did not pay any of its required assessment. Without revenue from the states, the nation struggled to pay the interest on its loans. Robert Morris, Philadelphia merchant and superintendent of finance for the Confederation Congress, proposed numerous measures to help the United States gain solvency, but Congress and the state legislatures staunchly opposed his proposals.

Congress further struggled to enforce the powers it did have, including authority over diplomacy with Native American and foreign nations and provisions of the 1783 Treaty of Paris regarding Loyalists and British creditors. Lacking the authority to compel compliance, the destitute Confederation Congress quickly lost international credibility. Britain refused to vacate forts and trading posts in the Northwest Territory, Spain limited American access to the Mississippi, and the Barbary States of North Africa seized American ships in the Mediterranean. As the nation teetered on ruin, George Washington remarked that the Confederation was "little more than an empty sound, and Congress a nugatory body."

On February 21, 1787, the Confederation Congress recognized its deficiencies, recommending that delegates meet in Philadelphia to revise the Articles of Confederation. However, the Philadelphia Convention soon embarked on the creation of an entirely new document, the United States Constitution, which took effect on March 4, 1789. While this transition helped to maintain the fledgling nation's fragile stability, the debate over the role and powers of the national government continued long after the Articles of Confederation became defunct.

Constitutional Convention of 1787

Stuart Leibiger

From May 25 to September 17, 1787, at the Pennsylvania State House in Philadelphia, the Constitutional Convention drafted the United States Constitution, the world's oldest written national constitution still in use. The document, which divides power between the federal government and the states, launched a new phase of the American "experiment" in republican government (representative democracy). After being ratified by the American people, the Constitution began operation in 1789 in New York City (the federal capital until 1790) with the convening of the First Congress and the inauguration of George Washington as the first president.

By the mid-1780s, several problems had arisen under the Articles of Confederation, which went into effect in 1781. In particular, Congress needed the authority to tax and to regulate commerce. It also needed the means to solve foreign policy problems, such as opening the Mississippi River to American navigation and expelling British troops from several forts in the Northwest Territory. On February 21, 1787, the Confederation Congress endorsed assembling the Constitutional Convention in response to the call by an earlier convention that met in Annapolis, Maryland, in September 1786 to discuss giving Congress control of commerce. Congress tasked the 1787 convention with revising the Articles to render the federal government "adequate to the exigencies of the union." All agreed that the convention must strengthen the federal government at the expense of the states. The new constitution needed separate, coequal executive, legislative, and judicial branches restrained by checks and balances so that it could avoid repeating what many regarded as the injustices of the state governments, where, according to conservatives, popular majorities acting through unchecked legislatures often trampled the rights of religious or propertied minorities.

Fifty-five delegates, representing all of the states except Rhode Island, attended the convention in Philadelphia, a geographically central location. The biggest city in the United States, this metropolis of about forty thousand people featured boardinghouses, such as the Indian Queen Tavern and the City Tavern, where the delegates could reside, caucus, and dine. In addition to shops, theaters, and other cosmopolitan amenities, Philadelphia offered a religiously and ethnically diverse and tolerant atmosphere, where men of varying cultures felt comfortable. Many of the delegates found Philadelphia, the former national capital, a familiar place. Southerners, however, considered the antislavery views of the Quakers and like-minded residents troubling. With the windows of the State House's Assembly Room sealed shut to prevent eavesdropping, the delegates spent the humid summer months deliberating in sweltering conditions.

The convention, scheduled to open on May 14, did not achieve a quorum until May 25. On the first day, Robert Morris of Pennsylvania nominated George Washington to be the convention president, to which the delegations unanimously assented. After agreeing to meet from 10 a.m. to 3 p.m. six days a week and settling on rules (including keeping the proceedings secret, allowing one vote per state, and permitting any decision to be debated again and changed), the convention took up a proposal for the structure of the government. The Virginia Plan, drafted by the Virginians and supported by the Pennsylvanians in the preconvention days, proposed a bicameral legislature with representation in both houses based on either each state's free population or federal taxes paid, along with executive and judicial branches. The South Carolina delegation backed the Virginia Plan even though its members considered it favorable to the wealthiest and most populous states. In return, Pennsylvania supported counting three-fifths of enslaved people toward representation in Congress.

The small states, led by William Paterson of New Jersey, countered with the New Jersey Plan in opposition to the sweeping changes proposed by the Virginia Plan, especially elimination of the confederation's one-vote-per-state system. The New Jersey Plan would essentially add executive and judicial branches to the existing confederation and grant Congress power over taxation and commerce. At stake were not just the interests of large versus small states, but whether the new framework would be a national government of people or whether it would continue a confederation of states. Upon reaching an impasse and nearly dissolving, the convention turned the divisive matter over to a grand committee composed of a member from each state. The committee, which included

FIGURE 16. *Signing of the Constitution*, by Howard Chandler Christy, 1940, depicting the scene at Independence Hall on September 17, 1787. ARCHITECT OF THE CAPITOL.

Benjamin Franklin of Pennsylvania, devised the Great Compromise (or the Connecticut Compromise) in which each state's representation in the House of Representatives would be based on population (including three-fifths the number of enslaved people), and each state would receive two seats in the Senate. Appropriations bills could only originate in the House. This breakthrough created what James Madison of Virginia called a partly national, partly federal "compound republic."

At the end of July, the convention recessed for ten days while a five-man Committee of Detail incorporated the agreed-upon resolutions into a draft constitution. The committee, dominated by John Rutledge and James Wilson, replaced a blanket grant of power to Congress with a list of enumerated powers. At the same time, the draft included blank checks that undermined the concept of enumerated powers, such as the "necessary and proper," "general welfare," and "supremacy" clauses. In addition to the three-fifths compromise already agreed upon by the convention, the committee inserted a number of provisions favorable to the South, including a ban on export taxes and the requirement of a supermajority of two-thirds of Congress rather than a bare majority to pass commercial legislation. Nor could Congress prohibit the importation of enslaved Africans.

In August, the entire convention struggled with the issue of enslavement. Several northerners, led by Gouverneur Morris of Pennsylvania, eloquently attacked involuntary bondage as a moral abomination. The debate resulted in the South obtaining a fugitive slave provision in return for dropping the supermajority requirement for commercial legislation and allowing Congress to ban the international slave trade after twenty years, in 1808. Congress could also impose a tax on each imported enslaved person. The delegates also decided to use the word "persons" instead of "slaves." By threatening disunion if enslavement were not adequately protected, the South, especially Georgia and South Carolina, got the better of these compromises. The three-fifths compromise in particular secured enough additional seats in Congress to enable the "Slave Power" eventually to enact proslavery legislation such as the 1854 Kansas-Nebraska Act, which overturned the ban on enslavement imposed in those territories by the Missouri Compromise of 1820. Thanks to the electoral college, moreover, the three-fifths compromise also made it easier to elect southern presidents, who in turn often nominated proslavery Supreme Court justices.

The draft Constitution called for a president to be elected by Congress for one seven-year term. After considering myriad alternative arrangements, the delegates, at the beginning of September, turned the disposition of the presidency over to the Committee on Postponed Parts. Chaired by David Brearly of New Jersey, this committee redesigned the office, giving the executive a four-year term to be elected without a term limit by an electoral college. In accepting this change, the convention created a truly independent executive, coequal with the federal government's other branches. The convention's expectation that Washington, the likely first president, would not abuse his power convinced the delegates to take this bold step.

With all of the Constitution's major provisions decided upon, the convention on September 8 appointed a Committee of Style to prepare the final draft. Gouverneur Morris, an eloquent writer, finalized the preamble and organized the document into its various articles and sections. Not knowing which states would ratify, Morris changed the preamble's opening from a list of the thirteen states to "We the People of the United States."

On September 17, the convention met one last time to sign the engrossed manuscript. Franklin called on the forty-one delegates still present to add their signatures to the document; George Read signed for absent delegate John Dickinson, making thirty-nine signatures total. George Mason of Virginia, Edmund Randolph of Virginia, and Elbridge Gerry of Massachusetts remained unwavering in their opposition. As the delegates one by one affixed their names, Franklin pointed to the half sun carved into the backrest of Washington's chair. The Pennsylvanian remarked that after wondering all summer whether it was a rising or setting sun, he now knew that it was in fact a rising sun.

The convention forwarded the Constitution to Congress with resolutions specifying that the ratification decision be made by conventions "chosen in each state by the people." Congress voted unanimously not to endorse but merely to transmit the document to the states for ratification. Article VII provided that the Constitution would take effect when ratified by nine states. Delaware, Pennsylvania, and New Jersey became the first three states to ratify the Constitution, all by lopsided margins. The Delaware ratification convention, meeting in Dover, happy with the Great Compromise and not wishing to see such a small state become a separate nation, ratified on December 7 by a 30-0 vote. The Pennsylvania convention, held in the State House, approved the Constitution on December 12 by a vote of 46 to 23, rejecting the anti-federalists' request to postpone ratification until they had time to propose amendments. The bitter response of Pennsylvania's unreconciled anti-federalists to the federalists' heavy-handed approach caused remaining states to conduct a more thorough and sincere ratification debate. New Jersey's convention in Trenton, eager for commerce (and import duties) to be controlled by the federal government because of the state's dependence on out-of-state ports in New York City and Philadelphia, ratified on December 18 by a 38–0 vote. Philadelphians celebrated the Constitution's ratification on July 4, 1788, with a Grand Federal Procession to the Bush Hill estate of William Hamilton, three miles outside of town, where James Wilson delivered a spirited address to a crowd of seventeen thousand. Toasts and a sumptuous feast followed.

EXPLORE MORE

Many locations central to the nation's founding can be visited in the Philadelphia region on both sides of the Delaware River. Independence National Historical Park, situated primarily between Second, Sixth, Walnut, and Arch Streets in Philadelphia, contains the Pennsylvania State House (now Independence Hall), Carpenters' Hall, City Tavern, Franklin Court, and other eighteenth-century sites. The Museum of the American Revolution, National Constitution Center, and American Philosophical Society are located nearby. Military sites in the region include Washington Crossing state parks in Pennsylvania and New Jersey; the Old Barracks Museum, Trenton; Brandywine Battlefield Historic Site, Chadds Ford; Valley Forge National Historical Park, King of Prussia; Red Bank Battlefield Park (Fort Mercer), National Park New Jersey; Fort Mifflin, Philadelphia; and Hancock's Bridge, Lower Alloways Township. The American Philosophical Society, Delaware Public Archives, New Jersey State Archives, Historical Society of Pennsylvania, Library Company of Philadelphia, and other historical societies, archives, and libraries in the area have a wealth of original documents on the Revolutionary era.

A range of books demonstrate the impact of the Greater Philadelphia region during the Revolutionary era including works such as Gary B. Nash, *The Urban Crucible: Social Change, Political Consciousness, and the Origins of the American Revolution* (Harvard University Press, 1979); Eric Foner, *Tom Paine and Revolutionary America*, rev. ed. (Oxford University Press, 2005); Pauline Maier, *American Scripture: Making the Declaration of Independence* (Knopf, 1997); Gregory Evans Dowd, *A Spirited Resistance: The North American Indian Struggle for Unity, 1745–1815* (Johns Hopkins University Press, 1992); and Richard R. Beeman, *Plain, Honest Men: The Making of the American Constitution* (Random House, 2009).

Several collections encompassing the larger history of Philadelphia, Pennsylvania, and New Jersey offer insightful essays on the Revolutionary period: Russell F. Weigley, ed., *Philadelphia: A 300-Year History* (Norton, 1982); Randall M. Miller and William Pencak, eds., *Pennsylvania: A History of the Commonwealth* (Pennsylvania State University Press and Pennsylvania Historical and Museum Commission, 2002); John B. Frantz and William Pencak, eds., *Beyond Philadelphia: The American Revolution in the Pennsylvania Hinterland* (Pennsylvania State University Press, 1998); and Maxine N. Lurie and Richard Veit, eds., *New Jersey: A History of the Garden State* (Rutgers University Press, 2012).

More closely focused research on the Revolutionary period in Philadelphia includes Richard A. Ryerson, *The Revolution Is Now Begun: The Radical Committees of Philadelphia, 1765–1776* (University of Pennsylvania Press, 1978); Billy G. Smith, *The "Lower Sort": Philadelphia's Laboring People, 1750–1800* (Cornell University Press, 1990); Thomas M. Doerflinger, *A Vigorous Spirit of Enterprise: Merchants and Economic Development in Revolutionary Philadelphia* (University of North Carolina Press, 1986); Michael H. Taylor, *James Wilson: The Anxious Founder* (Lexington Books, 2021); Gary B. Nash, *Forging Freedom: The Formation of Philadelphia's Black Community, 1720–1840* (Harvard University Press, 1988); Owen S. Ireland, *Sentiments of a British-American Woman: Esther DeBerdt Reed and the American Revolution* (Pennsylvania State University Press, 2017); Richard Godbeer, *World of Trouble: A Philadelphia Quaker Family's Journey Through the American Revolution* (Yale University Press, 2019); and Aaron Sullivan, *The Disaffected: Britain's Occupation of Philadelphia During the American Revolution* (University of Pennsylvania Press, 2019).

Recent works on the Revolutionary era in New Jersey and Delaware include Maxine N. Lurie, *Taking Sides in Revolutionary New Jersey: Caught in the Crossfire* (Rutgers University Press, 2022); Barbara J. Mitnick, ed., *New Jersey in the American Revolution* (Rutgers University Press, 2005); James J. Gigantino II, ed., *The American Revolution in New Jersey: Where the Battlefront Meets the Home Front* (Rutgers University Press, 2015); Gary B. Nash, *Warner Mifflin: Unflinching Quaker Abolitionist* (University of Pennsylvania Press, 2017); and the documentary collection edited by Jane E. Calvert, *The Complete Writings and Selected Correspondence of John Dickinson*, of which the first two volumes were published in 2020 and 2021 by the University of Delaware Press.

Studies focusing on military action in the Delaware Valley include Stephen R. Taaffe, *The Philadelphia Campaign, 1777–1778* (University Press of Kansas, 2003); Thomas J. McGuire's two-volume *The Philadelphia Campaign* (Stackpole Books, 2006–7); Jeffery M. Dorwart, *Fort Mifflin of Philadelphia: An Illustrated History* (University of Pennsylvania Press, 1998); John W. Jackson, *The Pennsylvania Navy, 1775–1781: The Defense of the Delaware* (Rutgers University Press, 1974); Wayne K. Bodle, *The Valley Forge Winter: Civilians and Soldiers in War* (Pennsylvania State University Press, 2002); and David Hackett Fischer, *Washington's Crossing* (Oxford University Press, 2004). The special expanded issue on the Revolutionary War of *SoJourn: A Journal Devoted to the History, Culture, and Geography of South Jersey* (Summer 2018), edited by Paul W. Schopp and Tom Kinsella, confirms the national significance of Revolutionary battles and naval engagements in the Philadelphia region and the widespread impact of these battles and the British army's occupation of the city on residents across the countryside.

mbia happy land hail! ye Heroes heav'n born band Who fought a
ns caufe who fought & bled in freedoms caufe and when the ftorm of
d the peace your valor won let Inde pen - dence be our boaft
what it coft ever grateful for the prize let its Alt
2d time Chorus
Firm uni - ted let us be rallying round our Li - ber

Chapter 4

NATION'S CAPITAL

Introduction

For a decade, the politics and culture of Philadelphia and the nation were intertwined. The United States capital returned to the city from New York in December 1790, after President George Washington moved into the mansion owned by Robert Morris at 190 High Street (now Sixth and Market Streets) and members of the U.S. Congress took their seats in the Philadelphia County Court House (Congress Hall) at Sixth and Chestnut. Philadelphians had lobbied for return of the capital since the Confederation Congress left in 1783 in the face of protests by Pennsylvania troops wanting back pay and promised bonuses. After prolonged debate among national leaders, the city obtained the status of temporary capital until construction of Washington, D.C., on the Potomac River. Despite summer heat and yellow fever epidemics, Philadelphia offered the new government a vibrant economic, social, and cultural environment in which to establish its political authority and national institutions.

In 1790, Philadelphia, including its suburbs Southwark and the Northern Liberties, had 44,096 residents, the largest urban population in the United States. By 1800, the population of the city and these suburbs grew to 61,559. Philadelphia's commerce prospered from international trade with the West Indies and Europe with exports of wheat, flour, pork, beef, lumber, and other goods produced and transported to the city by farmers, craftspeople, and traders throughout southeastern Pennsylvania and southern New Jersey. Philadelphia merchants expanded trading partnerships after the American Revolution, importing spices, tea, porcelain, and silk from China. Wealthy residents built large homes, commissioned portraits, and purchased expensive carriages, clocks, foods, clothing, and other luxuries from local artisans and shopkeepers who obtained iron, lumber, and coal from furnaces and sawmills throughout the region. Guided by financier Robert Morris, in 1781 elite Philadelphians invested in the Bank of North America, the first nationally chartered bank, providing capital to fight the Revolution, prop up the Confederation government, and fund entrepreneurs. The first Bank of the United States (1791), also founded in Philadelphia, similarly supported the nation's credit and encouraged commercial and industrial growth.

The diverse income levels and ethnic backgrounds among the city's population distinguished Philadelphia from a nation composed mostly of plantations, farms, small towns, and hamlets. Philadelphia remained a walking city in which merchants situated their homes and businesses on the waterfront or located their mansions centrally in the Market Street corridor, while in some cases also building country houses to escape summer heat and urban pests and pestilences. Laborers found less expensive housing in the northern, southern, and western sections and in alleys throughout the city, while many poor Philadelphians lived in "Hell Town," a neighborhood extending three blocks north of Market

Street along the Delaware River. During the 1790s, approximately 180 taverns operated in Philadelphia, many on the waterfront. Throughout the city, bakers sold bread daily to their neighbors.

Black residents of Philadelphia challenged President Washington and many members of the U.S. Congress who were enslavers and refused to abolish enslavement nationally. The number of enslaved people in the region declined as some successfully escaped, Quakers and other enslavers chose emancipation, and Pennsylvania's abolition act (1780) gradually took effect. Free Black people built a strong community with institutions such as the African Episcopal Church of St. Thomas and Mother Bethel African Methodist Episcopal Church that offered mutual support and protected new migrants who arrived from outside the Philadelphia area. As Washington, his family, and many affluent residents escaped the devastating yellow fever epidemic of 1793, ministers Absalom Jones and Richard Allen led Black Philadelphians in providing medical and burial services for the city's sick and poor.

Within the Philadelphia region during the 1790s, residents witnessed, joined, and contested the federal government's efforts to establish authority. While President Washington sent military expeditions to defeat Native people in the Ohio Country, Philadelphia hosted Creek, Cherokee, Ottawa, Miami, Haudenosaunee (Iroquois), and many other delegations who negotiated with his administration. Between meetings with officials, the Native diplomats visited cultural sites such as theaters and churches and talked with members of the Quaker Indian Committee and other residents. In 1794, Washington sent troops against farmers in western Pennsylvania who rebelled against the federal excise tax on whiskey, returning some of the protesters to Philadelphia for trial. John Adams's administration similarly responded with armed force and indictments against agitators in the Fries Rebellion in Bucks, Montgomery, and Northampton Counties who opposed the House Tax Law and the Alien and Sedition Acts of 1798. In each instance, the federal trials of accused traitors unfolded in the U.S. District Court in Philadelphia. Newspapers in the U.S. capital such as the *Philadelphia Aurora* and *Gazette of the United States* published the increasingly hostile partisan rhetoric of the developing Republican and Federalist political parties.

Despite the departure of the federal government to the Potomac River in 1800, the Philadelphia region's commerce and diverse culture remained central to the nation's growth, just as hosting the capital had a permanent imprint on the city's heritage and identity. In subsequent years, Philadelphia remained the "Athens of America" with stately buildings referencing Greek architecture, institutions such as the Bank of the United States and the U.S. Mint, and intellectual and artistic centers, including the American Philosophical Society and Charles Willson Peale's portrait gallery and natural history museum.

Capital of the United States (Selection of Philadelphia)

Hillary S. Kativa

As the national capital from 1790 to 1800, Philadelphia was the seat of the federal government for a short but crucial time in the new nation's history. How and why Congress selected Philadelphia as the temporary United States capital reflects the essential debates of the era, particularly the balance of power between northern and southern states. These debates, as well as the creation of new national institutions and the rise of political parties, distinguished Philadelphia's decade as the capital city and created an enduring connection to the early national period.

Philadelphia's selection in 1790 as the temporary national capital followed the drafting of the new federal Constitution, which authorized Congress to enact legislation for establishing a permanent seat of government. As a candidate for the permanent capital, Philadelphia's size, wealth, and central location weighed in its favor, yet congressmen from both New England and the southern states considered Philadelphia too urban, as well as hot and prone to outbreaks of disease. In addition, sectional conflicts and whether or not the capital should be a commercial city animated the debate and guided Congress's efforts to find a location "consistent with convenience to the navigation of the Atlantic Ocean, and having due regard to the particular situation of the Western Country."

As the debate unfolded during the 1780s, western expansion informed the contest between northern and southern states to secure the capital, as each region adopted a different geographic calculus to advance its case. While northern advocates focused on current population centers, placing the city east of Pennsylvania's Susquehanna River, southern promoters emphasized future growth and the implicit and unstated elevation of the agrarian economy based on enslavement of Black people. Notably, both sides assumed a natural alliance between southern and western political interests, a crucial consideration given the capital's potential to enhance the power and leverage of the region in which it was located.

By 1790, two dozen sites located on or near the Delaware, Schuylkill, Susquehanna, and Potomac Rivers and Chesapeake Bay had been proposed publicly as candidates for the capital city. The Philadelphia region figured prominently in several proposals, which alternately incorporated portions of Southwark, Northern Liberties, Byberry, and Germantown. Several prominent Philadelphians, including Tench Coxe, Robert Morris, and Dr. Benjamin Rush, lobbied on the city's behalf, with Morris going so far as to offer his mansion on High Street as the presidential residence. For their part, Philadelphia's citizens flooded Congress with petitions and the city council pledged money for both remodeled federal housing and public buildings, including a new city hall and a courthouse built on the same square as the existing Pennsylvania State House.

Ultimately, the issue of assumption, Secretary of the Treasury Alexander Hamilton's plan for the federal government to assume the states' war debts, determined the capital's permanent location. Facing resistance from states like Virginia that had already resolved their debts, Hamilton wedded together the questions of assumption and the federal capital to strike a political bargain that advanced his cause. While Robert Morris negotiated with Hamilton to establish the capital in Germantown or at the Falls of the Delaware, a deal never came to fruition. Instead, wary of Virginia's opposition to the assumption plan, Hamilton struck a deal with Thomas Jefferson that provided enough northern votes for a federal capital on the Potomac. In exchange for the Pennsylvania delegation's support, Coxe and Morris negotiated a plan to relocate the capital from New York to Philadelphia for ten years; the final compromise, the Residence Act of 1790, passed both houses of Congress in July 1790.

As New Yorkers decried the loss of the capital, Philadelphians embraced the city's status as the temporary capital and hoped that, once the federal government settled in Philadelphia, inertia would keep it there permanently. While the Potomac seemed best situated to strengthen and preserve the connection between the North, South, and West, many were skeptical that a new capital constructed out of so-called "wilderness" was preferable to the nation's largest city. As one Baltimore newspaper argued, the "idea of fixing their Residence in the Woods, can only be agreeable to *a Congress of hermits*." A Connecticut humorist similarly proposed a constitutional amendment banning Congress from establishing itself "in an Indian wigwam . . . [or] in the howling wilderness." Nonetheless, under the leadership of President George Washington, plans for a Potomac capital continued apace as Congress reconvened in Philadelphia.

In December 1790, Philadelphia stretched approximately nine blocks west from the Delaware River. Per the first federal census, the population of the city and its adjacent districts was 44,096 inhabitants. While the U.S. Supreme Court occupied city hall, the House of Representatives and Senate convened in what became known as Congress Hall, a Philadelphia County courthouse recently erected just west of the Pennsylvania State House. Over the ensuing decade, these walls bore witness to several key events in the nation's formative period, including ratification of the Bill of Rights and Jay's Treaty, President John Adams's inauguration, and passage of the federal Fugitive Slave Act and the Alien and Sedition Acts. Congress also enacted legislation to establish the first Bank of the United States, the U.S. Mint, and the federal tariff, thereby approving Secretary Hamilton's plan to create the nation's first financial center and spur maritime trade and commercial growth.

As the federal capital, Philadelphia boasted a diverse population that included foreign dignitaries, representatives of many Native peoples, and a significant free Black community, all of whom animated its political culture and enhanced the city's reputation as the most cosmopolitan city in the new republic. The concentration of government activity around Sixth and Chestnut Streets notably afforded constituents easy, daily access to their representatives and increased Philadelphians' political participation to levels

This Plan of the City of Philadelphia and its Environs, (shewing the improved Parts) is Dedicated to the MAYOR, ALDERMEN and CITIZENS thereof, By their most obedient Servant, John Hills,
May 30th 1796.
Surveyor and Draughtsman.
Sir, I have the pleasure of presenting to You the thanks of the Corporation, agreeably to their resolution of this day, for the Elegant Plan of the City of Philadelphia, which You have Inscribed to them, and with which their Chamber is decorated.
I am Sir,
Philad. Sep. 5. 1796. Your most humble Servant,
Mr. Jno. Hills. Matth. Clarkson, Mayor.
REFERENCE
No. 1. Christ Church, 2. St. Peters, 3. St. Pauls — Protestant Episcopal Churches
4. St. Thomas — for the Africans
5. St. Michaels, 6. Zion Church — German Lutheran
7. German Reformed Church
8. The Old Roman Chapel, 9. St. Marys — Roman Catholic
10. Holy Trinity — German
11. First Presbyteran, 12. Second Do., 13. Third Do. — Church
14. Friends Meeting house
15. Pine Street Friends Mg. and School house
16. Keys Alley Friends Meeting
17. Fourth Street Friends Mg. and School house
18. Free Friends Meeting house
19. Secedars Meeting house
20. Moravian Church
21. Baptist Church
22. Methodist Episcopal Meeting
23. Secedars Meeting
24. Universalists Meeting
No. 25. Jews Synagogue
26. Pennsylvania, 27. Christ Church — Hospitals
28. Friends Alms House
29. University of Pennsylvania
30. German Lutheran Free School
31. Library with the Loganian Library
32. Carpenters, 33. Philosophical, 34. Surgeons — Halls
35. United States, 36. North America, 37. Pennsylvania — Banks
38. State House
39. City Hall
40. County Court house (the Seat of Congress)
41. House of Employment & Alms house
42. New Theatre
43. Circus
44. Goal for Debtors
45. Goal for Felons
46. Market
47. Fish house
48. Burying Grounds
In Southwark
No. 1. Swedes Church
2. Methodist Meeting house
3. Old Theatre
In the Northern Liberties
No. 1. Presbyteran Church
2. School house
3. Market
NB. The Line from Federal Street Public Landing to Cedar Street was fixed by the Port Wardens as the Boundary of the Wharfs, April, 2nd 1788. The Line from Vine Street Public Landing, to Eyres Wharf was fixed by the Port Wardens, March, 21st 1796.
The Street and Roads that are dotted thus are to be opened according to Law.
Brick Yards & Kilns.
PART OF THE NORT
SCHUYLKILL RIVER
From Lancaster
Middle Ferry
Turnpike Road from Lancaster
Public Landing
Callow Hill Street
Vine Street
North West Square of Eight Acres
South West Square of Eight Acres
Broad Street
PART OF PASSYUNK
MOYAM
Federal Road from Grays Ferry to Southwark

FIGURE 17. *This Plan of the City of Philadelphia and its Environs, (showing the improved Parts)*, by John Hills, 1796. LIBRARY OF CONGRESS.

FIGURE 18. *Back of the State House, Philadelphia*, by William Birch, 1800. This view of the courtyard features several visitors, including a delegation of Native Americans. LIBRARY COMPANY OF PHILADELPHIA.

unmatched over the next century. Between 1790 and 1800, Philadelphia's elections were watched for signs of national political developments, most critically Federalists' declining support and the rise of a two-party system. The growth of partisan politics was likewise evident in the city's print culture, especially newspapers like the *Philadelphia Aurora* and *Gazette of the United States* that increasingly aligned with either the Jeffersonian or Federalist factions. As the federal government prepared to depart Philadelphia in 1800, change was on the horizon for both the nation and the city, whose loss of the federal capital arguably marked the end of its role as the preeminent American metropolis. Nonetheless, the legacy of Philadelphia's tenure as the national capital endures in the national institutions that first took root in Philadelphia and whose buildings provide a boon for historical tourism and a trademark of civic identity.

U.S. Congress

Coxey Toogood

During the 1790s, while Philadelphia served as the nation's temporary capital, the United States Congress met problems and threats to the nation that tested the endurance of the Constitution and the republic it framed. Domestic issues of finance, taxation, sectionalism, Native American affairs, and enslavement divided the delegates into bitter political camps, and international relations fomented disagreements as well. Partisan politics aside, Congress during this decade forged a government that remained intact, despite expectations to the contrary from monarchies overseas.

Many members of Congress during the 1790s knew Philadelphia well. The Continental and Confederation Congresses had met in the Pennsylvania State House from 1775 through 1783, and dozens who had served, including some of the signers of the Declaration of Independence and Constitution, were elected to the First Congress. Delegates to Congress now operated under a new frame of government, with different political realities. They worked with a sense that they were setting precedent for future legislators.

Congress opened its first Philadelphia session in December 1790, after the recently constructed (1787) county courthouse at the corner of Sixth and Chestnut Streets had been renovated to accommodate the House of Representatives and Senate. The House met in the large first floor room and the senators met above them in the second floor's southern room, with offices and committee rooms filling its northern end. Next door, the Pennsylvania General Assembly and governor worked in the Pennsylvania State House, while the mayor and his court occupied Philadelphia City Hall (1791) on the Fifth Street end. It was a unique time when all three levels of government sat on State House Square together.

Philadelphia raced to meet the demands of the enormous influx of people from New York who migrated south with Congress. Property owners spiked room and house rentals, sometimes more than doubling the former rates, much to the congressmen's annoyance. Carpenters rushed to build more accommodations, not just for Congress and the federal government, but for the many artisans and shopkeepers who followed behind. Congressmen, however, found the city filled with commodities they could send home to grateful families and many amusements—libraries, theaters, gardens, spas, balls, a museum, and constant invitations for socializing.

Congress convened on December 6, 1790, in the third session of the First Congress. Sixty-five members of the House sat in curved rows facing the Speaker. Twenty-six senators (two from each of thirteen states) climbed the steep staircase to their desks that faced Vice President John Adams, until he became president in 1797. When the 1790 federal census (congressional act in March 1790) increased the number of representatives to 105, the city enlarged the building to make room for the new members. The Senate grew as well, from twenty-six to thirty-two members, as Congress admitted three new states—Vermont (1791), Kentucky (1792), and Tennessee (1796).

To handle the heavy load of business, Congress created the first standing committees—commerce, banking, taxes, and the national debt. Early in 1791, Congress passed the act incorporating the hotly debated Bank of the United States, which carried the federal debt until its twenty-year charter expired. In 1792, Congress passed the Coinage Act that created the first U.S. Mint, which was built in Philadelphia. Secretary of the Treasury Alexander Hamilton had masterminded the details for this legislation, to secure a stable economy, regular debt payment, and a unified currency for the nation.

The issue of abolishing enslavement remained contested through the 1790s as certain southern delegates threatened that their states would abandon the union if the subject came to a vote. In 1793, Congress passed the Fugitive Slave Act that strengthened the terms established by the Constitution for returning fugitives. Petitions against enslavement made no headway on the floor, including those from members of Philadelphia's free Black community, Quakers, and the Pennsylvania Abolition Society. Although Congress limited American participation in international trafficking with the Slave Trade Act in 1794, the fate of the nation's enslaved people remained a topic too difficult for Congress to address.

Congress tackled multiple obstacles to address conflict west of the Appalachians, as the Senate ratified and the House funded peace treaties with Native Americans, Spain, and Great Britain. Native people in the Ohio Valley, after defending their territory against white settlement, met defeat at the Battle of Fallen Timbers in 1794 and signed the Treaty of Greenville the next year. Spain's troublesome control of New Orleans and navigation along the Mississippi found resolution with ratification of the Pinckney Treaty in 1796.
The most controversial treaty during the decade was negotiated by Chief Justice John Jay in 1794 to address Great Britain's failure to remove troops from western

forts in blatant denial of the 1783 Treaty of Paris, continued seizure of American cargo in the West Indies, and impressment of American seamen. Though Jay had considerable success, the treaty inflamed partisan animosities as Republicans in Congress railed against it and demonstrators marched in protest. When President George Washington showed his approval, the Federalists gained popular support and the Senate finally ratified it in 1795. House Republicans tried to block funding for the treaty, but failed, and the House finally voted its financing.

By the close of the decade, politics had become rife with personal attacks in the halls of Congress and in the press. Partisan newspapers, discreetly funded by party leaders, lashed out at their political opponents, incensing public opinion and demonstrations. There seemed to be no limit to the slander and animosity printed in the Federalist and Republican press.

When the nation unexpectedly faced the threat of war with France (the Quasi-War), however, the patriotism of citizens dampened the strident political rivalry. With war pending, the Fifth Congress, still dominated by Federalists, passed the Alien and Sedition Acts in 1798 to suppress opposition to the Adams administration. Republicans immediately denounced these four laws as unconstitutional; the party leaders Thomas Jefferson and James Madison anonymously published the Kentucky and Virginia Resolutions in protest. The resolutions contributed to the election of Jefferson as president in 1800. The turbulent decade of Federalist reign had ended, but not without a record of impressive accomplishments in forming and securing the emerging nation.

U.S. Presidency

Stuart Leibiger

The decade when Philadelphia hosted the national government proved pivotal in the evolution of the United States presidency, with emergence of an independent but democratic chief executive under the U.S. Constitution. This formative period from 1790 to 1800 included nearly seven years of the administration of George Washington and more than three years of the single term of John Adams. Among other notable events, Philadelphia witnessed Washington's second inauguration and John Adams's inauguration, significantly the first transfer of power from one president to another.

Washington took up residence in Philadelphia in December 1790. For his executive mansion, he rented from the city for £500 a year the house of Robert Morris at 190 High Street (526–30 Market Street today) near the corner of Sixth Street. One of the largest homes in the city, the President's House (as it became known) stood three stories tall and featured a spacious backyard with several outbuildings including a washhouse, kitchen, icehouse, smokehouse, coach house, and stables. Amenities also included a walled garden, a paved yard, and a woodyard. Before moving in, Washington had a two-story bow added to the southwest corner of the house to enlarge the State Dining Room and State Drawing Room and also built quarters for enslaved people and servants in the backyard. In addition to one or two secretaries, a staff of about a dozen white servants and three or four enslaved African Americans from Mount Vernon served the president's family, which included Martha Washington and two of Martha's grandchildren, Eleanor "Nelly" Parke Custis and George Washington Parke Custis. Washington regularly rotated his enslaved people out of Pennsylvania to keep them from becoming free through the state's 1780 Gradual Abolition Act, which freed nonresident enslaved people who had lived there continuously for six months. Enslaved seamstress Ona Judge fled to freedom from the city, while a cook named Hercules escaped on Washington's birthday in 1797 after returning to Mount Vernon.

Washington enjoyed Philadelphia's amenities (especially the theater and shops) and admired the industrious economy of the middle states. Like many others, however, the Washingtons fled the city during the 1793 yellow fever epidemic, traveling to Virginia then returning in November 1793 to Germantown, first to the Dove House and then to the Deshler-Morris House. Despite lobbying by Philadelphians, Washington declined to occupy an immense residence built by the city on Ninth Street and pushed forward construction of the new capital of Washington, D.C., on the Potomac River.

Entertainments at the President's House consisted of Tuesday afternoon "levees," Thursday afternoon state dinners, and Friday evening "drawing rooms," which Martha Washington hosted and her husband informally

FIGURE 19. *The Residence of Washington in High Street*, by William Breton, 1795–96. The President's House, owned by Robert Morris, was located at Sixth and Market Streets (then 190 High Street). COLLECTION OF THE HISTORICAL SOCIETY OF PENNSYLVANIA.

attended. At the levees, Washington appeared in formal dress, stood in the bow of the State Dining Room, and exchanged greetings with gentlemen attendees formed in a circle. "On fryday Evenings mrs. Washington has a drawing Room which is usually very full of the *well Born and well Bred*," wrote Abigail Adams. "Some times it is as full as her Britanick majesties Room, & with quite as Handsome Ladies." The "company are entertained with Coffee Tea cake Ice creams Lemonade &c . . . this shew lasts from seven, till Nine oclock comeing & going . . . as it is not Etiquette for any person to stay Long." Wealthy Philadelphians such as Samuel Powel and his wife Elizabeth Willing Powel also hosted a variety of parties for socializing and political networking, forming what became known as the "Republican Court." Abigail Adams witnessed "Parties upon Parties, Balls & entertainments" in Philadelphia "equal to any European city."

In Philadelphia, President Washington continued the challenging task of establishing presidential precedents that he had begun in New York. For example, he conferred with his department heads—Treasury Secretary Alexander Hamilton, Secretary of State Thomas Jefferson, Secretary of War Henry Knox, and Attorney General Edmund Randolph—as a group advisory board that became known as the cabinet. Washington issued the first presidential veto in 1792 when he rejected a bill to reapportion congressional representation.

Philadelphia witnessed the emergence of political parties, with Washington endorsing the use of implied powers and loose construction of the Constitution advocated by Hamilton and the Federalist Party to create a strong federal government and to promote an industrial economy. In 1791, for example, he signed the controversial bill creating the Bank of the United States (the institution moved into its home on Third Street in 1797). The opposition Republican Party led by James Madison and Jefferson favored an agrarian republic of limited federal power and feared that the administration's "high toned" policies foreshadowed a return of monarchy to the United States. Washington, who deplored partisanship and who viewed parties as special interests hostile to the public good, tried unsuccessfully to reconcile cabinet members Hamilton and Jefferson. In response to pleas from both parties, Washington reluctantly accepted a second term as president starting in 1793.

President Washington used military force to protect white settlement on Native lands and to suppress the Whiskey Rebellion in western Pennsylvania. Against Native Americans in the Ohio Country, the administration sent expeditions led by General Josiah Harmer in 1790 and General Arthur St. Clair in 1791 that ended in disastrous American defeats. The latter loss led to the first congressional investigation of the executive in U.S. history. A third expedition led by General Anthony Wayne defeated the Native people in 1794 at Fallen Timbers in present northwestern Ohio. In 1794, after failing to redress grievances of western Pennsylvania farmers angry over a 1791 federal excise on whiskey, Washington federalized 12,950 militiamen from New Jersey, Pennsylvania, Maryland, and Virginia to suppress the Whiskey Rebellion. This action established a precedent that President Abraham Lincoln followed in 1861 to resist the secession of the Southern states.

Hoping to steer clear of war between Great Britain and France, Washington issued the 1793 Proclamation of Neutrality. The following year he appointed Chief Justice John Jay as special envoy to Great Britain to negotiate an end to British seizures of American ships and impressment of sailors. Washington signed the controversial Jay's Treaty in 1795 even though it did not end ship seizures and impressment, because he was determined to keep the new nation at peace. Mobs celebrating the French Revolution and critical of the agreement soon roamed the city and even threatened the president's safety. A major dispute between the executive branch and the Republican-controlled House of Representatives occurred when Washington refused to turn over sensitive documents pertaining to the treaty negotiations, citing executive privilege. By holding political gatherings and public meetings to rally public opinion behind the president, the Federalists pressured the House into appropriating funds to implement the treaty. In exploiting Washington's popularity to win the battle over the treaty, however, the Federalists unleashed democratic forces in American politics that lost them the war for control of the federal government when the Jeffersonian Republicans won the election of 1800. The Republicans, whose democratic ideology proved more appealing to common voters than the deferential, aristocratic ideology of the Federalists, also began seeking support directly from the voters on specific issues.

On September 19, 1796, Washington's farewell address announced that he would not serve a third term as president. A printed message, not a public speech, the farewell appeared in the *Philadelphia American Daily Advertiser* published by David C. Claypoole. In addition to warning against entangling foreign alliances, the address called on the American people to place national interests and the common good ahead of political partisanship.

John Adams and Thomas Jefferson were sworn in as the second president and vice president, respectively, at Congress Hall on March 4, 1797. This first transfer of executive power marked a great triumph for the new republic and a milestone in the history of representative democracy. By choosing to occupy the High Street house (despite a doubling of the rent and the building's severe state of disrepair), rather than the palace on Ninth Street, Adams helped guarantee the removal of the capital to Washington, D.C., in 1800. Adams hosted weekly "great dinners," each attended by about "36 Gentlemen," as well as Fourth of July celebrations. Like Washington, the second president admired Philadelphia. "It is a great City," he wrote, "and has Science, Litterature, Wealth and Beauty." But he found the presidency even more trying and disagreeable than his predecessor and spent much of his term at home in Massachusetts with his wife, Abigail, who suffered poor health.

Faced with French anger over Jay's Treaty, Adams sent diplomats to Paris to seek a peaceful resolution. Instead, the envoys received an insulting demand from the French for a bribe. This failure of diplomacy led to the Quasi-War in 1798, an undeclared naval war with France on the Atlantic Ocean. Republican opposition to a military buildup, the presence in Philadelphia of hundreds of French refugees fleeing the rebellion of enslaved people in Haiti, and vicious attacks on Adams in the partisan press convinced the Federalists in Congress to pass, and Adams to sign, the Alien and Sedition Acts. These laws made it a crime to falsely or maliciously criticize the president or Congress, authorized the president to deport aliens without due process, and increased the residency requirement for U.S. citizenship from five to fourteen years. The unpopularity of these acts, tax increases caused by the military buildup, and an ongoing divide between the Adams and Hamilton factions in the Federalist Party, intensified by the president's decision in 1800 once again to try to negotiate peace with France, contributed to the 1800 defeat of Adams and the Federalists by Jefferson and the Republicans.

Early in the nineteenth century the President's House, located in a thriving commercial neighborhood, was converted into shops. All but the side walls of the building were knocked down in 1832 to accommodate bigger stores. Early in the twentieth century, confusion arose over the exact size and location of the President's House. In 1951, the Commonwealth of Pennsylvania, not realizing the historical significance of the site, demolished the surviving exterior walls of the building to clear land for Independence Mall and then erected a restroom on the site. In 2000, the icehouse pit was unearthed while building the Liberty Bell Center. The ironic location of the quarters of Washington's enslaved workers near the entrance to the Liberty Bell Center drew considerable public attention. Archaeologists excavating the site in 2007 discovered significant portions of the original foundations. Beginning in 2010, visitors to the President's House Site (an open-air exhibit within Independence National Historical Park) could view the building's original footprint and underground remains.

U.S. Supreme Court

Laura Michel

As the nation's capital from 1790 to 1800, Philadelphia also served as the seat of the United States Supreme Court. Sharing a space with the Mayor's Court in Old City Hall at Fifth and Chestnut Streets, the Supreme Court of the 1790s was very much an institution in progress. Established by Article III of the Constitution and further elaborated by the Judiciary Act of 1789, the court's power of judicial review—generally considered to be at the heart of the institution's authority and prestige—was not specifically articulated until *Marbury v. Madison* in 1803, after the capital moved to Washington, D.C. Despite its relative weakness, scholars have come to identify the Supreme Court's time in Philadelphia as a period of important procedural groundwork that allowed the court to evolve into an independent and powerful branch of government.

The Supreme Court of the 1790s was smaller than its modern iteration. In accordance with the Judiciary Act of 1789, it had six members: one chief justice and five associate justices. With a firm belief in the importance of a strong judiciary to effective governance, President George Washington approached the selection of these early justices deliberately, prioritizing geographic diversity and jurists with established records of service to the young nation. The men who served during the court's first terms in Philadelphia included well-known figures such as *Federalist Papers* coauthor John Jay (New York); Constitutional Convention delegates James Iredell (North Carolina), John Rutledge (South Carolina), and James Wilson (Pennsylvania); as well as established jurists William Cushing from the Massachusetts Superior Court and John Blair of the Virginia Court of Appeals. During the court's tenure in Philadelphia, six additional appointments were made, including the third chief justice, Oliver Ellsworth.

The justices met as a whole body for two one-month terms in February and August and spent much of their time away from Philadelphia performing their "circuit riding" duties. The Judiciary Act of 1789 had established a series of lower federal courts: one district court per state and three superior circuits (Eastern, Middle, and Southern). Drawing from English judicial tradition, two Supreme Court justices were assigned to each "circuit" and would "ride" to hear cases in their respective regions. The justices almost universally loathed these duties. While neither February nor August was the most salubrious time in Philadelphia, circuit riding presented more of a threat to life and limb. Justice Iredell's leg was broken in a road accident, Justice Samuel Chase nearly drowned when his carriage driver misjudged the depth of a river, and Justice Wilson died of malaria while on circuit duties in North Carolina. While the Judiciary Act of 1793 reduced this burden and required only one justice to be present at a hearing, the practice of circuit riding meant that justices were not part of the everyday social or political life of Philadelphia in the 1790s.

Constrained by the burden of circuit riding and its as-yet unsettled powers, the Supreme Court heard only an average of seven cases per year during its time in Philadelphia. While few, these cases nevertheless reflected the role of the court in the broader Federalist project of establishing and enhancing federal authority. *Van Staphorst v. Maryland* (1791), the first case docketed before the Supreme Court, involved a dispute over the repayment of a loan made by Dutch bankers Nicolaas and Jacob van Staphorst to Maryland during the

FIGURE 20. *John Jay*, 1794, by Gilbert Stuart. GIFT OF THE JAY FAMILY, NATIONAL GALLERY OF ART, SMITHSONIAN INSTITUTION.

Revolution. While it was ultimately settled out of court, by agreeing to hear the case, the court held that it had jurisdiction to enforce contracts made between foreign nationals and states.

Subsequent cases continued to build on this articulation of federal power and authority, perhaps most controversially in *Chisholm v. Georgia* (1793). In this landmark case, Alexander Chisholm, executor of the estate of a South Carolina merchant, sued the state of Georgia for the nonpayment of goods provided by his client during the Revolutionary War. Georgia, citing the long-held British common-law doctrine of sovereign immunity, claimed that a state could not be sued without its consent and called for the case to be dismissed. In a 4–1 decision in favor of Chisholm, the court ruled that Article 3, Section 2, of the Constitution superseded states' claims of sovereign immunity and made them subject to the jurisdiction of the Supreme Court. With the ratification of the Constitution, Chief Justice Jay wrote in his decision, the ultimate sovereignty of the people was placed in the federal government, to which the states were subordinate. In the context of the emerging first party system and debates over federalism, the decision met with vocal opposition, particularly from the states. In response, Congress moved quickly to adopt the Eleventh Amendment (1795), which limited the ability of individuals to sue states in federal courts. Despite this apparent setback, the Supreme Court continued to place limits on states' sovereignty throughout the 1790s, including in *Ware v. Hylton* (1796), which ruled that federal treaties had precedence over any conflicting state laws.

In addition to cases heard, the court fashioned its place in the federal system in what it opted *not* to do. Rather than defer to the stronger and better-defined executive and legislative branches, the justices asserted their own vision of the extent and limits of judicial power. This was particularly apparent in the career of John Jay, the first chief justice of the Supreme Court. In 1793, Secretary of State Thomas Jefferson—acting on behalf of Jay's longtime friend President Washington—asked the court to prepare an official advisory opinion related to American neutrality amid ongoing conflict between Great Britain and France during the wars of the French Revolution. Jay, who was respected for his role in negotiating the Treaty of Paris (1783), was certainly qualified to advise on this matter of foreign policy. Nevertheless, he declined to offer an official opinion in order to protect the impartiality of the Supreme Court should any related cases appear on its docket in the future. Only by doing so, Jay asserted, could the separation of powers and system of checks and balances established by the Constitution truly succeed. At the same time, Jay saw no issue with continuing to serve as a personal advisor to Washington. He even offered to help the administration draft its 1793 Proclamation of Neutrality, publicly defended the policy in an ex-officio capacity, and in 1794 negotiated Jay's Treaty with Britain.

In terms of the accepted scope of its authority, prestige, the amount of time spent in session, and the number of decisions made, the Supreme Court of the 1790s was a less powerful and less robust institution than it became under leadership of Chief Justice John Marshall. Nevertheless, the importance of its evolution while in Philadelphia should not be underestimated.

The court's role in the articulation of federal supremacy and assertion of independence as the third branch of government laid the groundwork for its emergence in later years as a powerful and prestigious institution.

Bank of North America

Robert F. Smith

Chartered May 26, 1781, by the Confederation Congress and officially titled The President, Directors, and Company of the Bank of North America (BNA) until 1825, the BNA was the first commercial bank created by the national government to do business with and for the government. Robert Morris, congressional superintendent of finance, crafted the charter and used the bank to stabilize the national currency and save the Confederation from bankruptcy. The BNA's first building was at 307 Chestnut Street, Philadelphia, in the home of Tench Francis, the first cashier.

The BNA received funding from a variety of sources, opening on January 7, 1782, with ninety-nine Philadelphians, along with congressmen, subscribing to its shares. During 1782, subscribers to the Pennsylvania Bank, which had been founded in 1780, sold their shares to BNA. Morris, famous for furtive dealings, used a $450,000 French silver shipment to Congress to fund the bank, which lent the money back to Congress. Later, when the bank feared congressional loan default, Morris sold the government's shares to repay the bank, which then re-lent the money to Congress. Through maneuvers like this, the bank kept Congress funded through the Revolution and built itself a secure reputation.

BNA initially faced political controversy as opponents argued it was an overreach of congressional power and a bastion for moneyed interests. Fears eased when bank directors chartered the bank in Pennsylvania, giving BNA the unique distinction of holding two charters simultaneously. State politicians briefly revoked the charter in 1786. When the Confederation ceased, the national charter vanished and the bank operated under its state charter until 1864. Out of the national spotlight, the bank increasingly became a tool of the Pennsylvania government, which protected it in exchange for favorable loan conditions. BNA was a model for the federal Bank of the United States, chartered in 1791 by Congress at the behest of Alexander Hamilton, a protégé of Morris. BNA, however, did little business with the federal government, aside from relatively small loans to the government during the War of 1812 and the Civil War.

In 1863, seeking security, BNA applied to become "national" under the National Banking Act. Participating banks received national charters but were required to purchase government bonds with fixed interest rates as well as accept minimum reserve requirements. Banks benefited from consistent interest income and a federal guarantee that if the bank failed, bank depositors would be reimbursed by the sale of bank-held government bonds. Granted national status in 1864, BNA was the only bank exempted from the requirement to add the word "national" to its title.

BNA became part of the Federal Reserve System in 1914. It merged with Commercial Trust Company in 1923 and with the Pennsylvania Company for Insurances on Lives and Granting Annuities in 1929.

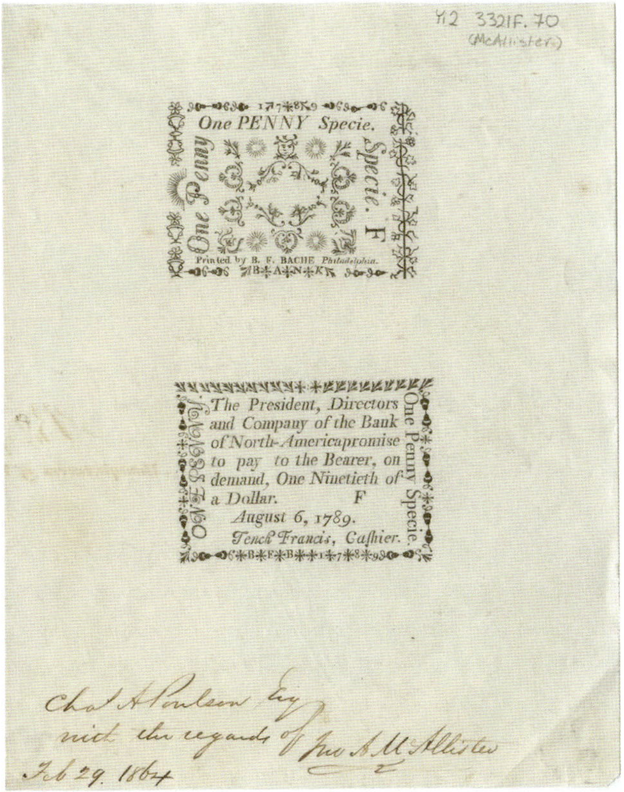

FIGURE 21. One penny specie note of the Bank of North America, printed by Benjamin Franklin Bache, 1789. LIBRARY COMPANY OF PHILADELPHIA.

BNA's legacy became the First Pennsylvania Banking and Trust Company in 1955 after another merger, this time with the First National Bank of Philadelphia. In 1990, CoreStates acquired "First Penny," which First Union in turn acquired in 1998. In 2001, First Union merged with Wachovia, which was then purchased by Wells Fargo in 2008.

First Bank of the United States

Jordan AP Fansler

The first Bank of the United States, chartered in 1791 as part of the financial and economic reform plans of Secretary of the Treasury Alexander Hamilton, played an instrumental role in establishing the nation's credit. Based in Philadelphia, it followed the precedent of the nationally chartered Bank of North America (1781), drawing many principal investors from the region and augmenting the city's role as a commercial center. During its twenty-year existence, the Bank of the United States was politically controversial and a foundational point of disagreement between developing political parties.

When Hamilton took office as Treasury secretary in 1789, economic instability and the Revolutionary War debt threatened the nation and the individual state governments. Capitalizing on those circumstances and using powers he believed the U.S. Constitution granted, Hamilton put forth a plan that included the Bank of the United States, chartered by Congress. The bank would stabilize currency, act as a depository for and lender to the government, and raise money for the nation to pay war debts. Hamilton also recommended that the federal government assume the outstanding war debts of the states. By consistently paying down this debt, the nation would reestablish good faith for future loans. As an organ of the national government, the bank would also tie private citizens financially to the well-being of the United States, and those who held a stake in the war loans would likewise want to see the nation prosper to ensure their repayment.

The bank immediately ignited controversy and, with other early disputes, fueled a developing political divide that led to the first rival political parties, the Federalists and Republicans. Each side argued that failure to follow their policies was tantamount to abandoning the Revolution, to the ruin of the nation. Federalists, who supported the bank, tended to be urban merchants and lawyers. They supported the bank, deeming it necessary for strengthening the nation's economy and the union in general. They believed that the Articles of Confederation had failed on both of those counts and that the Constitution was adopted to enact vigorous national programs such as those Hamilton suggested. Their rivals, often rural residents and debtors rather than creditors, argued that the bank was unconstitutional. They believed it would further enrich urban elites who had stockpiled wealth during the Revolution and increase emphasis on volatile financial markets. Furthermore, it would do little to aid destitute veterans requiring immediate debt relief. These opponents, led by Secretary of State Thomas Jefferson in the cabinet and James Madison in the House of Representatives, also argued that by encouraging speculation and financiers, the bank would run counter to the Revolutionary principles and virtuous agrarian ideal that best suited a republican form of government. Despite the controversy, Congress passed the legislation necessary to establish the bank, and President George Washington signed the bill into law, granting it a twenty-year charter to 1811.

Originally headquartered in Carpenters' Hall, the meeting place of the First Continental Congress, after 1797 the Bank of the United States moved to its own building on Third Street (later part of Independence National Historical Park). The building, an example of neoclassical architecture emulating that of Greece and Rome, featured a colonnaded, marble façade alluding to the ancient republican ideals that the new nation espoused.

As with the Bank of North America, the Bank of the United States drew many of its major stockholders from the Philadelphia region. Thomas Willing, formerly president of the Bank of North America and business partner to Robert Morris, became the national bank's first president. Willing, Samuel Howell, and David Rittenhouse, all Philadelphians, served as the bank's first appointed commissioners. Another of Hamilton's initiatives, the U.S. Mint, also located in Philadelphia, assisted the bank with its capacity to regulate the money supply. In addition to its local presence, the Bank of the United States connected Philadelphia to the nation through its branches in Boston, Baltimore, New York,

FIGURE 22. *Girard's Bank, late the Bank of the United States in Third Street, Philadelphia*, engraving based on William Birch's 1800 image. Stephen Girard purchased most shares of the Philadelphia branch after Congress allowed its charter to expire in 1811. LIBRARY OF CONGRESS.

and Charleston (opened in 1792); Norfolk, Virginia (1800); Washington, D.C., and Savannah, Georgia (1802); and New Orleans (1805). Despite difficulty in coordination, the far-flung branches assured the bank's opponents that it would be truly national and serve more than simply Philadelphia's merchant class.

While the national controversy surrounding the Bank of the United States abated after its creation, the partisanship it engendered continued. Within months of its incorporation, the bank, through the initial branch in Philadelphia, helped to set off the Panic of 1792, seemingly confirming accusations about economic volatility. Nevertheless, by the end of the bank's twenty-year charter in 1811, national credit was largely established. The Republicans controlling Congress allowed the charter to expire with the assets liquidated relatively peacefully, at least in Philadelphia. Stephen Girard of Philadelphia bought most of the Philadelphia branch's shares, operating the institution as a private concern, the Girard Bank. Only five years later, in the midst of depressed trade after the War of 1812 and European Napoleonic Wars, Congress instituted a second Bank of the United States (also headquartered in Philadelphia).

The first Bank of the United States played a pivotal role in establishing the nation's credit. It drew from the traditions of banking already present in Philadelphia during the Revolution, was supported by Philadelphia's merchant class, and set a precedent of national banking. It contributed to the growing partisanship of the 1790s and helped the Philadelphia region and its wealthy elite remain at the epicenter of national finance and the economy into the nineteenth century, even after the seat of government shifted to Washington, D.C.

FIGURE 23. *Famous Whiskey Insurrection in Pennsylvania*, wood engraving, 1880. NEW YORK PUBLIC LIBRARY.

Whiskey Rebellion Trials

Patrick Grubbs

The first two convictions of Americans for federal treason in United States history occurred in Philadelphia in the aftermath of the Whiskey Rebellion, an uprising against the federal excise tax on whiskey that took place primarily in western Pennsylvania in 1791–94. During the crucial first decade under the U.S. Constitution, Philadelphia served as a testing ground for federal authority as Congress passed excise legislation to help pay Revolutionary War debts, President George Washington issued proclamations against the rebels and sent troops, and the U.S. District Court in Philadelphia tried accused rebels for their resistance to federal law.

The Whiskey Rebellion developed after the First U.S. Congress, seated at Congress Hall at Sixth and Chestnut Streets, passed on March 3, 1791, an excise tax on domestic whiskey. This legislation, pushed through Congress by Secretary of the Treasury Alexander Hamilton, was designed to help pay off state debts assumed by Congress in 1790. The law required citizens to register their stills and pay a tax to a federal commissioner within their region. Almost immediately, residents in areas such as North Carolina, Kentucky, and particularly western Pennsylvania protested because they had little money to pay the tax and had used whiskey for decades to barter within their regions. They believed the tax represented government intrusion into their domestic lives that Americans had fought against during the American Revolution.

The first resistance to the excise tax in western Pennsylvania occurred in September 1791 when sixteen men assaulted an excise collector in Washington County by cutting his hair, tarring and feathering him, and leaving him in the woods. Protests continued through 1791, although they were not always violent. Citizens also organized mass meetings in July and September 1791 to draft petitions to Congress to repeal the tax. Western Pennsylvania then remained relatively peaceful until fall 1792, when John Neville, the regional supervisor for collecting the excise tax, rented an office from a local man named William Faulkner. Within days, roughly twenty men ransacked Faulkner's home and forced him to evict Neville. On September 15, 1792, President Washington issued a proclamation condemning the resistance, which nevertheless continued into 1793.

Despite a lull after Congress passed an amendment to the law allowing distillers to sell whiskey to the army to help pay the excise tax, the conflict flared once again. In 1794, U.S. District Attorney William Rawle obtained federal writs requiring more than sixty western distillers to appear in federal court in Philadelphia. U.S. Marshal David Lenox and tax supervisor Neville reignited the resistance when they arrived in western Pennsylvania with the writs. On July 16, 1794, a gun battle at Neville's home in Allegheny County resulted in the death of one resister. The next day, in reaction to this "murder," an estimated five hundred resisters returned to Neville's house, where they fought ten soldiers from Fort Pitt, burned Neville's home, and captured Lenox, who somehow escaped with his life. Lenox returned to Philadelphia, where Hamilton and Washington called for military force to suppress the rebellion.

As Washington prepared his 12,950-man army, drawn from New Jersey, Pennsylvania, Maryland, and Virginia state militia troops, citizens in Philadelphia and other cities including Hagerstown and Baltimore, Maryland, protested the use of military force against their countrymen. By the time troops reached western Pennsylvania in October 1794, Washington's army found little opposition and easily rounded up many potential resisters but not the supposed leaders of the rebellion, who had fled farther west. The army returned to Philadelphia with twenty suspects by Christmas Day, parading them through the city as trophies.

Many of these prisoners languished in prison for nearly six months while they awaited federal trial for treason. Eventually, only ten of the accused whiskey rebels were tried for treason at the U.S. District Court for the District of Pennsylvania, which sat in Philadelphia City Hall (later known as Old City Hall, Fifth and Chestnut Streets). Two of these ten men, John Mitchell and Philip Vigol (or Weigle), were convicted largely because William Rawle successfully offered an expanded definition of treason: that combining to defeat or resist a federal law was the equivalent of levying war against the United States and therefore an act of treason. This set a precedent for defining treason that was used in the aftermath of Fries Rebellion in Bucks, Montgomery, and Northampton Counties. Mitchell and Vigol were the first two Americans convicted of federal treason in American history though, on November 2, 1795, Washington pardoned them after finding one to be a "simpleton" and the other to be "insane." While these pardons unofficially ended the saga of the Whiskey Rebellion, the government's use of military force to repress this "rebellion" and its use of the expanded definition of treason remained controversial.

Alien and Sedition Acts

Nathaniel Conley

A culmination of political battles between Republicans and Federalists while Philadelphia served as capital of the United States, the federal Alien and Sedition Acts imposed stringent new rules governing political speech and writings, immigration rights, and non-naturalized immigrants. The acts also had an immediate impact on the political life of Philadelphia as they inflamed passions in the region, resulted in charges against many newspaper publishers, and contributed to the outbreak of Fries Rebellion.

When President John Adams assumed office in 1797, relations between France and the United States had deteriorated, leading to the Quasi-War of 1798–1800. Though the United States in 1793 had taken a position of neutrality in France's war with Great Britain, the French seized American ships and rejected Adams's efforts to negotiate peace. In what became known as the XYZ Affair, the revolutionary French government demanded a large loan, bribe, and official apology from Adams before negotiations could begin. The American mission rejected these terms and news of the XYZ Affair created a political firestorm across the United States, especially in Philadelphia.

In response to concerns about invasion by France, the Federalist-dominated Fifth U.S. Congress enacted legislation in 1798 to shore up national defense from both foreign and domestic threats, including an increase in military spending for the army and navy. In addition, the Federalists passed the Alien and Sedition Acts, four laws dealing with perceived domestic threats, including criticism by Republicans that the Federalists thought undermined national security.

The first of the Alien and Sedition Acts was the Naturalization Act, which increased the residency requirement for American citizenship from five to fourteen years. The Federalists intended to stop newly arrived immigrants from voting because they were a major constituency for the Republican Party. The second law was the Alien Act, which allowed the president to imprison or deport aliens considered dangerous to the United States at any time. The third was the Alien Enemies Act, which allowed the president to deport any male citizen of a hostile nation during times of war.

The last of these laws, the Sedition Act, was perhaps the most controversial. The Sedition Act outlawed actions or conspiracies against government policies and banned false or malicious publishing against federal officials, including members of Congress and the president. This represented one of the strongest attacks on the First Amendment in American history and created a major political backlash against President Adams and the Federalists in Congress. Notably absent from the protections of false or malicious publishing was the vice presidency, at the time occupied by Vice President Thomas Jefferson, leader of the Republican Party.

The Sedition Act, despite attacking the First Amendment rights of newspaper editors and contributors, substantially liberalized the law of seditious libel. Under English common law, the truth of a published allegation was no defense from accusations of sedition, indeed, it could be worse if it was true. Under the new Sedition Act, the truth could be used as a defense against the charge of sedition. Regardless of this liberalization, the Sedition Act was wildly unpopular to Americans.

The Sedition Act was particularly important to the Federalists because it allowed them to clamp down on rival political newspapers. Throughout the 1790s, newspapers were by far the most important political battleground, particularly in Philadelphia. The Republican press, led by editors such as the grandson of Benjamin Franklin, Benjamin Franklin Bache at the *Philadelphia Aurora*, had been gaining on their Federalist rivals. Indeed, by 1800, Republican-leaning newspapers far outnumbered Federalist newspapers despite the Sedition Act. Bache was one of seventeen publishers jailed under the provisions of the act; he died of yellow fever in 1798 awaiting trial. Bache's successor at the *Aurora*, William Duane, was tried but acquitted. Matthew Lyon, a Republican member of the House of Representatives from Vermont was also jailed under the Sedition Act. He was later reelected from jail by his constituents.

The Alien and Sedition Acts helped incite the Fries Rebellion in rural Pennsylvania counties northwest of Philadelphia. With passage of the 1798 war program, including new taxes and the Alien and Sedition Acts, German Americans of the region protested. President Adams declared the area in rebellion and sent troops to arrest the insurgents.

Republican leaders James Madison and Thomas Jefferson opposed the Alien and Sedition Acts by authoring, respectively, the Virginia and Kentucky Resolutions passed by the Virginia and Kentucky legislatures in 1798. The Virginia Resolutions called upon other states to declare that the Alien and Sedition Acts violated the First Amendment while the Kentucky Resolutions went further and asked the states to declare "these acts void and of no force." None of the other state legislatures agreed. Delaware, Pennsylvania, and New Jersey discussed but rejected the resolutions, which are widely seen as precursors to later nullification principles espoused during the antebellum period.

As home to the federal government and a large, partisan press corps, Philadelphia in the 1790s stood at the center of political and legal battles over the Alien and Sedition Acts. The Republicans gained support in the city and state as Federalists used severe tactics against publishers Bache and Duane and sent troops to arrest the protesters of Fries Rebellion. This Federalist overreach in southeastern Pennsylvania and Philadelphia in large part hastened the splintering and decline of the Federalist Party before the election of 1800.

Fries Rebellion

Patrick Grubbs

In 1798, the Alien and Sedition Acts and a new federal tax on property sparked resistance in rural Bucks, Montgomery, and Northampton Counties of Pennsylvania, less than fifty miles from Philadelphia. The reputed ringleader, John Fries, was twice convicted of treason but received a presidential pardon. Beyond local disruption, the rebellion played a national role in helping to fracture the Federalist Party and contributed to the first (and only) impeachment of a Supreme Court justice, Samuel Chase.

In response to growing tensions with France and confiscation of American ships, the Federalist administration of John Adams expanded the American military to prepare for a potential war. To fund this expansion, on July 9, 1798, the Fifth Congress of the United States, meeting in Congress Hall, passed the House Tax Law, which imposed a direct tax on lands and dwelling houses. The Federalist government also passed the Alien and Sedition Acts, a set of four laws that curtailed the rights of immigrants and punished critics of the Federalist government.

Similar to the Whiskey Rebellion of 1791–94, rural Pennsylvanians during the Fries Rebellion resisted federal legislation, resulting in mobilization of troops, imprisonment, and trial for treason in Philadelphia. In this case, the House Tax and Sedition Laws angered many citizens in Northampton, Montgomery and Bucks Counties, particularly the Germans, who viewed these acts as unconstitutional and designed to rob them of their property and liberty.

Resistance began in August 1798 and increased through December with public denouncements of the acts and erection of liberty poles. After the rebels threatened violence against the tax assessors, the federal government in January 1799 issued arrest warrants for obstructing assessment of the House Tax. U.S. Marshal William Nichols left Philadelphia on February 25 to serve the warrants, which required resisters to appear for trial in Philadelphia. Nichols arrived in Northampton County on March 1, took twelve men into custody the next day, and served the remainder of his warrants over the next three days. He then retired on March 6 to his new headquarters and temporary jail for his prisoners, the Sun Inn in Bethlehem.

The next day nearly four hundred armed resisters entered Bethlehem to attempt to free the prisoners. As the highest-ranking militia officer present, John Fries assumed command of the men. Once they reached the Sun Inn, Fries began negotiations with Nichols. As the negotiations dragged late into the day the uneasy crowd grew anxious. Nichols finally agreed to release the prisoners in order to calm the crowd and also to protect his deputies. In response to this event President Adams issued a proclamation from Philadelphia urging all insurgents to retire peacefully by March 18, 1799. The insurgents complied with Adams's proclamation by March 18, but by that point Adams had already set the military into motion.

On March 22 the *Philadelphia Aurora* printed a notice from Secretary of War James McHenry calling for Pennsylvania militia to assemble to put down the insurrection. In the same issue *Aurora* editor William Duane severely criticized the Adams administration for its use of military force, a bold move when the Sedition Act was in place. The troops left Philadelphia on April 4 to quell the insurrection, meeting little resistance as they marched into Northampton County. They promptly arrested thirty-one insurgents, including John Fries, and returned to Philadelphia on April 20.

Fries and two others faced trial under the expanded definition of treason that Philadelphia lawyer William Rawle put forth during the Whiskey Rebellion trials. Rawle, the lead prosecutor in the trial, had argued in 1795 that combining to defeat or resist a federal law was the equivalent of levying war against the United States and therefore was an act of treason. Fries was convicted of treason on May 9, 1799, in the U.S. District Court for the District of Pennsylvania and was sentenced to death, but on May 17 a mistrial was declared when evidence surfaced that a juror had expressed a desire, before the trial began, to see Fries hang.

The second trial opened on April 16, 1800, with Judge Richard Peters and Supreme Court Justice Samuel Chase presiding. To expedite the trial Justice Chase issued a legal brief upholding the expanded definition of treason. The House of Representatives in 1804 cited Chase's brief and actions during this trial among the articles of impeachment, of which the Senate acquitted him.

Fries was again found guilty of treason on April 25, 1800, and sentenced to hang on May 23. President Adams issued a presidential pardon for Fries and two other men who were convicted of treason on May 21. This pardon was the last straw in a developing dispute between Adams and Alexander Hamilton, who wrote to colleagues that the pardon was the "most inexplicable part of Mr. Adams' conduct." When published, this letter created a schism in the Federalist Party, helping Republican Thomas Jefferson to defeat Adams in the 1800 election. More generally, the harsh Federalist prosecution of the Fries insurgents and enforcement of the Alien and Sedition Acts encouraged Pennsylvania Germans and other voters to shift their allegiance to the Republicans.

"Hail, Columbia"

Jack McCarthy

"Hail, Columbia," written in Philadelphia in the closing years of the eighteenth century, became a popular patriotic song in early America and served for many years as an unofficial national anthem. Philadelphia lawyer Joseph Hopkinson created "Hail, Columbia" in the spring of 1798 when he put lyrics to the tune of the "President's March," a patriotic instrumental piece composed in 1789 by Philip Phile, a German immigrant musician active in Philadelphia in the 1780s and 1790s.

In his later years, Hopkinson related the story behind the song: In April 1798 a young singer-actor named Gilbert Fox asked Hopkinson to write a song for Fox to perform at an upcoming benefit concert in Philadelphia. Fox needed a rousing song for the concert and asked if Hopkinson could write lyrics to Phile's "President's March." Hopkinson obliged and came up with lyrics that opened with the stirring proclamation "*Hail Columbia, happy land! Hail, ye heroes, heav'n born band.*" With Philadelphia then serving as the nation's capital and the United States on the verge of war with France, Hopkinson envisioned the song as a patriotic rallying cry.

The public first heard the song when Fox performed it at the Chestnut Street Theatre on April 25, 1798. The audience loved it and demanded multiple encores. A Philadelphia music publisher issued a sheet music version a few days later and the song quickly became very popular in both Philadelphia and New York.

Unlike other early American patriotic songs such as "The Star-Spangled Banner" and "America (My Country 'Tis of Thee)," which featured new lyrics set to traditional English melodies, both the words and music to "Hail, Columbia" were written in the United States. Philip Phile, who wrote the tune, first appeared in the mid-1780s as a performer, composer, and music teacher in Philadelphia and New York. In 1785 he led the orchestra at Philadelphia's Southwark Theatre. He wrote the "President's March" reportedly in honor of the presidential inauguration of George Washington. Philadelphia music publisher Benjamin Carr first published the piece in 1793, not long before Phile died in Philadelphia, perhaps a victim of the 1793 yellow fever epidemic.

Joseph Hopkinson was a prominent lawyer who later served as a U.S. congressman and federal judge. He followed in the footsteps of his father, Francis Hopkinson, a signer of the Declaration of Independence, in mixing law, statesmanship, and the arts. Francis Hopkinson, in addition to being a lawyer and judge, was considered the country's first "poet-composer" and was the first native-born American to write a secular song, "My Days Have Been So Wondrous Free" (1759).

"Hail, Columbia" remained popular through the centuries. Bands began playing the tune in honor of the U.S vice president in the 1830s, and later it became the official song of that office. It was one of several songs that served as an unofficial American national anthem until Congress officially gave that designation to "The Star-Spangled Banner" in 1931. Written in the capital during a formative period in U.S. history, "Hail, Columbia" was one of the first pieces of music to define the emergent nation in song.

FIGURE 24. "Hail Columbia, The favorite new Federal Song," by Joseph Hopkinson, 1798. LIBRARY OF CONGRESS.

The favorite new Federal Song
Adapted to the Presidents March
Behold the Chief who now commands!
Sung by Mr. FOX
Written by J: HOPKINSON Esqr.
For the Voice, Piano Forte, Guittar and Clarinett.
Hail! Columbia happy land hail! ye Heroes heav'n born band Who fought and bled in
freedoms cause who fought & bled in freedoms cause and when the storm of war was gone en-
joy'd the peace your valor won let Inde-pen-dence be our boast ever mindful
what it cost ever grateful for the prize let its Altar reach the Skies
2d time Chorus
Firm uni-ted let us be rallying round our Li-ber-ty as a band of

EXPLORE MORE

Independence National Historical Park features many sites from Philadelphia's decade as capital for the U.S. government, including Congress Hall at Sixth and Chestnut Streets; Old City Hall, where the Supreme Court held sessions, at Fifth and Chestnut Streets; the printing office at Franklin Court, on Market Street between Third and Fourth Streets; the first Bank of the United States, at Third and Chestnut Streets; and the President's House (Robert Morris mansion), Sixth and Market Streets. The open-air exhibit *The President's House: Freedom and Slavery in the Making of a New Nation* explores the work of enslaved people in George Washington's household and, more generally, the history of enslavement in the early republic. Mother Bethel African Methodist Episcopal Church at 419 S. Sixth Street and the African American Museum in Philadelphia, 701 Arch Street, explore the history of the free Black community.

Other relevant sites in Philadelphia include the American Philosophical Society, 105 S. Fifth Street; National Constitution Center, 525 Arch Street; site of the Bank of North America (home of Tench Francis), 307 Chestnut Street; and the Germantown White House (Deshler-Morris House), 5442 Germantown Avenue, where Washington avoided yellow fever in November 1793 and the city's heat in summer 1794. Elfreth's Alley, located between Front and Second Streets north of Arch Street, includes a museum about the neighborhood that started in 1703 as a cart path and has survived for more than three hundred years. The home of Joseph Hopkinson, lyricist of "Hail, Columbia," is a private residence at 338 Spruce Street, marked with a historical plaque.

Beyond Philadelphia, locations marking Fries Rebellion include the Sun Inn, 556 Main Street, Bethlehem, and the Fries Rebellion historical marker, Main and Broad Streets, Quakertown, Pa. Museums interpreting agriculture and industry during the period include the Colonial Pennsylvania Plantation in Ridley Creek State Park, Gradyville; the Colonial Industrial Quarter of Historic Bethlehem Museums and Sites in Bethlehem; and Batsto Village, which preserves a Pinelands ironworks in Wharton State Forest near Hammonton, N.J.

Many research collections related to the U.S. government and the city's history during the 1790s can be found in the Historical Society of Pennsylvania at 1300 Locust Street, such as the Coxe Family Papers, James Wilson Papers, Bank of North America Records, Robert Morris Papers, and Hopkinson Family Papers. The Benjamin Franklin Bache Papers are located at the American Philosophical Society, while the Keffer Collection of Sheet Music is available at the Kislak Center for Special Collections, Rare Books and Manuscripts, University of Pennsylvania Library, 3420 Walnut Street. A vast array of printed works (maps, pamphlets, constitutions and reports, woodcut drawings) from private associations and institutions organized in the region during the late eighteenth century are available at the Library Company of Philadelphia, 1314 Locust Street.

Excellent sources on the people, economy, and culture of Philadelphia during the 1790s include the essay by Paul Sivitz and Billy G. Smith, "Philadelphia and Its People in Maps: The 1790s," in the online edition of the *Encyclopedia of Greater Philadelphia*; Billy G. Smith, *The "Lower Sort": Philadelphia's Laboring People, 1750–1800* (Cornell University Press, 1990); Charlene Mires, *Independence Hall in American Memory* (University of Pennsylvania Press, 2002); Simon Finger, *The Contagious City: The Politics of Public Health in Early Philadelphia* (Cornell University Press, 2012); Thomas M. Doerflinger, *A Vigorous Spirit of Enterprise: Merchants and Economic Development in Revolutionary Philadelphia* (University of North Carolina Press, 1986); Robert E. Wright, *The First Wall Street: Chestnut Street, Philadelphia, and the Birth of American Finance* (University of Chicago Press, 2005); Gary B. Nash, *Forging Freedom: The Formation of Philadelphia's Black Community, 1720–1840* (Harvard University Press, 1988); Richard S. Newman, *Freedom's Prophet: Bishop Richard Allen, the AME Church, and the Black Founding Fathers* (New York University Press, 2008); Edward Lawler Jr., "The President's House in Philadelphia: The Rediscovery of a Lost

Landmark," *Pennsylvania Magazine of History and Biography* 126, no. 1 (January 2002): 5–95; Russell F. Weigley, ed., *Philadelphia: A 300-Year History* (Norton, 1982); Catherine E. Hutchins, ed., *Shaping a National Culture: The Philadelphia Experience 1750–1800* (Henry F. DuPont Winterthur Library and Museum, 1994); and C. Dallett Hemphill, *Philadelphia Stories: People and Their Places in Early America*, ed. Rodney Hessinger and Daniel K. Richter (University of Pennsylvania Press, 2021).

Among many important books on the early history of the U.S. government, see Stanley Elkins and Eric McKitrick, *The Age of Federalism* (Oxford University Press, 1993); Stuart Leibiger, *Founding Friendship: George Washington, James Madison, and the Creation of the American Republic* (University Press of Virginia, 1999); Joanne B. Freeman, *Affairs of Honor: National Politics in the New Republic* (Yale University Press, 2001); Thomas P. Slaughter, *The Whiskey Rebellion: Frontier Epilogue to the American Revolution* (Oxford University Press, 1986); Paul Douglas Newman, *Fries's Rebellion: The Enduring Struggle for the American Revolution* (University of Pennsylvania Press, 2004); and Jeffrey L. Pasley, *"The Tyranny of Printers": Newspaper Politics in the Early American Republic* (University Press of Virginia, 2001). Erica Armstrong Dunbar's *Never Caught: The Washingtons' Relentless Pursuit of Their Runaway Slave, Ona Judge* (37 Ink/Atria, 2017) underscores the paradox of freedom and enslavement in the early republic, while emphasizing the entangled legacy of Philadelphia and the nation.

15

Chapter 5

REVOLUTION REMEMBERED

Introduction

The generations of Americans born after the nation's founding inherited the task of conveying the significance of the American Revolution into the future. This was especially the case in Philadelphia and the nearby region, where sustaining memory of the Revolution depended on stewardship of distinctly important sites and symbols of the founding era. Local people acted to honor their ancestors, to venerate the nation's founders and ideals, and to cultivate attractions for tourism. Their motives varied, but over time they produced a rich mosaic of historic sites, museums, monuments, and commemorative events that continued into the twenty-first century.

While the Revolutionary generation remained alive, recalling the American Revolution required little concerted effort apart from celebrations on the Fourth of July. But by the 1820s, as that generation passed from the scene, Philadelphians and Americans generally began to take interest in preserving material relics. During this period, the old Pennsylvania State House in Philadelphia gained the name "Independence Hall," first applied to the room where independence had been declared and later extended to the entire building. The name emerged as Philadelphians prepared to welcome a returning hero of the Revolution, the Marquis de Lafayette, on his celebrated tour of the United States during 1824–25. As Lafayette traveled around the country, his presence stirred efforts to preserve relics of the Revolution. After he departed, Philadelphia officials insisted that a new steeple for the State House resemble the spire of 1776 instead of adopting a different, more structurally sustainable design to support a new fire bell for the city.

The nineteenth century also propelled the Liberty Bell to fame as a symbol of the American Revolution, even though the known evidence of whether the bell rang for independence in 1776 is largely circumstantial. More than sixty years later, local novelist, journalist, and labor activist George Lippard popularized the story of the bell ringing to announce the Declaration of Independence. Lippard's fiction, published in the 1840s, subsequently appeared as fact in guidebooks and schoolbooks. The association with the American Revolution grew exponentially when the bell toured the country as a symbol of national unity in the decades following the Civil War. The supposed connection with the Revolution for many years superseded recollection of the bell's service as an abolitionist symbol, which predated Lippard's story. Its role in promoting freedom for Black people enslaved in the American South gained greater attention later, in the twentieth century, as the African American civil rights movement accelerated.

Devotion to ancestry drove much of the work of preserving memory of the American Revolution, locally and nationally. Hereditary associations such as the Daughters of the American Revolution, Colonial Dames, and Sons of the Revolution preserved places honoring their predominantly white, Anglo-Saxon ancestors. But they were joined in this project by European immigrant groups, who celebrated their contributions to American history with parades and monuments honoring such figures as Irish Commodore John Barry and Polish General Thaddeus Kosciuszko. The power of ancestry also played a role in shining light on contradictions within an American story rooted in the pursuit of freedom. In the first decade of the twenty-first century, activism by Black Philadelphians assured that the experience of enslaved and free Black people would be acknowledged in an outdoor exhibit at Sixth and Market Streets, where George Washington lived while president of the United States, and in the adjacent Liberty Bell Center.

Whenever Americans turned to patriotism to celebrate, defend, or critique their nation, their embrace of Revolutionary sites and symbols enhanced the Philadelphia region's reputation as a significant place in American history. At fifty-year intervals, Philadelphians hosted commemorations of the Declaration of Independence and the U.S. Constitution, including the magnificent Centennial Exhibition in Fairmount Park in 1876 and the ambitious but less successful Sesquicentennial International Exhibition in South Philadelphia in 1926. The historic preservation movement of the nineteenth century assured that sites and landscapes of the Revolutionary era would be available not only for their intrinsic value but as destinations for a growing tourism industry. The arrival of the automobile in the twentieth century, especially when combined with the patriotic impulses stirred by World War I, World War II, and the Cold War, drew vacationers to the Philadelphia area to pay homage to the nation's founding.

The more time passed, the more effort seemed to be necessary to sustain the memory of the American Revolution. Independence Hall became the centerpiece of a national park created in the 1950s by demolishing surrounding blocks of nineteenth-century commercial buildings. The Liberty Bell moved from a display case inside Independence Hall to its own pavilion in 1976 and then to a much larger Liberty Bell Center with exhibits in 2003. Museums proliferated and institutionalized the project of recalling the Revolution with exhibits and programming. By the twenty-first century, a visitor to the Philadelphia region could tour a vast network of local, state, and federal parks, museums, and other historic sites spanning Pennsylvania, New Jersey, and Delaware. Together with volunteer stewards of the region's history, professional public historians and tourism agencies created a visitor experience to benefit the region's economy while also sustaining the memory of the American Revolution.

Independence Hall

Charlene Mires

Originally the Pennsylvania State House, Independence Hall gained fame from its associations with the Declaration of Independence and the U.S. Constitution and evolved from a workplace of government to a treasured shrine, tourist attraction, and World Heritage Site. Its history encompasses more than 275 years of creating, preserving, and debating the founding principles of the United States.

The history of Independence Hall dates to 1729, when the Pennsylvania Provincial Assembly authorized construction of "a House for the Assembly of this Province to meet in." The site chosen, on Chestnut Street between Fifth and Sixth Streets, was then on the outskirts of Philadelphia and therefore pulled the city's development westward. In architectural style, the building constructed beginning in 1732 was Georgian—a common choice for American public buildings but also a statement of British elite culture at a time when Pennsylvanians were concerned about a surge of immigration by Germans and Scots Irish.

Assembly Speaker Andrew Hamilton led the committee to select the site and is credited with the building's design, which closely resembled architectural pattern-book plans for English country houses. Edmund Woolley, a member of the Carpenters' Company, supervised the craftsmen and laborers who built the structure, which was ready for use by the assembly by 1736. In 1749, the assembly again called upon Woolley to add a tower and steeple to the south side of the building, thereby creating the building's distinctive, church-like silhouette and providing a place to hang a new bell—the same bell that later became known as the Liberty Bell.

The Pennsylvania State House served many purposes in its first half century, as the seat of provincial

FIGURE 25. *Election Day in Philadelphia*, by John Lewis Krimmel, 1815. Without its tower and flanked by office buildings, the old Pennsylvania State House served as a place for delivering ballots on election days. MUSEUM PURCHASE WITH FUNDS PROVIDED BY HENRY FRANCIS DU PONT, COURTESY OF WINTERTHUR MUSEUM, GARDEN & LIBRARY.

government, a banquet hall for occasions such as celebrations of birthdays of British monarchs, and a meeting place for learned societies such as the American Philosophical Society and the Library Company of Philadelphia. But it secured its lasting place in American history during the era of the American Revolution, when Pennsylvania's central location and relatively moderate politics made Philadelphia the logical gathering place for the First and Second Continental Congresses.

Despite resistance to independence by the Pennsylvania Provincial Assembly, the Second Continental Congress met in the State House beginning in May 1775. In the east room on the first floor, the Congress resolved to break from Great Britain on July 2, 1776, and approved the Declaration of Independence on July 4. Within the State House, Pennsylvania government also changed. In July 1776, the Pennsylvania Constitutional Convention created a constitution regarded as the most democratic among all the former British colonies, and in 1780, the Pennsylvania General Assembly passed the nation's first law mandating the gradual abolition of slavery. The State House served as capital of both the state and national governments during the War of Independence, interrupted by the British occupation of Philadelphia in 1777–78, when the building served as jail and hospital ward for American prisoners.

A second hallmark event in the building's history occurred between May and September 1787, when the State House served as meeting place for the Constitutional Convention. Activity in and around the State House then shifted to whether Pennsylvania would ratify the new frame of government, and violent street confrontations occurred between supporters (Federalists) and dissenters. After lengthy public debates by a ratifying convention in the State House, Pennsylvania became the second state (after Delaware) to ratify the U.S. Constitution.

The State House continued as the seat of Pennsylvania government through the 1790s, when Philadelphia also served as the nation's capital. In 1799, however, it became the "old" State House after Pennsylvania followed its westward-growing population by moving the state capital to Lancaster and later to Harrisburg. When the federal government also left Philadelphia for the new District of Columbia in 1800, the old State House faced an uncertain future. Through the 1790s and the early decades of the nineteenth century, the second floor gained a new purpose under the management of artist Charles Willson Peale, whose museum aimed to cultivate a new national culture through appreciation of the arts and natural sciences. But the building and square surrounding it between Chestnut and Walnut Streets became surplus state property at risk of being sold for redevelopment as building lots.

Philadelphians also showed little regard for the original fabric of the old State House when, in 1812, they allowed the structure's wings and arched piazzas to be replaced by rows of brick buildings for city offices. However, when state proposals in 1813 and 1816 called for selling off State House Square, Philadelphia city officials acted to preserve the building and opened a period of local guardianship that continued until the mid-twentieth century. The city agreed to buy the building and square from the state in 1816, an act regarded as important in the history of historic preservation in the United States.

The old State House began to acquire the name "Independence Hall" when the Marquis de Lafayette, a hero of the American Revolution, visited the United States in 1824. Philadelphians welcomed him at the old State House. While planning this event, they began to refer to the first-floor east room as "the Hall of Independence" and "Independence Hall"—a name that gradually came to be applied to the entire building. The surrounding square was named Independence Square in 1825, when the city also gave names of historic figures (Washington, Franklin, Rittenhouse, and Logan) to other squares. In 1828, Philadelphia city councils also ordered a new steeple for the old State House and insisted that it resemble the original, which had rotted away four decades before. Such actions reflected a growing dedication to preserving the memory of the American Revolution as the founding generation passed from the scene.

As a public building associated with the nation's founding events but surviving amid a growing, industrializing city, Independence Hall served as a focal point for engaging the political, economic, and social issues of the nineteenth century. Other than the first-floor room where independence was declared, through the mid-nineteenth century the building housed courtrooms where judgments determined the freedom or loss of freedom for individuals accused of crimes; apprentices who sued for release from their contracts; and African Americans suspected of being fugitives from enslavement.

Outside in the square, laborers demonstrated for improved working conditions, immigrants demonstrated in sympathy with revolutions in Europe, and Frederick Douglass spoke against slavery in 1844. In 1876, Susan B. Anthony and other women's rights activists distributed a *Declaration of Rights of the Women of the United States*. Independence Square remained a forum for public dissent until the early twentieth century, when the City of Philadelphia responded to a planned demonstration by the Industrial Workers of the World (IWW) by restricting activity to officially designated "patriotic purposes." After the creation of Independence National Historical Park in the mid-twentieth century, the National Park Service tolerated demonstrations during the civil rights and Vietnam eras, but federal regulations subsequently placed new limitations on the use of the square, especially following attacks on the United States on September 11, 2001.

Under the guardianship of Philadelphians, Independence Hall gradually transformed from a working government building to a national shrine, with traces of other local uses often erased in the process. The first-floor east room became a shrine to the founding fathers in 1854 under the sponsorship of nativist politicians, who gained control of the city government that year and created new city council chambers on the second floor. During the Centennial celebration of 1876, the building's first floor became the "National

FIGURE 26. Independence Hall visitors, 1978. PHOTOGRAPH BY WILLIAM OWENS, SPECIAL COLLECTIONS RESEARCH CENTER, TEMPLE UNIVERSITY LIBRARIES.

Museum," featuring portraits and early American artifacts. At the end of the century, after the city councils left the building for the new city hall, the Daughters of the American Revolution renovated and redecorated the second floor in Colonial Revival style. The despised "row buildings" that had flanked the central structure since 1812 were replaced by new, graceful archways that resembled the original piazzas and opened a view and passageway from Chestnut Street to the square.

With the building fully dedicated to historic purposes, in the first decades of the twentieth century Philadelphians also advocated creating expanded parks to buffer the treasured landmark from its dense, heavily industrialized surroundings. They succeeded. The resulting Independence Mall and Independence National Historical Park at midcentury led to demolition of six city blocks of buildings not regarded as "historic," an urban renewal project that also opened a new era of professional stewardship by the National Park Service. Independence Hall gained additional recognition in 1979, when it was designated a World Heritage Site by the United Nations Educational, Scientific, and Cultural Organization (UNESCO).

Independence Hall, the scene of events of national and international importance, also influenced the development and redevelopment of its home city and served as an impetus for the growth of the region's tourist industry. By the first decades of the twenty-first century, Independence Hall anchored a historic district devoted to tourism and civic education, including the National Constitution Center, the Liberty Bell Center, the Independence Visitor Center, the Weitzman National Museum of American Jewish History, and a memorial to the President's House and individuals enslaved there by George Washington. Surrounded and dwarfed by larger institutions, expertly restored, Independence Hall is experienced as a time capsule of the past, and it has many stories to tell.

The Liberty Bell

Gary B. Nash

It began inconspicuously as a two-thousand-pound mass of unstable metal. It nearly ended up in the scrap heap. It cracked and lost its voice. It was all but forgotten. But then, gradually, it became a national symbol. The Liberty Bell became a stand-in for the nation's vaunted values: independence, freedom, unalienable rights, and equality. It became a touchstone of American identity representing justice, the rule of law, sovereign rights, and the ongoing struggle to fully realize the nation's founding ideals.

The Liberty Bell started out simply as the bell commissioned by the colonial Pennsylvania Assembly in 1752 to hang in the steeple of the Pennsylvania State House to announce meetings of the legislature and toll for notable events. Cast in London, it cracked at its first testing at which point two artisans in Philadelphia, John Pass and John Stow, recast the bell. Around its brim

FIGURE 27. Liberty Bell talk, 1984. The Liberty Bell gained symbolic importance apart from its original setting in Independence Hall. NATIONAL PARK SERVICE.

it carried words from the Old Testament: "Proclaim LIBERTY throughout all the Land unto all the Inhabitants thereof" (Leviticus, XXV, 10).

During the Revolutionary era the State House bell became an accomplice in Revolutionary politics. It rang in 1765 to warn of an English ship sailing up the Delaware River to deliver stamped paper for implementing the hated Stamp Act. It tolled in 1768 to attract thousands gathering to protest the Townshend duties. Again it rang to assemble the citizenry in 1773 to protest the Tea Act. And in 1774, the bell summoned Philadelphians to protest the Coercive Acts. On July 8, 1776, the bell is believed to have pealed as people massed in the State House yard to hear the sheriff of Philadelphia read the Declaration of Independence.

During the British occupation of the city in 1777–78, Philadelphians wrestled the bell down from the State House steeple and carried it by wagon to Allentown, lest it be melted down and converted into bullets to be aimed at insurgent Americans. But the bell was back in Philadelphia to toll the British surrender at Yorktown on October 24, 1781, and again to announce the signing of the Treaty of Paris with Great Britain on April 15, 1783.

The bell escaped a narrow brush with death in 1812 when Philadelphia officials considered demolishing the rotting hulk of the State House, which had lost its function since the state capital had moved inland to Harrisburg. But the city brokered a deal in 1816 to acquire the old State House, along with the bell, from the state. After construction of a new steeple with a new bell in 1828, the old bell remained suspended in the building's brick tower.

The bell's elevation to symbolic importance began in the 1830s when New York and Boston abolitionists, drawn by the bell's inscription about proclaiming freedom throughout the land, appropriated the bell as an emblem of the growing campaign to abolish slavery. The New York Anti-Slavery Society's *Anti-Slavery Record* named the "old bell," as it was familiarly known in Philadelphia, as "The Liberty Bell"—"the tocsin of freedom and slavery's knell," as one abolitionist put it in a poem reprinted in the abolitionist paper the *Liberator.* New York abolitionists egged on their Philadelphia counterparts, reminding them that "Hitherto, the bell has not obeyed the inscription and its peals have been a mockery, while one sixth of 'all inhabitants' are in abject slavery."

After almost one hundred years of ringing in important commemorative moments, the Liberty Bell cracked in 1843. A legend developed that the bell had cracked earlier, on July 8, 1835, when it tolled for the funeral procession of Chief Justice John Marshall. It is almost certain, however, that the fissure occurred while it rang eight years later in remembrance of the birthday of George Washington. Once damaged, the bell rested on the first floor of Independence Hall in elaborate settings.

The bell did not rest in the public's admiration. In 1847, it began to gain new but fictional fame when the journalist George Lippard wrote a story, "Ring, Grandfather, Ring," for the *Saturday Courier* that related how an old bellman rang the bell to pronounce independence, after his grandson heard Congress's resolve. The popular tale, though fictional, was retold as truth in guidebooks and schoolbooks and thereafter linked the bell to the Declaration of Independence.

The bell's association with the Declaration muffled its earlier antislavery message in the decades after the Civil War, when the Liberty Bell was sent across the continent by train to be exhibited at world's fairs and exhibitions. The bell served as a messenger of reconciliation between the North and South at the World's Industrial and Cotton Exposition in New Orleans in 1885. At each stop of its journey, people surged forward to touch, stroke, and kiss the bell. At Chicago's World's Columbian Exposition in 1893, millions of visitors gazed at the bell, displayed in the Pennsylvania building, and heard "The Liberty Bell March" composed by John Philip Sousa. Other trips took the Liberty Bell to expositions in Atlanta, Charleston, St. Louis, and Boston. On the last of its seven trips out of Philadelphia, to San Francisco and San Diego in 1915, a journalist in San Diego opined that "there is not a single person in any state of the union who does not feel a personal interest in the bell." Marketing helped to make it an American icon, an image repeated in millions of trinkets, postcards, miniature versions, postage stamps, and other memorabilia. On New Year's Eve in 1924, 1925, and 1926, the tapping of the Liberty Bell, broadcast by radio across the nation, welcomed in the New Year.

The price of immortality was co-optation. Organizations of multiple political stripes and causes enlisted the Liberty Bell to pursue their causes. The Pennsylvania Woman Suffrage Association, campaigning amid World War I, commissioned a Liberty Bell of their own to tour the state. Dubbing their bell the "Justice Bell," they added two words to the famous inscription: the bell would not only proclaim liberty throughout the land but "establish justice," which meant enfranchising women. Other groups followed their lead, including a citizens group called the Loyal Fraternity of the Liberty Bell, which formed to fight the resurgent Ku Klux Klan in the 1920s, and the "Liberty Bell Ringers" in Michigan, dedicated to keeping alive some of the unrealized Progressive reforms.

During World War I and World War II, the U.S. government enlisted the Liberty Bell in liberty bond campaigns to finance the struggle to protect democracy. Ships and airplanes were named after the Liberty Bell, and the Liberty Bell itself, standing in Independence Hall, formed the backdrop for many patriotic gatherings. At the urging of President Franklin Roosevelt, the bell was tapped for his radio broadcasts to pump up patriotism. The tapping went out over the radio waves throughout the war to celebrate patriotic occasions, victories, and the opening of war bond drives. But while the United States fought a war in the name of freedom, African Americans recognized that the nation's freedoms were not equally shared. In Philadelphia, Black banker Richard R. Wright Sr. instituted an annual Freedom Day commemoration at the bell to call attention to the continuing struggle for freedom and equality.

During the Cold War, the federal government frequently deployed the Liberty Bell as the beacon demonstrating American unity and strength, and it was further immortalized when *Liberty Bell 7* carried Gus Grissom into space in 1961. By this time, organizations from far right to far left claimed the Liberty Bell as their own. These ranged from the Liberty Belles, who saturated the country with messages that the Sixteenth Amendment (authorizing the federal income tax) was unconstitutional, to civil rights activists who staged sit-ins at the Liberty Bell, to members of the Quebec Separatist Movement who planned to dynamite the bell in 1965, and to environmentalists thronging to the bell on the first Earth Day in 1970. Meanwhile, entrepreneurs happily appropriated the Liberty Bell, plastering its image on everything from skimpy women's underwear, to cat and dog pillows, to the gigantic electrified Liberty Bell at the Phillies' Citizens Bank Park.

In 1976, to celebrate the bicentennial of the American Revolution, the National Park Service (which assumed custodianship of the bell, along with Independence Hall, in 1948) moved the Liberty Bell from Independence Hall, where it had rested for more than two centuries, to a pavilion facing Independence Hall a block away. Then in 2003 it found a new home in a spacious exhibit building at Sixth and Market

Streets. This location, adjacent to the site where enslaved Africans labored in the household of President George Washington, forced a new reckoning over the legacies of freedom and enslavement in American history. Visitors to the Liberty Bell, numbering about 1.5 million annually in the early twenty-first century, encountered the bell's long and varied history in exhibits as they moved toward the sacred bell, to be viewed but seldom touched.

Valley Forge

Siobhan Fitzpatrick

In 1777 the Continental army, unable to prevent the British forces from taking Philadelphia, retreated to Valley Forge for the winter of 1777–78. Selected for its strategic location between Philadelphia and York, along the Schuylkill River, Valley Forge had natural defensive positions, access to water, enough land to support the army, and was far enough from Philadelphia to prevent a surprise attack by the British. While preserved for its eighteenth-century significance as a winter encampment site for the Continental army, Valley Forge has a more extensive past and continues to play an integral role in the region's history and environment.

Indigenous people inhabited the area that became known as Valley Forge as early as the Archaic period (8000 BCE to 1000 BCE). Following the 1681 grant of land to William Penn, however, European plantations displaced the Native people. In 1699, the Pennsylvania Land Company of London bought the land that later became the north side of Valley Forge National Historical Park; most of it was subsequently purchased by two families, the Pawlings and the Morgans. By the early 1700s they had established substantial plantations called Pawlings and Mill Grove.

At the start of the American Revolution Valley Forge was one of several farming towns that supplied Philadelphia. Along with large farms, the town had several mills, a forge, and a predominantly Quaker population. The Revolution came to Valley Forge in December 1777, after British troops moved south from New York and captured Philadelphia and the Continental army retreated. At Valley Forge, generals and their staffs rented homes of farmers, most of whom stayed to care for their livestock and safeguard their property. Soldiers initially lived in tents, but for this long-term encampment they also constructed log cabins, sixteen by fourteen feet in size, each housing sixteen men. The soldiers suffered from lack of basic supplies due to mismanagement and weather conditions. Contrary to popular belief, Valley Forge was not the coldest encampment of the War for Independence (Morristown, New Jersey, was). Mild weather with heavy rain resulted in muddy roads and swollen rivers that prevented supplies from reaching the camp.

During this encampment the newly appointed Prussian-born Inspector General Baron von Steuben began drilling the Continental army. The Battle of Monmouth (1778), while not a victory for the Americans, proved that the new skills learned under the general were essential to the army's survival.

During the Revolutionary War the farms at Valley Forge were ransacked by the British troops and used by the Americans. Archaeologists later uncovered saw-cut animal bones from cattle and pigs, uniform buttons, musket balls, and redware shards to verify these events. Following the war, the land continued to be farmed, and the community embraced scientific farming. The first permanent bridge over the Schuylkill was built in 1810, and the canals came into place during the 1820s.

Initial preservation efforts at Valley Forge did not start until the mid-nineteenth century, when poets began romanticizing the site and it became a place of interest for the Colonial Revival movement. By the 1880s, trains brought tourists from Philadelphia to Valley Forge.

The Centennial and Memorial Association, modeled after the Mount Vernon Ladies' Association, set about opening Washington's Headquarters as a historic house museum for the encampment's centennial. Fundraising efforts, spearheaded by Anna Morris Holstein, initially were very successful. The first "march out" commemoration of the end of the encampment occurred on June 19, 1878. With the aid of the Patriotic Order Sons of America (POSA) and a grant from the state, the restored house was eventually purchased from private owners and opened to the public.

In 1893 the Commonwealth of Pennsylvania took further interest in Valley Forge and established it as a state park. The state park commission began acquiring land that encompassed remnants of the inner

FIGURE 28. Park ranger William Troppman instructs recruits for a "Join the Continental Army" program at Valley Forge, 2018. Historic sites helped convey memory of the American Revolution to new generations. NATIONAL PARK SERVICE.

and outer line defenses from the encampment and eventually accrued several historic structures, including Washington's Headquarters, as well as a thin strip of property north of the Schuylkill River.

The area remained popular into the 1920s with city dwellers seeking to escape the oppressive heat of the city and return to nature. The south side of the park remained a historic tourist destination, but the popularity of the north side declined. With the strong connection to the American Revolution, Valley Forge became a symbolic site for reflection, commemoration, and occasionally protest. During the Vietnam era, Vietnam Veterans Against the War organized Operation RAW (Rapid American Withdrawal), a march from Morristown to Valley Forge culminating with a rally in Valley Forge on Labor Day 1970.

In 1976 the National Park Service acquired stewardship of Valley Forge when President Gerald Ford signed legislation creating Valley Forge National Historical Park. In the early twenty-first century Valley Forge National Historical Park embraced more than five square miles of green landscape, a refuge for recreation as well as historical memory amid Philadelphia's suburban sprawl.

Lafayette's Tour

Charlene Mires

When the Marquis de Lafayette, a French hero of the American Revolution, returned to the United States in 1824–25, Philadelphians joined in a wave of nationwide affection for the nobleman who had volunteered for service in the Continental army at the age of nineteen. Lafayette's return to the region stirred increasing regard for preserving relics of the Revolution, especially the old Pennsylvania State House, which began to acquire a new name: Independence Hall.

Lafayette (Marie Joseph Paul Yves Roch Gilbert de Motier, Marquis de Lafayette) returned to the United States as the "nation's guest" by invitation of his longtime friend President James Monroe. With the Declaration of Independence nearly fifty years in the past, Lafayette represented a generation of heroes soon to pass from living history into memory. Throughout the United States, his presence touched off elaborate preparations, pageantry, and a lively market for Lafayette keepsakes. The tour, originally intended to last four months, triggered such intense public enthusiasm

FIGURE 29. The Nation's Guest, 1825. This lithograph by Joseph Perkins, published in Philadelphia, hailed the Marquis de Lafayette as "magnanimous and illustrious." His visit stirred interest in preserving relics of the American Revolution. NATIONAL PORTRAIT GALLERY, SMITHSONIAN INSTITUTION.

that Lafayette stayed for thirteen months and traveled to all twenty-four states in the nation. He visited Thomas Jefferson at Monticello and the Mount Vernon tomb of his general and friend George Washington.

Lafayette came to the Philadelphia region twice, near the beginning and end of his tour. In September 1824, after arriving in New York from France, he journeyed through northern New Jersey to Trenton, where he crossed the covered bridge over the Delaware River to Morrisville, Pennsylvania. Entertained at an evening ball at Holmesburg and then lodged overnight at the Frankford Arsenal, the next day Lafayette entered Philadelphia in a carriage pulled by six horses and accompanied by a three-mile-long procession of citizens on horseback, public officials from Pennsylvania and New Jersey, military units, veterans of the Revolution, tradesmen, and farmers. The parade followed a route calculated to pass impressive neighborhoods, landmarks, and cheering throngs of onlookers on the way to the old State House. Temporary triumphal arches ushered the marchers and riders through Northern Liberties into the city.

For nearly two months, Philadelphians planned for the moment of Lafayette's arrival. For his reception, an arrangements committee commissioned architect William Strickland to refurbish the room in the old State House where independence had been declared. By that time in a state of neglect, the east room on the building's first floor attracted renewed attention as it became transformed for the occasion. Philadelphians acquired new mahogany chairs and sofas, draperies, and carpets to create a suitably lavish reception, and they coined a name for the room: the "Hall of Independence" or "Independence Hall." Originally applied only to the first-floor east room, over subsequent decades the name became applied to the building as a whole.

Lafayette's reception in the Hall of Independence, where he and Philadelphia's mayor exchanged greetings and reflected on the historic events that transpired where they stood, established a precedent for other nineteenth-century guests, from dignitaries to visiting fire companies. Lafayette's eight-day visit also created new attachments to the memory of the American Revolution for thousands of school children who assembled in the State House yard to be in his presence, for residents who attended a celebratory civic ball at the Chestnut Street Theatre, and for those who adorned themselves and their homes with mass-produced souvenirs. "Everything is Lafayette, whether it be on our heads or under our feet," the *Saturday Evening Post* commented in the aftermath. "We wrap our bodies in Lafayette coats during the day, and repose between Lafayette blankets at night."

Departing Philadelphia, Lafayette traveled by steamboat on the Delaware River to Chester, Pennsylvania, which celebrated him with a parade and banquet, and from there to Wilmington, Delaware. When he returned to the region for a somewhat longer, but quieter, stay near the end of his tour in July 1825, his itinerary included Germantown, Mount Airy, and Chestnut Hill. On the way south for departure from Washington, he stopped in West Chester (where an estimated ten thousand people gathered to witness his procession) and joined military units and aged veterans to tour the area of the Battle of Brandywine, where he had been wounded during the Philadelphia campaign.

Lafayette's tour left lasting effects around the United States in the form of towns, counties, colleges, and streets bearing his name, projects to create monuments, and new regard for material relics of the American Revolution. In Philadelphia, historically minded citizens formed the Historical Society of Pennsylvania in 1824. Some who served on the arrangements committee for Lafayette's visit mobilized again in 1828 to replace the steeple on Independence Hall, which had lacked this distinctive feature since the original rotted away more than four decades before. The new steeple served contemporary needs for a clock and bell, but members of the Philadelphia city councils showed their regard for the past by insisting that the steeple must resemble as closely as possible the building as it stood at the time of the American Revolution.

Constitution Commemorations

Hillary S. Kativa

As a cause for commemoration, the signing of the U.S. Constitution historically has struggled to compete with the Declaration of Independence for national recognition and ardor. In contrast to the dramatic act of independence, the framing of the national government is a more sober and complex narrative not easily celebrated with barbecues and fireworks. In Philadelphia, the site of the Constitutional Convention of 1787, commemoration of the document's major anniversaries has reflected how regard for the Constitution and its connections to the city have evolved over time.

For Philadelphia and the nation, the Constitution's major anniversaries often occurred in times of conflict that inspired and informed the celebrations. The Golden Jubilee in 1837 passed largely unobserved, but September 17, the date on which the convention signed the Constitution, was recognized occasionally throughout the early 1800s. Such commemorations often served political purposes. In the 1850s, for example, Philadelphia's Democratic Party staged commemorations as a counterpoint to the anti-immigrant nativist politicians who dominated city government. Similar tributes also cropped up during the strife of the Civil War.

In contrast to these limited observances, the Constitution's one hundredth anniversary in 1887 was treated as an opportunity to demonstrate national progress with a three-day spectacle reminiscent of the 1876 Centennial Exhibition. A lack of congressional interest and funding effectively ceded responsibility for the festivities to Philadelphia, which organizers styled the "Mecca of America," much to the chagrin of rival cities such as New York. In an era of rising immigration and agitation from groups including laborers, suffragists, and African Americans, proclamations of national unity and reverence for the storied Revolutionary past dominated the proceedings, which began on September 15 with a Civic and Industrial Procession on Broad Street. The procession featured 21,029 representatives from the city's trade and commercial organizations, as well as 2,106 musicians and 497 massive floats depicting key moments in American history. A military parade, the largest in the nation's history, followed the next day, and celebrations concluded on September 17 at Independence Square. Attended by President Grover Cleveland, the ceremonies included a Marine Corps band led by John Philip Sousa. Speeches venerated constitutional principles while overlooking any conflict regarding the document's drafting and ratification.

Approximately five hundred thousand visitors and one million local residents observed the Centennial proceedings, which emphasized mass participation even though the contributions of African Americans, women, and ethnic groups were largely scripted or overlooked. Despite resistance from Black and tribal leaders, participation by both African Americans and Native Americans was limited to a series of "object-lessons" that celebrated progress toward the Anglo-Saxon ideal. The Carlisle Industrial Indian School, which removed youth from reservations and sought to assimilate them into American society, was a centerpiece of the Civic and Industrial Procession, and a series of floats glorified the African American journey from slavery to emancipation. In both instances, organizers downplayed social conflict and stressed national harmony and unity, themes echoed in the sesquicentennial celebrations fifty years later.

Amid the tumult of the Great Depression, anxiety about the strength and endurance of national principles colored the Constitution's 150th anniversary, and the festivities captured a prevailing nostalgia for early

25 Cts.
25 Cts.
GA. S.C. N.C. VA. MD. DEL. PA. N.Y. N.J. CONN. R.I. MASS. N.H.
OFFICIAL PROGRAMME
OF THE
CONSTITUTIONAL
CENTENNIAL CELEBRATION.
PHILADELPHIA, SEPTEMBER 15-16-17.
·1887·
J. F. DICKSON & CO.
PRINTERS, BINDERS AND PUBLISHERS.
SEVENTH AND ARCH STREETS, PHILADELPHIA.

American traditions and culture. Compared to the Centennial, the 1937 commemoration was a more national affair that, in the wake of the New Deal, reflected the federal government's activist role in national life. Under the leadership of Congressman Sol Bloom, the U.S. Constitution Sesquicentennial Commission gave scant attention to Philadelphia, choosing to highlight the Constitution's history and meaning rather than the place where it was crafted. Centered in Washington, D.C., festivities were to begin on September 17, 1937, with commemorations of key dates and events following throughout the country until April 30, 1939, the anniversary of the inauguration of President George Washington.

To the commission's dismay, Philadelphia disregarded the national plan and began its festivities on May 14, the date the Constitutional Convention convened in the city. The proceedings commenced at Independence Hall, where teachers gathered dressed as the fifty-five delegates and Mayor S. Davis Wilson struck the Liberty Bell thirteen times with a wooden gavel made from a tree at Valley Forge. Over the next four months, local interest and pride in Philadelphia's constitutional legacy was evident in festivities staged throughout the city, including a mummers parade on the Benjamin Franklin Parkway and a water carnival on the Schuylkill featuring speedboat races, fireworks, and a floating reenactment of the signing of the Constitution. The Pennsylvania Constitution Commemoration Committee also organized school programs and essay contests that stressed Independence Hall's connection to the Constitution, a bond reinforced by ceremonies held there on June 20, 1938, to mark Pennsylvania's ratification of the document.

The Constitution's bicentennial anniversary in 1987 was also a nationwide, ongoing celebration in which Philadelphia's commemoration was one among many. Once again, a lack of national planning and funding plagued the proceedings, which nonetheless featured a calendar of observances that built momentum to the Bicentennial itself. In Philadelphia, the coordinating committee "We the People 200" identified key themes for programming, including the Constitution's evolution, Philadelphia's legacy as the first national city, and the growth of the nation. Through exhibitions, tours, and historic dramas, organizers sought to underscore how historic sites like Independence Hall and the second Bank of the United States created an enduring connection between Philadelphia and constitutional history.

In comparison to earlier anniversaries, the Bicentennial celebrations placed greater emphasis on the Constitution's evolution, including the progress of African Americans and women. In Philadelphia, however, the Constitutional Convention remained at the forefront, allowing the city to briefly reclaim its mantle as the preeminent American city. The Constitution Heritage Act of 1988 likewise affirmed the city's constitutional legacy, authorizing creation of a National Constitution Center in Philadelphia. The center, which broke ground at 525 Arch Street on September 17, 2000, and opened to the public on July 4, 2003, aspired to increase public understanding of the history and ideas of the Constitution, a purpose that likewise pervaded each commemoration of the Constitution's major anniversaries.

FIGURE 30. Constitutional Centennial program, 1887. Philadelphians merged historic commemoration with a demonstration of national progress that downplayed social and political conflicts. FREE LIBRARY OF PHILADELPHIA.

Centennial Exhibition

Stephanie Grauman Wolf

The International Exhibition of Arts, Manufactures and Products of the Soil and Mine, more simply known as the Centennial, opened in Fairmount Park to great fanfare on May 10, 1876, and closed with equal flourish six months later. Modeled after the Crystal Palace Great Exhibition in London in 1851, and the first in a long line of major "world's fairs" in the United States, the Centennial exhibited national pride and belief in the importance of education and progress through industrial innovation. An additional mission of the Centennial grew from a desire to forgive and forget the Civil War.

Philadelphia had precedent for such a fair. The Great Central Fair of 1864, one of many held throughout the Union during the Civil War, anticipated the combination of public, private, and commercial efforts that were necessary for the Centennial. The Great Central Fair, held on Logan Square, had a similar gothic appearance, the waving flags, the huge central hall, the "curiosities" and relics, handmade and industrial exhibits, and even a visit from the president and his family.

The idea for a world exposition in Philadelphia honoring the hundredth anniversary of the Declaration of Independence was first presented to Mayor Morton McMichael in 1866 by Professor John Campbell of Wabash College, Indiana. In 1871, with support from prominent businessmen such as John Wanamaker, the Republican political machine, and the Franklin Institute, the city and state successfully petitioned Congress to authorize the Centennial and set up a commission to oversee planning and implementation. The legislation explicitly excluded federal funding for the fair. The commissioners, led not by political appointees but by leaders in business, had confidence that the undertaking could be handled by private enterprise.

Although rich in historic associations, Philadelphia presented problems as a site for the fair. Business sponsors and nonprofit organizations quarreled over whether to focus on commercial achievements or on American progress in the arts and sciences. Outside Pennsylvania, some suspected that the Centennial was merely an attempt to promote Philadelphia and its industries, and the nationally publicized kidnapping of four-year-old Charley Ross from Germantown in 1874 painted the Philadelphia police force as corrupt and incompetent, raising fears for the safety of visitors.

The Panic of 1873 dried up private financing. Fair organizers devoted the next several years to attracting attention and money from national, state, and foreign governments; from organizations like churches and universities; and from industrial and commercial associations. They enlisted newspapers all over the country in the cause. Members of the Women's Centennial Committee had the most success raising funds, going door-to-door in thirty-one states, selling stock and bringing in $100,000 in contributions. Still, with insufficient capital on hand as the opening neared, and the prestige of the United States at stake, the federal government was forced to step up. The government required repayment as first creditor, thus dooming the fair corporation to financial failure.

As a popular attraction, however, the Centennial was a great success. At a time when the population of the United States was forty-six million and that of Philadelphia less than one million, almost 10 million paid admissions were recorded, with most people paying fifty cents to attend. While most visitors were from Pennsylvania and its neighboring states, 20,000 signed in from Illinois and more than 2,000 from California. On their special state days, Pennsylvania and New York each recorded over 250,000 attendees, while New Jersey, Delaware, and Maryland listed over 10,000 each.

The Centennial overlooked the Schuylkill River, with 250 pavilions and seven miles of avenues and walkways occupying a 285-acre tract of Fairmount Park's 3,160 acres. Many visitors arrived at the temporary "Centennial station" of the Pennsylvania Railroad and entered through the newly invented automatic turnstile. They found numerous fountains and statuary placed strategically throughout the grounds, prominent among them the arm and torch of the Statue of Liberty. Concessionaires, who paid up to 50 percent of their take for the privilege of doing business within the fair, operated stands selling cigars, soda water, and popcorn and theme-oriented restaurants, including French, Turkish, and Viennese.

The Centennial Commission owned and managed thirty-four structures, including five central buildings that covered more than fifty acres. The largest, the Main Exhibition Hall, included exhibits on education and science but concentrated largely on the industrial arts and on selling merchandise. Machinery Hall housed the huge Corliss engine, both the power source for the fair and perhaps its most popular attraction. Exhibitors demonstrated manufacturing processes while also offering products for sale, increasing the interest of visitors. Agricultural Hall, with demonstrations of the latest in farm equipment along with forty-two acres of farm and livestock exhibits, held particular significance for the still largely agricultural nation. Horticultural Hall with its Victorian gardens and Memorial Hall with its exhibit of international fine arts were the smallest of the main group of buildings. Other structures run by the commission included fire and police stations, a medical department, and seven "public comfort" stations.

The remainder of the buildings, just over two hundred, represented several interests. The United States government contributed seven structures, including a main exhibit hall housing the Smithsonian collection,

FIGURE 31. Main Building of the Centennial Exhibition, 1876. The array of flags suspended in the cavernous structure featured figures of Benjamin Franklin and George Washington. Below, an orchestra entertained visitors and manufacturers displayed wares of silver and gold. FREE LIBRARY OF PHILADELPHIA.

which later formed the nucleus of the Smithsonian Institution museum. Of the twenty-six states that erected buildings, most were either Pennsylvania's neighbors or from the mid- or far West. Most of the South, still smarting from its loss of the Civil War, resented the request to spend money in the North. Only Mississippi participated from the Deep South, frustrating the attempt of the Centennial Commission and the federal government to present a picture of a country reunited. While thirty-eight foreign countries had a presence, only eleven provided their own buildings. Forty buildings, the largest number, housed commercial enterprises like the Singer Sewing Machine Company or community service groups like the Bible Society.

The commission advertised the main value of the fair as educational, urging visitors to compare the contemporary strides in technology and learning with the state of the country one hundred years earlier, but the growth of a consumer society made shopping one of the most popular activities. The fair also offered frequent entertainment by musical groups from symphony orchestras to minstrel bands, special days sponsored by states and nearby businesses, and events like hot-air balloon ascensions and fireworks displays. Huge crowds turned out for the music, speeches, and celebrations that marked the opening and closing of the fair and the Fourth of July. "Curiosities" such as a full-sized Liberty Bell made of soap, "Liberty accompanying Washington" done in human hair, and a Centennial medallion carved in butter attracted attention.

Outside the gates, a small, temporary city grew up along what later became Parkside Avenue. Flimsy, wooden structures housed dubious hotels, low-end restaurants, ice cream saloons, beer gardens, and "shows" and were sandwiched two or three deep on narrow lots. They stretched a mile in each direction from the main gate and provided entertainment the commissioners deemed inappropriate on the grounds proper. Profits trumped morality, however, and when attendance flagged at the fair, the organizers allowed the sale of wine and beer. Still, they resisted opening on Sundays, and amusement-park rides and "hoochie koochie dancers" had to await the Chicago Fair of 1893.

Other values of the times were also on display, although not intentionally. White contempt of African Americans and non-Anglo-Saxon foreigners often found expression in crude humor, such as exaggerated dialect, cartoons, and stories found in books written about the Centennial. Victorian sensibilities demoted the graphic painting *The Gross Clinic* (1875) by Thomas Eakins to the army medical hall and banned all works by women from the Memorial Hall Art Exhibit.

A patronizing attitude toward women pervaded the Centennial. Women responded with their own pavilion, built with funds completely raised by women, with all exhibits created and operated by them. Labor-saving devices for domestic use, invented by women, formed part of the exhibit. While traditional forms of women's work in needlework, china painting, and fine arts were not ignored, women also acted as engineers, woodworkers, and printers, turning out newspapers and furniture and operating fabric-producing machinery. The chair of the Women's Centennial Committee, Elizabeth Duane Gillespie, a descendent of Benjamin Franklin, sat on the platform for the fair's closing ceremonies, but when rain curtailed the number of invited guests, admission was "refused to ladies' tickets."

Almost immediately after the Centennial closed, most physical remains were removed, either taken elsewhere or broken down and sold for parts. Much of the statuary and many of the fountains remained, as did the Ohio state building and two small, brick buildings used as "comfort stations."

Two buildings were intended to be permanent, but Horticultural Hall was destroyed by a hurricane in 1954. Memorial Hall ceased to be an art museum in 1928 and in subsequent years served as a gymnasium, swimming pool, and police station. In 2008 it was renovated and reopened as the Please Touch Museum, a children's museum with a *Centennial Exploration* exhibit featuring a tabletop diorama of the fair on a scale of 1:192 feet. Commissioned in 1889 by John Baird, a former member of the Centennial Finance Committee, the model fulfilled its intended mission of educating future generations about the Centennial Exhibition of 1876.

Sesquicentennial International Exposition

Martin W. Wilson

In 1926, Philadelphia hosted the Sesquicentennial International Exposition, a world's fair to commemorate the 150th anniversary of the signing of the Declaration of Independence. Although it opened to great fanfare, the exposition failed to attract enough visitors to cover its costs. While inviting attention from across the nation and around the world, the Sesquicentennial marginalized participation by African Americans in its home city.

The idea to commemorate the signing of the Declaration of Independence by holding a world's fair originated in 1916 with John Wanamaker, owner of Wanamaker's department stores. Wanamaker, the lone survivor of the 1876 Centennial Exhibition's Finance Committee, called upon Philadelphia to host an industrial and commercial exposition that would fittingly mark the birth of the United States. World War I temporarily derailed planning, but in 1920, Mayor J. Hampton Moore and a group of leading citizens took up the effort; they incorporated the Sesquicentennial Exhibition Association (SCEA) in 1921.

Planning for the fair suffered from struggles for control of the SCEA and from members' divergent visions for the exposition. Moore and the Chamber of Commerce, headed by Alba B. Johnson, favored a commercial vision for using Philadelphia's historic legacy to attract visitors (and their dollars) to the city. A competing view, championed by *Ladies Home Journal* publisher Edward W. Bok, sought to broaden the fair's appeal nationally and internationally by avoiding crass commercialism and emphasizing Philadelphia's role in American history with "The Liberty Fair for World Peace and Progress." He tried to wrest control of the SCEA from Moore in 1922 by offering to pay a director general for the fair a $50,000 salary from his own pocket. Additional hopes for the exposition appeared in the *Philadelphia Tribune*, which served the city's Black residents. The *Tribune* saw not only economic benefits but also an opportunity to showcase African American progress.

Limited public enthusiasm hampered the planning. Attempts to get city residents to fund the exposition by buying shares in the SCEA failed. Residents also protested the Fairmount Park site originally proposed. Worried that taxes would be increased for an enterprise that would only benefit real estate and commercial interests, they argued that Philadelphia needed housing and new infrastructure, not an international party. Church leaders warned the fair would attract criminals and other undesirables. Labor feared higher prices resulting from increased numbers of visitors to the city. Because unemployment was low, they saw no need for temporary jobs, which they believed would attract out-of-towners who would compete for jobs after the fair. Management feared higher wages and losing workers to jobs at the fair ground.

Opposition coalesced in the Anti-Sesquicentennial League. Even Mayor Moore, who resigned as SCEA president in May 1922 in part because of his clash with Bok and in part because he realized public support for the enterprise was thin, came out publicly against the fair by the end of 1923. By the time W. Freeland Kendrick became mayor in 1924, little planning for the event had been accomplished.

Kendrick, a member of the Republican political organization headed by William Vare, took charge of the SCEA. He abandoned the Fairmount Park site in favor of previously undeveloped land in Boss Vare's backyard in South Philadelphia just north of the Navy Yard at League Island. Vare and his associates cared little about the vision for the fair. Instead, they focused on the profits they would earn from city contracts and increased property values. The swampy land was drained and filled in (with dirt excavated from the N. Broad Street subway project), and construction began on the exposition's buildings in the fall of 1925.

Kendrick also reached out to African Americans, who coincidentally had staged their own exposition in the same location in 1913 to mark the fiftieth anniversary of the Emancipation Proclamation. He encouraged Black leaders to stage an exhibit of African American progress, but the Committee on Negro Activities did not receive exhibit space until a month before the Sesquicentennial opened, leaving little time to organize. Despite promises that the fair would not be segregated, African American singers were not allowed to join the Sesquicentennial Chorus and none of the many Black soldiers who had served in World War I marched in the opening day parade.

The Sesquicentennial International Exposition opened to great fanfare on May 31, 1926, and ran through November 30 in South Philadelphia between the Naval Yard and Packer Avenue and between Tenth and Twenty-Third Streets. On hand to participate in the opening ceremonies with Mayor Kendrick were Secretary of Commerce Herbert Hoover and Secretary of State Frank B. Kellogg. Although not listed in the program, the opening day speakers also included African American labor activist A. Philip Randolph, whom Kendrick invited at the urging of local Black leaders. At a time when Philadelphia remained a highly segregated city, Randolph called for racial equality as a means for fulfilling the nation's founding ideals.

Unfortunately for early fairgoers, the fair was not quite finished. Several structures remained under construction until late July, nearly two months into a six-month run. But when completed, the Sesquicentennial offered an impressive collection of buildings. Five large "palaces," or exhibition halls, provided acres of indoor exhibition space, and pavilions represented thirty-one states, four territories, and nine nations. The city built the horseshoe-shaped Municipal Stadium (renamed John F. Kennedy Stadium in 1964 and torn down in 1992), measuring 710 by 1,020 feet, on the fairgrounds. It became the site of a recurrent patriotic pageant called "Freedom," large outdoor religious services, and sporting events, including the September 23 championship boxing match

FIGURE 32. The Luminous Liberty Bell, 1926. Spanning Broad Street, the symbol of liberty became a colossus of electric light fitting for the 1920s. PHOTOGRAPH BY JOHN D. CARDINELL, FREE LIBRARY OF PHILADELPHIA.

between Gene Tunney and Jack Dempsey. In pouring rain, more than 120,000 people watched Tunney prevail in a ten-round decision. The Sesquicentennial had a ten thousand–seat auditorium, an emergency hospital, a fire station, and its own working post office.

History also had its place at the fair, but with 1920s flair. The Sesquicentennial Women's Committee generated national publicity by re-creating a colonial Philadelphia "High Street" featuring more than twenty buildings. A Forum of the Founders consisting of thirteen pylons, each 39 feet high, represented the original colonies. And an 80-foot-high replica of the Liberty Bell straddled Broad Street just north of the fair's entrance on Packer Avenue. Lit with twenty-six thousand fifteen-watt bulbs, it formed part of an elaborate lighting scheme for the fair. The exhibition halls, each painted a different pastel shade, were lit at night with mechanically rotating lights. Stadium lighting allowed sports to be played at night. Fair organizers also began to build a 175-foot-tall Tower of Light to cast a beam for seventy miles, but they ran out of money before the tower was completed.

Although 50 million people lived in the region within fifty miles of the fairgrounds, leading to predictions that

30 million people would visit, only 4,622,211 people actually paid to attend (of 6.4 million total attendees). Attendance was so bad by the end of June that the organizers decided to violate the city's 132-year-old blue laws and open on Sunday. The act allowed people who worked six days a week to attend, but it angered the city's Sabbatarians, still a force in 1926. Poor attendance prompted fair organizers to keep the grounds open in December to give concessionaires a chance to sell remaining stock.

Several factors contributed to the fair's failure. Bickering among its organizers and public opposition was compounded by bad word-of-mouth advertising that stemmed from delayed construction and bad weather—it rained 107 of the 184 days the fair was open. Some scholars have suggested that mass availability of automobiles and motion pictures after World War I rendered world's fairs obsolete (a notion challenged by later successful fairs). Whatever the reason, after the fair closed, four hundred creditors presented bills totaling $5.8 million. The fair organization went into receivership in 1927, and its assets were sold at auction. It took until May 1929 for the city to pay off the Sesquicentennial's tab.

Freed for development after the fair, the grounds of the Sesquicentennial International Exposition became Franklin Delano Roosevelt (FDR) Park, Marconi Plaza, the Packer Park neighborhood, and the South Philadelphia sports complex. Following the great success of the Centennial Exhibition in 1876, the Sesquicentennial of 1926 proved to be a disappointment. When the city initiated planning of another fair for the Bicentennial in 1976, it refused to host another exposition without funding from the federal government.

FIGURE 33. Salesmen at the Sesquicentennial, 1926. Cashing in while commemorating the American Revolution, vendors encouraged fair visitors to drink their "Valley Forge Special" beverage. PHOTOGRAPH BY JOHN D. CARDINELL, FREE LIBRARY OF PHILADELPHIA.

Bicentennial

Madison Eggert-Crowe
and Scott Gabriel Knowles

FIGURE 34. Bicentennial pinback button, 1976. DREXEL UNIVERSITY ATWATER KENT COLLECTION.

Planners of Philadelphia's Bicentennial celebration in 1976, aware of the incredible success of the 1876 Centennial as well as the flop of the 1926 Sesquicentennial, hoped to showcase the growth and ambitions of the city while also commemorating the two hundredth anniversary of the Declaration of Independence. While the big celebrations drew crowds of Americans, the summer of '76 also produced conflict and ultimately failed to fulfill the dreams of the city and its planners.

In the early 1960s, more than a decade before the event, city planning director Edmund Bacon initiated bold plans for a Bicentennial commemoration with an additional element: a world's fair. He wanted to use the nation's birthday and the international profile of the world's fair—and the federal dollars these would bring—to advance the agenda of the Philadelphia City Planning Commission. Bacon imagined a thorough redevelopment of the waterfronts in Center City as well as a midway that would close Chestnut Street to vehicles except for open-side electric streetcars. An overhead tram would move visitors across the Schuylkill to fairgrounds in Fairmount Park, the same location as the Centennial of 1876.

In short order, however, the initial planning group and Bacon's early vision were pushed aside by a vocal coalition of architects, planners, and reformers billing themselves as the "young professionals." Including figures like attorney Stanhope Browne, editor Herbert Lipson, and architect Richard Saul Wurman, this group advocated a much grander concept, a model city to be built on a four-mile "megastructure" above the Pennsylvania Railroad yard on the west bank of the Schuylkill. Meanwhile, planning also grew tense around the lack of inclusion of African Americans in the process. In response, the Bicentennial Corporation appointed Catherine Sue Leslie, a housing reform activist, to lead an "Agenda for Action" to include minority voices in Bicentennial planning. Leslie developed a low-cost rival vision for the Bicentennial built around a scattered-site concept that would highlight the racial and ethnic diversity of Philadelphia.

At the national level, in 1966 the administration of President Lyndon B. Johnson created the American Revolution Bicentennial Commission (ARBC), which was charged with recommending a site and making content and funding decisions. In Philadelphia, meanwhile, a Bicentennial Corporation chartered in 1967 began to raise funds, gather public support, and elaborate the theme and design elements of the Bicentennial and world's fair. Philadelphians also sought to gain a competitive edge over Boston, a rival for the celebrations.

In 1969 a Philadelphia delegation presented the ARBC with its "Toward a Meaningful Bicentennial" plan, with the megastructure at the center and five different "core" areas in the city to demonstrate innovative ways to solve America's urban problems. Anticipating an estimated 100 million visitors, the projected costs totaled more than $1 billion. The ARBC rejected the plan, and in Philadelphia a bitter divide developed along racial lines over the thematic focus and location. By 1972 progress stalled, and Mayor Frank Rizzo canceled the world's fair bid, leaving only the Bicentennial commemoration to go forward. On the national level, the ARBC encouraged celebrations throughout the nation, not just in Philadelphia.

A year packed with Bicentennial-themed events began on December 31, 1975, as thousands came to Philadelphia to witness the Liberty Bell being moved from Independence Hall to a new pavilion on Independence Mall on New Year's Eve. From January through October daily events included activities such as puppet shows, street theater, and concerts. The city hosted the NCAA Final Four basketball tournament as well as all-star games for professional baseball, basketball, and hockey. The week leading up to July 4, named Freedom Week, featured even more daily celebrations, street parties, parades, picnics, and concerts. A 2076 time capsule was buried at Second and Chestnut Streets, a fifty thousand–pound Sara Lee birthday cake was served at Memorial Hall, and fireworks filled the sky throughout the week.

On July 4, 1976, a ceremony on Independence Mall featured President Gerald Ford, Pennsylvania's Governor Milton Shapp, and Mayor Rizzo, with actor Charlton Heston as the master of ceremonies. Following the ceremony a five-hour parade featured floats from every state and an estimated forty thousand marchers. An estimated two million visitors came to Philadelphia to attend these events. On July 6, Queen Elizabeth II of Great Britain visited and, with Prince Philip, presented a Bicentennial Bell made in the same foundry as the original Liberty Bell.

During the year-long celebration, Valley Forge, up to this time a state park, became Valley Forge National Historical Park. On July 3, the winter campsite of the Continental army served as final destination for a commemoration of the westward wagon treks of the nineteenth century. Six wagon trains totaling around two hundred wagons, which had traveled for months from all over the nation, converged in Valley Forge in front of a crowd of nearly half a million people.

Along with the patriotic events came counterdemonstrations. Two groups of Philadelphia citizens, the July 4th Coalition and Rich Off Our Backs Coalition, staged marches and demonstrations during Freedom Week to oppose the celebration. Their plans prompted Mayor Rizzo to request fifteen thousand federal troops to maintain order, a request that was denied. Despite Mayor Rizzo's concerns, the demonstrations in Fairmount Park and Norris Square Park were peaceful.

Philadelphia's Bicentennial celebration concluded to mixed reviews. The event introduced thousands of Americans to the urban renewal and historic preservation successes of the postwar period in the city. The three blocks composing Independence Mall had been added to Independence National Historical Park in 1973, and historic buildings in the park had been refurbished. The Afro-American Historical and Cultural Museum (later renamed the African American Museum in Philadelphia) and the Mummers Museum both opened in 1976. The Port of History Museum on Penn's Landing at Walnut Street (later the site of the Independence Seaport Museum) was designed as a Bicentennial gift from the state to the city, but it did not open until 1981. The Society Hill neighborhood, Elfreth's Alley, and Penn's Landing were all popular sites during the celebration.

While Freedom Week brought large crowds to Philadelphia, attendance at Philadelphia's historical sites dropped quickly afterward. Between fourteen and twenty million people visited Philadelphia in 1976, far short of the planners' expectations. Much of the shortfall may be attributed to fear of violence spread by media attention to the protests and the mayor's reaction to them. Also during the Bicentennial, hundreds of members of the American Legion staying at the Bellevue-Stratford Hotel contracted an infectious disease through the hotel's air conditioning system, killing more than thirty and giving the ailment its name—Legionnaires' Disease.

Despite Philadelphians' initial visions for a transformative event, the planning price tag of more than $50 million may have been too high considering the lack of long-term benefits. Features meant to bring lasting value, like a Living History Center or the Chestnut Street Transitway, were considered a thorn in the city's side just five years later. It would be hard to imagine a more challenging period of time—with civil rights struggles, the Vietnam War, and Watergate fresh in mind, and the effects of racial strife, white flight, crime, and deindustrialization apparent in American cities—to hold a patriotic celebration. Philadelphia could not alter the calendar or reshape the larger context of the Bicentennial year.

1776

Alexandra Jordan Thelin

The story of American independence came to life in the musical *1776*, which dramatized the debates, drafting, and signing of the Declaration of Independence by the Second Continental Congress. The musical, which debuted on Broadway in 1969 and became a film in 1972, highlighted Philadelphia as the site of the fateful decisions made at the Pennsylvania State House (Independence Hall) and featured the pivotal roles of delegates from Pennsylvania and Delaware.

Created by composer and lyricist Sherman Edwards with book writer Peter Stone, *1776* depicts historical events from May 8 through July 4, 1776, with a sprinkling of dramatic license. Produced on the eve of the nation's bicentennial, in the charged political climate of the 1960s and 1970s, *1776* dramatizes the conflicts of the nation's beginnings. The musical opens in Independence Hall's Assembly Room with John Adams complaining that Congress cannot come to an agreement on whether to separate from Great Britain. Frustrated, he states, "I have come to the conclusion that one useless man is called a disgrace, that two are called a law firm, and that three or more become a congress!"

The tone of fundamental disagreement escalates as Virginia's Richard Henry Lee proposes independence. John Dickinson, from Pennsylvania, moves to indefinitely postpone this notion, but Adams buys time by calling for postponement until a written Declaration of Independence can be prepared. Thomas Jefferson is then nominated to write the Declaration, despite missing his wife and claiming he is unable to concentrate without her. The film version of *1776* shows Jefferson walking up the stairs to his rented rooms at Seventh and High (Market) Streets to write, play the violin, and spend time with his wife, which enabled him to successfully write.

Jefferson's draft, when completed, triggers additional disagreements, including conflict between North and South over whether the text should denounce King George III as responsible for the slave trade—a reminder that the roots of racial tensions run deep in American history. The story ends as the names of delegates from every colony are called and they sign the Declaration of Independence (depicted as occurring on July 4, although signing did not begin until August 2). The bell in the State House, later known as the Liberty Bell, is heard ringing dramatically (a myth invented later, in the nineteenth century).

Throughout, the show calls attention to Philadelphia's stifling heat. The song "The Egg" playfully refers to hot and humid Philadelphia acting as an incubator for the unborn majestic eagle that will ultimately represent the United States. Philadelphia figures play key roles in the suspenseful vote for independence. Within the Pennsylvania delegation, Benjamin Franklin favors independence while John Dickinson does not, and James Wilson tends to follow Dickinson's actions. After all other colonies have voted "yea," the divided Pennsylvania delegation has the final vote. Wilson's choice assures Pennsylvania's approval and a unanimous vote in favor of independence. Dickinson is shown leaving Congress. He did not sign, but he did, however, join the Pennsylvania militia.

The musical also portrays Caesar Rodney as the tiebreaking vote in favor of independence for the Delaware delegation. After riding approximately eighty miles on horseback through a thunderstorm, Rodney arrives in Philadelphia on July 2 still wearing his muddy boots just as the vote for independence is about to take place. New Jersey also plays a role in the show as Franklin notes the strain in his relationship with his son William Franklin, a Loyalist who served as royal governor of New Jersey from 1763 to 1776.

The Broadway production of *1776*, directed by Peter Hunt and choreographed by Onna White with musical direction by Peter Howard, received warm reviews. Critics found the book for the show to be well researched and written. Although they commented that musical numbers often sounded alike and acted as filler with large gaps in between, the show was a smash hit with audiences. *1776* won the Tony Award for Best Musical in 1969, and it came back to Broadway as a revival in 1997. Numerous professional, regional, community, and school theaters performed the show, including at least nine regional theater companies during the year of the Bicentennial. In Philadelphia, the Walnut Street Theatre produced the show in 1997. The production came back to Philadelphia in 2023 with a touring company of a new revival in which female, transgender, and nonbinary actors played the traditionally male roles.

The director of the 1969 Broadway production also directed the screen version, and many actors from the stage repeated their roles in the movie, including William Daniels as John Adams, Howard Da Silva as Benjamin Franklin, and Ken Howard as Thomas Jefferson. Although set in Philadelphia, filming for the movie of *1776* took place in California at the Columbia Ranch (later known as the Warner Brothers Ranch, or Warner Ranch) in Burbank and Sunset Gower Studios in Los Angeles. A fire at the Warner Ranch in the 1970s destroyed the film's re-creation of a colonial Philadelphia street and other sets. The movie cost an estimated $4 million to make and grossed $6.1 million, but it was not generally admired by critics.

Throughout *1776*, Adams's character repeats the words "Is anybody there? Does anybody care?" These words have continued to resonate and take on new meanings to viewers of all ages. Set in and around Independence Hall, *1776* has helped to sustain recognition of Philadelphia's role in history.

National Parks

Seth C. Bruggeman

National parks have figured prominently in Greater Philadelphia's cultural, economic, and natural landscapes. Morristown (1933), Independence (1948), Valley Forge (1976), and First State (2015) National Historical Parks all preserve and provide access to sites associated with the American Revolution and early American history. Together they welcome millions of visitors each year and create thousands of jobs in surrounding communities, thereby generating considerable economic activity throughout the region. Alongside other regional units of or supervised by the National Park Service, including historical sites, memorials, heritage areas, historic landmarks, historic properties, an agency headquarters, and a sprawling nature reserve, the national parks reflect a longstanding and ongoing investment by the federal government in protecting the region's rich natural and cultural resources.

Established in 1916 amid a Progressive impulse to preserve the nation's scenic treasures, the National Park Service began its work primarily in western states, far removed from the East's burgeoning population centers. Agency leaders worked to shift the balance by establishing parks throughout the eastern states and expanding their scope to include sites of historical significance. Doing so, however, put the National Park Service into competition with state and local preservation organizations, which had spread throughout the country following the Civil War. Also at odds with this mission was the War Department, which since the 1890s had been charged with supervising national military parks.

Despite the increasingly competitive heritage landscape, National Park Service leaders scoured the region looking for footholds to expand the agency's stewardship across all federal parks. Their search led to Morristown, New Jersey, in 1932. Although no battles occurred there, Morristown was storied for its association with George Washington and two encampments of the Continental army, particularly during the hard winter of 1779–80. Because Morristown was not a battlefield, it was not subject to the War Department's supervision. A private organization formed to protect Morristown's historic structures during the 1870s, but it struggled financially during the 1920s and 1930s despite growing public interest in the site. Against the backdrop of George Washington's two hundredth birthday celebrations in 1932, National Park Service leaders together with local enthusiasts convinced Congress to establish the nation's first national historical park at Morristown. President Herbert Hoover signed the act into law in 1933.

Morristown was not the agency's first historical unit—it had established two historical monuments in Virginia in 1930—but was the first to be designated a historical park, which implied a scale and significance akin to iconic wilderness parks like Yosemite and Grand Canyon. It was a crucial step in prompting a massive reorganization in 1933 that placed all of the nation's federal parks, monuments, and historic sites under National Park Service supervision. In the Historic Sites Act of 1935, Congress authorized the agency, for the first time, to seek out and preserve historic sites and properties of particular significance. In this regard, Morristown was a catalyst for creating an expansive history program within the agency that, in coming years, employed corps of researchers, architects, and preservationists.

The impact of the reorganization was immediately evident throughout Greater Philadelphia, in part because of additional New Deal initiatives of President Franklin Roosevelt. With the country deep in economic crisis, the Roosevelt administration sought to ease anxieties and provide job relief by commissioning a network of recreational areas on past-prime lands bordering the nation's urban areas. These included nearly six thousand acres reclaimed in 1935 from a centuries-old iron plantation on the border of Chester and Berks Counties forty miles northwest of Philadelphia. Hundreds of men employed by Roosevelt's Civilian Conservation Corps restored buildings and landscapes. By 1936, when administration of federal recreation areas passed to the National Park Service, agency leaders inherited a ready-made historic site. Hopewell Furnace National Historic Site entered the system in 1938, only the second historical site designated as such under the Historic Sites Act.

In Philadelphia, meanwhile, citizens motivated by patriotism and concern for the deteriorating urban environment around Independence Hall clamored to leverage the Historic Sites Act to create a national monument encompassing the hall and other buildings associated with the nation's founding. Making the case for a large park was difficult, however, given a complex web of competing private property interests. The National Park Service made inroads during 1939 when it acquired the building of the second Bank of the United States, just vacated by the U.S. Customs Service, and designated it the Old Philadelphia Custom House National Historic Site. In 1942, the National Park Service brokered a cooperative partnership with stewards of Old Swedes' Church in South Philadelphia to establish Gloria Dei Church National Historic Site. Meanwhile, a coalition of power brokers including politicians, lawyers, architects, and members of hereditary societies leveraged wartime patriotism to generate support for a stronger federal presence. It came in 1943 when, with a special presidential waiver of a wartime prohibition against new parks, the National Park Service established Independence Hall National Historic Site. In 1948, having spent the remaining war years haggling over plans with park boosters and city officials, agency leaders and local supporters convinced Congress to authorize Independence National Historical Park.

Although born of World War II, Independence very much embodied the Cold War era. It was, after all, a park committed squarely to promoting the success of American democracy. Its singular focus on the Revolutionary era conveniently excused it from contending with Constitutional failures such as those that prompted civil rights activism in the postwar years. What's more, the National Park Service's development plan literally created the park's historical landscape. Throughout the 1950s, bulldozers cleared nineteenth- and twentieth-century buildings to create a mall (initially a state park) north of Independence Hall and a landscaped park extending three blocks to the east. Although some within the agency warned against this approach of displacing people and businesses that did not harmonize with Independence's historical aesthetic, it reflected the considerable influence of postwar-era urban renewal strategies, which favored "slum" clearance and the expansion of public space in city centers. The National Park Service's energies in Philadelphia advanced a radical transformation of the city's landscape that was more broadly coordinated by the City Planning Commission and its executive director, Edmund Bacon. The opening of a restored Independence Hall to the public in 1972 thus reflected Philadelphia's new cachet as a center of historic preservation, but it also bespoke a new vision for urban life at the end of the twentieth century.

The popularity of that vision during the 1970s owed, in part, to the remarkable breadth of activities associated with the nation's Bicentennial celebration in 1976. Bicentennial fervor made Independence a locus of veneration and protest. But, even beyond Independence, the Bicentennial intensified National Park Service commitments throughout Greater Philadelphia. A campaign emerged to put Valley Forge State Park—set aside in 1893 as Pennsylvania's first state park—under federal supervision. Washington's Continental army suffered a difficult though transformative encampment at Valley Forge during the winter of 1777–78. Public memory of its travails inspired significant commemorations, but a shifting economy and runaway suburban growth exceeded the park's capacity to protect its resources. After considerable debate throughout the early 1970s, Congress agreed in 1976 to make Valley Forge the region's third national historical park.

FIGURE 35. Cleared block north of Independence Hall, 1953. Demolition created a blank canvas for expanded commemoration of the nation's origins. NATIONAL PARK SERVICE.

Large historical parks ranked among only the most visible of National Park Service initiatives throughout the region at the end of the twentieth century. Bicentennial energies brought Philadelphia's Thaddeus Kosciuszko National Memorial (the agency's smallest unit at .02 acres) into the system in 1972 as well as the Edgar Allan Poe National Historic Site in 1978. The agency's capacity to serve the region owed also to the presence of a thriving field office, established in Philadelphia in 1956. Although the purview and the name of the Northeast Regional Office shifted over the years, its purpose has been to provide a corps of planners and technicians to nearly eighty parks and other units spread across thirteen states. Regional officers figured prominently in brokering the 1978 establishment of the New Jersey Pinelands National Reserve across nearly a million acres of ancient forest in southern New Jersey.

The Pinelands project heralded a new direction for the National Park Service favoring cooperative management—with state, local, and private interests—of mixed-use natural and heritage areas rather than exclusive federal control typical of national parks. This strategy shaped much of the agency's work throughout the Greater Philadelphia area during the early twenty-first century. Beyond sustaining its legacy units, the agency took an advisory role in managing the Delaware and Lehigh National Heritage Corridor (1988), the Schuylkill River Valley National Heritage Area (2000), the Lower Delaware National Wild and Scenic River (2000), the Crossroads of the American Revolution National Heritage Area (2006), and the Washington-Rochambeau National Historic Trail (2009). In

FIGURE 36. George Washington's tent, 2019. As a focal point of the Museum of the American Revolution, the artifact became a star attraction. MUSEUM OF THE AMERICAN REVOLUTION.

addition, through its supervision of the National Register of Historic Places, the agency provided assistance to hundreds of historic properties and landmarks.

The Greater Philadelphia region's distinctive concentration of natural and cultural resources created significant responsibilities for the National Park Service. Despite dwindling budget appropriations in the twenty-first century, Congress continued to create new units to be managed. In 2015 these included First State National Historical Park, Delaware's first national park, which was designated to preserve and provide access to sites associated with colonial Dutch, English, Finnish, and Swedish settlements (reaching also into southeastern Pennsylvania). National politics and regional needs thus mixed again with shifting landscapes and the tides of memory to ensure an ongoing and dynamic role for the National Park Service throughout Greater Philadelphia.

Museum of the American Revolution

Virginia Mulligan

Founded in 2000, Philadelphia's Museum of the American Revolution sought to create a single museum experience capturing the full story of the nation's origins. While highlighting the promises of freedom, self-governance, and equal rights, the museum explored the contradictions within the American Revolution in all its complexity.

The origins of the museum date to 1907, when the Rev. W. Herbert Burk, an Episcopal priest, sought to honor George Washington and the importance of the American Revolution by constructing the Washington Memorial Chapel at Valley Forge. At its completion, the chapel included a small museum holding several significant artifacts. In 1909, Burk added to the museum's stature by buying George Washington's marquee (war tent) from Mary Custis Lee, great-granddaughter of Martha Washington. Lee chose Burk over others who bid for the tent because it had been used during Washington's Valley Forge encampment in 1777–78. Nine years later, Burk established the Valley Forge Historical Society, which added an extensive and distinguished collection of artwork, rifles, swords, sculptures, rare books, and manuscripts. To support the growing collection, in 2000 the historical society created a new nonprofit organization, the Museum of the American Revolution, in Valley Forge to educate visitors about the complex story of the nation's founding.

Although the historical society proposed in 1999 to construct a new facility in Valley Forge National Historical Park, concerns about the museum's projected size and cost delayed construction. It was not until 2005, when H. F. "Gerry" Lenfest joined the board of directors and became chairman, that the project started to move forward again. Lenfest, a well-known philanthropist and devoted Philadelphian, loved the city and its history. His enthusiasm for a museum devoted to the Revolution led him to contribute considerable financial support.

In 2007, Lenfest bought seventy-eight acres in Valley Forge for $4.1 million for the envisioned museum as well as a hotel, restaurant, and conference center. However, the site was blocked in court after residents objected to the traffic they expected the mixed-use project to bring. Following that setback, Lenfest enlisted Pennsylvania governor Edward G. Rendell to identify an alternate site. Their solution was to exchange the seventy-eight acres Lenfest had purchased in Valley Forge for less than an acre at Third and Chestnut Streets in Philadelphia, formerly the Independence National Historical Park visitor center.

The new location across from the first Bank of the United States building and just a few blocks from Independence Hall lent itself naturally to the new museum. Although it presented some measure of competition to the nearby National Constitution Center, supporters managed to raise funds necessary for its creation. Besides Lenfest's donation of more than $63 million, the American Revolution Center (then the museum's name) matched a challenge grant for $40 million set by Lenfest. Other significant donors included the venue management firm SMG, Wawa, the Bank of America Charitable Foundation, and the Church of Jesus Christ of Latter-day Saints. The Oneida Indian Nation gave $10 million because it wanted the museum to demonstrate the Oneidas' multiple roles in the Revolutionary War, allying with the Revolutionaries, actively aiding the British, or remaining neutral in hopes of securing independence, protection, and trade agreements.

The museum's design and construction companies observed the stringent zoning and deed restrictions imposed in the historic district and set in place by the National Park Service. A required archaeological survey, which took place between July and October 2014, uncovered eighty-two thousand artifacts dating to Philadelphia's founding. The artifacts became a part of the museum's collection, the most notable being the *Triphena* bowl, a punch bowl from the eighteenth century. After completing the new building's foundation in April 2015, workers used a tower crane to lift in large exhibits and objects, including the wood that helped recreate a deck of a privateer ship and the Liberty Tree, as well as the museum's grand staircase.

The museum opened on April 19, 2017, the 242nd anniversary of the Battle of Lexington and Concord. The permanent exhibit's central narrative focused on the war's political and military history, but displays also revealed the subtle social transformation of British subjects into Revolutionaries. By featuring not just the military's viewpoints but also those of women, enslaved African Americans, free Black people, and Native Americans, the museum provided visitors with a broad social understanding of the war. The exhibits moved on a snakelike path to show the war's complexity. Exhibits engaged visitors by asking them, for instance, to consider what role they would have chosen in particular moments rather than just presenting them with facts about what happened.

The permanent exhibit opened with "Prologue: Tearing Down the King," explaining events leading up to the war. Following an account of the Seven Years' War, visitors encountered a life-size reproduction of the Boston Liberty Tree, the first symbol of resistance against British tyranny. Surrounding the Liberty Tree, which incorporated a fragment from the surviving tree, stood important figures who opposed the British, including Mercy Otis Warren and Phillis Wheatley. The second part of the museum, "The Darkest Hour," progressed from the Battle for New York in the fall of 1776 to the winter at Valley Forge 1777–78. Visitors could line up to march into battle for the Battle of Brandywine under heavy fog, gunfire, and rumbling, to protect Philadelphia from falling. In the Oneida Nations Theater, a video explored the experiences of Native American women and children refugees.

Next, in "The War at Sea" section, visitors could walk on a life-size replica of a privateer ship and learn how women dressed as men to become privateers and how sailors persuaded Benjamin Franklin to support voting rights for the poor. Continuing, "The War in the South, 1778–1780" presented a central contradiction of enslaved African Americans fighting for the British because of the promise for freedom even as many American patriots sought liberty while continuing to hold slaves.

Finally, "A New Nation" recounted the establishment of the United States, from the Peace of Paris to the Constitution and the Bill of Rights. Not merely celebratory, this section noted that some were disillusioned with the new country and its laws. The exhibit suggested that free African Americans never felt free due to racism and prejudice and explained how and why Native Americans continued to fight the United States for decades. The exhibit also delved into how, in the 1790s, some women sought to demonstrate their intellectual equality with men through a growing movement for women's education. At the end of the exhibits, visitors walked past portraits of veterans who fought to secure the new nation. Inside the Alan B. Miller Theater, the centerpiece of the earlier collection at Valley Forge—Washington's marquee—drew visitors' attention with a video about the tent's journey from the American Revolution to the present. When the video faded, visitors gained a glimpse of the actual tent, a reminder of the role of museums in preserving objects from the past.

In the first year after opening in April 2017, the Museum of the American Revolution welcomed over three hundred thousand visitors, including thirty thousand students, a strikingly high number given that the museum charged an admission fee while many other museums in the area of Independence National Historical Park were free. In the second year, the museum received three major awards: a Pennsylvania Museum 2019 Institutional Achievement Award for its family-oriented discovery center, Revolution Place; an American Alliance of Museums Award for Sustainability; and an American Association for State and Local History Award for Revolution Place. The museum also extended its digital reach through social media. By bringing the American Revolution to life in an animated fashion through touchscreen displays, re-creations, human-sized re-created spaces, and hands-on experiences for children, the museum established itself as a central destination in Philadelphia's historic district.

National Constitution Center

Mabel Rosenheck

Created in 1988 by the Constitution Heritage Act, the National Constitution Center in Philadelphia played a role in debates about the future of the Independence Mall area of Independence National Historical Park as a tourist draw and as a historic site that represented American national identity even before it was built. From its opening in 2003, the National Constitution Center museum used exhibits, programs, and performance to engage with the Constitution not only as a historical document but also as a legal framework, a set of ideas, and a site of struggle. In the late 2010s, the center found new relevance by presenting a diverse and inclusive history of the United States and serving as a reliable, fact-based resource for a polarized nation.

The sponsors of the Constitution Heritage Act imagined an institution that would carry on the educational aims of the 1987 bicentennial observance of the Constitution. Beyond constitutional history as a vital part of American law, politics, democracy, and citizenship, advocates argued the Constitution Center should inspire citizens to participate in democracy and celebrate American ideals. Its educational mission aimed "to increase the awareness and understanding of the Constitution." A 1998 opinion poll conducted by the museum found that more teenagers could name the Three Stooges than the three branches of government.

Philadelphia mayor Edward G. Rendell, a key supporter, incorporated the Constitution Center into

FIGURE 37. National Constitution Center, 2017. PHOTOGRAPH BY M. KENNEDY FOR VISIT PHILADELPHIA.

his push for redeveloping Independence Mall, the three blocks extending north of Independence Hall. Rendell sought to bolster the tourism economy in Philadelphia by revitalizing its familiar historic resources and building new ones. Ultimately, Rendell, Senator Arlen Specter, the Constitution Center's founding president Joseph Torsella, and others mobilized $86 million from the state and federal governments, $5 million from the city, and $10.5 million from the Delaware River Port Authority for the center. Despite its federal mandate and its public funding, the center itself was a private institution, which made individual gifts equally important to creating and sustaining it. Key early contributions came from Walter and Leonore Annenberg and Richard and Helen DeVos, each couple donating $10 million.

The National Constitution Center opened on July 4, 2003, at Fifth and Arch Streets with a view of Independence Hall three blocks to the south. The center invited visitors to "Enter a visitor. Leave a citizen," suggesting that engaging with the ideas of freedom and democracy were more central to the museum experience than learning the names and dates associated with a two hundred-year-old document.

The museum housed the main exhibit—*The Story of We the People*—in a massive, round exhibit hall. In the middle a sharply stepped 360-degree theater staged an hourly live, multimedia performances titled *Freedom Rising*. Around the perimeter a circular exhibit offered a timeline of American history from the Stamp Act of 1765 to the Patriot Act of 2001. It brought legal history together with the history of politics and democracy to explore key themes of national identity. A dizzying array of text, primary sources, secondary sources, objects, sculpture, sound, video, and interactives—both digital and analog—narrated these histories with traditional text-based displays and participatory engagement. The museum updated displays periodically to include post-2003 events like the election of President Barack Obama. It also revised its discussion of the Civil War and Reconstruction to reflect the historiography of a later exhibit that explored both the successes and failures of the Thirteenth, Fourteenth, and Fifteenth Amendments.

To uphold its nonpartisan mission, the museum sought to straddle party lines and ideological divides. Supreme Court justices Antonin Scalia and Stephen Breyer served on the advisory board for the opening and, despite their opposing political ideologies, both were pleased with the exhibits. On the contemporary Supreme Court, interpreting the Constitution was the subject of an ongoing ideological battle between originalists like Scalia and pragmatists like Breyer. At the Constitution Center, however, exhibits highlighted more familiar debates, such as those over voting rights or race and gender equality as narratives of progress and an evolving national consensus. Educational programs and speakers sometimes were more contentious. Together, the whole of the institution, from funders to supporters to school groups, offered multiple approaches that ultimately created balanced discussion as the ideal way to understand politics and the Constitution.

The timeline format of the main exhibit showed how the Constitution changed over time, usually in favor of equality and inclusivity. Highlighting these changes further, on panels mounted above the visitor the text of the Constitution was etched in glass with notes marking changes that later amendments made to the original document. The Interactive Constitution, an online digital resource, used a similar method of annotation as well as essays and commentary to explore constitutional history and debate in-depth. The development of the Interactive Constitution began in 2015 with funding from the John Templeton Foundation. It was a collaboration with the Federalist Society, a conservative and libertarian think tank, and the American Constitution Society, a progressive counterpart.

Since its opening, the National Constitution Center also has featured an array of temporary exhibits, some more closely related to the Constitution than others. The center's concerns about generating public interest, and thus admissions, factored into programming decisions and worried some critics that the efforts to be popular were causing it to drift from its mission. A 2009 exhibit on Diana, Princess of Wales was a particularly glaring attempt to attract visitors. In the first decade of the 2000s, many museums turned to flashy exhibits produced by for-profit entertainment companies to enhance revenues. However, the Constitution Center's own internal financial struggles should also be understood in context of the unique competition it faced from free historical and educational sites like Independence Hall and the Liberty Bell nearby.

In the 2010s, the Constitution Center adopted new strategies while retaining old ones. The museum produced exhibits that engaged more directly with constitutional issues and showed their relevance to everyday life. Some of those exhibits also toured. In 2010, the museum revitalized its educational mission with the interactive theater program *The Living News*. In 2015, it also took on a local collaboration in curating *Speaking Out for Equality: The Constitution, Gay Rights, and the Supreme Court* with the William Way LGBT Community Center in Philadelphia.

In 2013, the National Constitution Center hired Jeffrey Rosen as its sixth—and by 2021 its longest serving—president and CEO. He was the first legal scholar to lead the institution. While education and K-12 school groups continued to be a focus, Rosen also led multipartisan academic engagement with the Constitution through programs like the Interactive Constitution and America's Town Hall, which brought together conservative and liberal scholars to discuss historic and contemporary issues in law and politics. In the name of balanced debate, these programs showed the Constitution as a site of struggle whose meaning was unsettled.

In 2019 and 2021, the museum opened large exhibits curated in-house about the Civil War and on the Nineteenth Amendment. These extended the traditional display strategies—artifacts and text labels informed by historical scholarship—used elsewhere. The Civil War exhibit also contained digital interactives that, like other Constitution Center projects, used the process of revision—in this case revision of the Reconstruction amendments prior to their passage—to show the complex trajectories that led to the evolution of the law and society. In addition, the museum launched *FOURTEEN*, another educational theater program, about lesser-known histories of the Black experience after the Civil War. The Pew Foundation funded the program with Black writers and performers from Philadelphia leading its creation.

Consideration of race and gender in the history of a document authored by white men, many of whom enslaved people, reflected the progressive ethos of a moment when many Americans were reconsidering the stories they had long told about their national past. However, the Constitution Center captured other political currents as well. It became a place to turn to for civil discourse and trustworthy, balanced information about the law, the Constitution, and American history amid attacks on all three. Said Rosen in 2020: "People are hungry for an alternative to the partisan paralysis and clashes that are paralyzing Washington, and that is what the framers intended: A constitution shaped by the understanding of the people." The center embodied what people often imagine museums—and the Constitution—to be: neutral, trusted authorities. At the same time, its programs and new exhibits showed that the Constitution was actually defined by partisan clashes. It was not neutral and in fact had always been a site of constant struggle for freedom, equality, and democracy.

EXPLORE MORE

The Greater Philadelphia region is a landscape of memory of the American Revolution, from pristinely restored historic sites to the names of suburban streets and service plazas on the New Jersey Turnpike. Books that trace the evolving regard for sites of the American Revolution include Charlene Mires, *Independence Hall in American Memory* (University of Pennsylvania Press, 2002), and Lorett Treese, *Valley Forge: Making and Remaking a National Symbol* (Pennsylvania State University Press, 1995). For a broader view, see Michael A. McDonnell et al., eds., *Remembering the Revolution: Memory, History, and Nation Making from Independence to the Civil War* (University of Massachusetts Press, 2013). Philadelphia's dedication to remembering the past, including but not limited to the Revolution, is the subject of Gary Nash, *First City: Philadelphia and the Forging of Historical Memory* (University of Pennsylvania Press, 2002). The symbolism of Marquis de Lafayette in the United States is the subject of Anne C. Loveland, *Emblem of Liberty: The Image of Lafayette in the American Mind* (Louisiana State University Press, 1971).

Monuments throughout the region recall Revolutionary heroes and principles. Many are clustered at Valley Forge, including the Patriots of African Descent Monument and statues of George Washington, General Friedrich von Steuben, and Brigadier General Anthony Wayne, among others. The park's reconstructed log cabins evoke the memory of the winter encampment of 1777–78; the nearby Washington Memorial Chapel is a living monument to the Revolution with an active Episcopal parish and stained-glass windows depicting the role of Washington and others in the nation's expansion. Monuments to the Revolution are also plentiful in Philadelphia, including Commodore John Barry behind Independence Hall and General Thaddeus Kosciuszko at Eighteenth Street and the Benjamin Franklin Parkway. Throughout the region, monuments mark sites of important battles, including the Trenton Battle Monument and Princeton Battle Monument in New Jersey.

The major events commemorating anniversaries of the nation's birth in 1876, 1926, and 1976 remain evident in the landscapes and streetscapes of Philadelphia. The avenues of the Centennial Exhibition in Fairmount Park remain in use, and two structures still stand: Memorial Hall, which became home to the Please Touch Museum for children in 2008, houses an intricate twenty-by-forty-foot scale model of the exposition. One state building, the Ohio House, remains. The park also retains the 1876 Catholic Total Abstinence Fountain, a demonstration of ethnicity and national identity featuring Irish-Catholic heroes of the Revolution. For the story of the fair, begin with Dee Brown, *The Year of the Century: 1876* (Scribner's, 1966).

Some monuments that originated on the Centennial grounds later moved to more visible locations: a Christopher Columbus monument given by the Italian people moved in 1976 to Marconi Plaza in South Philadelphia, where it was highly valued by Italian Americans but challenged as a representation of white imperialism during the 2020 social justice uprisings that followed the killing of a Black man, George Floyd, in Minneapolis, Minnesota. The *Religious Liberty* statue commissioned for the Centennial by B'Nai B'rith moved in 1984 to a site a block from the Liberty Bell adjacent to the National Museum of American Jewish History. A bust of Black religious leader Richard Allen sculpted for the Centennial, long thought to be lost or destroyed, was discovered more than a century later at Wilberforce University in Ohio and came back to Philadelphia for temporary exhibit at Mother Bethel African Methodist Episcopal Church in 2010.

The landscape created for the Sesquicentennial in then-undeveloped South Philadelphia became a footprint for the future FDR Park and the sports complex. The fair's history is the subject of Thomas H. Keels, *Sesqui!: Greed, Graft, and the Forgotten World's Fair of 1926* (Temple University Press, 2017). The Bicentennial, while more decentralized across the nation, produced notable museums that expanded the scope of local historical memory: The Afro-American Historical and Cultural Museum (later renamed the African American Museum in Philadelphia), at Seventh and Arch Streets, which in 2022 announced plans to move to the Benjamin

Franklin Parkway; the Port of History Museum at Penn's Landing, whose building became home to the Independence Seaport Museum in 1995; the Mummers Museum, 1100 S. Second Street; and the Living History Center, whose building at Sixth and Race Street became headquarters for WHYY public media. The *LOVE* sculpture by Robert Indiana, an iconic addition to the plaza at Fifteenth Street and JFK Boulevard, also came to Philadelphia for the first time during the Bicentennial. The impact of the Bicentennial is examined in Tammy S. Gordon, *The Spirit of 1976: Commerce, Community, and the Politics of Commemoration* (University of Massachusetts Press, 2013).

New museums added in the vicinity of Independence Hall in the early twenty-first century reflected the ongoing role of the Revolution in civic education and the region's tourism economy: the National Constitution Center, 525 Arch Street (opened 2003); the Liberty Bell Center, Sixth and Chestnut Streets (2003); *The President's House: Freedom and Slavery in the Making of a New Nation*, Sixth and Market Streets (2010); and the Museum of the American Revolution, 101 S. Third Street (2017). Exhibits and programs at these locations and at parks and historic sites throughout the region daily renew the memory of the American Revolution.

Chapter 6

Contradictions of Enslavement and Servitude

Introduction

In 1686, neighbors in Burlington, West New Jersey, listened and watched as the affluent Quaker James Wills beat an enslaved woman more than one hundred times because she resisted his commands. He was acquitted of her death but fined for burying her without notifying authorities. Two years later, four Germantown, Pennsylvania, Friends issued their protest against enslavement, the first by colonists in North America. They believed that potential emigrants from Europe would be appalled by news that "Quakers do here handle men as they handle there the cattle." Francis Daniel Pastorius and his colleagues summed up the contradiction of freedom and bondage in colonial America: "Here is liberty of conscience, which is right and reasonable; here ought to be likewise liberty of the body."

Despite resistance by Black people and appeals by Quakers such as George Fox, William Southeby, and the Germantown Friends, many colonists, including Quakers, endorsed enslavement. Though an enslaved man arrived in New Sweden as early as 1639, involuntary servitude remained limited before the 1680s. The Delaware Valley, including the city of Philadelphia, then developed with a mixed labor system of indentured servants, enslaved workers, family members, and free laborers, which suited the labor requirements of grain agriculture, livestock raising, crafts, shopkeeping, and overseas commerce. This hybrid system also accommodated changes in the labor supply caused by immigration and demographic trends. These same considerations operated in other colonies such as Virginia, Maryland, and South Carolina, where planters to a greater degree turned to enslavement to produce staple crops such as tobacco, rice, and cotton.

As employers throughout North America made conscious choices to purchase people who had been kidnapped, sold, and transported from Africa, colonial governments enacted severe laws to constrict the actions and opportunities of enslaved and free Black residents. In the early eighteenth century, Pennsylvania, New Jersey, and Delaware established separate courts for trying enslaved persons, with harsher penalties for certain crimes than for accused white people. In 1726, Pennsylvania curbed emancipation by requiring an enslaver to post a £30 bond upon manumission. Free Black inhabitants could be re-enslaved if they married a white person; they were restricted in trading with and entertaining enslaved people in their homes. New Jersey required a £200 bond for emancipation and prevented freed people from owning real estate. Along with colonial legislation facilitating the international slave trade, these laws reinforced a caste system based on skin color that persisted in the Delaware Valley despite growth of abolitionist sentiment.

Pennsylvania's Gradual Abolition Act of 1780, the first legislation against enslavement in the nation, built upon resistance by enslaved Black people before and during the American Revolution as well as the Quaker

Philadelphia Yearly Meeting's ban on enslavement among its membership. Yet the Pennsylvania law perpetuated bondage by emancipating no enslaved people born before March 1, 1780, and requiring servitude to age twenty-eight for the children of enslaved women. Black activists and the Pennsylvania Abolition Society, which had been founded in 1775 and revived in 1784, fought to emancipate individuals under the law and expand the scope of its provisions. In the late eighteenth and early nineteenth centuries, they tried but failed to convince the Pennsylvania and United States governments to abolish enslavement completely. New Jersey passed its gradual abolition law in 1804 but extended the grasp of enslavers by requiring servitude from the children—and grandchildren—of enslaved women. Because Delaware failed to enact an abolition act, enslavement remained legal in the state until ratification of the Thirteenth Amendment to the U.S. Constitution in 1865.

In collaboration with white abolitionists who helped to propel the Philadelphia region forward in antislavery reform, Black activists risked their lives and freedom to end enslavement and the caste system. Starting with rebels such as the woman killed in 1686 by James Wills and the hundreds who escaped during the colonial period and American Revolution, Black people used disobedience, violence, and escape to undermine involuntary bondage. Richard Allen, Absalom Jones, James Forten, and their supporters petitioned against enslavement and the Fugitive Slave Act of 1793, passed while Philadelphia served as capital of the United States. Black Philadelphians opposed the colonization movement whose goal was exportation to Africa of Black people freed by southern enslavers. Robert Purvis and other Black abolitionists formed vigilance committees in the 1830s to protect fugitives from southern enslavement and free Black residents from kidnapping. In the 1850s, William Still operated the Philadelphia Underground Railroad in coordination with Black communities and Quaker activists throughout the region.

Despite racism, discrimination, and continued bondage, by 1810 the Philadelphia region was home to a significant free Black population, including communities and churches in southwestern New Jersey. In Philadelphia, where free Black inhabitants numbered nine thousand (10 percent) of the total population, the Mother Bethel African Methodist Episcopal Church and other congregations anchored neighborhoods. During the nineteenth century, in addition to battles against enslavement, kidnapping, and colonization, Philadelphia Black residents endured race riots and struggled for the right to vote, equal opportunity in education and jobs, and an end to segregation on streetcars. In the twentieth century, Black Philadelphians honored activists who had fought against enslavement with the 1913 Pennsylvania Emancipation Exposition at Broad Street and Oregon Avenue. During World War II, Richard R. Wright Sr., who had been enslaved as a child in Georgia, created National Freedom Day, which remains a national holiday.

Enslavement

James Gigantino

Enslavement was central to the economy of the Philadelphia region in the late seventeenth and eighteenth centuries despite growing opposition to the institution among Black people, Quakers, and other activists. Early Philadelphia, an Atlantic trading hub, became a focal point for the Atlantic slave trade and home to a community of enslaved Africans. While enslaved Native Americans were occasionally imported from the Carolinas and other colonies during the early eighteenth century, most enslaved people were Africans or African descendants. Enslaved people created their own family and social networks while simultaneously integrating into the dominant white population, shaping the region's political, economic, and social evolution into the nineteenth century.

Enslavement was integral to the Delaware Valley even before William Penn founded Pennsylvania. The first enslaved African laborer in the region was Anthony, who in 1639 arrived in the New Sweden colony. By 1677, according to a census taken by the Duke of York's government, nine enslaved people worked on the west bank of the Delaware River and one resided in the Salem colony in West New Jersey. After Penn founded Pennsylvania, enslavement became integral to his infant capital and its environs with the 1684 arrival of the ship *Isabella* with 150 enslaved Africans. As the Delaware Valley developed a diverse economy based on wheat, corn, and livestock, enslaved people filled labor needs in many occupations including agricultural workers, artisans, laborers, stevedores, mariners, and household servants.

The Philadelphia region created a hybrid labor system in which family members, free wage laborers, indentured servants, and enslaved workers toiled alongside one another. This system created flexibility for meeting labor needs as the cost and supply of workers fluctuated throughout the colonial period. Enslavers routinely hired out their enslaved laborers on long- and short-term contracts, which added to the labor system's flexibility and the regional impact of enslavement. With growing European immigration before 1755, the absolute number of enslaved people increased in Philadelphia, but their percentage in the population declined. By 1710, enslaved residents numbered an estimated 630 people, or almost 20 percent of Philadelphia's population; their number grew to 1,375 by 1770, or just over 8 percent of the total population.

The transportation of enslaved people from Africa to the western hemisphere was significant in the Philadelphia region's relationship to the Atlantic world, with networks formed by trade, migration, and political associations between Europe, Africa, and the Americas. While ships outfitted in Philadelphia traveled to the West African coast, however, most enslaved people arrived in the Delaware Valley after toiling in the Caribbean. They filled labor shortages, especially when disruptions limited the supply of indentured laborers. For example, when the Seven Years' War interrupted the flow of European immigration, Delaware Valley residents imported almost 1,300 enslaved people from 1757 to 1766, including many directly from Africa. Nevertheless, the slave trade to the region largely ended by the time Pennsylvania levied a high duty in 1773 and the First Continental Congress prohibited the trade in 1774 with its boycott of British commerce. At the Constitutional Convention of 1787, South Carolina and Georgia insisted on continuation of the international slave trade.

Enslaved men and women in the Philadelphia region developed strong kinship and community networks that facilitated support for abolition and resistance to enslavement in the late eighteenth century. As part of the region's hybrid labor force, enslaved Black people

FIGURE 38. *Alice*, engraved by Mackenzie and published in London, 1803. Alice was born enslaved and held memories of William Penn and early settlers. She lived for more than one hundred years and died in 1802. LIBRARY COMPANY OF PHILADELPHIA.

labored for individuals who in most cases held one or two enslaved workers, which could restrict their ability to have families and develop a distinct culture, while increasing the enslavers' control. Despite these arrangements, enslaved Philadelphians established kinship networks throughout the city and its environs. They interacted with enslaved people living in rural areas who traveled with their enslavers to sell at the city's markets or for other business or social purposes. Enslaved people in the Delaware Valley formed romantic relationships, maintained family connections across long distances, sustained African cultural institutions, and developed new social and

FIGURE 39. *London Coffee House*, Philadelphia, depicting enslaved people being auctioned during the colonial period, lithograph by William Breton, ca. 1830. LIBRARY COMPANY OF PHILADELPHIA.

religious institutions. Enslaved mariners who worked for the region's ship captains created extensive Atlantic networks that allowed for an exchange of culture, information, and possibly the tools to achieve freedom.

Though early historians portrayed enslavement in the North as benign, physical force and violence pervaded the institution. Pennsylvania, New Jersey, and Delaware, like all other colonies, passed strict regulations in the early eighteenth century to govern the behavior of enslaved laborers, including travel limits and harsh punishment for violent acts against white persons. As in the Caribbean and the American South, enslaved people resisted in many ways, often escaping to reject the enslavers' control and to maintain kinship ties with distant families and communities.

Discussions of abolitionism developed in the Delaware Valley in tandem with continuation of enslavement. Though members of the Society of Friends held enslaved workers throughout the colonial period, sentiment grew among Quakers that the practice was sinful and should be ended. In 1776, Philadelphia Yearly Meeting required its members to emancipate enslaved people in their households or be disowned. In the midst of the American Revolution, abolitionists routinely used the same language that Patriots utilized in their quest for freedom from British "tyranny" or "enslavement" to highlight the hypocrisy of holding enslaved people amid a crusade for freedom.

In Pennsylvania, this Revolutionary rhetoric motivated the state legislature to enact the first legislative emancipation in history: the Gradual Abolition Act of 1780. This law freed no enslaved people immediately, providing freedom for children born to enslaved mothers after its enactment. These children were required to labor for their mothers' enslavers for twenty-eight years and therefore, in effect, paid oppressors the cost of their own freedom. These children, caught within an entirely new legal category, were often worked, beaten, and sold in the same way as their enslaved parents. Enslavement, therefore, died a very slow and painful death. Among other initiatives, Pennsylvania abolitionists sought to enforce a provision of the Gradual Abolition Act that freed enslaved people brought into the state after six months' residence. The rule exempted congressmen and foreign ministers but applied to other nonresident enslavers such as federal officials. George Washington, who brought nine enslaved people to the President's House, continued to hold enslaved workers in Pennsylvania indefinitely by moving them temporarily to New Jersey or Mount Vernon to restart the six-month limit.

By 1800, enslavement declined significantly in the southwestern counties of New Jersey, within the Philadelphia area, to a large extent because of Quaker influence, but remained important and grew between 1790 and 1800 in northern parts of the state. In 1804, New Jersey became the last northern state to adopt a gradual abolition law. Delaware discussed gradual abolition but never approved it because of the interests of enslavers in the southern part of the state. However, after Delaware and Maryland relaxed requirements for manumission, enslavement gradually declined in the areas bordering Pennsylvania.

Though the number of enslaved people in the Philadelphia region decreased by the 1810s, enslavement remained legal in New Jersey until 1846 and in Pennsylvania until 1847 because of the terms of gradual abolition. During the early nineteenth century, Philadelphia's status as a port city and Pennsylvania's border with slaveholding Maryland and Delaware attracted increasing numbers of enslaved people who sought escape. The border also put free Black people at risk of being kidnapped to feed the hungry markets for enslaved workers in Louisiana and Mississippi. Concern over kidnapping led white and Black Philadelphians to action. For instance, Absalom Jones, who had been enslaved and was a leading Black abolitionist and minister, helped author a 1799 petition to Congress with other free Black activists asking for revisions to the 1793 Fugitive Slave Law. When relief did not come from the federal government, Philadelphia's Mayor Joseph Watson used city resources in the 1820s to recover Black people kidnapped to the South. This new dimension of enslavement continued debates over the institution until the Civil War.

Indentured Servitude

Jean R. Soderlund

As in many parts of colonial North America, employers in and around Philadelphia recruited workers through indentured servitude, a system of bound labor that obligated individuals to serve for a term of years. Servitude began in the Delaware Valley with the seventeenth-century Swedish, Dutch, and English settlements, expanding after 1720 when a new wave of immigrants responded to the colonization of lands of the Lenapes and other Native people in Pennsylvania, Delaware, and New Jersey. While indentured servitude declined among white workers by the late eighteenth century, term bondage gained new life into the nineteenth century when Pennsylvania and New Jersey gradual abolition acts bound Black children to serve the masters of their enslaved mothers. In addition, many of the enslavers throughout the region who agreed to emancipate Black people required them to labor additional years before becoming free.

Indentured servitude encompassed a number of conditions that legally bound an individual, voluntarily or involuntarily, to serve a master for a term of years. The contract could include a signed document, spoken agreement, or arise from a legislative act or judicial decision. Among the earliest New Sweden settlers were men who had been convicted of crimes in Sweden, then given the option of immigrating to the colony as bound servants. Peter Cock, for example, worked as a cook and tobacco laborer before obtaining freedom, land, and an appointment as presiding justice of the Upland Court. During the seventeenth century, servitude became widespread in the North American colonies and Caribbean. In Delaware, Dutch and English households employed servants in New Castle and the Whorekill by 1671, and more arrived in subsequent years with plantation owners from the Chesapeake. Households brought Quaker and non-Quaker servants to West New Jersey after Salem founder John Fenwick in 1675 offered transportation and freedom dues of clothing, tools, and one hundred acres in return for a term of four years. Servants also accompanied the Quakers who founded Burlington where, in 1682, Sarah Biddle and other women persuaded the men's meeting to require members to obtain permission before selling their servants' terms of labor to non-Friends.

During the colonial period, many indentured servants who immigrated to the Philadelphia region received transatlantic transportation in return for laboring a term such as three, four, or five years. Upon arrival, the servant worked for a farmer, artisan, or shop owner who provided housing, food, and clothes and promised freedom dues at the end of the individual's term. John Fenwick and William Penn briefly offered land as incentives for servants to immigrate, though many failed to accumulate the capital to pay required fees and build farms. As demonstrated by newspaper advertisements for escaped servants, some men and women considered flight from onerous conditions worth the risk of punishment if caught.

While England remained an important source of servants in the eighteenth century, by the late 1720s growing numbers of Scots Irish, Irish, and German-speaking servants arrived in the Delaware Valley as part of larger immigrant flows. Spurred by a disastrous famine, more than five thousand people in 1729 landed in Philadelphia and New Castle from Ulster and southern Irish ports. Though fewer migrants arrived annually in subsequent years, many individuals and families took advantage of established routes in the transatlantic trade. Merchants welcomed the opportunity to transport servants along with customers who prepaid fares, thus making profits on the westward route and returning to Europe with flaxseed and other colonial products. Young single men composed a large proportion of the Scots Irish and southern Irish immigrants who obtained credit for their passage by agreeing to serve as indentured servants.

The flow of German-speaking immigrants grew from the late 1720s to peak in the early 1750s, as residents of the Rhine lands of southwestern Germany, Switzerland, and Alsace-Lorraine sought economic opportunity, lower taxes, and religious and political freedom in the Philadelphia region. Families and individuals who lacked sufficient capital for transportation turned to the redemptioner system in which, upon arrival, they agreed to fulfill a specific term of bound service according to their level of debt. German-speaking residents who had arrived earlier, sometimes relatives or friends, often facilitated the new immigrants' settlement, including purchasing the time of teenage children. The teenagers thus helped to pave the family's success by becoming redemptioners to resolve the family's debt.

Though Scots Irish, Irish, English, and German immigration resumed after disruption caused by the Revolutionary War, the share of European bound servants in the region's workforce declined as wage labor increased. At the same time, the emancipation practices of individual enslavers and provisions of the gradual abolition acts passed by Pennsylvania in 1780 and New Jersey in 1804 forced thousands of African Americans into bound servitude. Many enslavers from Pennsylvania, New Jersey, Delaware, Maryland, and Virginia who manumitted Black people required additional bondage prior to freedom. The gradual abolition acts codified this practice for children born to enslaved women whom the laws failed to emancipate. In Pennsylvania, for example, children born after March 1, 1780, were obligated to serve their mothers' enslavers until age twenty-eight; under the 1804 New Jersey law the ages were twenty-five for men and twenty-one for women. Like enslaved people and indentured servants, these children and young adults could be assigned long hours of plantation, craft, or domestic labor; punished with beatings; and sold at the enslaver's whim. The Pennsylvania Supreme Court in 1826 somewhat limited the range of enslavement for a term by ruling that it would not extend to another generation. With no similar decision in New Jersey, the grandchildren as well as children of enslaved Black women remained subject to involuntary bondage until ratification of the Thirteenth Amendment in 1865.

Indentured servitude, including various forms of bound labor for a term, contributed in tandem with enslavement and wage labor to the economic growth of the Delaware Valley. Despite arduous conditions, many poor European immigrants gained economic opportunity by agreeing to serve in exchange for transportation. Some evaded death sentences by accepting deportation and servitude. With high mortality rates, many died before completing their terms. For enslaved Black persons and the descendants of enslaved mothers in the era of gradual abolition, enslavement for a term represented a long path to economic independence and political freedom.

Abolitionism

Richard S. Newman

Few regions in the United States can claim an abolitionist heritage as rich as the Delaware Valley. By the time Boston abolitionist William Lloyd Garrison launched the *Liberator* in 1831, the Philadelphia area's confrontation with human bondage was more than 150 years old. Still, Philadelphia abolitionism has often been treated as a distant cousin of the epic nineteenth-century antislavery struggle. The milestone 2013 documentary *The Abolitionists* (PBS), for example, celebrated Garrison as the antislavery struggle's first great innovator. Before him, the documentary declared, there was barely an abolitionist movement anywhere in America.

Perhaps it is fitting that a place long associated with Quaker circumspection ceded the abolitionist spotlight to other locales. But Philadelphia's ambivalent relationship to the abolitionist struggle, particularly during the nineteenth century when the movement became more diverse and aggressive, also explains its marginalized status. The city had vast economic ties to the South and Atlantic world, connecting Philadelphians to the mighty engine of enslavement. Brotherly Love was not always accorded to reformers—particularly Black Americans and women. For a city steeped in notions of tolerance, that is a difficult reality to confront.

For many years, abolitionism in the Philadelphia region was a story of firsts. The 1688 Germantown Protest, which challenged the Society of Friends to treat African-descended people as brethren and not bondsmen, was the first formal protest against enslavement in North America. While generations of Quakers gained wealth from the institution, the Philadelphia region soon became a seedbed of abolitionist thought. By the early 1700s, monthly meetings stretching from Burlington in West Jersey to Chester south of Philadelphia began debating the morality of enslavement. The visible saints of this inaugural abolitionist wave—William Southeby, Ralph Sandiford, Benjamin Lay, John Woolman, Anthony Benezet—rejected bondage as a necessary part of the modern world, but they were not always popular, even within the Society of Friends. Yet by crafting printed antislavery discourses steeped in secular as well as sacred tones, they also charted new directions for humanitarian reform. No longer was the righteous figure an inward-looking perfectionist; rather he or she was motivated to improve society too. By the Revolutionary era, when Philadelphia Yearly Meeting banned bondage, Philadelphia-area Quakers could look proudly on a long history of abolitionism.

The second wave of abolitionism was also defined by firsts. The creation of the Pennsylvania Abolition Society (PAS) in 1775, and its reorganization and expansion in the 1780s, marked the beginning of secular abolitionism in the United States. Agitating for abolition at the state and federal levels and protecting Black people in courts of law, the PAS gained a glowing reputation throughout the Atlantic world. Pennsylvania's gradual abolition law of 1780—the world's first such statute, which liberated enslaved people born after the law's passage at age twenty-eight—relied on PAS agitation and the matrix of ideas established by Benezet and his abolitionist colleagues. Over the next several decades, the PAS perfected legal and political lobbying by gaining support from respectable figures such as William Rawle, David Paul Brown, and Evan Lewis, noted lawyers all. With the American Convention of Abolition Societies, a biennial meeting of gradual antislavery groups created in 1794, often convening in the City of Brotherly Love, Philadelphia was again an abolitionist stronghold.

Yet cracks emerged by the early 1800s. While the PAS aided many African Americans, the group failed to forcefully condemn the rising colonization movement, which supported the exportation of Black people as a means of encouraging southern manumission. Popular in the North as well as the South, colonization deemed free Black people anathema to white liberty. Still, the PAS did not launch an anti-colonization campaign—even as African Americans in Philadelphia did. Some PAS members also believed that abolitionism must never endanger the Union, no matter how much enslavement expanded. The abolitionist cause sagged.

Hoping to reignite the movement, a third wave of abolitionism washed over the region between the 1820s and 1850s. Drawing energy from Black and female reformers, so-called "modern" abolitionists embraced more aggressive forms of protest. Following in the footsteps of Black founders like Richard Allen and James Forten, who advocated racial equality but were prevented from joining the PAS (which did not admit its first Black member—Robert Purvis—until 1842), Philadelphia's Black abolitionist community supported new abolitionist ventures. These included both the *Liberator* and the American Anti-Slavery Society (a national organization formed in 1833 in Philadelphia), both of which espoused immediate, uncompensated, universal abolition and no compromises with enslavers. Black activists played critical roles in antebellum antislavery circles. Serving as lecturers, fundraisers, and authentic voices of the oppressed, they pictured enslavement and racism as twin evils haunting American society. With antislavery contacts in Pennsylvania, New Jersey, and Delaware, Black activists formed vigilance committees to aid Black people who escaped from southern enslavers and to protect members of free Black communities in the Philadelphia region from kidnappers.

Female reformers also emerged as key antebellum abolitionists, locally and nationally. During the 1820s Elizabeth Chandler, who worked alongside Garrison at Benjamin Lundy's *Genius of Universal Emancipation*, wrote powerfully about female abolitionists' potential to reshape American antislavery struggles. At nearly the same time, Lucretia Mott helped build the Free Produce Society (which disavowed goods produced by enslaved workers) into a powerful movement aimed at undercutting enslavement's economic standing in northern households. Angelina Grimké and Sarah Grimké, South Carolinians who rejected bondage after settling in Philadelphia, became perhaps the most prominent female abolitionists in the nation during the 1830s when they began agitating against bondage. Angelina, who married celebrated abolitionist orator Theodore Dwight Weld and subsequently moved to Belleville, New Jersey, became the first woman to address a political body when she spoke before the Massachusetts legislature in 1838.

Women demonstrated their radicalism by establishing Philadelphia's first integrated abolitionist organization in December 1833: the Philadelphia Female Anti-Slavery Society (PFASS). Predating both the Philadelphia Anti-Slavery Society (1834) and the Pennsylvania Anti-Slavery Society (1837), the group was composed of Black and white women who espoused immediate abolitionism. Between the 1830s and 1850s, members of the PFASS led petition drives, ran antislavery fairs, and served as the organizational backbone of area abolitionism. Little wonder that, by the early 1860s, a woman became perhaps the city's leading antislavery voice: Republican Party activist Anna Dickinson.

This newly aggressive brand of abolition caused a severe backlash. Indeed, Philadelphia witnessed a series of anti-abolition and anti-Black riots in the 1830s and 1840s that cast a long shadow over politics in the city. The infamous burning of Pennsylvania Hall (a newly built abolitionist meeting place) in May 1838 reminded activists that seemingly tolerant Philadelphia supported a violent brand of anti-abolitionism. Viewing reformers—rather than their foes—as disturbers of the peace, many Philadelphia leaders kept a wary eye on abolitionists for years to come. At both the Great Central Fair of 1864 and the Centennial Exposition of 1876, civic authorities suppressed civil rights activity to prevent a reprise of 1838.

Ironically, while the Civil War vindicated northern abolition, it did not compel Philadelphians to honor living abolitionists in their midst. Instead, distant previous generations of Quakers became the face of Philadelphia abolitionism for their seeming quietude (a notion forgetting that they too were one-time agitators). It took new rounds of activism to overturn streetcar segregation in Philadelphia (in 1867) and return voting rights to African American men in Pennsylvania (via the Fifteenth Amendment in 1870). Perhaps for that reason Black abolitionists like Octavius Catto, an egalitarian reformer who was gunned down on Election Day in 1871, were still viewed as rabble rousers during Reconstruction. More than a century passed before Philadelphians truly reappraised antebellum reformers as civil rights heroes.

Escape, Vigilance, and the Underground Railroad

Beverly C. Tomek

From the 1600s, enslaved people in the Philadelphia region resisted oppression through noncompliance, violence, and escape. Enslaved and free Black people became abolitionists before white abolitionism gained momentum, then joined with Quakers and other allies

FIGURE 40. *Destruction by Fire of Pennsylvania Hall, On the night of the 17th May, 1838,* by J. C. Wild. LIBRARY COMPANY OF PHILADELPHIA.

to oppose enslavement, the slave trade, and fugitive slave acts. After passage of Pennsylvania's Gradual Abolition Act, Black and white abolitionists assisted fugitives and helped to protect free Black people from kidnapping and sale to southern enslavers. A network of activists provided transportation, food, and shelter on Underground Railroad journeys through Delaware, Pennsylvania, and New Jersey.

The Delaware Valley, and particularly Pennsylvania, became a focal point of sectional tension in the United States after passage of the Gradual Abolition Act in 1780. Pennsylvania became a destination for enslaved Black people who escaped from neighboring states, putting the state at odds with enslavers throughout the South and causing conflict with Maryland in particular. Black communities and Quakers in southern New Jersey assisted people who crossed the Delaware River to arrive at Greenwich or Salem, guiding many toward New York. Though white residents in both states had mixed reactions to the newcomers, Pennsylvania's location on the Mason-Dixon Line—the Pennsylvania-Maryland border—created a unique situation that influenced local and national attitudes about enslavement and abolition.

Abolitionists in the Philadelphia region operated within a framework established by the U.S. Constitution that required states to return people who fled enslavement across state lines. The Fugitive Slave Act of 1793, enacted while Philadelphia served as the nation's capital, authorized local judges to return accused fugitives to enslavers without a jury trial. As sectional

FIGURE 41. Jane Johnson and her two sons escaped their North Carolina enslaver in Philadelphia in 1855. Illustration from William Still, *The Underground Rail Road*, 1872. WIKIMEDIA COMMONS.

animosity between the North and South reached its zenith prior to the Civil War, Congress passed a second Fugitive Slave Act in 1850 that required federal marshals, state and local authorities, and citizens to assist in returning people accused as fugitives to southern enslavers. Self-emancipated people could not testify in their own behalf.

From the 1780s, the Pennsylvania Abolition Society (PAS) sought stronger legislation to stop kidnapping and to protect people who escaped enslavement in other states. The Pennsylvania General Assembly in 1820 passed the first state personal liberty law, which imposed fines and jail sentences of seven to twenty-one years at hard labor for convicted kidnappers. The law also directed that only judges from higher courts could issue writs to return fugitives, not aldermen or justices of the peace. In 1826, when Maryland challenged the law and Pennsylvania legislators considered revisions, the PAS, free Black activists, and Quakers lobbied successfully for stronger protections against kidnappers and enslavers. New Jersey passed personal liberty laws in 1826 and 1837, the latter permitting jury trials.

Starting in the 1780s, PAS lawyers such as William Rawle and Evan Lewis defended accused fugitives in court. Quaker attorney David Paul Brown represented and won freedom for a number of Black Americans during his forty-year career. Freedom suits grew even more complicated after passage of the Fugitive Slave Act of 1850 when the old Pennsylvania State House (Independence Hall) became the scene of heated cases in which white people accused Black individuals of being fugitives and the accused and their abolitionist allies fought to establish their freedom. In one case, Henry Garnet ran out of the courtroom celebrating his newly granted freedom, only to be arrested by police who assumed he was attempting an escape. This case illustrates the precarious position of the men and women who pleaded their cases in the building that, by that time, was celebrated by many as the birthplace of American liberty.

As enslaved people sought refuge in Pennsylvania, New Jersey, and other northern states, free Black and white activists organized vigilance (or vigilant) associations to protect fugitives and potential kidnap victims. After Black abolitionist David Ruggles in 1835 formed the first such organization in New York City, Robert Purvis and his father-in-law, the influential businessman James Forten, convinced associates in 1837 to organize the Vigilant Association of Philadelphia. A year later, women formed the Female Vigilant Association to assist in fundraising, with Elizabeth White as president. The women held West Indian Emancipation Day celebrations on August 1 and fairs in December to raise money. Citizens in rural counties soon founded vigilance committees and women's associations throughout the region.

Vigilance committees collaborated in loose and irregular regional networks, concealing the details of their efforts to help enslaved people break the law by claiming liberty. While the work of the committees was kept secret, their existence was well-known. In Philadelphia, members published their names and addresses in the *Pennsylvania Freeman* newspaper and in flyers so that fugitives and others in need could easily find them. Purvis's home at Ninth and Lombard Streets contained a hidden room in the basement for emergencies, and his country home, Byberry (near Bristol in Bucks County), served as a temporary home for many.

The Philadelphia Vigilant Association reorganized annually in 1839, 1840, and 1841, changing leadership and staff as it struggled for financial stability. The group offered shelter, clothing, medical attention, legal counsel, and guidance further north to a growing number of fugitives. From June to December 1839, the committee handled more than fifty cases and sent forty-six people to freedom. Most had escaped from Virginia and Maryland, and most went to Canada via New York. Other destinations included Trinidad and England. By the fall of 1841, the group was handling more than three cases per week. A race riot in Philadelphia on August 1, 1842, then stifled the committee as rioters targeted the Purvis home, leading the family to relocate to their property in Byberry.

In December 1852, in response to the 1850 Fugitive Slave Act, the Vigilant Committee reemerged under Purvis's guidance. The committee operated under leadership of New Jersey native William Still, whose name became synonymous with the Philadelphia Underground Railroad. His wife, Letitia (George) Still, played an important role by raising money, using her skills as a seamstress to sew clothing, and offering the Still home. The Stills hosted a number of famous fugitives, including Jane Johnson and her sons, whom Still and fellow abolitionist Passmore Williamson dramatically rescued in 1855. In addition, Still received a number of now-famous fugitives in the Pennsylvania Anti-Slavery Society office, including Henry "Box" Brown, who had himself shipped there from the South, and Still's own brother Peter. Much of what historians know about these encounters comes from Still's meticulous records and his resultant book, *The Underground Railroad*, published in 1872.

With its deep abolitionist history and a large free Black population, Philadelphia and the surrounding region played a prominent role in the famed Underground Railroad. The loosely connected organization of white and Black activists helped hide and guide enslaved people as they sought freedom in the North and Canada. A system of routes led people north from the Chesapeake toward Havre de Grace, Maryland, and across the Susquehanna River to Lancaster and Chester Counties. Several routes developed in south central and southeastern Pennsylvania and in southwestern New Jersey, regions with vibrant free Black communities and strong Quaker abolitionist networks.

FIGURE 42. William Still, photograph published in Wilbur Henry Siebert, *The Underground Railroad from Slavery to Freedom*, 1898. WIKIMEDIA COMMONS.

Conflict developed between border South states like Maryland and border North states like Pennsylvania and New Jersey as abolitionists put up armed resistance to enslavers' efforts to recapture enslaved people, often from courthouses and jails. Two famous incidents led to considerable violence as fugitives and their allies fought hard to thwart the efforts of slave catchers. In 1836, rescuers in Swedesboro, New Jersey, saved a Black family from a professional slave catcher from Philadelphia. In 1847, however, the efforts of activists in Carlisle, Pennsylvania, ended in convictions for eleven rescuers. Perhaps the most famous of these rescue "riots" occurred in 1851 in Christiana, Pennsylvania, when a Maryland enslaver was killed by Black men as they defended themselves against recapture. Despite the rising violence along the North-South border, escapes continued throughout the 1850s. An estimated nearly nine thousand fugitives made their way to Philadelphia by the beginning of the Civil War, some heading to other destinations and others choosing to stay.

During the antebellum years, Black people who escaped from southern enslavers and free Black and white abolitionists forced the issue of enslavement to shape political rhetoric throughout the United States. They developed a mindset of "free soil" in the North long before its emergence in the 1840s with the Liberty and Free Soil Parties, which aimed to outlaw enslavement in new states. The conflict on the Mason-Dixon Line over freedom and bondage helped to move the nation toward Civil War.

Christiana Riot Trial

James Kopaczewski

In 1851, armed conflict between proslavery and antislavery factions at a Pennsylvania town twenty miles north of the Mason-Dixon Line riveted national attention. Bloodshed at Christiana and the subsequent trial in Philadelphia became flashpoints that deepened sectional divisions between the North and South.

Enslaver Edward Gorsuch and his party of eight men rode into Christiana on September 11, 1851, from Baltimore County, Maryland, with warrants for the arrests of four fugitive Black people. Upon reaching the home of William Parker, who had escaped enslavement, Gorsuch and his party met armed resistance. A large group of Black men and women surrounded Gorsuch's party and demanded that they leave Pennsylvania immediately. Gorsuch's men fired guns as Black men and women attacked with clubs, corn cutters, and similar weapons. Numerous individuals on both sides were injured and Gorsuch died of wounds sustained during the fight.

In the immediate aftermath of the Christiana Riot, Parker and other men escaped for Canada. U.S. officials hastily arrested anyone possibly connected with the riot, including a white miller from Christiana named Castner Hanway, who was mistakenly identified as the mastermind of the riot. Hanway was one of forty-one men charged with treason for "wickedly and traitorously" intending "to levy war" against the United States. Hanway's trial began on November 24, 1851, at the old Pennsylvania State House in Philadelphia (Independence Hall) with Supreme Court justice Robert C. Grier and U.S. District Court judge John K. Kane presiding.

The defense of the Christiana Riot participants became a popular cause for the abolitionist movement. Fiery abolitionist and U.S. representative for Lancaster County Thaddeus Stevens led Hanway's defense team, and abolitionist Lucretia Mott sat in the courtroom on the second floor of Independence Hall throughout the trial. The prosecution was directed by the U.S. attorney for the Eastern District of Pennsylvania, John W. Ashmead, and a team of lawyers from the state of Maryland. After opening arguments, Ashmead called the prosecution's key witness, U.S. Deputy Marshal Henry Kline, to the stand. Kline had been among Gorsuch's party on the day of the riot and testified that Hanway was responsible for inciting Parker and the resisters. Under cross-examination, Kline admitted that he had hidden in a cornfield during the riot, so his view was obstructed. Following Kline's testimony, the defense called twenty-nine character witnesses, including Judge William D. Kelley, who portrayed Kline as a liar and a known kidnapper. This testimony was devastating for the prosecution. Indeed, for many Pennsylvanians—even those who were not in sympathy with the abolitionist cause—there was little interest in prosecution, because the 1850 Fugitive Slave Law seemed to represent an incursion of federal power into state sovereignty. After fifteen minutes of deliberation by the jury, Hanway was found not guilty of treason. Subsequently, federal and state officials declined to press further charges against the resisters.

The verdict served as fuel for the abolition movement as it gained momentum in the 1850s. African American men and women organized at Christiana to actively resist any attempts to kidnap people who had escaped enslavement or disturb their communities. Nevertheless, southerners viewed the verdict as a product of northern radicalism and a failure to equally apply the law. The sectional divisions made clear by the Christiana Riot trial deepened throughout the 1850s and ultimately led to the Civil War.

Pennsylvania Emancipation Exposition (1913)

Charlene Mires

Held in 1913 in South Philadelphia, the Pennsylvania Emancipation Exposition marked the fiftieth anniversary of the Emancipation Proclamation with events and exhibits celebrating African American progress. At a time when the Black population in Philadelphia was growing and gaining in political influence, the event's organizers also experienced a backlash of criticism as they secured $95,000 in state funds to stage the exposition.

In Pennsylvania and elsewhere, Black Americans organized state and local events to mark the fiftieth anniversary of the Emancipation Proclamation after Congress declined to support a national commemoration. Pennsylvania's exposition took place at Broad Street and Oregon Avenue, then undeveloped but designated on maps as "City Plaza" (later Marconi Plaza). Three exposition buildings, including a two-story, Beaux-Arts style administration building designed by African American architect C. Henry Wilson II, housed exhibits, a dining room, an auditorium, and a lecture and concert hall. The Emancipation Exposition opened on September 14, 1913, with a religious congress attended by more than five thousand people. The next day, marching bands led a parade of floats down Broad Street from Girard Avenue to the exposition grounds, a four-mile route that presented a moving pageant of floats marking African American achievements on display for the white establishment occupying the city's office buildings, hotels, and city hall. The exposition continued through October 4 with events including education and medical congresses, athletic contests, and musical performances. An estimated one hundred thousand people visited the exhibits, which stressed advancements in education and industry.

The exposition sparked racial conflict as white-owned Philadelphia newspapers, especially the *North American*, portrayed the event as a corrupt scheme to funnel public money into the pockets of the ruling Republican Party political machine. The state funding was obtained by the first Black state legislator to be elected in Pennsylvania, Republican Harry W. Bass, who was born in West Chester. Exposition organizers rented an office from the Republican Party at 1352 Lombard Street, which the *North American* labeled "the notorious Senate Club." Development in the area of Broad Street and Oregon Avenue would potentially benefit property owned by political boss William Vare in South Philadelphia. Such accusations were vigorously challenged by the African American–owned *Philadelphia Tribune*. Claims of corruption were never substantiated, but the exposition ran over budget by $4,000 and a sculptor and exposition workers protested afterward that they had not been paid.

After 1913, the site of the Emancipation Exposition was landscaped according to plans by the Olmsted Brothers of Brookline, Massachusetts, and in 1926 the resulting park became the location for the eighty-foot-tall, electrified Liberty Bell that served as gateway to the Sesquicentennial International Exposition. With South Philadelphia dominated by Italian immigrants and their descendants, the square in 1937 was renamed Marconi Plaza to honor Guglielmo Marconi, the recently deceased Italian inventor of wireless telegraphy. Later additions to the plaza, including the Christopher Columbus monument originally located in Fairmount Park, added to the site's recognition as a place for Italian American community and commemoration. The Pennsylvania Emancipation Exposition of 1913, significant in its time for Black residents of Philadelphia, left little trace on the landscape or in published histories of Philadelphia.

National Freedom Day

Charlene Mires

Created in 1942 by a Philadelphian who had been enslaved as a child, the annual National Freedom Day is commemorated each February 1. The holiday calls attention to the Thirteenth Amendment to the United States Constitution, which ended enslavement, and the continuing struggle for African American justice and equality.

National Freedom Day began in the early months of the United States' involvement in World War II. Upon hearing President Franklin D. Roosevelt speak of the Four Freedoms, Richard R. Wright Sr. wrote in the *Philadelphia Tribune* that Americans would not be free until everyone, including Black Americans, shared fully in those freedoms. Born into bondage in Georgia, Wright had moved to Philadelphia in 1921 following a long career as an educator, including the presidency of the State College of Industry for Colored Youth and Mechanic Arts in Savannah. Also well-known as a political activist and journalist, he was among the thousands of African Americans who migrated north during and following World War I. After joining several of his children in Philadelphia, including Richard R. Wright Jr., later bishop of the African Methodist Episcopal Church, he cofounded the Citizens and Southern Bank and Trust Company at Nineteenth and South Streets.

Wright had a longstanding interest in commemoration, including involvement in the fiftieth anniversary of the Emancipation Proclamation, a "Seventieth Anniversary Celebration of Negro Progress" in 1933, and creation of the *All Wars Memorial to Colored Soldiers and Sailors* (initially in Fairmount Park, later moved to Logan Circle). For National Freedom Day, he selected February 1 because it was the date when President Abraham Lincoln signed the congressional resolution proposing the Thirteenth Amendment. Promoted vigorously and nationally by Wright until his death in 1947, the earliest observances of National Freedom Day included parades and gatherings of delegates from around the nation at Independence Hall and Congress Hall. Such prominent speakers as Thurgood Marshall and Dr. Martin Luther King Jr. stressed harmony and good will while also calling attention to issues such as political participation and economic opportunity for Black Americans. A consistent feature of the commemoration has been the laying of a wreath at the Liberty Bell.

Resonating with national and global concerns for freedom and civil rights in the early years of the Cold War, National Freedom Day became a national holiday in 1949 by proclamation of President Harry S. Truman. Over time, however, the observance became more local, including the wreath laying at the Liberty Bell, a banquet, scholarships awarded by the National Freedom Day Association, and observances by pupils at Richard R. Wright School, Twenty-Seventh and Dauphin Streets. Despite the continuing efforts of dedicated Philadelphians, National Freedom Day garnered less attention than Martin Luther King Jr. Day (the third Monday in January) and Juneteenth (June 19), which observes the end of slavery on the date in 1865 when news of the Emancipation Proclamation reached Galveston, Texas.

In the twenty-first century, however, National Freedom Day gained increased visibility on the Internet as creators of websites posted and expanded upon lists of federally recognized holidays. In 2010, President Barack Obama directed new attention to the Philadelphia-born event and linked it to a global cause when he designated the month of January as National Slavery and Human Trafficking Prevention Month, culminating with February 1—National Freedom Day.

FIGURE 43. Employees from the Veterans Administration singing at the Liberty Bell for the annual National Freedom Day, photograph by Joseph Wasko, 1964. SPECIAL COLLECTIONS RESEARCH CENTER, TEMPLE UNIVERSITY LIBRARIES.

EXPLORE MORE

For opportunities to explore exhibits about the history of enslavement, abolition, and the Underground Railroad in the Delaware Valley, visit the African American Museum in Philadelphia, 701 Arch Street; Independence Seaport Museum, 211 S. Columbus Boulevard; Johnson House Historic Site, 6306 Germantown Avenue; Mother Bethel African Methodist Episcopal Church, 419 S. Sixth Street; Museum of the American Revolution, 101 S. Third Street; President's House (Robert Morris mansion), Sixth and Market Streets (all in Philadelphia); and, in New Jersey, the Peter Mott House, 26 Kings Court, Lawnside, and Harriet Tubman Museum, 632 Lafayette Street, Cape May. Several historic trails document the courage of Harriet Tubman and other Underground Railroad conductors, including the Harriet Tubman Underground Railroad Byway, which includes more than thirty sites through Maryland's Eastern Shore and Delaware; and the Underground Railroad Freedom Trail that continues the Tubman Byway through southern Chester and Delaware Counties, Pa., to Independence Hall in Philadelphia. In 2022, the New Jersey Historical Commission received funding for the Black Heritage Trail from the New Jersey state government.

The Historical Society of Pennsylvania at 1300 Locust Street holds the Pennsylvania Abolition Society Papers, William Still Journals, and Vigilant Committee of Philadelphia Records. The Library Company of Philadelphia, 1314 Locust Street, continues to develop its African Americana Collection of over thirteen thousand newspapers, periodicals, graphics, books, pamphlets, and broadsides. The Charles L. Blockson Afro-American Collection at Temple University, 1330 Polett Walk, contains more than five hundred thousand items on global Black history and culture from 1581 to the twenty-first century. Quaker meeting records and other papers related to abolitionism can be consulted at Quaker and Special Collections, Haverford College, Haverford, and Friends Historical Library, Swarthmore College, Swarthmore; the Passmore Williamson Papers are located at the Chester County History Center, 225 N. High Street, West Chester, Pa. For records of the Pennsylvania Emancipation Exposition, see the *Philadelphia Tribune*; for National Freedom Day, see Papers of Governor Edward Martin at the Pennsylvania State Archives in Harrisburg, and the R. R. Wright Family Collection, Moorland-Spingarn Research Center, Howard University, Washington, D.C.

Sources on enslavement, emancipation, and the extension of bondage under the gradual abolition acts in the Philadelphia region include Erica Armstrong Dunbar, *Never Caught: The Washingtons' Relentless Pursuit of Their Runaway Slave, Ona Judge* (37 Ink/Atria, 2017); James J. Gigantino II, *The Ragged Road to Abolition: Slavery and Freedom in New Jersey, 1775–1865* (University of Pennsylvania Press, 2015); Gary B. Nash and Jean R. Soderlund, *Freedom by Degrees: Emancipation in Pennsylvania and Its Aftermath* (Oxford University Press, 1991); Richard S. Newman, *The Transformation of American Abolitionism: Fighting Slavery in the Early Republic* (University of North Carolina Press, 2002); Richard Newman and James Mueller, eds., *Antislavery and Abolition in Philadelphia* (Louisiana State University Press, 2011); Paul J. Polgar, *Standard-Bearers of Equality: America's First Abolition Movement* (University of North Carolina Press, 2019); Billy G. Smith and Richard Wojtowicz, *Blacks Who Stole Themselves: Advertisements for Runaways in the* Pennsylvania Gazette, *1728–1790* (University of Pennsylvania Press, 1989); Jean R. Soderlund, *Separate Paths: Lenapes and Colonists in West New Jersey* (Rutgers University Press, 2022); Beverly C. Tomek, *Pennsylvania Hall: A "Legal Lynching" in the Shadow of the Liberty Bell* (Oxford University Press, 2014); Crystal Lynn Webster, *Beyond the Boundaries of Childhood: African American Children in the Antebellum North* (University of North Carolina Press, 2021); William H. Williams, *Slavery and Freedom in Delaware, 1639–1865* (SR Books, 1996); Jean Fagan Yellin and John C. Van Horne, eds., *The Abolitionist Sisterhood: Women's Political Culture in Antebellum America* (Cornell University Press, 1994); and Cory James Young, "For Life or Otherwise: Abolition and Slavery in South Central Pennsylvania, 1780–1847" (Ph.D. diss., Georgetown University, 2021).

On indentured servitude among European immigrants, see Susan E. Klepp and Billy G. Smith, eds., *The Infortunate: The Voyage and Adventures of William*

Moraley, an Indentured Servant (Pennsylvania State University Press, 1992); Sharon V. Salinger, *"To Serve Well and Faithfully": Labor and Indentured Servants in Pennsylvania, 1682–1800* (Cambridge University Press, 1987); and Marianne S. Wokeck, *Trade in Strangers: The Beginnings of Mass Migration to North America* (Pennsylvania State University Press, 1999).

Among many works on the Underground Railroad, vigilance, and resistance, see Nat Brandt and Yanna Kroyt Brandt, *In the Shadow of the Civil War: Passmore Williamson and the Rescue of Jane Johnson* (University of South Carolina Press, 2007); Stanley Harrold, *Border War: Fighting over Slavery Before the Civil War* (University of North Carolina Press, 2010); Charlene Mires, *Independence Hall in American Memory* (University of Pennsylvania Press, 2002); Nilgun Anadolu Okur, "Underground Railroad in Philadelphia, 1830–1860," *Journal of Black Studies* 25, no. 5 (May 1995): 537–57; Thomas P. Slaughter, *Bloody Dawn: The Christiana Riot and Racial Violence in the Antebellum North* (Oxford University Press, 1991); and William Still, *The Underground Railroad* (Porter & Coates, 1872).

Sources on the Pennsylvania Emancipation Exposition and National Freedom Day include Mitch Kachun, *Festivals of Freedom: Memory and Meaning in African American Emancipation Celebrations, 1808–1915* (University of Massachusetts Press, 2003); Mitch Kachun, "'A Beacon to Oppressed Peoples Everywhere': Major Richard R. Wright Sr., National Freedom Day, and the Rhetoric of Freedom in the 1940s," *Pennsylvania Magazine of History and Biography* 128, no. 3 (July 2004): 279–306; and Charlene Mires, "Race, Place, and the Pennsylvania Emancipation Exposition of 1913," *Pennsylvania Magazine of History and Biography* 128, no. 3 (July 2004): 257–78.

After more than two centuries, Philadelphia-area residents continued to reflect on the contradiction of enslavement and freedom in the region's history through popular culture, scholarship, museum exhibits, and celebration of national holidays. The designation of Juneteenth as a federal holiday in 2021 provided an opportunity for Black and white people to reflect on the long struggle against involuntary bondage that ended only in 1865.

Morning View of the African Episcopal Church of St Thomas *in Philadelph*

Chapter 7

CAPITAL OF BLACK AMERICA

Introduction

In 1899, W. E. B. Du Bois published his landmark sociological study, *The Philadelphia Negro: A Social Study*, analyzing historical, social, and economic data. He considered the growth of Mother Bethel African Methodist Episcopal (AME) Church "so phenomenal that it belongs to the history of the nation rather than to any one city." Indeed, the men and women of Philadelphia's Black communities assumed leadership beyond the city's bounds, establishing influential Black organizations and convincing white allies to take more robust action against enslavement, discrimination, and violence. The efforts of Black activists made the Philadelphia region a destination for tens of thousands of African Americans during the antebellum period, through the Great Migration of World Wars I and II, to the late twentieth and early twenty-first centuries.

The awe-inspiring lives of Black founders Richard Allen, Absalom Jones, and James Forten illuminate the history of Black activism in a region slowly and unevenly disengaging from its entanglement with bondage. Allen was born enslaved in the household of Pennsylvania jurist Benjamin Chew, then sold to a Delaware farmer, who in 1780 agreed that Allen could purchase his freedom. Allen worked as a sawyer and wagon driver while preaching on the Methodist circuit from South Carolina to New York until 1786, when he settled in Philadelphia to lead Black worshippers at St. George's Methodist Church and in the Northern Liberties and Southwark. Absalom Jones was born enslaved in Delaware, then moved to Philadelphia at age fifteen with his enslaver, who eventually allowed him to buy his freedom at age thirty-eight. Allen and Jones joined other emancipated Philadelphians in 1787 to establish the Free African Society, which became the institutional foundation for Allen's Mother Bethel AME Church, Jones's African Episcopal Church of St. Thomas, and many other churches and organizations. Through these societies, Black Philadelphians provided mutual aid, educational and employment opportunities, and a leadership structure for opposing enslavement, discrimination, and kidnapping by southern enslavers.

James Forten's life followed a somewhat different trajectory. He was born free in Philadelphia and, during the Revolution, enlisted at age fourteen on an American privateer. He survived imprisonment on a disease-ridden British prison ship, worked for a white sailmaker, then took over and expanded the business after the owner's retirement. Forten employed Black and white craftspeople, becoming a wealthy businessman in antebellum Philadelphia. He joined Allen, Jones, and many other Black leaders in fighting enslavement and injustice. For example, Forten published *Letters from a Man of Colour* (1813) in which he successfully opposed plans by Pennsylvania legislators to ban Black people from settling in the state and to require that African American residents obtain certificates of registration. Forten also collaborated with William Whipper in establishing the American Moral Reform Society (1835–

41), which grew out of the national Colored Convention movement. At Richard Allen's invitation, the convention movement had been founded in 1830 at Mother Bethel Church.

Leadership at the state and national levels continued among Black Philadelphians in subsequent generations. James Forten's son-in-law Robert Purvis, for example, took the lead in fighting the 1837–38 Pennsylvania Constitutional Convention's proposal to restrict voting to white men. Purvis's *Appeal of Forty Thousand Citizens* employed historical and economic data demonstrating the substantial contributions of Black citizens to Pennsylvania society yet failed to prevent the change. Black men in Pennsylvania won back the vote only with ratification of the Fifteenth Amendment to the U.S. Constitution in 1870. By that time, Octavius V. Catto and other civil rights activists had successfully fought to desegregate public transportation in Pennsylvania. Catto was murdered on Election Day in 1871.

Black women contributed to abolitionism and community development despite the legal and cultural obstacles they confronted as African Americans and as women. Among founders of the Philadelphia Black community, Sarah Allen established the charitable society Daughters of Conference in the 1820s and supported the work of her husband, Richard Allen, the female preacher Jarena Lee of Cape May, New Jersey, and many other AME ministers. Charlotte Vandine Forten, wife of James Forten, and their daughters Margaretta Forten, Harriet Forten Purvis, and Sarah Forten Purvis helped to found the Philadelphia Female Anti-Slavery Society (PFASS), a major force in the Delaware Valley for immediate abolition and equality. Black women filled key leadership roles, including Margaretta Forten, who served as recording secretary, treasurer, and manager, and Sarah Mapps Douglass, who was an officer and for eleven years taught the school for Black students partially funded by PFASS. The abolitionist writer and lecturer Frances Ellen Watkins Harper became active in the Women's Christian Temperance Union in Philadelphia and helped to establish the National Association of Colored Women's Clubs in 1896. Educator Fanny Jackson Coppin served as a teacher and principal of Philadelphia's Institute for Colored Youth and as a missionary for the AME Church.

As the Black community grew in the Philadelphia area with the Great Migration of the twentieth century, African American men and women took leadership in many areas of employment, education, the arts, health care, and politics. Throughout, they faced and resisted discrimination. In time for the nation's Bicentennial, Temple University professor Lawrence Dunbar Reddick prompted the Bicentennial planning commission to advocate for establishment of the African American Museum in Philadelphia, which offers insightful exhibits and preserves collections on Black history and art. Black Philadelphians also gained a share of power in the late twentieth century through community leaders such as Judge A. Leon Higginbotham Jr., Reverend Leon Sullivan, and the city's first Black mayor, W. Wilson Goode. Philadelphia activists joined the national Black Lives Matter movement in 2015 to oppose police violence, judicial bias, and economic injustice. In 2020, after more than fifty years of efforts by Charles "Poppy" Sharp's Black People's Unity Movement and subsequent organizers, the reformed policing system in Camden, New Jersey, became a model for fighting crime and police brutality.

Free Black Communities

Andrew Diemer

In the Philadelphia area during the nineteenth century, free Black communities developed that by most measures were the most vibrant, dynamic, and influential in the United States. Free African Americans relied on each other to confront the persistent power of enslavement and white supremacy in Philadelphia and the region, while looking outward to become leaders in the national fight against those same threats.

The emergence of free Black communities was not a foregone conclusion. In the mid-eighteenth century, despite the fact that Philadelphia had produced some of the earliest protests against enslavement in the English-speaking world, involuntary bondage remained an important part of the region's economy. In 1765, of approximately 1,500 Black Philadelphians, about 1,400 were enslaved. This dramatically changed in the next quarter century: By 1790, the number of enslaved people who lived in Philadelphia had declined to 300, while the city's free Black population had grown to approximately 2,000. During the Revolutionary era, some supporters of independence came to recognize a clear contradiction between their calls for liberty and enslavement. Others, in particular some of the region's significant Quaker minority, grew to acknowledge enslavement as a violation of deeply held religious beliefs. In 1780, the Pennsylvania legislature enacted the gradual abolition law that freed no enslaved people, but stipulated that all children born to enslaved mothers after the law's passage would become free upon their twenty-eighth birthday. More than two decades later, New Jersey legislators passed similar legislation in 1804, delayed by the political power of enslavers in the eastern part of the state.

Most importantly, free Black communities emerged as African Americans across the region seized opportunities during the Revolutionary War and its aftermath. Many supported the British army as the most likely agent of emancipation, others supported the Patriot cause in hopes of turning the American Revolution into a war for emancipation, and still others took advantage of the chaos of war to escape from their enslavers' control. During the late eighteenth and early nineteenth centuries, a significant number of free Black people found their way to Philadelphia from the upper South, where legislatures rejected calls for abolition. Numerous enslavers in Delaware, Maryland, and Virginia manumitted some enslaved people in response to ideological critiques of enslavement and changing regional economics, often requiring additional service as indentured servants. Enslaved people played a crucial role in this process, often negotiating contracts in which they purchased their own freedom over time, while others found opportunities to disappear into the region's growing free Black communities.

As some southern states required emancipated people to leave the state and others increased restrictions on free Black people, many manumitted people moved to Philadelphia, the free city nearest to the slave South. By 1810, the city's free Black population increased to nine thousand, or 10 percent of Philadelphia's total population. In 1820, free Black people made up more than 6 percent of the population in Chester County and 7 percent in Delaware County. Free Black residents accounted for more than 15 percent of the population in New Castle County, Delaware. In New Jersey, Salem County's free Black population topped 7 percent, while free African Americans made up more than 4 percent of the population in Burlington and Gloucester Counties.

FIGURE 44. The Peter Mott House in Lawnside, N.J., built ca. 1844 and preserved by the Lawnside Historical Society. Peter Mott and his wife, Elizabeth Ann Thomas Mott, assisted people escaping enslavement as part of the Underground Railroad. WIKIMEDIA COMMONS.

One of the great draws of Philadelphia was the lure of economic opportunity. Newly emancipated African Americans from rural areas across the region and beyond saw promise in the burgeoning city. Once there, though, they often found that they were shunted into the lowest paying and least desirable kinds of work, competing with European immigrants, who also sought employment. While white workers found jobs in the city's robust industrial sector, free Black people were largely excluded from this sort of work and relegated to employment as physical laborers and in the low-status service economy. Many free Black people worked on the city's docks and aboard ships that plied the Delaware River, while some Black Philadelphians found a greater measure of economic success as teachers, ministers, and entrepreneurs. Among the most celebrated Black businessmen was James Forten, whose sailmaking

FIGURE 45. James Forten, 1818. COLLECTION OF THE HISTORICAL SOCIETY OF PENNSYLVANIA.

business thrived in Philadelphia's multiracial waterfront. The most successful Black waiters and caterers capitalized on their expertise and skill to establish themselves as an indispensable part of Philadelphia high society. Perhaps the most famous was Robert Bogle, celebrated by financier Nicholas Biddle in a poem, *Ode to Bogle*.

In this period, New Jersey also saw the growth of thriving Black communities such as Timbuctoo in Burlington County, Gouldtown in Cumberland County, and the Snow Hill and Free Haven settlements that became Lawnside in Camden County. Enslavement's end was slower in New Jersey than in Pennsylvania, casting a shadow over free Black workers who often toiled alongside enslaved people in a complex labor market. As in Philadelphia, newly emancipated African Americans in New Jersey struggled to achieve independence in the face of significant limitations on their economic opportunities. While most Black farmers were tenants, a significant minority purchased their own farmland, which was often economically marginal. Whether they lived in cities or in the countryside, Africans Americans found their economic status to be tenuous.

The dramatic growth of the region's free Black population provoked anxiety among many white residents. Pennsylvania legislators considered a series of bills to stop Black migration into their state but were thwarted by the cooperative activism of Black and white abolitionists. In 1813, for example, James Forten published his pamphlet, *Letters from a Man of Colour*, denouncing proposed legislation requiring Black people in Pennsylvania to obtain certificates of registration and banning African Americans from entering the state. Free Black residents, especially abolitionists and affluent members of the community, faced the persistent threat of mob violence. New Jersey officially denied the vote to Black people in 1807. In 1838, Pennsylvania voters ratified a new state constitution that explicitly restricted the vote to white men. Black Pennsylvanians had attempted to prevent this action, publishing the *Appeal of Forty Thousand Citizens, Threatened with Disfranchisement*, written by Black abolitionist Robert Purvis, but were unsuccessful and would not regain the right to vote until 1870.

One of the primary ways in which free Black people dealt with economic, social, and political discrimination was through building autonomous institutions. One of the first was the Free African Society, founded in 1787 by leading Black Philadelphians including pastors Richard Allen and Absalom Jones. This religious mutual aid society promoted education and provided aid to those in need. Allen and Jones then founded their own independent Black churches, Mother Bethel African Methodist Episcopal Church and the African Episcopal Church of St. Thomas, only the first of many Black congregations in the Philadelphia area. Black Philadelphians also helped to establish institutions that extended beyond the region, including the African Methodist Episcopal Church, an independent Black denomination cofounded by Allen in 1816. Many African Americans joined Black fraternal organizations and intellectual clubs, especially in Philadelphia but also in smaller Black communities across the region. Black Philadelphians played a leading role in the Colored Convention movement, which brought together Black leaders from across the United States to strategize about political issues.

FIGURE 46. *A Sunday Morning View of the African Episcopal Church of St. Thomas in Philadelphia*, by William Breton, 1829. COLLECTION OF THE HISTORICAL SOCIETY OF PENNSYLVANIA.

Perhaps the most urgent goal of free Black communities, especially in areas like Greater Philadelphia that bordered on slave states, was the protection of Black citizens from enslavement, kidnapping, and white violence. Black communities were constantly on the lookout for kidnappers, resisting them with force when necessary and forming vigilance committees to protect the Black community from such threats. Free Black people also worked with white abolitionists to provide legal and political expertise and to offer shelter, food, and transportation as part of the escape network called the Underground Railroad. Black abolitionists, especially Black Philadelphians, played a crucial role in radicalizing white abolition and in convincing white abolitionists to abandon the colonization movement. Black abolitionists coupled their opposition to enslavement with demands for Black equality, and they supported white abolitionists who did the same.

Free African Americans made up a significant portion of the population of the Greater Philadelphia region during the decades between the American Revolution and the Civil War. Such numbers, though, tell only part of the story. The Black community of Philadelphia played a critical role in the history of the city, and Black Philadelphians helped to lead the cause of abolition and the fight for Black citizenship rights, in the city and beyond.

African American Migration Since 1820

James Wolfinger

People of African descent have migrated to Philadelphia since the seventeenth century, first arriving in bondage, either directly from Africa or by way of the Caribbean. They soon developed a small but robust community that grew during the colonial period, then continued to expand in the 1800s despite employment discrimination, disfranchisement, and periodic riots by white mobs. During the twentieth century, the promise of jobs during the two world wars attracted tens of thousands of people who helped to create one of the largest African American communities in the urban North. While deindustrialization and suburbanization from the post–World War II period to the early 2000s contributed to rising rates of poverty, racial tensions, and disinvestment in Black neighborhoods, the Black community continued to attract new migrants.

During the decades leading up to the Civil War, Philadelphia attracted the largest Black population outside the slave states even though the city's acceptance of African Americans was mixed at best. The number of Black Philadelphians stood at fifteen thousand in 1830, grew to nearly twenty thousand by 1850, and topped twenty-two thousand in 1860. The population clustered in South Philadelphia near what is today Center City, while smaller concentrations developed in Kensington, Northern Liberties, and Spring Garden. With their reputation as vibrant political, cultural, and economic centers, these Black communities attracted African Americans. Philadelphia, true to its antislavery reputation, became a major stop on the Underground Railroad, especially for enslaved people escaping through Maryland and Delaware. But jobs—the great lure for most immigrants—were mostly physically demanding and low paying, with only a few people managing to secure positions as barbers, caterers, doctors, ministers, and teachers. Competition for work, coupled with anti-abolitionist sentiment, fired attacks by working-class people, especially Irish immigrants. Between 1828 and 1849, Philadelphia experienced a series of racial attacks that destroyed Black homes, businesses, and the abolitionist Pennsylvania Hall, leading one observer to call the city "illiberal, unjust and oppressive." Sentiment against Black people was not limited to the city: In 1838, Pennsylvania ratified a new constitution that officially disfranchised African Americans.

Despite the problems confronting Black Philadelphians, the community attracted many migrants in the second half of the nineteenth century. The population grew to nearly thirty-two thousand in 1880 and almost doubled to sixty-three thousand by 1900. The Black Philadelphia community was large enough to muster eleven regiments to serve in the Civil War, and in the ensuing decades it supported approximately three hundred Black-owned businesses, including the *Philadelphia Tribune* (established in 1884) and Frederick Douglass Memorial Hospital and Training School (opened in 1895). By the 1890s, the community had the size and vitality to command sociological investigation, which took the form of W. E. B. Du Bois's classic study *The Philadelphia Negro* (1899).

In the years following the Civil War, Black Philadelphians, led by Octavius V. Catto, pushed to regain the right to vote, end segregation of the city's schools, and desegregate the streetcars. Feeling the pressure, the Pennsylvania state legislature in 1867 passed a law requiring street railways to carry passengers regardless of color and in 1881 ended legal segregation of the educational system (although the city's schools remained segregated by custom for decades afterward). The Fifteenth Amendment to the United States Constitution compelled Pennsylvania to grant African Americans the franchise in 1870, but, signaling Philadelphia's continuing racial difficulties, Catto was shot and killed on Election Day in 1871.

The greatest wave of Black migrants in Philadelphia's history to that point came during World War I when the conflict overseas choked off European migration and northern businesses across the United States looked to the South for labor. This population movement, known as the Great Migration, changed the face of American cities from Boston and New York City to Detroit, Chicago, and beyond. Philadelphia's Black population more than doubled, rising from 63,000 in 1900 to 134,000 in 1920, with most of the migrants coming from the Eastern Seaboard. Most Black immigrants to the region moved to Philadelphia, though Black communities also grew in industrial cities such as Camden, New Jersey, and Chester and Norristown, Pennsylvania. Women played a critical role in the migration, helping to establish communal and kin networks that brought migrants to the Philadelphia area.

Most newly arrived African Americans were best described as the "working poor," seeking employment at major companies such as the Pennsylvania and Reading Railroads, Baldwin Locomotive, Midvale Steel, Cramp Shipbuilding, and the Philadelphia Rapid Transit Company. White Philadelphians, many of them recent immigrants to the United States, considered African Americans as competitors for jobs and decent housing. Racial conflicts included the 1911 lynching of a steelworker named Zachariah Walker in Coatesville (thirty-five miles west of Philadelphia), and attacks in Chester (1917) and Philadelphia (1918) resulted in fatalities in each city. Surveys showed that Philadelphia was so inhospitable that many new residents contemplated returning to the South. Some formed the Colored Protective Association or supported the National Association for the Advancement of Colored People (NAACP) to assert their rights.

Philadelphia's in-migration continued in the ensuing decades, tapering off only during the Great Depression. By the end of the 1920s, Philadelphia's Black population grew to 220,000 people and the community established a much larger presence in North and West Philadelphia. Enough African Americans enjoyed the era's prosperity that some critics accused better-off Black Philadelphians of shirking their responsibilities to the poor and working class. Such criticisms diminished in the 1930s when the Depression devastated the city, especially its Black community where unemployment exceeded 50 percent. Across Philadelphia, at textile mills and metal shops, African Americans faced the age-old problem of "last hired, first fired." For many working-class Black residents, like the city's white ethnic groups, economic hard times led them to support Franklin Delano Roosevelt and the New Deal, a sea change in a city dominated by the Republican Party for a century. Only with the coming of World War II and its attendant federal military supply contracts did the situation improve. African Americans, although some of the last people to gain employment, found jobs at Sun Shipbuilding, the Philadelphia Transportation Company, and elsewhere. Still, they faced discrimination as Sun Ship created a segregated yard and the transit company endured one of the costliest hate strikes of World War II.

Despite continued workplace discrimination, Philadelphia attracted thousands of migrants during the war and for decades afterward. The city's Black population stood at 250,000 in 1940, grew to 375,000 in 1950, and peaked at some 655,000 residents in 1970. By that year, African Americans represented one-third of the population. Unfortunately for Black Philadelphians, their numbers grew just as the city's economy declined. For generations a national industrial leader, especially in smaller craft occupations, Philadelphia lost textile, metal manufacturing, and electronic production jobs by the tens of thousands from the 1950s to 1970s. Some of the positions moved to the South and foreign countries while others migrated to the suburbs. African Americans found that because of discriminatory housing practices they could not follow the jobs to suburban Bucks and

FIGURE 47. Absalom Jones, 1810, by Raphaelle Peale. DELAWARE ART MUSEUM.

Montgomery Counties, and they increasingly became locked in poor inner-city neighborhoods shorn of employment and resources. These circumstances led to a more radicalized civil rights movement championed by Cecil B. Moore as well as activism by women who demanded the support of public institutions for their families.

In the last three decades of the twentieth century, Philadelphia's Black population stabilized at between 630,000 and 655,000 people. As white Philadelphians moved to the suburbs, African Americans became a larger portion of the overall population, 43 percent in 2000. The changing population mix created tense political contests, with law-and-order candidate Frank Rizzo serving two mayoral terms from 1972 to 1980. W. Wilson Goode finally secured a representative share of political power for the Black community when he served as mayor from 1984 to 1992, although his first term was marred by an infamous conflict with the Black liberation group MOVE.

Goode's emergence along with that of Judge A. Leon Higginbotham Jr., Reverend Leon Sullivan, and others showed the vitality of Philadelphia's African American community that continued into the first decades of the twenty-first century. The 2020 census demonstrated that Philadelphia remained attractive to Black migrants: the total population stood at 1,603,797 with African Americans comprising 38 percent of total residents and white residents comprising 34 percent. Philadelphia attracted more Latino and Asian immigrants in the late twentieth and early twenty-first centuries (15 percent and 8 percent of the population, respectively, in 2020), but it remained a magnet for African American migrants who continued to find opportunities as well as stony ground in the city. Unemployment, high public school dropout rates, and other problems persisted, but the vibrancy of Philadelphia's Black community continued, a vibrancy built by migrants for 350 years.

Free African Society

Elise Kammerer

Headed by Black founding fathers Richard Allen and Absalom Jones, the Free African Society was founded on April 12, 1787, as a nondenominational mutual aid society and the first dedicated to serving Philadelphia's burgeoning free Black community. Members contributed one shilling per month to fund programs to support their social and economic needs.

The Free African Society emerged from discussions among Allen, Jones, and other men in early 1786, when Allen was leading prayer meetings and early morning services for Black congregants of St. George's Methodist Church. Concerned that the majority of Philadelphia's Black community was illiterate and did not go to church, these men decided to form a nondenominational religious society to promote religion and literacy, as well as assist members' families cover the costs of burial after a member's death.

To join the Free African Society, prospective members agreed to pay the monthly dues and to abide by moral requirements to be temperate and refuse to engage in disorderly behavior. Members of any religious denomination could join, but individuals who behaved in disorderly ways, abused alcohol, or did not pay their dues faced expulsion. By demanding that members abstain from feasts, drinking, and gambling, the society's officers sought to combat beliefs that Black people were lazy, disorderly, or frivolous—claims often deployed as a justification for enslavement. They also argued that indulgence in the "sins" of drinking, gambling, or idleness showed a lack of respect for Black people still enslaved.

Members in good standing could expect a number of benefits from the mutual aid fund. Particularly in the first years of the society, important aspects of support for members included payments for burials and financial aid for widows and other family members of the deceased, finding apprenticeships for children to learn a trade, and paying tuition for members' children if places in free schools were not available. Over time, the society expanded to care for the social and economic well-being of its members by providing moral guidance, by helping newcomers to the city feel welcome, and by giving assistance during periods of financial difficulty brought on by unemployment or sickness. The society also took on the task of assisting the sick during the yellow fever epidemic in 1793. Members nursed the sick, dug graves and buried the dead, and transported the ill to quarters outside of the city where they could be quarantined and given medical aid.

Ultimately, the nondenominational nature of the Free African Society brought about a schism, which led to the society's demise. Allen, a Methodist, became disillusioned with the society's reliance on Quaker principles such as observing fifteen minutes of silence before meetings or having a committee visit members' houses to ensure they were living morally. Allen and his followers broke away from the society, establishing the Mother Bethel African Methodist Episcopal Church in 1794. Many other members of the society chose to worship at Absalom Jones's African Episcopal Church of St. Thomas.

Though the Free African Society was not particularly long-lived, it spurred the creation of many similar African American mutual aid societies, more than one hundred in the Philadelphia region by 1838. The society's mission of community building and assisting one another also contributed to the self-sufficiency of Philadelphia's growing free Black community. Not only did the churches founded by Jones and Allen become cultural and religious centers of the community, but free Black Philadelphians also began moving to the neighborhoods around the churches, close to shops, businesses, and schools operated by former members of the Free African Society.

Mother Bethel AME Church: Congregation and Community

Ricardo Howell

Established in the crucible of the American Revolutionary era, Mother Bethel African Methodist Episcopal (AME) Church is recognized as the genesis of Black religious organizing spirit. The church is mother church of the African Methodist Episcopal denomination, formed in 1816. Located at Sixth and Lombard Streets in Philadelphia's Society Hill neighborhood, the church sits on the oldest continuously Black-owned parcel of land in the country. It remains a symbol of the struggle for justice and freedom in the twenty-first century.

Mother Bethel was founded by Richard Allen of Delaware, who purchased his own freedom in 1783. He began preaching the gospel in Delaware, Maryland, New Jersey, and Pennsylvania. In 1786, a Methodist elder asked Allen to minister to Philadelphia's growing free Black community at the city's St. George's Methodist Church, where he preached to Black worshippers at pre-sunrise services, so as not to get in the way of white church members. He also evangelized Black people in nearby neighborhoods. By 1787, Allen joined Absalom Jones, who was born in bondage in Delaware, and other Black community leaders to press for a religious and social fellowship of their own. The causes of faith, mutual financial benefit, and community support were central to the Free African Society they formed in 1787. No less important were Black claims to personal and organizational independence in an age marked by enslavement and demands for liberty.

From the onset, the Free African Society's activist goals were to argue for the abolition of enslavement and to aid free Black people whose lives were compromised by the racial prejudices and proscriptions of the day. In practice, the society's members aimed to show themselves as valuable and trustworthy citizens. As one notable example, the society ably filled the void as emergency health workers when yellow fever overran Philadelphia in 1793. Mother Bethel Church, the descendant of the Free African Society, recognizes its birth in the formative 1787 moment of first independent organization—a "Liberty Bell for Black folks" as one of the church's pastors has said.

Despite the religious activities undertaken by the Free African Society, its adherents remained as worshippers at St. George's until the early 1790s. With their numbers rising—and with tensions rising with white congregants—Richard Allen and Absalom Jones and other Black leaders began fundraising and petitioned Methodist elders to create a distinct Black church. When their designs were denied, confrontation was inevitable. Allen and Jones led Black parishioners in a walkout when white people at St. George's attempted to push Black worshippers to segregated seating and physically bar them from kneeling in prayer during a Sunday service.

Three Black congregations originated from this historic act of protest. Some Black residents preferred to associate themselves with the Episcopal (formerly Anglican) denomination—founding in 1794 the African Episcopal Church of St. Thomas, with Jones as their leader. Black congregants who remained at St. George's were soon allowed to meet separately and would formally organize the African Zoar Methodist Church, a Methodist satellite, in 1796. Allen, who believed deeply in Methodism's antislavery bona fides and its virtues of plain living and speaking, remained committed to establishing an independent Methodist church. On land located at Sixth and Lombard Streets that Allen had purchased in 1791, Bethel AME Church was dedicated in July 1794. The church remains at this location today, hence its claims to being the oldest continuously Black-owned plot of land in the country.

Allen's Bethel AME Church was highly active, organizing the first Black Sunday school—and perhaps a separate night school—in 1795. Mother Bethel assumed moral leadership, with Allen shepherding and instructing newly liberated and free alike in rectitude. Allen's method was to prove that Black people were fit for equality—while they took the moral high ground *and* action against discrimination. He, along with Jones and others, petitioned Congress in 1799 to end the African slave trade well before its constitutionally possible 1808 expiration date, and to take action to free Black people who remained in bondage. By the 1810s, Mother Bethel claimed more than one thousand members. Allen and Mother Bethel's efforts went beyond Black self-help; during the War of 1812, Mother Bethel helped to raise twenty-five hundred Black troops in the efforts against the British.

In the antebellum era, Mother Bethel's reach spread throughout the republic. In 1816 Allen solidified a regional network of churches in an act that would transform Mother Bethel into the "abbey of African Methodism." Delegates from five churches in Baltimore Washington, Wilmington, Philadelphia, and Salem, New Jersey, whose experiences with white Methodist parent churches were similar, agreed to ally in a new denomination, the African Methodist Episcopal (AME) "connection" with Richard Allen elected the organization's first bishop. The seed of religious independence that was sowed in 1787 and germinated in 1794 grew quickly in the first five years of the AME denomination's emergence, absorbing congregations in New York, New Jersey, Pennsylvania, and Maryland. Evangelists with talents like Richard Allen's were tasked with organizing AME congregations in Ohio and parts of the emerging West.

If Bethel AME Church was mother church of the burgeoning AME connection, it was also a beacon to the still enslaved, serving as a Philadelphia sanctuary along the Underground Railroad to freedom. In 1830, Allen, who had long helped shape conversations about the destiny of Black people in America—including the merits of African colonization—oversaw planning of the first national meeting of Black leaders. Delegates to the convention, the American Society of Free Persons of Colour, met for five days in September 1830 at Mother Bethel Church. While this was Allen's final act before his death in 1831, it reflected only a portion of his legacy.

At the time of Allen's death, the AME Church had congregations in every northern state and several southern states with ten thousand members. By the Civil War, AME membership was two to five times that size, according to various estimates. During and after the war, ministers who were Richard Allen's successors moved like dynamos through the South and the West, founding churches, promoting Black involvement in politics, and establishing a growing roster of AME

FIGURE 48. *Goal, in Walnut Street, Philadelphia*, by William Birch, 1799. This scene, in front of Walnut Street Prison, likely shows the move of the blacksmith shop that became Richard Allen's Mother Bethel African Methodist Episcopal Church in 1794. LIBRARY COMPANY OF PHILADELPHIA.

institutions of higher education and an increasing set of departments and missions. By 1900, the AME Church was a sprawling denomination with churches in places as far-flung (from Philadelphia) as South Africa. In the second half of the 1800s, Mother Bethel could tout among its leaders the journalist and activist Frances Ellen Watkins Harper and famed educator Fanny Jackson Coppin. Mother Bethel was still the AME Church's home, and Philadelphia its headquarters.

During the late nineteenth and twentieth centuries, thousands of formerly enslaved African Americans and their descendants sought opportunity in Philadelphia, finding work primarily in domestic service or other manual labor. As a matter of familiarity and necessity, since they faced discrimination when seeking housing, Black people who migrated were funneled into the city's most aging housing stock, often into overcrowded conditions, including the Seventh Ward neighborhood surrounding Mother Bethel. The Seventh Ward was particularly worrisome to Philadelphia's social reformers. In his book *The Philadelphia Negro* (1899), W. E. B. Du Bois observed among Mother Bethel's congregation "the best of the great laboring class—steady, honest people, well dressed and well fed, with church and family traditions." Empowered by its members, Mother Bethel was able to construct its current structure in the late 1880s.

In the 1890s, Mother Bethel claimed the most members of fourteen AME congregations in the city. An influx of Black migrants to Philadelphia expanded many of the city's churches and denominations. Mother Bethel played an important part in encouraging migration by Black southerners, sending southward information about conditions in Philadelphia and promising migrants a church home. But the influx of newcomers to the church, as in other established congregations, also created tensions between the church's more staid worship service and leadership and the "country" ways of the rural Black people coming into the city. Such tensions contributed to some church members leaving to join other congregations.

As a testament to the vitality of the institution, Mother Bethel paid off its debt in 1945. The church was designated a historic shrine by the Department of the Interior in 1965, and a historic landmark in 1974. Mother Bethel's efforts to create a museum detailing its history led to the 1976 opening of the African American Museum in Philadelphia—in time for the nation's Bicentennial. In a story that parallels Mother Bethel's origins, white residents of the church's Society Hill neighborhood, and Black residents from other sections of the city, fought against an effort to have a Black history museum erected adjacent to the church.

Mother Bethel symbolizes the legacy of Richard Allen and the AME pressing for religious, economic, and social freedom. Among those who have graced the church and spoken from its pulpit are freedom fighters Desmond Tutu, the South African archbishop, in 1986; and Rosa Parks, a pioneer of the modern civil rights movement, in 1995. Mother Bethel is one of more than two dozen AME churches in Philadelphia in the AME's First District Conference, headquartered since 1986 in West Philadelphia. The global AME Church that has grown up around Mother Bethel is a sprawling international conference of churches, with seven thousand places of assembly and more than four million members. As W. E. B. Du Bois observed, the "growth of Bethel Church . . . has been so phenomenal that it belongs to the history of the nation rather than to any one city."

FIGURE 49. Bishop Richard Allen, founder of the Mother Bethel African Methodist Episcopal Church. COLLECTION OF THE HISTORICAL SOCIETY OF PENNSYLVANIA.

National Colored Convention Movement

Lucien Holness

During the antebellum period, when Philadelphia was home to one of the North's largest free African American communities, the city's Black leaders launched the national Colored Convention movement to address the hostility, discrimination, exclusion, and violence against African Americans by white people in northern cities. As national forums, the national Colored Conventions brought together African Americans to debate and adopt strategies to elevate the status of free Black people in the North and promote the abolition of slavery.

The idea for a national Colored Convention first emerged among Black leaders in response to events in Cincinnati, Ohio, during the late 1820s. Following Cincinnati's enforcement of Ohio's "Black laws" in 1829 and subsequent violence unleashed by white mobs against the city's Black community, in the spring of 1830 Hezekiah Grice, a Baltimore activist, appealed to African American leaders throughout the North to devise a plan for emigration to Canada. His appeal went unanswered for several months until Richard Allen, minister and founder of Mother Bethel African Methodist Episcopal Church in Philadelphia, called a national meeting of Black leaders to address this issue.

The delegates who gathered at Mother Bethel Church from September 20 to 24, 1830, selected Allen as president of the newly formed American Society of Free Persons of Colour. The purpose of this organization was to establish a settlement in Canada because it had a similar climate and shared language with the United States and was thought to lack institutional racial discrimination. (This purpose later changed when Black people encountered hostility in Canada and many activists were convinced that Black people should have rights in the United States.) Before returning home from the 1830 Philadelphia meeting, delegates adopted a resolution that called for a general convention the following year in Philadelphia, thus launching the national Colored Convention movement.

In addition to the first gathering in 1830, Philadelphia hosted national conventions in 1831, 1832, 1833, 1835, and 1855. Guided by middle- and upper-class Black delegates, the conventions adopted a philosophy of respectability centered on education, temperance, and thrift. Black leaders believed this strategy would dispel popular stereotypes that portrayed African Americans as lazy, ignorant, and susceptible to vice. By demonstrating economic independence and success, convention delegates hoped that white residents would see Black people as responsible and productive citizens worthy of equal rights. They also believed that respectability would lead to greater support for immediate abolitionism among moderate white reformers. Delegates used the egalitarian rhetoric of the American Revolution, arguing that enslavement and discrimination were incompatible with the nation's founding documents.

Although strategies of respectability and moral persuasion dominated, a younger generation of activists in the 1840s and 1850s began to endorse more militant solutions. Black nationalism was one option, a controversial position that called for African Americans to establish a separate colony in Africa, the Caribbean, or Central America. Many Black Philadelphians rejected this strategy, believing that respectability and interracial cooperation were the best route to ending enslavement and securing equality.

Launched during an important period of Black political activism, the national Colored Convention movement created a stronger collective voice among African Americans and a forum for devising national strategies to confront the growing racial hostility. Although the convention movement did not end enslavement or gain equal rights for African Americans, by the outbreak of the Civil War some other notable goals were achieved. Delegates established manual labor schools that trained a number of Black people in skilled trades. The 1835 convention created the American Moral Reform Society (1835–41), an organization headquartered in Philadelphia and led by local businessmen James Forten and William Whipper. This group attempted to uplift Black communities through education and promoting moral behavior such as temperance. The conventions also united African American communities from across the country into a national network of political activism. Finally, delegates formed a coalition with radical white antislavery activists to oppose movements such as the American Colonization Society, an organization with ties to enslavers that encouraged free Black people to relocate to Africa.

During the Civil War the convention delegates began to devise plans for the postwar Reconstruction period. At the October 1864 meeting in Syracuse, New York, delegates created the National Equal Rights League, which lobbied the federal government for full citizenship rights for all African Americans on the premise of Black service in the Union army and the belief that all men were created equal. With numerous state and local chapters, the league's members became active in northern and southern politics. Members of the Pennsylvania State Equal Rights League lobbied members of Congress to ratify the Fifteenth Amendment to the U.S. Constitution in support of Black male suffrage and continued to demand protection of Black civil and political rights in a new era in which white hostility increased and government support waned.

Appeal of Forty Thousand Citizens

David Reader

The *Appeal of Forty Thousand Citizens, Threatened with Disfranchisement, to the People of Pennsylvania* attempted to persuade Pennsylvanians to vote against ratification of a new constitution for Pennsylvania in 1838 because the word "white" had been inserted prior to "freemen" as a qualification for voting. Written by African American

FIGURE 50. Executive Committee of the Pennsylvania Anti-Slavery Society, photograph by Frederick Gutekunst, 1851. Robert Purvis, author of the *Appeal of Forty Thousand Citizens*, is seated in the front row, third from right. FRIENDS HISTORICAL LIBRARY, SWARTHMORE COLLEGE.

leader Robert Purvis, the pamphlet highlighted the achievements, sacrifices, and value of the Black community to Philadelphia and its suburbs.

Under Pennsylvania's first two constitutions, ratified in 1776 and 1790, Article III limited voting rights and elections to "freemen," but definitions of "freeman" varied in individual counties depending on local politics and traditions. Some understood the term "freeman" to apply only to white individuals, while others did not. The commonwealth's western counties, which had small populations of free Black people, tended to allow them to vote. Eastern counties with larger populations of African Americans—especially Philadelphia—discouraged them from voting through intimidation at the polls.

The growth of Philadelphia's free Black community, the increasing demands by Black and white activists for immediate abolition, Nat Turner's rebellion in Virginia in 1831, and violence by white rioters against Black neighborhoods made race relations an explosive issue in the 1830s. Pennsylvania also faced many financial, governmental, and immigration problems when the legislature called a convention in 1837 to reform the state constitution. The convention began in May 1837 in Harrisburg but moved to Musical Fund Hall in Philadelphia for its concluding sessions in November 1837 and February 1838. Initially, delegates made no recommendations to alter the language of Article III to prohibit free Black people from voting. But Democrat John Sterigere of Montgomery County seized on public opinion against Black voting rights and proposed to the convention that the language of Article III be changed to include the word "white" prior to "freemen" in order to exclude all Black people, even if they paid taxes or owned property.

Thomas Earle, a Democrat from Philadelphia County, objected to changing the language and attempted to persuade the convention to seek a compromise by temporarily suspending Black voting rights throughout the commonwealth. He lost to a larger Democratic majority, which approved the change to Article III and proposed a new Constitution of 1838 for ratification. Similar actions occurred in other states during this period as politicians attempted to prevent Black people from gaining the same voting rights as white men, whose access to the polls was increasing with changes in voting qualifications such as reduced tax or land-owning requirements.

Philadelphia's Black community responded to Pennsylvania's proposed constitution with the *Appeal of Forty Thousand Citizens, Threatened with Disfranchisement, to the People of Pennsylvania*. In the tradition of African American leaders such as Absalom Jones, Richard Allen, and James Forten Sr., Robert Purvis emphasized the worthiness of Philadelphia's Black community. Purvis systematically presented an argument based on history, statistical data, economics, and politics to combat public misconceptions about African Americans.

The *Appeal of Forty Thousand Citizens* invoked the founding documents of Pennsylvania and the nation to argue that it would be consistent with previous generations to ensure suffrage to freemen without the mention of a specific race. The pamphlet pointed out that during the colonial period, white indentured servants as well as Black enslaved people were not permitted to vote because they lacked the status of freemen. "White" was not included as a qualification for voting in the 1776 and 1790 Pennsylvania constitutions.

To support the claims of the *Appeal of Forty Thousand Citizens*, the Pennsylvania Abolition Slavery compiled a census as evidence that Philadelphia's Black community provided the city with revenue, laborers, and taxpayers who contributed to its economic success. The census demonstrated that compared with white inhabitants, African Americans made up a substantially lower proportion of the poor and people receiving aid. In fact, the Black community paid more to provide relief for the poor than it received in return. Purvis used the statistics to rebuke a public image of idleness. Recognizing the connection between actions in Pennsylvania and increasing racial tensions in the nation, Purvis charged the Pennsylvania Constitutional Convention with having "laid our [Black] rights a sacrifice on the altar of slavery."

Voters ratified the Constitution of 1838 by a margin of a little more than one thousand votes—113,971 to 112,759—on October 9, 1838. African Americans continued to petition the legislature to reinstate suffrage for free Black people, but their petitions were left unanswered. Racial tensions turned to violent riots targeting African Americans and a newly erected abolitionist meeting place, Pennsylvania Hall. Although a new generation of leaders, including Jacob C. White Jr., continued the fight for suffrage, African Americans in Pennsylvania did not regain the vote until the Fifteenth Amendment to the U.S. Constitution (1870) extended voting rights to Black men throughout the nation.

The Philadelphia Negro

Steven McGrail

In 1899, the University of Pennsylvania published William E. Burghardt Du Bois's *The Philadelphia Negro: A Social Study*, the first scholarly study of the impact of racism on Black residents of an urban place. The comprehensive report about Philadelphia's Seventh Ward, one of a growing fleet of Progressive-Era social surveys, became a distinctive (and still relevant) landmark in the annals of sociological study and social advocacy.

Four years earlier, the publication of *Hull-House Maps and Papers* (1895)—a pioneering local study of immigrant, labor and living conditions in and about the Chicago settlement run by Jane Addams—signaled opportunity in the minds of Philadelphia Progressives. In spring 1896, at the suggestion of leading citizen Susan P. Wharton, the University of Pennsylvania and

FIGURE 51. W. E. B. Du Bois, photograph by C. M. Battey, 1919. LIBRARY OF CONGRESS.

Philadelphia's College Settlement convinced W. E. B. Du Bois, a rising African American scholar and professor at Ohio's Wilberforce University, to conduct a study of the city's Black community, which many critics held responsible for a post-depression (1893–96) rise in crime and disorder. Accepting the invitation, even at the lowly title of "Assistant Instructor," Du Bois arrived with his wife, Nina, in August 1896 and promptly set out on an immersive, yearlong study to "ascertain something of the geographical distribution of this race, their occupations and daily life, their homes, their organizations, and, above all, their relation to their million white fellow-citizens." The massive report that followed went far beyond the Hull-House model, and far beyond what its patrons anticipated or perhaps desired.

Despite its title, *The Philadelphia Negro*'s subject was both larger and smaller than the term "Philadelphia" connotes. It is really a neighborhood study, focusing on the central Seventh Ward running north-south for four blocks from Spruce to South Street and east-west for about eighteen blocks from Seventh Street to the Schuylkill River. Site of the city's oldest African American community, dating to the colonial era, the Seventh Ward by the 1890s was home to nearly a quarter of Philadelphia's forty thousand Black residents. Incredibly diverse, the ward mingled affluent white inhabitants (including Wharton), one of the nation's densest concentrations of Black elites along Lombard Street, and many poor Black and white people on the ward's eastern front.

For more than a year (1896–97), the Du Boises resided within the poorer quarters surrounding College Settlement, just to the east of the Seventh Ward. To many Seventh Ward Black residents, the Harvard-educated Du Bois looked the part of his genteel sponsors, who hoped to use his analysis to justify sweeping reforms in the Black community. Du Bois, meanwhile, preferred to demonstrate that Black people possessed their own internal class structure and should not be judged solely by the lowest rung (the "submerged tenth"). Pioneering sociological methods, Du Bois and his lone appointed assistant (College Settlement's Isabel Eaton, who herself published a trailblazing study of domestic labor as an appendix to the larger work) employed archival research, descriptive statistics, and questionnaires compassing occupations, health, and education as well as religious, social, and family life. Most crucially, they conducted a door-to-door canvass of the Seventh Ward, mapping out every Black residence, business, and church, amassing over five thousand personal interviews. The findings revealed a heterogeneous and accomplished community, a portion of which affirmed the reality of poverty, crime, and illiteracy that so many feared and which Du Bois himself often condemned as a moral failing. Du Bois was also uncommonly frank about the legacy of racism, placing blame squarely on socioeconomic and historical causes, notably the exclusion of Black people from the city's premier industrial jobs and single-family homes and the formidable legacy of enslavement and checkered race relations.

In stressing circumstance and contingency, Du Bois demonstrated *structural* inequities of which many white people were largely unaware, in the process leveling a powerful rejoinder to then prevalent arguments that used race theory, evolutionary science, and scriptural interpretation to justify discrimination. Du Bois hoped this work would be supplemented by similar studies of other cities, yet what began as a local study came, by default, to stand for all of urban Black America. Most of Du Bois's methods lay dormant, reemerging only in the 1920s—in Chicago again, with the rise of the Chicago School of Sociology. A fair hearing for his forthright and formidable conclusions, meanwhile, waited longer still. Du Bois's study has enjoyed a renaissance in contemporary scholars' investigations of poverty, race, and political economy, and *The Philadelphia Negro* continues to inform readers with its poignant representation of one of the great forgotten communities in modern American history, whose vitality, diversity, and challenges still linger in its pages.

African American Museum in Philadelphia

Mabel Rosenheck

Opened to the public in 1976, the African American Museum in Philadelphia (AAMP) was the first major museum of African American history and culture established by an American municipality. Founded as part of Philadelphia's Bicentennial celebration, the

FIGURE 52. African American Museum in Philadelphia, 2009. PHOTOGRAPH BY G. WIDMAN FOR VISIT PHILADELPHIA.

museum emerged at a moment when many Americans were reconsidering the place of Black history and culture in American history and arguing for its inclusion in Americans' understanding of their past and themselves. However, from the museum's inception tensions developed over who would lead it, where it would be located, what community it would serve, and what stories it would tell. Over the next fifty years, it struggled administratively and struggled to find an identity in a city already crowded with art and history museums. Still, the push for a more inclusive history and continued financial support from the city allowed it to survive.

The AAMP, originally called the Afro-American Historical and Cultural Museum, was part of a larger shift toward creating institutions for Black art and history collections. Although an independent 501(c)(3) nonprofit since its formal inception in 1975, the museum was unique because of the city's role in its founding and its creation as part of the United States Bicentennial. As part of the 1976 celebrations, the museum responded to the civil rights movements of the 1960s, which raised awareness of inequality in the legal treatment of African Americans and in the treatment of Black history in narratives of the past. While telling a more diverse and accurate history of the United States and Philadelphia, a Black history exhibit at the Bicentennial also had the potential to promote pride and positive self-image in Philadelphia's Black communities and cross-racial understanding in a racially divided city.

The need for a coordinated approach to the inclusion of Black history in the celebrations came to the attention of Bicentennial planners by 1974, although Philadelphia had chartered its Bicentennial planning commission (eventually known as Philadelphia '76 Inc.) seven years before, in 1967. In May 1974, Lawrence Dunbar Reddick, a professor of history at Temple University, wrote to the planners to raise concerns about the lack of representation of Black history at the Bicentennial. In a long letter to William Rafsky, chairman of Philadelphia '76, he asked: "How did it happen that the plans for the bicentennial celebration at Philadelphia resulted in virtual exclusion of blacks from active participation and a distortion of the role of the black people in the building of 'American civilization'?" Rafsky responded by sharing information about planned programs and existing collaborators. He also invited Reddick to meet with him and, ultimately, to be part of a steering committee for what became the AAMP.

This did not facilitate the smooth development of the project. In December 1974, Mayor Frank Rizzo cut funding for the Black history museum. He restored it a few days later, however, after public protests and questions about why a Mummers Museum could be built in time for the Bicentennial, but a Black history museum could not be.

Even more visible was the prolonged debate in 1975 over where the city should locate the museum. Following a survey of various sites across Center City and North Philadelphia by architect Theodore Cam, a site at Sixth and Pine Streets emerged as the most desirable. The site's advantages included proximity to the subway, the highway, and the historically significant Mother Bethel African Methodist Episcopal Church and the Seventh Ward, which in the nineteenth and early twentieth centuries had been the heart of Philadelphia's Black community. By the 1970s, however, the neighborhood had been redeveloped as predominantly white, upscale Society Hill. The Society Hill Civic Association, which was mostly white, protested that the size and scale of the proposed museum building would bring too much traffic and would be detrimental to the character of the neighborhood. The association members specified that they were objecting to the lack of input from the existing community rather than the concept of a Black history museum, but the events nonetheless highlighted racial exclusions in the city. Ultimately, the protests in Society Hill delayed the project long enough to force organizers to select a new site for the museum so it could open in 1976. The site at Seventh and Arch Streets was only a block from the Independence Mall tourist area, but it was awkwardly located behind modern office buildings. In addition, its hasty design was not ideal for exhibits or the care of collections.

From the start, the museum struggled to establish an identity. Among its problems was its inability to establish sustainable sources of revenue. The city funded construction, but the museum was meant to fund itself as an independent nonprofit with only partial governmental support. Without an endowment or a preexisting donor base, this proved difficult. Also, lacking funding and effective leadership, the museum could not develop as an institution on the level of its peer museums. It was meant to complement—and even critique—not only the Bicentennial but also legacy institutions like the Historical Society of Pennsylvania, Library Company of Philadelphia, and Atwater Kent Museum. However, collection building was difficult because of the lack of funds, competition for support from other institutions, and the seeming sparsity of surviving artifacts related to Black history. At the same time, its origins as a history museum often overshadowed its participation in the art world as seen, for example, in the works it commissioned from Romare Bearden and John Rhoden for its opening.

In its first decade, the museum went through seven directors and struggled to maintain a professional staff and an adequate environment for borrowed art and artifacts. It did collaborate with Charles Blockson to display items from his collection in the 1981 exhibit *Of Color, Humanitas and Statehood*, but Blockson had reservations about the museum's ability to properly care for the collection and ultimately donated it to Temple University in 1984.

Still, the museum's presence and its programs were meaningful for Black Philadelphians. In a rich challenge to mainstream histories, its narrative moved from life in Africa to enslavement and abolition in the United States and then followed the Black experience through the Great Migration, the Harlem Renaissance, and post–World War II fights for civil rights. It highlighted the disconnect between the equality and freedom promised in the Declaration of Independence and the reality of Black life in America and in Philadelphia over two hundred years.

The museum seemed to hit its stride after Rowena Stewart became executive director. During her seven-year tenure from 1985 to 1992, she focused on telling the story of Black Philadelphia with exhibits like *The Sounds of This City: Afro-American Music in Philadelphia* and *Let This Be Your Home*, which explored the Great Migration through the personal stories of Philadelphians. In 1986, she acquired the art and archives of Anna Russell Jones, a twentieth-century Philadelphia artist and designer, and Jack T. Franklin, a prominent photojournalist who worked locally and nationally from the 1940s through the 1980s. She also initiated ambitious programs in oral history and community collecting. Her efforts aimed to simultaneously engage the community and build a collection, twin problems that plagued the museum from the start.

Stewart and her immediate predecessor also made progress with fundraising, but it did not last beyond their tenures. At its lowest points, the museum survived because of financial support from the city, but the money it received was never enough to maintain an adequate facility, strong collection, and professional staff. For the twenty years following Stewart's leadership, the museum faced financial crises, at times because of internal mismanagement, at other times because of broader cuts to funding for arts and culture or chronic under-support for Black institutions. Amid these troubles, the museum changed its name in 1997 to the African American Museum in Philadelphia, which administrators hoped would better capture the museum's identity and the place it aimed to occupy in the city.

A new period of stability emerged when Romona Riscoe Benson served as the museum's director from 2005 through 2012. Benson built corporate and other partnerships, overseeing production of *Audacious Freedom*, a multimedia installation offering a sweeping history of Philadelphia's Black community in America's first hundred years. Benson's successors as director, including Patricia Wilson Aden from 2012 to 2020, maintained the stability of the institution and expanded its imprint in the Philadelphia arts scene with exhibits of Black artists and collaborations with community institutions, such as a much-heralded joint exhibit with the Pennsylvania Academy of the Fine Arts that opened in 2023. Plans also called for moving the museum to a new location near the Benjamin Franklin Parkway.

Despite its struggles, the AAMP strived to realize its potential for telling the stories of Black Philadelphians that too often had been neglected in histories of the city. The museum's founding as a city institution helped it survive, and its official status as the designated African American museum in Philadelphia made it a logical place for that storytelling. However, its origins in the city's white administration rather than the city's Black community and lack of centuries-old historical collections have situated the AAMP in an uncertain place among Philadelphia museums, often overshadowing its significant engagement with Philadelphia's Black art and artists.

EXPLORE MORE

Sources on Black communities in Philadelphia and southern New Jersey include Erica Armstrong Dunbar, *A Fragile Freedom: African American Women and Emancipation in the Antebellum City* (Yale University Press, 2008); James J. Gigantino II, *The Ragged Road to Abolition: Slavery and Freedom in New Jersey, 1775–1865* (University of Pennsylvania Press, 2015); Gary B. Nash, *Forging Freedom: The Formation of Philadelphia's Black Community, 1720–1840* (Harvard University Press, 1988); and Gary B. Nash and Jean R. Soderlund, *Freedom by Degrees: Emancipation in Pennsylvania and its Aftermath* (Oxford University Press, 1991).

A closer focus on the development of the Free African Society and Mother Bethel African Methodist Episcopal Church may be found in Carolyn Stickney Beck, *Our Own Vine and Fig Tree: The Persistence of the Mother Bethel Family* (AMS Press, 1989); Carol V. R. George, *Segregated Sabbaths: Richard Allen and the Rise of Independent Black Churches, 1760–1840* (Oxford University Press, 1973); Robert Gregg, *Sparks from the Anvil of Oppression: Philadelphia's African Methodists and Southern Migrants, 1890–1940* (Temple University Press, 1993); Roger Lane, *William Dorsey's Philadelphia and Ours: On the Past and Future of the Black City in America* (Oxford University Press, 1991); and Richard S. Newman, *Freedom's Prophet: Bishop Richard Allen, the AME Church, and the Black Founding Fathers* (New York University Press, 2008).

Works on Black Philadelphians and their battles for abolition and civil rights in the nineteenth century include Margaret Hope Bacon, *But One Race: The Life of Robert Purvis* (State University of New York Press, 2007); Daniel R. Biddle and Murray Dubin, *Tasting Freedom: Octavius Catto and the Battle for Equality in Civil War America* (Temple University Press, 2010); John Ernest, *A Nation Within A Nation: Organizing African-American Communities Before the Civil War* (Ivan R. Dee, 2011); Richard Newman and James Mueller, eds., *Antislavery and Abolition in Philadelphia: Emancipation and the Long Struggle for Racial Justice in the City of Brotherly Love* (Louisiana State University Press, 2011); William H. Pease and Jane H. Pease, "The Negro Convention Movement," in *Key Issues in the Afro-American Experience*, vol. I, *To 1877*, edited by Nathan I. Huggins, Martin Kilson, and Daniel M. Fox (Harcourt Brace Jovanovich, 1971): 191–205; Patrick Rael, *Black Identity and Black Protest in the Antebellum North* (University of North Carolina Press, 2001); William Still, *The Underground Railroad* (Porter & Coates, 1872); Julie Winch, *A Gentleman of Color: The Life of James Forten* (Oxford University Press, 2002); Julie Winch, *Philadelphia's Black Elite: Activism, Accommodation, and the Struggle for Autonomy, 1787–1848* (Temple University Press, 1988); and Jean Fagan Yellin and John C. Van Horne, eds., *The Abolitionist Sisterhood: Women's Political Culture in Antebellum America* (Cornell University Press, 1994).

For the history of African American migration to the region since 1820 and the struggle for equal rights, see John F. Bauman, *Public Housing, Race, and Renewal: Urban Planning in Philadelphia, 1920–1974* (Temple University Press, 1987); Matthew Countryman, *Up South: Civil Rights and Black Power in Philadelphia* (University of Pennsylvania Press, 2006); Kali N. Gross, *Colored Amazons: Crime, Violence, and Black Women in the City of Brotherly Love, 1880–1910* (Duke University Press, 2006); Lisa Levenstein, *A Movement Without Marches: African American Women and the Politics of Poverty in Postwar Philadelphia* (University of North Carolina Press, 2009); Joe William Trotter Jr. and Eric Ledell Smith, *African Americans in Pennsylvania: Shifting Historical Perspectives* (Pennsylvania State University Press, 1997); and James Wolfinger, *Philadelphia Divided: Race and Politics in the City of Brotherly Love* (University of North Carolina Press, 2007).

On W. E. B. Du Bois and his pathbreaking study, see *The Philadelphia Negro: A Social Study*, which was published originally by the University of Pennsylvania Press in 1899 and has been reissued with introductions by Elijah Anderson in 1996 and 2023. See also Michael B. Katz and Thomas J. Sugrue, eds., *W. E. B. Du Bois, Race, and the City:* The Philadelphia Negro *and Its Legacy* (University of Pennsylvania Press, 1998); and David Levering Lewis, *W. E. B. Du Bois: Biography of a Race, 1868–1919* (Henry Holt, 1993).

Manuscript collections on Black communities in the Philadelphia region include the Mother Bethel AME

Church Records, 1822–1972, twelve microfilm reels, at the Historical Society of Pennsylvania (HSP), 1300 Locust Street, Philadelphia. Also important are the HSP's Pennsylvania Abolition Society Papers, William Still Journals, and Vigilant Committee of Philadelphia Records; the Library Company of Philadelphia's African Americana Collection (1314 Locust Street); the Charles L. Blockson Afro-American Collection, 1330 Polett Walk, Temple University; and the Urban Archives, Special Collections Research Center, Temple University Libraries, Philadelphia.

Important sites for the late eighteenth and nineteenth centuries include Mother Bethel AME Church, 419 S. Sixth Street; African Episcopal Church of St. Thomas, 6361 Lancaster Avenue; Octavius V. Catto Memorial, southwest corner of city hall; Museum of the American Revolution, 101 S. Third Street, Philadelphia; and the Peter Mott House, 26 Kings Court, Lawnside, N.J. The African American Museum in Philadelphia (AAMP) is located at 701 Arch Street with plans to move to a site near the Benjamin Franklin Parkway. The AAMP is a landmark both for its exhibits on Philadelphia as capital of Black America and for its founding at the time of the nation's Bicentennial. It was the first major museum on African American history and culture established by a municipality—one of many "firsts" that Black Philadelphians have achieved over more than two centuries.

Chapter 8

Contesting and Expanding the Nation

Introduction

Long after Philadelphia ceased to be the capital of the United States, the work of creating a nation continued in the city and surrounding region. The United States had a frame of government that endured, but Americans struggled—sometimes violently—over competing claims to rights, liberty, and power. Riots, demonstrations, lawsuits, and the Civil War challenged and redefined the contours of nationhood. These struggles unfolded across the country, but they had heightened resonance in Philadelphia, the birthplace of the Declaration of Independence and the U.S. Constitution. Here, in the city known as the "Cradle of Liberty," citizens and others blocked from the full rights of citizenship leveraged the historic setting of the nation's founding to amplify calls for justice and equality.

The founding documents provided a vocabulary that could be embraced across the social and political spectrum. Striking laborers who paraded to Independence Square in the 1830s called for their rights to economic independence and equality by invoking the language of the Declaration of Independence; but defending the legacy of the nation's founders also animated anti-immigrant rioters who tormented Irish Catholics in Philadelphia and other cities during the 1840s. For a far different cause, Frederick Douglass chose to stand in the shadow of Independence Hall when he came to Philadelphia to speak against human bondage in 1844, and he expanded on his contrasts between enslavement and the nation's founding ideals in his 1852 address to an audience in New York, "What to the Slave Is the Fourth of July?" Women stated their claims to the full rights of citizenship by arguing that "all men and women are created equal" in the Declaration of Sentiments passed in 1848 in Seneca Falls, New York. The argument still needed to be made in 1876, when Susan B. Anthony again called for equality during ceremonies at Independence Hall to mark the nation's centennial, and again in the early twentieth century when suffrage activists created a copy of the Liberty Bell to campaign for the vote.

For much of the nineteenth century, Americans struggled over the balance of liberty and power—how much liberty should be accorded to individuals, states, and institutions, and what powers should be exercised by the federal government? The second Bank of the United States, a citadel of federal power located in Philadelphia, became the setting for a titanic struggle during the administration of President Andrew Jackson. The bank's Greek Revival building on Chestnut Street projected strength and confidence, but its directors could not prevail over Jackson's determination to dismantle the institution as a blow for democracy against federal power. When the president himself came to Philadelphia in 1833 to celebrate his veto of legislation to renew the bank's charter and his reelection, his reception in Independence Hall became so tumultuous and crowded that people resorted to exiting through the first-story windows.

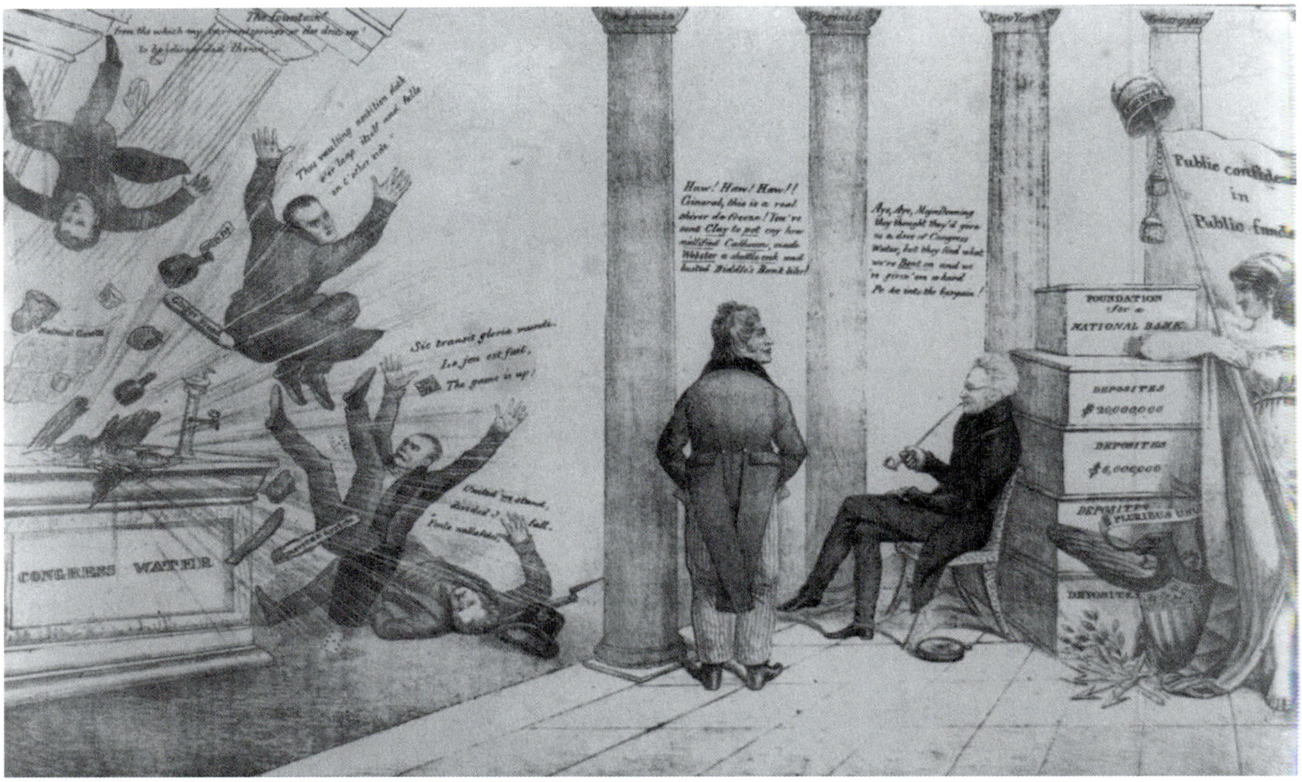

FIGURE 53. Bank War political satire, 1834. The cartoon depicts conflict between President Andrew Jackson and bank president Nicholas Biddle over rechartering the second Bank of the United States. LIBRARY OF CONGRESS.

The nation's greatest challenge, the Civil War, reached into Northern cities like Philadelphia even when the Union and Confederate armies fought on distant battlefields. The sectional struggle over enslaved labor, states' rights, and federal authority disrupted long-held economic and family ties between the Philadelphia region and the South. Most loyalties swung to the Union, although public opinion was by no means uniform in a region that had seen anti-abolitionist violence and fugitive slave hearings (ironically, in Independence Hall). Philadelphia served as a supply and transportation depot as well as a place where soldiers enlisted and Union supporters raised funds and organized civil defenses. The incursion of the war into Pennsylvania in 1863 raised fears for local security even though the Battle of Gettysburg took place more than 120 miles away. At Gettysburg, four months after the fighting, President Abraham Lincoln looked back to the nation's founding to single out a principle to guide the nation's future: "Four score and seven years ago our fathers brought forth, upon this continent, a new nation, conceived in liberty, and dedicated to the proposition that all men are created equal."

Lincoln's call for a "new birth of freedom" echoed loudly in the years that followed. Strivers for civil rights developed the mix of legal strategies and public action necessary to enact change, often leveraging the ideals of the nation's founding in the place where it happened. Black Philadelphians in the 1950s pursued the desegregation of Girard College all the way to the Supreme Court. During the 1960s, college students sat in at the Liberty Bell to support African American civil rights, and LGBT people and their allies demonstrated at Independence Hall on the Fourth of July. In the 1980s, people with disabilities donned colonial costumes to demonstrate in Philadelphia in support of a lawsuit to achieve greater accessibility in public transportation—the key to their personal independence.

It is tempting to see the civil rights achievements of the late nineteenth and twentieth centuries as a steady march of progress extending expanded benefits of American citizenship across the spectrum of race, class, ethnicity, gender, and sexuality. Activists achieved victories, to be sure, but they also faced backlash. In the most extreme local example, after Civil War veteran and educator Octavius Catto rallied Black votes to the polls, he was shot dead on South Street on Election Day in 1871. Advancing rights of African Americans, women, LGBT Americans, Native Americans, persons with disabilities, and others required perseverance against opponents and legal obstacles. Contesting and expanding the nation's commitment to freedom, equality, and justice remained an ongoing quest in the twenty-first century.

Bank War

Andrew T. Tremel

Conflict over renewing the charter of the second Bank of the United States triggered the 1830s Bank War, waged between President Andrew Jackson and bank president Nicholas Biddle. Operating from its Parthenon-style building on Chestnut Street between Fourth and Fifth Streets in Philadelphia, the bank served as a reliable depository for federal money and provided a sound national currency. The expiration of its federal charter in 1836 virtually ended Philadelphia's standing as the banking center of the United States, and New York's Wall Street supplanted Chestnut Street as the nation's financial hub.

In 1816, Congress issued a twenty-year charter for the second Bank of the United States, with the government controlling 20 percent of the bank's stock. Modeled after the first Bank of the United States, established in Philadelphia in 1791, the Second Bank handled all federal deposits and expenditures. The bank had a rocky start (overextension of loans helped trigger the Panic of 1819), but it became a dependable institution, and Biddle was generally considered a highly successful and respected leader. By the end of the 1820s, the bank had twenty-nine branches and conducted $70 million in business annually. Nevertheless, President Jackson's first annual message to Congress in 1829 alleged corruption and condemned the bank as an unconstitutional entity. He favored hard money over bank notes, but also blamed the bank for the Panic of 1819, particularly for his personal losses.

While Jackson, a Democrat, opposed the bank, National Republicans in Congress sought to renew the institution's charter in 1832 (four years early), believing a veto would cost Jackson reelection. The House approved the renewal by a 107–85 vote and the Senate by 28–20. Pennsylvania's two senators and all but one of its twenty-five congressmen were among the bill's advocates. The New Jersey and Delaware delegations were also strongly pro-bank. During congressional debates, pro-bank petitions came in from citizens of Philadelphia and Delaware County as well as from state banks, including fifteen from Pennsylvania. Despite nationwide support across various social groups, Jackson vetoed the bill.

Jackson handily won reelection in 1832, though his veto likely cost him votes. A majority of Philadelphians voted against Jackson (he did carry Pennsylvania); New Jersey voters elected an anti-Jackson state legislature, but the state's electoral votes went to Jackson, who was still personally very popular. When Jackson visited Philadelphia on the first anniversary of his charter veto in June 1833, a reception in Independence Hall—just one block from the Second Bank—became so crowded with enthusiastic supporters that some had to escape the throng through open first-floor windows.

Jackson insisted that the bank was "trying to kill me," and he vowed to destroy it at any cost. He believed his reelection a mandate and continued to portray the bank as a corrupt tool of foreign interests that worked against Americans. In 1833, President Jackson decided to withhold federal deposits, later transferring federal money to "pet banks" (state banks with Democratic ties). Jackson dismissed two treasury secretaries before finding a willing accomplice in Roger B. Taney. In response, Biddle contracted the bank's operations by calling in loans and exchanging state notes for specie to protect the institution and its investors. The bank's board of governors unanimously concurred.

As the Second Bank limited its operations, however, an economic depression began, businesses closed, unemployment rose, and inflation reached one of its highest rates in U.S. history. Biddle did not have the capital to make payments on the national debt. The

War Department forbade the bank from carrying out its responsibility of paying Revolutionary War pensions in an attempt to turn public opinion against it. Still, the bank initially lost little support and a new political party, the Whigs, emerged to challenge Jackson's supposed tyranny. At the height of the Bank War, 1833–34, the Senate received 243 memorials calling for the return of federal deposits and only 55 petitions supporting the president's actions. In January 1834, the Philadelphia Board of Trade issued a statement blaming the financial panic on the Jackson administration. Other Philadelphia banks also protested the president's actions. Tensions grew to the point that wealthy, pro-administration Philadelphians found themselves excluded or expelled from social organizations. In Congress, the Whig-controlled Senate censured Jackson for his actions against the bank. Each side blamed the other for the turmoil.

Biddle ultimately relaxed the bank's credit policies and the economic malaise lifted. The bank thus received the brunt of the blame for the previous years' problems. The public turned against the bank, viewing its actions as vindictive. In 1834, Election Day riots occurred in Philadelphia, and the Whigs lost seats in Congress and the state legislature. Finally, in 1836, two weeks before the U.S. charter expired, the Pennsylvania legislature granted the bank a state charter. By the time Biddle retired in 1839, the bank was in poor shape. Over the following two years, when it could not pay its debts, the bank suspended and resumed specie payments twice, closing its doors permanently in 1841.

The Bank War cost Philadelphia and the nation a central bank, and the nation's financial center shifted to New York City. Thereafter, local banks lacked any regulating authority and the resulting speculation triggered panics through the rest of the century.

Riots of the 1830s and 1840s

Patrick Grubbs

In the 1830s and 1840s, Philadelphia and its suburbs experienced a sharp increase in disorder as early industrialization caused economic tensions and the population grew rapidly and became more ethnically and religiously diverse. Philadelphia County's fragmented composition, with numerous municipalities, and the absence of a professional police department allowed demonstrations to escalate into full-scale riots. The city's inability to quell the riots ultimately aroused political support for consolidating twenty-nine jurisdictions into one municipality and creating one of the nation's earliest modern police forces.

During the early nineteenth century, industrialization, surging European immigration, and continued growth in the number of Black residents brought increased labor competition and ethnically mixed settlement patterns to the city. Philadelphia County's urban population more than doubled between 1830 and 1850, spilling beyond the original city limits (from South to Vine Streets between the Delaware and Schuylkill Rivers). This expansion put a strain on city resources not designed to accommodate such rapid growth.

The volatile environment created by economic and social change boiled over on August 11, 1834, when white and Black citizens quarreled over seats on a merry-go-round known as the "flying horses" near Seventh and South Streets. The next evening, as rumors spread that Black residents had insulted white people, fighting resulted in destruction of the carousel; later that night a group of white rioters smashed the taverns, homes, and furniture of Black residents in the Moyamensing quarter. Philadelphia constables and watchmen, called in to assist the helpless watchmen of Moyamensing, successfully broke up the mob and arrested nearly twenty rioters. Destruction continued over the next two days, however, as white mobs tore down an African American church in Southwark, sacked the First African Presbyterian Church, destroyed more than thirty homes of Black residents, and beat any Black citizen in their path. Despite more than forty arrests and the mayor's attempt to prevent violence, the undermanned constabulary and underprepared city could do little to prevent the devastation. After minor skirmishes over the next few days, Philadelphia's first widespread race riot ended on August 14, 1834.

Racial tensions continued over the next four years, growing worse with the Panic of 1837, increasing opposition to the national abolition movement, and controversy over the revised Pennsylvania State Constitution, approved in October 1838. The constitution rescinded the vote for free Black men despite

FIGURE 54. *Riot in Philadelphia, July 7th, 1844.* Nativists attacked militia defending a Catholic church in Southwark. COLLECTION OF THE HISTORICAL SOCIETY OF PENNSYLVANIA.

efforts by Robert Purvis and other activists to prevent the change. Amid this debate, abolitionists constructed Pennsylvania Hall on Sixth Street near Franklin Square, which opened on Monday May 14, 1838, with national abolitionist leaders such as William Lloyd Garrison, Maria Chapman, and the Grimké sisters in attendance. Two days later, a mob gathered outside the building and broke windows as Angelina Grimké spoke to a predominantly female audience inside. Although the meeting abruptly ended and the Thursday program was canceled, it was not enough to save the hall. Late Thursday evening, May 17, 1838, a crowd of nearly three thousand gathered in front and set the structure ablaze. After only four days of operation, Pennsylvania Hall burned to the ground as firemen refused to fight the fire and instead focused on protecting neighboring structures.

Over the next four years the city and nation suffered a severe business depression marked by widespread unemployment. Although Philadelphia remained relatively calm, economic, ethnic, and religious tensions simmered. The political fragmentation of Philadelphia County into twenty-nine jurisdictions did little to combat those tensions. Increased job competition among ethnic groups, in particular between Irish and Black workers, brought intermittent fighting that exploded into a full-scale riot in August 1842. When a Black temperance society began a parade on August 1 to promote temperance and celebrate Jamaican Emancipation Day, a flag they carried depicting an enslaved man breaking his chains and the rising sun of freedom offended white, in particular Irish, bystanders. As the parade reached the public market near Lombard and Sixth Streets, a mob chased the marchers, then torched an abolitionist meeting hall and the Second African Presbyterian Church on St. Mary's Street. The Lombard Street riot continued for two more days, causing many Black citizens to leave the city. Public order was restored only after the mayor called out seven militia companies with more than one thousand troops. This clash of predominantly Irish rioters with law enforcement officials stigmatized the Irish in Philadelphia and set the stage for the next large-scale riots in antebellum Philadelphia.

The rise of nativist and Protestant sentiment combined with a sharp increase in Irish Catholic immigration brought tensions to a fever pitch in spring 1844. Beginning as a contest over Catholic resistance to reading the Protestant King James Bible in public schools, unrest boiled into the streets when a nativist organization, the American Republican Association, attempted to hold meetings in the heavily Irish Kensington district. Catholic hecklers swiftly interrupted the meeting on May 3, 1844; a second meeting on May 6 was disrupted by Irish bystanders, then turned more violent with gunshots and rioting. Over the next three days, nativists burned more than thirty buildings, including a Catholic school and St. Augustine's Catholic Church at Fourth and Vine Streets, in Philadelphia. Militia companies and other troops restored order, which lasted for two months, then anti-Catholic sentiment boiled over again, this time in Southwark. On Sunday, July 7, 1844, a nativist mob rioted and exchanged cannon fire with militia protecting a Catholic church. The rioting stopped on July 8 after the governor ordered surrounding militia units into Philadelphia to quell the fighting in Southwark.

Explosive and destructive incidents of rioting occurred in many urban centers in the United States during the 1830s and 1840s, including Boston, Baltimore, and Philadelphia. While the riots brought destruction and death to Philadelphia, they also produced positive changes. Such violent events fueled discussion about consolidating the twenty-nine jurisdictions of Philadelphia County into one municipality, patrolled by a unified police force. This political consolidation was completed in 1854 followed by a professional police force in 1855, one of the first modern police forces in the nation.

Civil War

Theodore Zeman

The Philadelphia region in many ways was a microcosm of the issues and experiences that defined and troubled the Civil War era. With close economic, political, and social ties to both South and North, Philadelphia and the surrounding region were torn in their interests and loyalties. The sectional crisis of the 1850s, the secession of southern states in 1860–61, and the war (1861–65) forced people to choose sides. The war tested the region as it responded to the Union's military and manpower needs and felt the consequences of war. Connections to the South declined dramatically, especially in Philadelphia, as the region's identity and interests aligned more strongly with the nation and the Republican Party rose to prominence as a political force.

During the 1850s, expansion of slavery into western territories polarized the North and South, and southerners' demands for the return of fugitive enslaved people and silencing of antislavery critics became increasingly intolerable in the North. Philadelphia and regional newspapers amply reported and stirred public comment and conflict about events such as the Kansas-Nebraska Act (1854) and the ensuing bloodshed in Kansas as proslavery and antislavery forces fought a preview of the war that lay ahead. Further controversies arose over the Supreme Court's *Dred Scott* decision in 1857, the fracturing of the Democratic Party over enslavement, and the failed but far-reaching attempt by John Brown to foment an uprising of enslaved people in Harpers Ferry, Virginia, in October 1859.

Pro-southern sentiment ran strong in Philadelphia and the surrounding region. Economic ties with the South ran deep, especially in the textile, lumber, and coal industries, but also in education, banking, and marketing services. Some prominent families in the region owned many enslaved people and plantations in the South, especially in Atlantic Seaboard states. Feelings against Black people and abolitionists also ran high. As a result, the increasingly pro-southern Democratic Party dominated not only Philadelphia but also New Jersey and Delaware. Although the newly emerging antislavery Republican Party (known in Pennsylvania as the People's Party) gained supporters by the late 1850s, in the region it emphasized higher tariffs and a moderate position of opposing further extension of enslavement into the western territories. Local Republicans played down any ties to abolitionists who insisted on the immediate, universal, and uncompensated end to enslavement and the embrace of Black people as citizens.

The John Brown raid and his execution by Virginia authorities, which northern abolitionists and others likened to martyrdom, inflamed tensions in Philadelphia. Editorials in Democratic, pro-southern newspapers lashed out at abolitionists as revolutionaries bent on racial violence, lawlessness, and even disunion. They equated abolition with the Republican Party, asserting that it aimed to promote equality between white and Black people. Philadelphia's growing African American population and proximity to slave states made the city a magnet for enslaved persons fleeing bondage. The increasingly effective work of the Pennsylvania Abolition Society, vigilance committees, and the Underground Railroad network brought many freedom seekers into the city, further heightening tensions between abolitionists, African Americans, and Republicans on one side, and pro-southern supporters and Democrats on the other.

The sectional crisis came to a head in the election of 1860. "Fire-eating" southerners threatened to leave the Union if the Republicans won the presidency. But the Democratic Party had split into southern and northern wings, each nominating its own candidate for the presidency. Most northern Democrats threw their support behind Stephen A. Douglas, and southern Democrats, along with many Philadelphians, supported Vice President John C. Breckinridge. Complicating this already muddled field was the emergence of the Constitutional Union Party, a new third party committed to avoiding the issue of enslavement, which drew away votes from Democratic candidates. The Republicans offered a seemingly moderate ticket with Abraham Lincoln—the "rail splitter" from Illinois—at its head. To win the 1860 presidential election, Republicans needed only to hold on to the northern states they had won in 1856 and win Pennsylvania and either Illinois or Indiana. With fierce electioneering, the Republicans carried Pennsylvania. Douglas fared poorly, although he did win electors in New Jersey.

Following the Republican victory, seven southern states seceded, and efforts to bring them back during the "secession winter" from December 1860 to February 1861 failed, despite persistent efforts by prominent Philadelphia newspapers to rally support for compromise. As the Confederacy formed in the South, on February 21, 1861, president-elect Lincoln came to Philadelphia enroute to his inauguration and gave a powerful speech outside Independence Hall on the necessity of Union. His speech anticipated his inaugural address in Washington as he promised a firm hand to save the Union but an open hand to southerners that his administration would not disturb lawful existing institutions (meaning enslavement).

The new Confederacy's attack on Fort Sumter in Charleston, South Carolina, on April 12–13, 1861, immediately changed the attitude of people in the Philadelphia region from conciliation to defense of the Union. It also led four more southern states to secede from the Union and join the Confederacy. On April 15, Lincoln called for seventy-five thousand volunteers for ninety days to put down the rebellion.

In Philadelphia those who had voiced support for the South now kept a low profile. Most pro-Southern newspapers fell silent. Those that did not, such as the *Palmetto Flag*, came under threat of attack by enraged citizens. Philadelphia mayor Alexander Henry readied police to oppose violence against persons or property. Throughout the war, he sought to maintain order through police presence whenever rumors of trouble loomed.

Philadelphia woefully lacked military preparedness when the war began. The initial rush of local volunteers, however, amply filled the quotas established by the federal government. Enlistees came from a variety of ethnic and social backgrounds. Most units, including thousand-man regiments, were formed by prominent citizens who recruited from their neighborhoods and towns or appealed to common ethnic ties. During the war nearly fifty infantry and cavalry regiments were recruited in the Philadelphia area, forty in New Jersey, and eleven in Delaware.

Many of the Philadelphia-area regiments—infantry, cavalry, and artillery—distinguished themselves during the war, and successful officers parlayed their military exploits and reputations into political careers. Philadelphia and its surrounding counties provided more than 100,000 men for the Union army: the city of Philadelphia 93,300, Bucks County 3,300, Montgomery County 3,900, Chester County 4,800, and Delaware County 1,900. New Jersey sent close to 80,000, and Delaware sent more than 12,000, most recruited from New Castle County.

Philadelphia played a major role in mobilizing for the war and providing relief for soldiers and their families. Drawing on their experience in social reform and charitable efforts, faith-based and other private organizations offered aid and comfort to soldiers and widows and orphans of soldiers. Among them, the nationally organized United States Sanitary

FIGURE 55. *View of the Encampment of the Corn Exchange Regiment, 118th Penn. Vols.*, East Falls, Philadelphia, by John L. Magee, 1862. LIBRARY OF CONGRESS.

Commission and the United States Christian Commission were the most prominent. Many Northern cities organized fairs to fund these organizations by selling products, art, memorabilia, and other objects and charging admission. The largest such fair, held in Philadelphia's Logan Square, June 7–28, 1864, was supported by the governors of the three contiguous states. Contributions by businesses, industries, and private citizens raised over $1 million in support of the Sanitary Commission alone.

In the wake of the Battle of First Bull Run (First Manassas) in July 1861, Philadelphians and their neighbors began to understand that the conflict would be long and potentially devastating. This realization, coupled with a series of morale-sapping setbacks in the eastern theater of military operations and mounting Union casualties, spurred open opposition to the war by Southern sympathizers. Democratic newspapers pointed to the Lincoln administration's inability to defeat the Confederate armies and condemned wartime measures such as the suspension of habeas corpus in many Northern cites as examples of "tyranny." The preliminary Emancipation Proclamation issued by Lincoln in September 1862 stirred further opposition to the war by Peace Democrats in the region. Cries of Black-over-white and tyranny heightened with Lincoln's signing of the Emancipation Proclamation on January 1, 1863, and the call for African Americans to be recruited into the army. These reactions did not drown out jubilation by Black residents and other abolitionists, but anti-Lincoln sentiment deepened with the Enrollment Act of March 1863, which called for all able-bodied men, aged twenty to forty-five, to register for the draft. Many men in the region sought to evade conscription by paying a commutation fee of $300 or hiring substitutes. Conscription led to protests, defiance, and even violence in parts of Pennsylvania, especially in the anthracite coal region, but it helped to fill the ranks. Philadelphia escaped the protests and violent resistance that marked opposition to the draft elsewhere due to the presence of federal troops and the firm hand of the mayor enforcing law and order.

Needing manpower, the Lincoln administration sought to enlist Black troops. The president had been authorized to recruit African Americans as early as 1862, but he held off doing so for political reasons. Many white Americans believed recruiting Black soldiers was long overdue, for reasons of justice but, especially, to fill the ranks. Others held that Black men would make poor soldiers and run away at the first shots of battle, while some opposed arming African Americans because that would recognize their equality with white men. When Pennsylvania, New Jersey, and Delaware initially balked at accepting Black recruits, many Black men from the region joined the few state-level Black regiments in service such as the Fifty-Fourth and Fifty-Fifth Massachusetts Infantry (commanded, as was every other Black outfit, by white officers). Despite the army's efforts to limit their role in combat and often to confine them to fatigue or guard duty, Black soldiers from the Philadelphia area performed admirably during the war, and from that service called for the rights and respect due them as citizens. In Philadelphia, for example, Black soldiers and local Black women, angry over the inconvenience and disrespect of segregated public transportation there, pushed to end discrimination on the rails. After the war Black churches, veterans' organizations, and social clubs played major roles in setting up and staffing schools for the "freedpeople" in the South, attacking racial discrimination in public services, and lobbying for the vote.

The reemergence of resistance to the Lincoln administration appalled Republicans in Philadelphia, most of whom viewed opposition to the war and calls for a negotiated peace as treason. To meet the threat of the "Copperheads," as Republicans labeled Northern opponents of the war, a group of prominent Philadelphians in November 1862 established the Union League to counter the Peace Democrats and reenergize support for the war. As one of its first acts, the league created a military committee to help recruit, organize, and equip regiments for the Union army, including United States Colored Troops. The league also published tracts, posters, broadsides, and other printed materials and raised money to support the war effort, the Lincoln administration, and Republican policies during and after the war. The league's example encouraged hundreds of such organizations to form across the North.

Philadelphia and the surrounding region supported the Union war effort in a variety of ways. The government set up several military training camps in and around Philadelphia; the Frankford Arsenal supplied munitions; the Navy Yard built and repaired warships; and the DuPont Company in Delaware produced up to 40 percent of the black powder used by the Union army. Philadelphia served as the Northern station for receiving ships and contraband cargo seized in the blockade of the Confederacy. As the major railroad hub in the mid-Atlantic region, Philadelphia maintained and supplied rail transport for soldiers and matériel; indeed, most Union soldiers from Northern states east of the Appalachians who served in the eastern theater of the war passed through Philadelphia. This made the Philadelphia area a prime location also for wartime hospitals and refreshment stations.

Philadelphia also figured prominently in funding the war. Desperate to raise funds through bond sales, the Lincoln administration engaged Philadelphia financier Jay Cooke to organize a major bond drive, which succeeded by pitching the purchase of bonds to businesses and citizens as an investment in the nation. The mobilization of Philadelphia resources fostered a growing sense of national pride, purpose, and Philadelphia's importance to the nation, which Republicans used to move the city firmly into its camp.

Wartime mobilization created jobs for men and women in the area's many war-related industries. Men

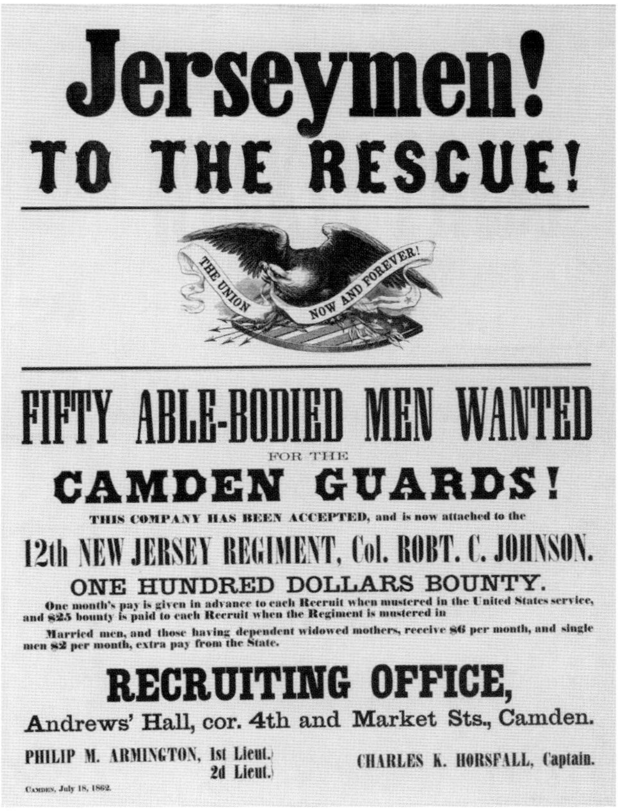

FIGURE 56. Recruiting poster for the Camden Guards attached to the Twelfth New Jersey Regiment, United States Army, 1862. LIBRARY COMPANY OF PHILADELPHIA.

found jobs in manufacturing and services. Women often took over businesses and farms when their men went to war, or they worked for pay as seamstresses making uniforms, as clerks in government offices, and doing various tasks in munitions factories. Because of wartime inflation, workers' pay did not keep up with the price of consumer goods, which led to workers protesting for more pay and better working conditions, although with mixed results.

The war came to Pennsylvania in June 1863 when Robert E. Lee's Army of Northern Virginia launched its northern campaign in hopes of defeating the Union army on Northern soil and dispiriting support for the Union. In Philadelphia fears of Lee's army marching into the city led to panicky calls for militia and the digging of defenses. The anxiety subsided when the Army of the Potomac, commanded by native Philadelphian Major General George Gordon Meade, defeated Lee's army at Gettysburg (July 1–3). This victory, coupled with Major General Ulysses S. Grant's capture of Vicksburg, Mississippi (July 4), led many to believe the war would end soon, but the worst of the fighting came the following year. In spring 1864, Grant assumed command of all the Union armies, which hammered relentlessly at the Confederates on multiple fronts. General William T. Sherman's army march through Georgia in 1864 helped secure Lincoln's reelection and raised Republican fortunes in Pennsylvania and elsewhere. Grant's armies forced Lee's surrender at Appomattox on April 9, 1865, and on April 26 Sherman received the surrender of General Joseph E. Johnston's Army of Tennessee, effectively ending the military war in the East. In the western theater the last Confederate army surrendered in late May 1865.

The assassination of Abraham Lincoln on April 14, 1865, cut short the victory celebrations. Philadelphia and the surrounding region, like the entire North, entered a period of mourning for the president, whose death soon became likened to martyrdom. The funeral train bearing the president's body arrived in Philadelphia on April 22 enroute to its final resting place in Springfield, Illinois. While Lincoln lay in state at Independence Hall, an estimated three hundred thousand mourners, who formed a line three miles long, waited up to five hours to pay their respects.

Although combat ceased with Union victory in 1865, the emotions it engendered continued as returning soldiers and their families and communities adjusted to resettling their lives, caring for the wounded, and remembering their service. The war also led to major efforts to define civil rights, not only for the newly freed people in the South but for Black people in the North. Such efforts renewed political and social conflict in Philadelphia and its environs. An influx of Black migrants into the area heightened racial tensions, while competition for jobs and controversy over the Radical Republican program of Reconstruction led to violence.

After the war, Republicans tried to consolidate their wartime gains by continuing to promote business, financial reforms, tariffs, and other economic measures, and especially by seeking to secure basic civil rights for "freedmen" in the South and an orderly return of the former Confederate states to the Union. Trading on the memory of the martyred Lincoln, the Union victory, and the supposed "betrayal" of Democrats in their lack of full support for the war effort, and pointing to their economic policies, Republicans emerged as the dominant party in Philadelphia and Pennsylvania and remained so well into the twentieth century. Democrats fared better in South Jersey and Delaware, where opposition to Reconstruction policies—especially expansion of civil rights to Black people—played well in public and at the polls.

Remembering the war became an important part of adjusting to the postwar world. While thousands of area soldiers died during the war from disease and battlefield wounds, no official count of casualties by county exists to know the exact numbers from the Greater Philadelphia area. Cemeteries filled with Union soldiers marking their service. The national dedication of the Union cemetery at Gettysburg, Pennsylvania, in November 1863, during which Lincoln delivered his Gettysburg Address, was part of a sustained national effort to memorialize the service of the soldiers. Local governments, church groups, ethnic associations, and other organizations put up statues, monuments, and memorials across the region. Philadelphia, for example, exalted its military leaders with statues of Pennsylvania native sons George B. McClellan and John Reynolds mounted on horses dominating the public square around city hall and George Gordon Meade at the entrance to Laurel Hill Cemetery, where many Civil War veterans were buried. By some accounts, the Philadelphia region built more Civil War monuments and memorials than anywhere else in the North.

Veterans also organized to lobby for pensions as well as public recognition. The Grand Army of the Republic (GAR), established in 1866, became the nation's most powerful veterans' organization, wielding a political influence through the end of the century. At one time the GAR had fifty-six posts in Philadelphia and its suburbs, twenty-eight in South Jersey, and twenty-nine in Delaware. Membership required an honorable discharge from the U.S. Army, Navy, or Marine Corps; all were considered equal in the post hall, whether general officer or private soldier, including African American veterans. The organization advocated voting rights for Black veterans as well as patriotic education for schools. It helped found Decoration Day (later Memorial Day), gained generous pensions for veterans, and staunchly supported the Republican Party. The first local Memorial Day ceremonies were held on May 30, 1868, in Doylestown, Bucks County, and at Laurel Hill Cemetery in Philadelphia, hosted by General George G. Meade Post #1 of the GAR. By 1890, the GAR's national membership exceeded four hundred thousand. Although its last surviving member died in 1956, the organization's mission continued into the twenty-first century through the efforts of the Sons of Union Veterans of the Civil War. Its museum and library in Philadelphia collected wartime memorabilia, printed material, military gear and uniforms, and more.

The Philadelphia region played a major role in mobilizing men and resources that brought Union victory in the Civil War and, afterward, raised questions about the meaning of emancipation and freedom. Working in relief organizations encouraged women to push for political rights and larger roles in civic affairs. Some industries that scaled up demand to meet wartime needs continued to prosper, while improvements in chemistry, medicine, and engineering developed in Philadelphia during the war yielded postwar benefits. Though Philadelphia-area businesses renewed commercial ties to the South after the war and many women served in freedmen's schools set up by churches and philanthropic organizations, Philadelphia was no longer a southern city. Its schools no longer enrolled many, or sometimes any, southerners, and its first families no longer enslaved people in southern places. The war consolidated Republican Party dominance in the region, and in Pennsylvania generally, though it did not weaken the Democrats altogether as their successes in local elections in the 1870s and after attested. The wartime generation also refused to forget the war or let those after them forget, as evinced in the monuments they constructed, the cemeteries they established, and the annual public invocations of soldierly valor and memory they celebrated.

United States Colored Troops

Lucien Holness

During the American Civil War (1861–65), Philadelphians raised eleven regiments of the United States Colored Troops (USCT). This division of the United States Army, consisting of Black soldiers led by white officers, provided much-needed manpower for federal forces in the final two years of the war.

When the Civil War began, many African Americans across the North sought to enlist, motivated by their belief that their military service would help win the war, end enslavement, and entitle them to rights that they were denied—the rights to vote, sit on juries, and testify against white people in court. Most white Americans opposed Black men serving in the army, believing that defending the republic was an essential element of citizenship reserved for white men only. Also, the federal Militia Act of 1792 prohibited Black men from serving in the militia.

By the summer of 1862, as casualties mounted from combat and disease and as fewer white men enlisted, Northern public opinion moved in favor of enrolling Black troops. On July 16, 1862, Congress passed the Second Militia Act, which allowed African Americans to be employed as soldiers, and in early 1863, Secretary of War Edwin M. Stanton authorized the governors of Rhode Island, Massachusetts, and Connecticut to organize Black regiments. Massachusetts was the first state to raise two regiments—the Fifty-Fourth and Fifty-Fifth Massachusetts Voluntary Infantry Regiments. About three hundred Black Philadelphians enlisted in these regiments. One company of the Fifty-Fourth was raised in Philadelphia.

In May 1863, the War Department established the Bureau of Colored Troops, which facilitated Black enlistment throughout the country and sent

Major George Stearns to Philadelphia to raise Black regiments. The local Union League—founded by elite white Philadelphians to foster support for the Union war effort—established a Supervisory Committee for Recruiting Colored Troops and received Secretary Stanton's permission to begin raising Black regiments with the aid of local and national Black leaders such as Octavius V. Catto, Jacob C. White, and Frederick Douglass. Mother Bethel African Methodist Episcopal Church and its denominational newspaper, the *Christian Recorder*, also encouraged Black men to enlist. Federal officials and local leaders (Black and white) campaigned extensively to attract Black recruits in Philadelphia, from Bucks, Chester, Delaware, Montgomery, and other counties in Pennsylvania, and from Delaware, New Jersey, and New York.

Eleven USCT regiments were raised in Philadelphia—the 3rd, 6th, 8th, 22nd, 24th, 25th, 32nd, 41st, 43rd, 45th, and 127th—totaling 10,940 men. These recruits trained eight miles north of the city at Camp William Penn, where they practiced weaponry, tactical formations and maneuvers, and guard duties. For these soldiers, weekdays began at 6 a.m. with reveille and roll call, followed by drills throughout the day and evening, and leading to a dress parade and then taps at 9 p.m. On Saturdays the men cleaned the camp, and on Sundays they assembled for inspection, attended a church service, and participated in dress parades.

Many white men seeking to become commissioned officers in the USCT regiments received training from the Free Military School for Applicants for the Command of Colored Regiments, formed by the Union League's recruiting committee, which operated from December 26, 1863, through most of 1864. Black men were not admitted to the school because most Northern white people believed that they were not capable or intelligent enough for command, but an auxiliary school trained Black men as noncommissioned officers.

The first Black regiments from the Philadelphia region, led by their white officers, arrived in the South in summer 1863 and participated in many subsequent campaigns. Their engagements included assaults on Fort Wagner and Fort Gregg (August 20–September 7, 1863) in South Carolina; the Battle of Olustee, also known as Ocean Pond (February 20, 1864) in the swamps of north Florida; the Richmond-Petersburg Campaign (June 1864–April 1865) in Virginia; and the Battle of Honey Hill (November 30, 1864) in South Carolina. The Forty-First Infantry Regiment USCT, which arrived in Virginia in the fall of 1864, contributed to the Union victory at Appomattox Court House on April 9, 1865.

Many local servicemen in USCT regiments earned recognition for their distinction in battle. Sergeants Alexander Kelly and Thomas R. Hawkins from the Sixth USCT received the Medal of Honor for their heroism in rescuing the regimental colors while under heavy fire at the battle of New Market Heights, Virginia (September 29–30, 1864). Kelly was also praised for rallying the men in his company during a period of confusion on the battlefield.

Military service did not guarantee equal treatment for African Americans on the battlefield or at home. For example, African American soldiers received pay of only ten dollars per month, with three dollars deducted for clothing, while white privates received thirteen dollars per month plus a clothing allowance. Many Black soldiers expressed their dissatisfaction by refusing to accept the reduced rate and went for more than a year without pay. Not until June 15, 1864—when many Black regiments teetered on the brink of mutiny—did Congress pass legislation that equalized the pay of Black and white soldiers, including retroactive pay.

At home, Black troops and African American women who provided aid and comfort to wounded soldiers faced discrimination. During the period of the Civil War, African Americans and their white abolitionist allies battled discrimination on Philadelphia's streetcars, where African Americans were excluded from riding or forced to ride on the front platforms. After the war, in March 1867, the campaign won legislation prohibiting segregation on all forms of public transportation in the state.

By early December 1865, most of the USCT regiments that had trained at Camp William Penn returned to Philadelphia and received a heroes' welcome for their service and sacrifice. When the Twenty-Fifth USCT returned to the city, the regiment attended a parade and flag-dedication ceremony at the Union League before being officially mustered out of service. Military service allowed Black men to establish their claims to full citizenship in Pennsylvania.

FIGURE 57. *United States Soldiers at Camp "William Penn" Philadelphia, Pa.*, lithograph by P. S. Duval & Son, 1863. LIBRARY COMPANY OF PHILADELPHIA.

Civil War Museum of Philadelphia

Mabel Rosenheck

Founded in 1888 by veteran officers of the Civil War, the Civil War Museum of Philadelphia was a monument to those who fought to preserve the Union. Originally known as the War Library and Museum, the institution operated in several sites in Philadelphia before settling in a town house near Rittenhouse Square from 1922 until 2008, when it closed for financial reasons. In 2016, the museum transferred its three-dimensional collections to the Gettysburg Foundation with artifacts also displayed at the National Constitution Center in Philadelphia. In their new homes, artifacts originally treated as memorial relics—including items from General Ulysses S. Grant, Abraham Lincoln, and lesser-known soldiers and officers—were given new meaning in the context of exhibits about such topics as enslavement, racism, and the broader causes and consequences of the Civil War.

The creation of a Civil War museum in Philadelphia originated with the Military Order of the Loyal Legion of the United States (MOLLUS), a fraternal association for veteran officers of the Civil War founded in 1865 at the Union League in Philadelphia. The group formed in the wake of Lincoln's assassination amid fear of a continuation of the Civil War, but when that fear subsided, commemoration became central to the association's mission. The chartering of the War Library and Museum in 1888 reflected new efforts at remembrance as veterans became older and events of the Civil War seemed to fade into history.

Members of MOLLUS, including John Page Nicholson, who had revived the organization a decade earlier, chartered the War Library and Museum to collect, preserve, and maintain books and artifacts—"implements, relics, and muniments of war"—pertaining to the "War of the Rebellion." The library and museum reflected a larger interest in documenting the memories of aging Union veterans to capture history before it was lost. The urge to collect their artifacts and to write and publish their recollections was also part of a contest over who would write the history of the Civil War.

Collections grew throughout the late nineteenth and early twentieth centuries, primarily from the donations of veterans and MOLLUS members, but the early history of the War Library and Museum focused primarily on finding a home. The State of Pennsylvania offered $50,000 to construct a building if MOLLUS could raise $100,000 more. Throughout the 1890s, the group wrote appeals, pursued various locations, and drew up designs for a grand structure that would house offices, banquet halls, and the library and museum. The veterans envisioned a repository of history and material objects, but also a space where they could socialize and reminisce. After pursuing various sites unsuccessfully, including council chambers at Independence Hall and properties near Philadelphia City Hall, in 1907 the organization rented rooms in the Flanders Building at Fifteenth and Walnut Streets and, in 1922, made a permanent home in a town house at 1805 Pine Street. The selection of a more modest home was a disappointment, but it enabled building funds to sustain the institution as an endowment for much of the twentieth century.

At the Flanders Building, for the first time, exhibits showcased the collections publicly. The displays included the Tiffany sword and scabbard that General Ulysses S. Grant received after the battle at Vicksburg, a uniform worn by General George Meade at Gettysburg, and casts of Lincoln's face and hands made by sculptor Leonard Wells Volk just before the war. Visitors could also see the cane Lincoln carried into Ford's Theater, a tree trunk hit by a cannonball at Gettysburg, a recruitment drum played in 1861 outside enlistment headquarters in Philadelphia, and the paisley smoking

FIGURE 58. Portrait of the preserved head of Old Baldy, General George Meade's war horse, 1883. COLLECTION OF THE HISTORICAL SOCIETY OF PENNSYLVANIA.

jacket worn by Jefferson Davis when he was captured by Union soldiers in 1865.

Ephemeral items and other personal relics donated by Union veterans contrasted strikingly with other Civil War commemorations in Philadelphia at the time, including the equestrian statues of Meade and General John Reynolds and the Smith Memorial Arch in Fairmount Park. While Nicholson and MOLLUS wanted the library and museum to be similarly monumental, the museum's collection was a mixture of official military history documented by the uniforms and firearms of commanding officers and a more subtle memory of the Civil War driven by everyday artifacts donated by individuals (albeit mostly officers) that revealed alternative, more personal histories. Debates arose in the 1920s over whether the collection needed to be better interpreted as veterans, who could recall their own experiences, were dying and MOLLUS membership passed to descendants, but a guide for visitors never emerged. In the members-only museum, the artifacts were largely left to speak for themselves and the library and archives, while available for use, were only partially cataloged or cared for.

MOLLUS remained involved with the museum until the 1970s, when the organization and the museum separated so that each could dedicate more resources to its narrower mission. In 1976, coinciding with the U.S. Bicentennial, the museum opened to the public on a day-to-day basis, and in the 1980s special exhibits began to interpret more diverse histories—including those of women or African Americans or even the Confederacy—in addition to the other long-standing displays of the collections.

By the early 2000s, a dwindling endowment and declining visitation threatened sustainability of the museum. Legal proceedings against former curator Russell Pritchard Jr. and his son for fraud and theft from a variety of Civil War institutions, including the Civil War Museum of Philadelphia, provided further evidence of the museum's longtime mismanagement. One proposed solution to address the state of the museum was to loan part of the collection to a planned Civil War museum in Richmond, Virginia. The backlash in Philadelphia against that idea resulted in a proposal to create a Center for Civil War Studies based at the Union League, with partners such as the Historical Society of Pennsylvania and National Civil War Museum in Harrisburg. The desire, beyond creating an exceptional network of research collections, was to make Philadelphia a destination for nineteenth-century history and Civil War tourism as well as for Revolutionary War tourism. Plans for such a consortium never came to fruition, nor did another plan for the museum to occupy Memorial Hall in Fairmount Park. Continuing the disappointments, in 2002 the State of Pennsylvania pledged $15 million toward a new facility but retracted the funds in 2009 during the recession.

While the quest for a new home signaled a desire for a more professional, authoritative institution, appreciation also remained for the small, quirky museum on Pine Street that displayed, among other things, the preserved head of Old Baldy, General Meade's horse. Rather than develop either of these identities, however, in 2003 the institution reemerged as the Civil War and Underground Railroad Museum with a new dual emphasis that reflected trends toward more inclusive histories of the Civil War era. With a limited collection of African American materials, the museum turned to living history with actors portraying historical figures, including Harriet Tubman and Absalom Jones. New outreach resulted in a 2006 program called "Faith and Freedom," co-produced with Black churches. One program featured an actor portraying Jones giving his "Thanksgiving Sermon" at St. Thomas's African Episcopal Church.

In 2004, a grant from the William Penn Foundation enabled the first complete inventory of the collection, which revealed objects previously unknown to the museum or the nation. In addition to the already celebrated items from well-known figures, the inventory uncovered items like a pocket watch belonging to Brevet Captain John O. Foering that was dented by a bullet; a jar of peaches from an orchard on the battlefield of Winchester, Virginia; the tombstone of John Butcher, a veteran of the United States Colored Troops; and an 1872 first edition of *The Underground Railroad* by William Still.

None of these developments could save the museum, which closed in 2008. The artifact collections transferred in 2016 to the Gettysburg Foundation—the private, nonprofit partner of Gettysburg National Military Park—with the promise that the National Constitution Center would still display some of the artifacts in Philadelphia. The museum retained the two-dimensional materials, including paintings, lithographs, and books that went on loan to the Union League and remained available to researchers there. Other artifacts—including the head of Old Baldy, which had been on loan from the Grand Army of the Republic Museum in Frankford—returned to the GAR Museum, which sustained Civil War memory in Philadelphia, although on a smaller scale.

In 2019, the National Constitution Center opened the exhibit *Civil War and Reconstruction: The Battle for Freedom and Equality*, which used Civil War Museum artifacts in an expansive history including the Civil War's causes, like enslavement and racism, and its consequences, like the Reconstruction amendments to the U.S. Constitution and the rise of Jim Crow segregation. At the Gettysburg National Military Park Museum, meanwhile, artifacts from the Philadelphia museum illustrated the story of the Civil War from the perspectives of both the North and the South.

Ultimately, the Civil War Museum faced several hurdles that it could not overcome. By the late twentieth century, Philadelphia museums—especially small, lesser-known museums—were suffering financially. The Civil War Museum's location was also challenging because Philadelphia never successfully cultivated a Civil War identity or Civil War tourism despite deep connections to that history. However, if, as a fundraising appeal from 1891 argued, the museum was meant to commemorate those "who gave their lives to the war which restored the Union and maintained the Constitution," then the collections found a fitting final resting place at the National Constitution Center in an exhibit about the simultaneous successes and failures of that document and a more critical memory of the Civil War for a new generation.

Woman Suffrage and Women's Rights

Tamara Gaskell
and Jean R. Soderlund

In 1915, Pennsylvania suffragists publicized their campaign for woman suffrage with a statewide tour of the Justice Bell, a replica of the Liberty Bell with its clapper silenced until women won the right to vote. A parade in Philadelphia with the bell attracted a crowd of one hundred thousand people. The suffragists sought to remind citizens of the region's role in the American Revolution while highlighting the nation's shortcomings in denying equal rights to women. Though the 1915 state referendum failed, five years later the Justice Bell rang for the first time on September 25, 1920, on Independence Square, after ratification of the Nineteenth Amendment to the United States Constitution.

The struggle for women's equality started early in the Philadelphia area as women organized for education, property ownership, political power, economic opportunity, and freedom. In the colonial era, Quakers took the vanguard in women's rights among European settlers by promoting women as ministers and overseers of discipline within the Society of Friends. Nevertheless, William Penn and other founders of West New Jersey, Pennsylvania, and Delaware followed English common law and culture to block women from suffrage, participation in government, control of property and wages, and guardianship of children. Black women were deprived of an even broader spectrum of human rights with enslavement by affluent colonists on both sides of the Delaware River. The Revolutionary and early national periods brought glimmers of change with New Jersey's provision (unique among the states) of voting rights to propertied women from 1776 to 1807, increased access to education, and passage of acts for the gradual abolition of slavery in Pennsylvania (1780) and New Jersey (1804).

In December 1833, Philadelphia-area women took a leading role to work collectively for social, legal, and economic change. The Philadelphia Female Anti-Slavery Society (PFASS), like other supporters of William Lloyd Garrison, promoted immediate emancipation and an end to discrimination against free Black people. Among the group's activists were Black leaders Margaretta Forten, Harriet Forten Purvis, and Sarah Mapps Douglass; Quakers Lucretia Mott and Sarah Pugh; and Mary Grew, of a Baptist family. PFASS circulated antislavery petitions, hosted abolitionist speakers, and held an annual fair to sell needlework and farm produce of abolitionist women and men throughout southeastern Pennsylvania and southwestern New Jersey. By contributing a large portion of the Pennsylvania Anti-Slavery Society's budget, PFASS gained leadership positions for Mott, Pugh, and Grew in the male-dominated state organization.

In the late 1840s and 1850s, PFASS members also played a vital role in launching the women's rights movement, as Lucretia Mott joined Elizabeth Cady Stanton in assembling the Seneca Falls, New York, convention. Stanton wrote the 1848 Declaration of Sentiments, modeled on the Declaration of Independence (1776), protesting the denial of woman suffrage; participation in government; ownership of property; equality in separation and divorce; access to well-paying employment, colleges, and education in the professions; and leadership in most religions. The signers insisted that women receive all rights as equal citizens, noting that anything less destroyed their self-confidence and self-respect. This first feminist movement

FIGURE 59. Women's Liberty Bell tour in Pennsylvania, 1915. The Justice Bell rang for the first time on September 25, 1920, on Independence Square, after ratification of the Nineteenth Amendment. COLLECTION OF THE HISTORICAL SOCIETY OF PENNSYLVANIA.

organized through state and national conventions, attracting large audiences to hear speakers on relevant issues. Philadelphian Sarah Tyndale, a wealthy businesswoman and reformer, served as vice president at the first national convention in 1850 in Worcester, Massachusetts. Lucretia Mott and Mary Ann White Johnson presided in 1852 at the first Pennsylvania convention in West Chester and, in 1854, Mott and Sarah Pugh organized the fifth national convention at Sansom Street Hall in Philadelphia.

In response to women's rights activists, increasing urbanization, and demographic and economic change, state legislatures gradually addressed inequities in married women's property rights. In Pennsylvania, for example, lawmakers passed the Married Women's Property Act of 1848, stipulating that wives owned personal property they brought into a marriage and received afterward, such as rents on their real estate. They could also independently write wills. The law did not give a married woman freedom to sell her real estate without her husband's permission but confirmed that he needed her consent before he attempted a sale. Women's rights reformers considered the 1848 Pennsylvania law a positive step, but they protested in 1855 when the legislature rejected the right of wives to control their earnings. The lawmakers reversed this decision in 1872 but still required women to file in local court their intentions to keep their separate wages. Through the nineteenth and twentieth centuries, legislatures and courts wrestled over women's economic rights versus the ideology of marital unity, gradually granting women more autonomy through piecemeal reforms.

Gaining woman suffrage required much energy and resilience before ratification of the Nineteenth Amendment. Formal agitation had begun in the region in 1844 when several men in Burlington County, New

Jersey, unsuccessfully petitioned the state constitutional convention to reinstate women's right to vote. In 1866, women's rights activists organized the American Equal Rights Association (AERA) to "secure Equal Rights to all American citizens, especially the right of suffrage, irrespective of race, color or sex." Lucretia Mott served as president. Philadelphia abolitionists and women's rights supporters formed the affiliated Pennsylvania Equal Rights Association in January 1867. Its founder, Robert Purvis, a former president of the Pennsylvania Anti-Slavery Society, was the only Black male abolitionist to support the idea that Black men should not be granted the vote until all women were also enfranchised. In December 1866, suffragists in the reform-minded community of Vineland, in Cumberland County, New Jersey, organized the Vineland Equal Rights Association and sent a petition to the Republican state convention for "Impartial Suffrage, irrespective of Sex or Color."

In 1869, the AERA splintered over support of the Fifteenth Amendment, which granted African American men, but not women, the right to vote. Those who believed that Black men should not receive the vote before women formed the new National Woman Suffrage Association (NWSA), led by Elizabeth Cady Stanton and Susan B. Anthony. Those who supported the Fifteenth Amendment formed the American Woman Suffrage Society (AWSA), led by Lucy Stone and Henry Blackwell of New Jersey.

Despite division at the national and local levels, advocates took vigorous steps for woman suffrage. In March 1868, Portia K. Gage of Vineland had attempted to vote in the municipal elections but was prevented because she was not registered. That fall she and 171 other women, Black and white, returned with their own ballot box and voted. The Vineland women continued the practice in 1869 and 1870. Their actions inspired women around the country to begin going to the polls to test the theory that women, as citizens, were enfranchised by the Fourteenth Amendment, suffrage being one of citizenship's "privileges and immunities." Carrie S. Burnham, a member of the Philadelphia Citizens' Suffrage Association, attempted to vote in October 1871. After a court ruled against her, she appealed to the state supreme court and also spoke before the state legislature. Burnham lost her appeal. In 1875, the U.S. Supreme Court, in *Minor v. Happersett*, ruled that voting was not a right of citizenship.

Suffragists also worked to change voting clauses in state constitutions, many of which were rewritten in response to ratification of the Fifteenth Amendment. Women sought to have the word "male" removed from voter qualifications at the same time that states removed the word "white." The Pennsylvania constitutional convention of 1872–73, however, changed its description of those eligible to vote from "white freeman" to "male citizens." The new constitution did allow women to run—but not vote—for school offices. Neither New Jersey nor Delaware updated their constitutions.

In 1876, at the instigation of the Philadelphia Citizens' Suffrage Association, NWSA determined to use the centennial celebration of American Independence, in Philadelphia, to point out the contradiction between the ideals of the Revolution and the reality of restricted suffrage. It also began lobbying for a sixteenth amendment for woman suffrage. The leaders of NWSA planned to read their *Declaration of Rights of the Women of the United States* at Independence Hall on July 4. When denied permission, they distributed it to the audience while Susan B. Anthony led a delegation onto the stage and handed it to the presiding officer. The AWSA, which had declined to sign the declaration, held its own meeting on July 3 at Horticultural Hall to recognize the centennial of woman suffrage in New Jersey and protest its loss in 1807.

When Congress in 1887 defeated a woman suffrage amendment, suffragists at the national level reassessed their strategy once again. The rival NWSA and AWSA reorganized in 1890 as the National American Woman Suffrage Association (NAWSA), with Anthony as its first president. In coordination, the New Jersey Woman Suffrage Association also reorganized that year. In 1892, Lucretia Longshore Blankenburg became president of the Pennsylvania Woman Suffrage Society and encouraged the formation of local societies, while Jane Campbell founded the Woman Suffrage Society of Philadelphia. Slow to organize, Delaware's first suffrage society, the Wilmington Equal Suffrage Club, formed in November 1895, under the leadership of Philadelphia's Rachel Foster Avery. A state suffrage society formed in 1896, with temperance advocate Martha S. Cranston as president. The Woman's Christian Temperance Union

(WCTU) had become an important ally of the suffrage movement with the result that issues of temperance and prohibition complicated arguments for woman suffrage, particularly in Philadelphia, into the final years of the suffrage campaign.

In the 1890s, some suffragists focused on securing more limited voting rights. New Jersey suffragists, working with the WCTU and the Grange, lobbied for an amendment to restore (for rural women) and expand (for others) women's right to vote for school commissioners; voters defeated the amendment in a special election in 1897. Suffrage activists were particularly interested in Delaware because it had a state constitutional convention scheduled for 1897. They were unsuccessful in getting "male" struck as a voting qualification, but Delaware did pass a law in 1898 that allowed tax-paying women to vote for school trustees.

New energy infused the woman suffrage movement in the region, and nationally, when Alice Paul, a Quaker from Mount Laurel, New Jersey, led a new generation to form the Congressional Union (CU), which originally affiliated with NAWSA but soon divided over strategy. The CU pushed for a federal suffrage amendment rather than NAWSA's state-by-state campaign and, following the lead of English suffragists, advocated the use of rallies, parades, and similar tactics to draw public attention to the cause. With the support of many Philadelphia suffragists, Alice Paul tested methods that she later took to the national stage. In May 1914, she planned May Day celebrations in every state. Many of Philadelphia's suffrage societies, including the Men's League, held the state's first suffrage demonstration in Rittenhouse Square before marching on Market Street to Washington Square.

The CU and Pennsylvania Woman Suffrage Society cooperated, sometimes uneasily, on the 1915 statewide referendum for woman suffrage, highlighted by the statewide tour of the Justice Bell with its silenced clapper. The referendum failed, with Philadelphia and most nearby counties in opposition, in part because of Philadelphia's machine politics and the power of the liquor interests in the region, which associated woman suffrage with the temperance cause. In 1915, New Jersey voters also defeated a suffrage referendum despite NAWSA's assignment of professional organizers to the state, including Camden, where Jenney G. Kerlin led the Camden Equal Suffrage League.

During World War I, while NAWSA suspended much of its work, the National Woman's Party, the CU's successor, lobbied representatives in Washington and held vigils outside the White House to underscore the hypocrisy of President Woodrow Wilson in fighting for democracy overseas while women were disenfranchised at home. Dora Kelly Lewis of Philadelphia was among those arrested during the protests in 1917, jailed, and force fed to end a hunger strike. The long struggle with Congress finally ended on June 4, 1919, with passage of the woman suffrage amendment. Suffragists in all states then turned to achieving ratification with the required minimum of thirty-six states. Pennsylvania quickly ratified within the month, but the New Jersey legislature waited until February 1920. Delaware rejected the amendment in 1920 and did not ratify until three years later, even though the Nineteenth Amendment gained the number of states needed for approval by August 1920.

Alice Paul then continued the battle for women's rights in opposition to reformers such as Florence Kelley of Philadelphia, who favored protective legislation for women workers. Paul and other members of the National Woman's Party in 1923 drafted the Equal Rights Amendment (ERA) to incorporate into the U.S. Constitution an unequivocal statement of equal rights regardless of sex. They lobbied until 1972, when Congress adopted the amendment and sent it to the states for ratification. Although Delaware, New Jersey, Pennsylvania, and twenty-seven other states endorsed the ERA within a year, the measure failed ratification by the required three-fourths of states.

Economic change in the Greater Philadelphia region from the nineteenth century to the post–World War II era highlighted the need for the ERA and inspired increasing numbers of women to fight for equal rights. In the 1800s, working-class women and girls worked as domestic servants and helped to industrialize the region in textile, garment, and other manufacturing. Despite low wages, women's earnings outside the home or from hosting boarders and manufacturing within the household provided essential support for their families. In the early twentieth century, female garment workers participated in strikes to obtain higher incomes and improve conditions. Black working-class women continued to face harsh discrimination in education and

FIGURE 60. Commemorating the centennial of the Declaration of Women's Rights at Independence Hall, photograph by Don Camp, July 5, 1976. SPECIAL COLLECTIONS RESEARCH CENTER, TEMPLE UNIVERSITY LIBRARIES.

business so labored primarily in domestic service, despite growing opportunities for white women in clerical and sales positions. World War II created openings for women in heavy industry and armaments that disappeared when the war ended. As described by Betty Friedan in her influential *The Feminine Mystique* (1963), American culture in the 1950s idealized middle-class households with male breadwinners and dependent wives and children.

With passage of the federal Civil Rights Act of 1964, the National Organization for Women (NOW) organized in 1966 to push the Equal Employment Opportunity Commission to fulfill its responsibilities under Title VII, which provided a platform for gender equity. NOW quickly added to its agenda the ERA, reproductive rights, childcare, and other goals. Philadelphia NOW launched in 1968 under the leadership of Ernesta Ballard, and Pennsylvania NOW formed in 1971, calling its first convention in 1973. The Philadelphia chapter published the *Philadelphia NOW Newsletter* and worked toward a range of goals including ratification of the national ERA; adding an ERA to the Pennsylvania state constitution; ending sex discrimination in employment, politics, education, and public accommodations; repealing Pennsylvania's restrictive abortion law; establishing government-funded childcare; and improving women's image in the media.

In 1968, the group New York Radical Women rallied feminists from New York, New Jersey, and elsewhere to demonstrate at the Miss America pageant in Atlantic City, New Jersey. They threw what they called "instruments of female torture" such as girdles, bras, hair curlers, and *Playboy* magazines into a "freedom trash can," gaining national publicity that helped to ignite the feminist movement in many cities. Philadelphia-area women in 1968 started consciousness-raising groups in which they gained motivation for collective action through discussions of how inequality and sexism affected their individual lives.

On August 26, 1970, Philadelphia NOW, the Women's Liberation Center, and more than twenty other organizations celebrated Women's Equality Day on the fiftieth anniversary of the woman suffrage amendment. In Rittenhouse Square, thousands of women and men heard speeches and talked to representatives of Philadelphia NOW, the Women's International League for Peace and Freedom, Women United for Abortion Action, and other feminist groups. Media coverage energized the movement, leading to the growth of consciousness-raising groups throughout the region.

While Black women helped to organize NOW, by 1973 feminists in New York City, including Florynce Kennedy and Margaret Sloan-Hunter, became convinced that a new organization, the National Black Feminist Organization (NBFO), was needed to address the challenges facing working-class women of diverse ethnic backgrounds. The NBFO established chapters in cities across the United States including Philadelphia in 1975. Women's rights groups collaborated to provide social services to women in the Philadelphia region, including literature and advice for finding jobs and health care, fighting sex discrimination, dealing with rape and sexual abuse, and transitioning through separation and divorce. Philadelphia feminists took the lead in creating women-led agencies such as the Elizabeth Blackwell Health Center for Women, Women Organized Against Rape, Women's Law Project, Pennsylvania Program for Women and Girl Offenders, and the funding coalition Women's Way.

By the early 2020s, a century after the Justice Bell rang for the first time on Independence Square, the status of women remained mixed. While many women in the Greater Philadelphia region had gained leadership in the arts, media, community service, health care, education, and business, and despite the important support of male allies, few women had reached high political office. No women had been elected to the U.S. Senate from New Jersey, Pennsylvania, or Delaware. In the U.S. House of Representatives, in 2023, Lisa Blunt Rochester held the at-large seat for Delaware and four women represented districts in eastern Pennsylvania, but none represented southern New Jersey. Pennsylvania has had no woman governor since the colonial period, while Delaware and New Jersey have each had one. After Cherelle Parker was elected the one hundredth mayor of Philadelphia, she became, in January 2024, the first woman to hold that office. The U.S. Supreme Court's reversal of *Roe v. Wade* (1973) in June 2022 highlighted the significance of political power in achieving and protecting women's rights. Movements such as Black Lives Matter and #MeToo, and lack of a national ERA, demonstrated how much change remained necessary.

Civil Rights (African American)

James Wolfinger
and Stanley Arnold

Black Philadelphians have fought for civil rights since the late eighteenth century. Early demands focused on the abolition of enslavement and desegregation of public accommodations. The movement gained greater power as the nineteenth century gave way to the twentieth and the World War I–era Great Migration brought tens of thousands of African Americans to the Philadelphia region. This exponential growth in the African American population gave Black Philadelphians the numbers and resources necessary to effect political change. Such efforts were never limited to the ballot box, which was gained by constitutional amendment, but were instead linked to community needs for adequate housing, economic opportunity, and social and educational services. As African Americans gained greater rights, especially in the post–World War II period, Black Philadelphians shifted more to emphasizing the need to achieve results based on their legal equality. The struggle to maintain civil rights and translate those rights into concrete results extended beyond the classic period of the 1960s and continued to shape Philadelphia into the twenty-first century.

After the Civil War, building on efforts of Black communities in the Philadelphia region to fight enslavement and discrimination, civil rights activists such as Octavius Catto and William Still worked to secure voting rights and equal access to public accommodations. Catto led the campaign for voting rights until he was assassinated on Election Day in 1871. Black men and women's efforts to desegregate the city's streetcars led the Pennsylvania state legislature to pass a law in 1867 requiring streetcar companies to carry passengers regardless of color. Such activism helped lead to the passage of the federal Civil Rights Act of 1875, which declared African Americans were entitled to equal treatment in public accommodations. Rev. Fields Cook tested the law and won a case against Philadelphia's Bingham House Hotel when he was denied a room in 1876.

The civil rights movement gained greater momentum in the early twentieth century with the Great Migration. The Black population in Philadelphia surged from some 63,000 people in 1900 to over 134,000 twenty years later. New arrivals lent their energy to the National Association for the Advancement of Colored People (NAACP), the National Urban League, and the city's Black newspaper, the *Philadelphia Tribune* (published by E. Washington Rhodes, est. 1884). Through these organizations, activists demanded greater access to jobs and adequate housing. Yet a brutal race riot over housing desegregation in 1918 that left four people dead and hundreds injured demonstrated that Philadelphia was not the land of hope that many prayed they had found.

FIGURE 61. Octavius V. Catto, 1871. After leading battles for suffrage and desegregation of Philadelphia streetcars, Catto was murdered on Election Day in 1871. LIBRARY OF CONGRESS.

Throughout the 1920s and 1930s, African Americans deepened their commitment to securing civil rights. In the 1920s, they expanded their access to residential areas in North, South, and West Philadelphia. They also supported a flowering of Black culture with authors such as Jessie Redmon Fauset from Fredericksville in Camden County, New Jersey, and venues such as the Dunbar Theatre at Broad and Lombard in Philadelphia, giving Philadelphia a smaller version of the Harlem Renaissance. The Great Depression devastated African American efforts to secure more housing and create a vibrant community and, in the process, radicalized Black political activism. In the early 1930s, African American unemployment crested at 61 percent, and tens of thousands of people lost their homes. In response, Black Philadelphians joined the Democratic Party, the National Negro Congress, and the Communist Party. They engaged in "Don't buy where you can't work" campaigns to pressure employers to end discrimination. And they demanded that political leaders meet a number of pressing needs: public housing to make up for the lack of decent and affordable housing, access to government-funded jobs, and an equal rights bill (passed by the state legislature in 1935) to once again guarantee access to public accommodations.

Demands for civil rights in the areas of jobs, housing, and political recognition continued into World War II. As the federal government poured billions of dollars into Philadelphia industries, African Americans flocked to the city. The Black population grew from some 250,000 in 1940 to 375,000 by the end of the war decade, and many of these residents supported the national Double V campaign that called for victory over fascism abroad and over Jim Crow at home. A presidential executive order, prompted by A. Philip Randolph's March on Washington movement, prohibited discrimination in hiring at industries receiving defense contracts and was a reminder that the federal government could be an ally in pushing for civil rights. Nonetheless, many companies tried to maintain a segmented system that confined Black workers to specific jobs. Employment practices at the Philadelphia Transportation Company, for example, led to a campaign promoted by the NAACP and its leader Carolyn D. Moore (who had started in the organization in Norristown, Pennsylvania) to secure driving jobs for African Americans. When the federal government ordered the desegregation of the workforce in August 1944, white workers staged one of the largest hate strikes of World War II, shutting down the city for nearly a week. African Americans also had to continue their struggle in the city's neighborhoods, where redlining and other discriminatory loan policies restricted African Americans to the most dilapidated communities. Federal Housing Administration policies as well as violence perpetrated by some white Philadelphians kept new public housing segregated as well.

The experience of World War II transformed civil rights in Philadelphia as the concerted efforts of the NAACP and local interracial organizations energized the Black community. Although there were fears that interracial strife would grow after the war, a strong economy and the diligence of the civil rights community prevented the rise of racial violence. Economic concerns took particular precedence in this era, as African Americans who had been hired in defense-related industries feared they would lose their jobs. Civil rights activists such as the Reverend E. Luther Cunningham seized the moment and in 1948 secured passage of a municipal fair employment practices ordinance that the state later adopted in similar form. New Jersey already had such a law on the books (passed in 1945), and Delaware added its own version of the law in 1960. Black Philadelphians also helped elect Democrat Joseph Clark as mayor in 1951, which cemented the political reorientation of the city and led to implementation of the Home Rule Charter that provided for a Commission on Human Relations, one of the first agencies in the nation dedicated to preventing discrimination.

Although the new Democratic administration paid greater attention to African American rights and increased civil service opportunities, deindustrialization and persistent housing segregation showed the need for continued civil rights agitation. Philadelphia lost some 250,000 industrial jobs between the 1950s and the 1980s, and as workplace opportunities evaporated many African Americans were disproportionately affected because they could not follow the jobs to the suburbs. Many white Philadelphians moved to suburban developments such as Levittown, Pennsylvania. Suburbanization freed up housing stock for some middle-class Black people to move into city neighborhoods that had previously been off limits, but racist lending practices and white violence meant most suburban housing excluded Black settlement. In 1957, a race riot broke out when white homeowners protested the arrival of the Myers family in Levittown.

White intransigence sharpened Black Philadelphians' commitment to a civil rights movement that transformed Philadelphia in the 1960s. Martin Luther King Jr. had been introduced to Satyagraha (Mahatma Gandhi's movement based on passive political resistance) in the late 1940s at Philadelphia's Fellowship House, an interracial organization. King studied at Crozer Theological Seminary in Chester, Pennsylvania, and lived in Camden, New Jersey, from 1949 to 1951. As a result, King was well acquainted with Philadelphia's civil rights community. Local civil rights activists provided moral and material support to King, who visited the city several times in the 1960s. Inspired by the national movement, local civil rights leaders such as the Reverend Leon Sullivan and NAACP branch president Cecil B. Moore employed new tactics. In 1960, Sullivan and other Black ministers launched a boycott of Tasty Baking Company, one of the city's largest businesses, over its refusal to hire Black workers. The success of the boycott influenced Moore to initiate street protests against racial discrimination in the construction industry and in food markets that did not hire Black people. This activism drew greater power with the passage of federal affirmative action legislation and found support from white allies in the Northern Student Movement, Fellowship House, and other area organizations.

While increasing protests contributed to a rising level of consciousness among Black Philadelphians, they were unable to stem the tide of frustration in the city's poorest communities, especially in North Philadelphia. In the early 1960s, North Philadelphia had the city's highest poverty and unemployment rates and tense relations with the police. On August 28, 1964, rioting broke out after an altercation between two Black motorists and two police officers. Hundreds were arrested and injured, and the

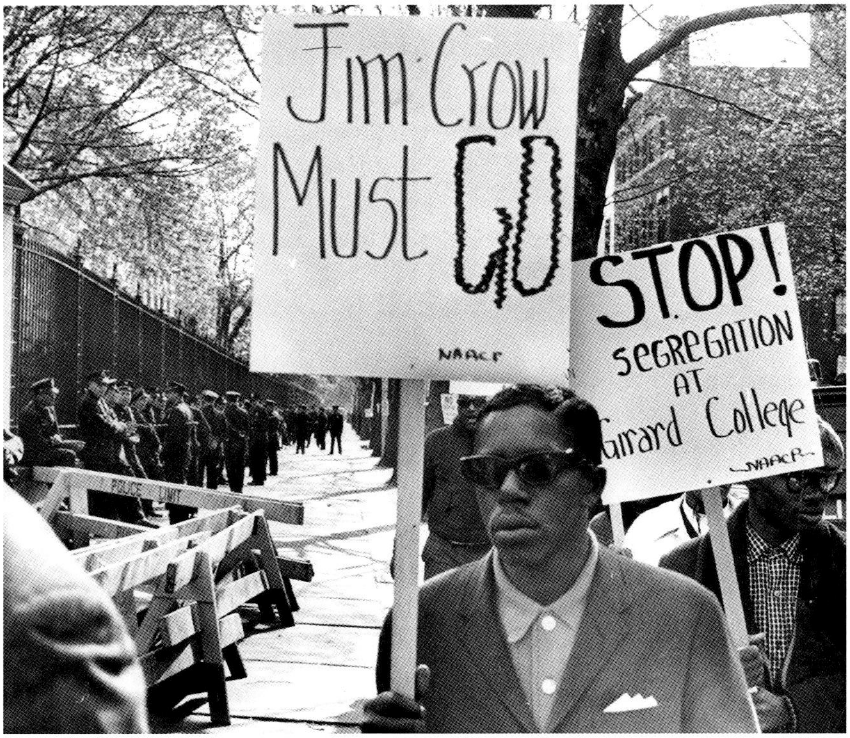

FIGURE 62. Demonstrators called for desegregation outside Girard College, 1965. SPECIAL COLLECTIONS RESEARCH CENTER, TEMPLE UNIVERSITY LIBRARIES.

uprising indicated the emergence of a new militancy among many Black Philadelphians. Some activists turned to more militant organizations such as the Nation of Islam, the Black Panthers, and the Black People's Unity Movement in Camden. Although the Philadelphia area had a long history of interracial civil rights organizing, an increasing number of activists influenced by Black Power ideology criticized the role of white people in the movement.

By the late 1960s, the Black Power movement had significant influence in the civil rights community. Both traditional civil rights activists and younger Black militants coalesced around the issue of education. Thousands protested the exclusion of African Americans from an all-white private school, Girard College, located in North Philadelphia. The movement against educational racism involved parents (mainly African American women), educators, and students. Black students criticized their inferior schools and dress codes that excluded traditional African garb, and they demanded a curriculum that included Black history. In late 1967, Black students launched a major protest at Board of Education headquarters and were attacked by police. The clash exemplified persistent tensions between the Black community and the police.

While street protests continued in the late 1960s, an increasing number of civil rights activists sought public office. Buoyed by the passage of significant federal civil rights legislation such as the Civil Rights Act of 1964 and the Fair Housing Act of 1968, these activists believed that they could considerably influence the political process. C. Delores Tucker became the first Black Pennsylvanian appointed to the office of secretary of state. David P. Richardson was elected to the Pennsylvania House of Representatives in 1972. In 1984, W. Wilson Goode became Philadelphia's first Black mayor. Although this new generation of political leaders had their roots in activism, their different power bases reflected an increasing maturation of the movement. Tucker had been active in the mainstream civil rights struggle and the rapidly emerging feminist movement. Richardson began his activism as a community organizer, while Goode's rise was propelled by his support among the city's Black religious establishment. Goode's success was in part fueled by the work of the city's first Black deputy mayor, Charles W. Bowser, who had run unsuccessfully for mayor in the 1970s. In turn, Goode's administration paved the way for future Black mayors John Street and Michael Nutter. While Black officials took power at a more formal level, a growing number of community-based organizations recognized the limits of their offices. The Kensington Welfare Rights Union, for example, articulated the demands of poor and working-class people of all races beyond what was provided in legislation.

Although the election of President Barack Obama demonstrated the gains made by civil rights activists, Black Philadelphians recognized the many problems they still faced. In the 2000s, Philadelphia's civil rights movement witnessed the emergence of organizations that addressed crime, joblessness, education, and immigration among other issues. In all, the changing demographics and economic environment of the Philadelphia region represented new challenges and extensions of old ones for the next generation of civil rights activists. Yet despite these challenges, the history of Philadelphia's civil rights movement demonstrated the gains African Americans made.

Black Power

Holly Genovese

Black Power, a movement significant to the Black freedom struggle in Philadelphia, came to prominence in the 1960s and 1970s through the combined efforts of local and national organizations including the Church of the Advocate, the Black Panther Party, the Black United Liberation Front, and MOVE. Before and after Stokely Carmichael of the national Student Nonviolent Coordinating Committee (SNCC) invoked the term Black Power in 1966, African American activists in the Philadelphia region fought for economic equality, educational equity, improved living conditions, and an end to police brutality.

Many advocates of Black Power had ties to the civil rights movement, but during the 1960s they diverged from its nonviolent stance and emphasized Black identity and empowerment through anti-poverty programs, self-defense, and diasporic connections with other oppressed people. Black Power stressed that Black people should be in control of Black communities. In Philadelphia, early Black Power initiatives included projects to raise awareness of African and African American history and culture, including the Freedom Library on Ridge Avenue in North Philadelphia, opened in 1964 by John Churchville. Churchville and other activists who gathered at Freedom Library formed Philadelphia's first Black Power political organization, the Black People's Unity Movement (BPUM), in 1965. An organization by the same name formed in Camden, New Jersey, in 1967.

In North Central Philadelphia, the Church of the Advocate, with a congregation becoming increasingly African American as white members moved from the city, became an important center of Black Power. Under the leadership of Father Paul Washington, one of the Freedom Library activists, the church and BPUM hosted a Black Unity rally in February 1966 that drew a capacity crowd to hear civil rights leader Julian Bond. Black Power rallies followed in locations around the city during the following summer, including two attended by Stokely Carmichael. In 1968, the church and BPUM also hosted the Third National Conference on Black Power, attended by two thousand people and leading to the creation of the Advocate Community Development Corporation and a Black activist newspaper, *Voice of Umoja*.

Church of the Advocate members included Reggie Schell, who in 1969 became the defense minister (leader) of the Philadelphia chapter of the Black Panther Party. The Black Panthers originally formed in 1966 in Oakland, California, to patrol and protect African American neighborhoods from police brutality. In Philadelphia, under Schell's leadership the local chapter expanded from its base in North Philadelphia to become influential throughout the city through a "Free Food for Survival" program, education programs, rallies, and other political events. The Black Power movement also spread to the region's college campuses, where sit-ins called for Black faculty and Black studies programs, and to high schools. Activism focused especially on control of the Philadelphia public schools. When Black students from a dozen Philadelphia high schools marched on a Philadelphia Board of Education meeting on November 17, 1967, with demands including Black history classes taught by Black teachers, many wore Black Power buttons.

The rising tide of Black activism and militancy so alarmed the Philadelphia Police Department that even the students marching on the school board were met with nightstick-wielding officers, commanded by then commissioner and future mayor Frank Rizzo. Police raided homes of Black Power activists and offices of organizations, and many local activists were followed by

FBI agents from COINTELPRO, a counterintelligence program that aimed to infiltrate U.S. political organizations, including the Black Panther Party. (COINTELPRO was discovered in 1971, when activists raided the Media, Pennsylvania, office of the FBI.)

On August 31, 1970, shortly before the Revolutionary People's Constitutional Convention held at Temple University and following a shooting of a white police officer by an African American man, Philadelphia police raided three Black Panther Party headquarters, including one near the campus on Columbia Avenue. The raids became internationally known for their brutality and visibility. Panther members were held at gunpoint, and many were publicly strip-searched before being taken to the police station. The bail for the Panthers was set at $100,000, but it was posted by the Philadelphia Yearly Meeting of the Society of Friends. The raids, ordered by Rizzo, did much to unite the NAACP and other stalwarts of the nonviolent civil rights movement with the Panthers. Although not entirely aligned politically, many Philadelphia activists united in their opposition to police brutality.

Despite the raids, the Revolutionary People's Constitutional Convention took place as scheduled at Temple University's McGonigle Hall in September 1970. The convention drew fourteen thousand participants, including Black Panther Party leaders from across the country, to hear speakers including Huey Newton. Activists gathered to draft a new constitution and attend workshops at the event, which the Black Panther Party declared successful. Many attendees, primarily women, felt differently and critiqued the masculinity and misogyny apparent in many of the activities. Still, the convention was one of the largest gatherings of radical activists in the United States.

Although the Black Panther Party declined in influence in the early 1970s, many advocates turned their interests toward diasporic connections and global injustice. Black Power activists in Philadelphia, for example, founded the Philadelphia Coalition to Stop Rhodesian and South African Imports to protest apartheid in South Africa. By the early 1970s, the Philadelphia chapter of the Black Panther Party disbanded but Reggie Schell and other local Panthers started the Black United Liberation Front, which continued much of their activism.

The legacy of Black Power lived on among other Philadelphia organizations and individuals. Black Power activism changed Philadelphia-area politics by making issues important to African Americans central to local governance and, eventually, by electing movement veterans to office. W. Wilson Goode, a West Philadelphia community organizer, became managing director of Philadelphia and its first African American mayor, serving from 1984 to 1992. Other veterans of the Black Power movement gained seats in the Pennsylvania General Assembly.

Although many have seen the disbanding of the Black Panther Party and the pursuit of prominent Black Power activists by law enforcement as failure of the movement, the Black Power movement left an important legacy in Philadelphia and across the country. The Church of the Advocate in North Philadelphia remained active in community-centered actions and social justice work, hosting a daily soup kitchen and youth programming. Prominent Philadelphia Black Panthers included Mumia Abu-Jamal, who joined the Black Panther Party at fourteen and became the local chapter's "lieutenant of information." His incarceration for the 1981 murder of Philadelphia police officer Daniel Faulkner and assertions of an unfair trial prompted global activism on his behalf. While imprisoned, Abu-Jamal became a vocal writer and activist for the rights of incarcerated people. Activists also pursued the release of jailed members of MOVE, the Black nationalist and anarcho-primitivist organization famously bombed by Philadelphia police in a 1985 standoff at a MOVE compound in West Philadelphia.

In both city government and radical activism across Philadelphia, the teachings and legacy of Black Power in Philadelphia remained prevalent. The Black Power movement of the 1960s and 1970s created the space for continued activism and political presence for African Americans in Philadelphia.

Lenape People (Continuing Presence)

Matthew J. Soderblom

As the original inhabitants of Pennsylvania, Delaware, New York, and New Jersey, the Lenape people have maintained an enduring presence in the region and a role in its development and heritage. Despite displacements

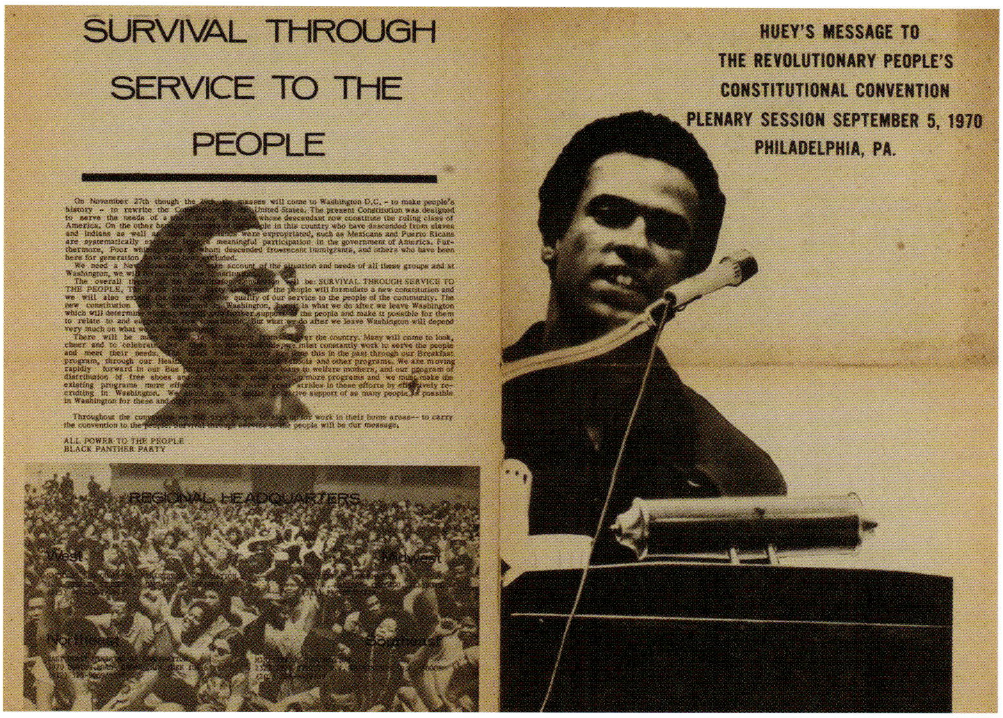

FIGURE 63. Report of the Plenary Session, Revolutionary People's Constitutional Convention, 1970. COLLECTION OF THE HISTORICAL SOCIETY OF PENNSYLVANIA.

by coercion and force during the seventeenth to nineteenth centuries, Lenape people remained in the Delaware Valley. Many hid their ancestry and embraced Anglo-American identities until the twentieth century, when groups emerged in southeastern Pennsylvania, Delaware, and New Jersey to continue tribal traditions through education and cultural preservation.

Prior to European colonization, Lenape territory (the *Lenapehoking*) encompassed the areas of later New York City, western Connecticut, southern New York, eastern Pennsylvania, the entirety of New Jersey, and, in Delaware, the land along the western bank of the Delaware River and Bay to at least Cape Henlopen. From the moment of first contact with Europeans in the sixteenth century, the Lenape people engaged in cultural and commercial exchanges with Europeans in the *Lenapehoking*, including Swedish, Finnish, Dutch, English, French, German, and other colonists. While influential in the region throughout the sixteenth, seventeenth, and eighteenth centuries, under the pressure of European settlement Lenape people faced removal to the western United States or Eastern Canada. Among the latest to move were the residents of the Brotherton reservation in New Jersey, who relocated to areas near Oneida Lake in New York, selling their lands in 1802 and their remaining hunting and fishing rights in 1832.

Lenape descendants stayed in the region in various small communities, but records of their lives and public presence in the nineteenth century are rare. In New Jersey, records document Lenape children who served as indentured servants to white merchants and farmers. Lenape existence remained somewhat obscure to non-Native people until the middle of the twentieth century. Then, on the heels of the civil rights movement and influenced by the American Indian Movement (AIM), Lenape people of the Greater Philadelphia region pursued greater self-determination, seeking to exercise their right to define their own identities and cultural expression. The many groups that formed in Pennsylvania, New Jersey, and Delaware included the Nanticoke Lenni-Lenape Tribal Nation (NLL), which became a formal entity on August 7, 1978, with New Jersey state recognition granted in 1982, and the Lenape Nation of Pennsylvania (LNPA), which formed in the 1990s.

Among the numerous groups in eastern Pennsylvania, southern New York, New Jersey, and northern Delaware, the LNPA became one of the most active. While neither a federally recognized nor a state-recognized tribe (Pennsylvania did not have an office of Indian affairs or any process of state recognition), the organization gained 501(c)(3) status in 2001. Headquartered in Easton, Pennsylvania, the LNPA has hosted traditional ceremonies, maintained a cultural heritage center and museum, organized Lenape language education programs, and engaged in community service. The group has sought to explain Indigenous history and assert that the original inhabitants of Pennsylvania did not simply disappear in the face of aggressive European American expansion. Its activities have included a quadrennial "Rising Nation River Journey" trip down the length of the Delaware River (from Hancock, New York, to Cape May, New Jersey), which had a mission of signing new treaties of friendship and brotherhood with local churches, educational institutions, environmental preservation groups, and historical societies. This activity sought to continue traditions of goodwill that began with meetings and treaties between William Penn and Chief Tamanend in the 1680s. The LNPA also initiated yearly friendship treaty signings at Temple University and other Philadelphia-region universities. Close ties with Temple also resulted in a celebration of Indigenous Peoples' Day on October 14, 2019. The LNPA's relationship with the Tri-College Consortium (Haverford, Bryn Mawr, and Swarthmore Colleges) culminated in the offering of Lenape language classes at Swarthmore and presentations, conferences, and other events at Haverford and Bryn Mawr.

The Nanticoke Lenni-Lenape Tribal Nation has maintained a strong presence in southern New Jersey. Centered in Bridgeton, they became one of the state's three recognized tribes, which also included Ramapough Lenape Indian Nation of Mahwah, Bergen County, and the Powhatan Renape of Rancocas, Burlington County. The NLL has taken a confederated approach to the process of recognition with members from various Nanticoke and Lenape groups. Led for many years by Mark "Quiet Hawk" Gould, the group sought to unite the Indigenous community within southern New Jersey and further assert Indigenous identity in their historical homeland. The tribe has held many gatherings, participated in community outreach programs in Bridgeton and Philadelphia, and worked alongside other Lenape and Nanticoke entities within the region.

Among the most vibrant Indigenous groups in the area, in 1995 the NLL community resecured their tribal grounds in Fairton, New Jersey. Their church, Saint John United Methodist Church (UMC) in Fordville, was designated a historically Native American church by the New Jersey annual conference of the UMC. This led to similar recognition by the national General Conference of the Methodist Church in 2017. During the 2020 coronavirus pandemic, members of the church and NLL provided food and relief to the community (especially in Fairfield Township).

Together with the Nanticoke Tribe of Delaware and the Lenape Indian Tribe of Delaware, the Nanticoke Lenni-Lenape formed the Confederation of Sovereign Nentego-Lenape Tribes on May 20, 2007. Akin to the NLL, the Nanticoke Tribe of Delaware, based in Sussex County, and the Lenape Indian Tribe of Delaware, in the Dover area, also sought to preserve the region's Indigenous heritage. Both tribes received state recognition. The Nanticoke of Delaware maintained a museum and cultural center in Millsboro, Delaware. Both Delaware groups participated in powwows, helped maintain the confederation's online museum, and fostered community among Indigenous peoples of the region.

Descendants of the original inhabitants of the Greater Philadelphia region persisted despite the ravages of colonization and forced assimilation. Their resilience has been a testament to the strength of their ancestors; their efforts in education and community outreach have had an enduring effect on the region and its citizens. By preserving their culture, these groups have ensured the place of Lenape people not only in the history of the region but in its future.

Civil Rights (LGBT)

Dan Royles

In the second half of the twentieth century, a growing number of lesbian, gay, bisexual, and transgender (LGBT) Americans claimed political rights as people whose same-sex desire or gender presentation challenged prevailing social mores. As movements for African

American, Latino American, and women's rights gained traction and visibility, so too did movements for LGBT civil rights. In this context, LGBT activists in Greater Philadelphia pressed for the extension of the rights and protections that would signal their inclusion in American society. By the time the Supreme Court legalized same-sex marriage in the landmark case of *Obergefell v. Hodges* in 2015, LGBT Philadelphians could point to victories at the local and state levels, achieved through a combination of theatrical protest and political advocacy. At the same time, however, Pennsylvania lagged behind New Jersey, Delaware, and other northeastern states in the civil rights afforded to LGBT residents.

Displays of homosexual affection and cross-dressing had been part of public life in cities like Philadelphia going back to the colonial period. However, it was not until the decades following World War II that such practices, and the sexual and gender identities associated with them, became explicitly politicized. During the 1950s and 1960s, the first gay and lesbian civil rights protests in Philadelphia reflected the growing political consciousness of homophile activists. These demonstrations also borrowed tactics from the much more widespread movement for Black civil rights unfolding at the same time.

The first documented public protest for LGBT civil rights in the city began with a sit-in. On April 25, 1965, Dewey's, a diner near Rittenhouse Square with a large clientele of gay youth, drag queens, and sex workers, began refusing to serve customers who appeared to be gay or lesbian, as well as those wearing clothing that did not match their gender. After more than 150 such customers had been denied service, three teenagers refused to leave and were arrested. Over the next five days, members of the Janus Society, a local gay and lesbian political group, protested outside of Dewey's, distributing their literature to passersby. On May 2, one week after the first sit-in, a group of teenagers staged a second protest. This time, no arrests were made, and the restaurant resumed serving LGBT customers.

Although the Dewey's sit-ins showed that some gay and lesbian activists were willing to stand up for those who publicly dressed and acted in unconventional ways, most hewed to a politics of respectability. They described themselves as "homophiles" rather than "homosexuals" in order to distance themselves from sexual acts, a strategy that many saw as a necessary step toward inclusion in American society. The Annual Reminder demonstrations, held in front of Independence Hall every Fourth of July from 1965 to 1969, also reflected this concern. As they protested anti-sodomy laws, the firing of gay men and lesbians from federal employment, and their exclusion from military service, Annual Reminder marchers dressed professionally and in ways that conformed to gender expectations, with men in suits, jackets, and slacks, and women in dresses. The choice of time and place for the demonstrations underscored the marchers' political claims. In contrast to the counterculture and anti-war movements, which criticized U.S. society as crassly commercial and militaristic, Annual Reminder marchers situated themselves squarely within American identity by marching on July Fourth in the place where the nation's founding documents had been written and signed.

In the early 1970s, homophile activism gave way to gay liberation, although the more radical goals and tactics of gay liberation groups did not preclude their involvement in conventional politics. The Homophile Action League and the Gay Activists Alliance, which staked out more militant positions than their Annual Reminder predecessors, pressed local lawmakers to extend Philadelphia's antidiscrimination protections to gay men and lesbians. In 1974 the city council held hearings on a bill to add sexual orientation to the city's Fair Practices Ordinance, to outlaw anti-gay discrimination in employment, housing, and public accommodations. However, with vocal opposition from both council members and religious leaders, including members of Philadelphia's Black clergy, the bill failed to make it out of committee. Opponents of the measure contended that race and sexual orientation were fundamentally different and questioned gay and lesbian activists' attempts to claim protections as an aggrieved minority alongside African Americans, Jews, and other historically persecuted groups.

In 1978, activists with the Christian Association, a philanthropic group at the University of Pennsylvania, organized the Philadelphia Lesbian and Gay Task Force (PLGTF) to advocate for sexual rights in the city. Under the leadership of Rev. James Littrell and Rita Addessa, the group's first two executive directors, PLGTF forged alliances with local African American

FIGURE 64. Picket line outside of Independence Hall, first Annual Reminder demonstration, July 4, 1965, photograph by Kay Tobin. ©MANUSCRIPTS AND ARCHIVES DIVISION, THE NEW YORK PUBLIC LIBRARY.

political and religious leaders. When a second effort to amend the Fair Practices Ordinance went before city council in 1982, W. Wilson Goode, the city manager who later became Philadelphia's first African American mayor, and members of the newly visible Black gay community testified in support. With broadened support for gay and lesbian civil rights, the bill passed. In 1983, Harrisburg, the state capital, revised its City Code to include protections against discrimination based on sexual orientation and gender identity. Lancaster similarly added sexual orientation as a protected class to its Codified Ordinances in 1991. York added an antidiscrimination measure covering sexual orientation to its City Code in 1993 and a measure covering gender identity in 1998.

In the 1990s, LGBT activists, along with allies in local government, pressed for domestic partnership laws in the city. City council member Angel Ortiz and Mayor Edward G. Rendell introduced different bills providing for domestic partnership recognition and benefits in 1993. The bills failed as opponents, including Council President John F. Street, argued that domestic partnerships would undermine traditional family structures. In June 1996, Rendell signed an executive order granting benefits to the domestic partners of some five hundred city employees, representing only a fraction of the almost twenty-six thousand working in local government. Street vocally opposed the measure, joining with Catholic archbishop Anthony Bevilacqua and the Black Clergy of Philadelphia and Vicinity to reverse the order. Rendell refused, and a trio of domestic partnership bills passed the council in 1998, granting health and pensions benefits to the "life partners" of city employees.

In 2013, the city council expanded life partnership provisions to include hospital visitation with the passage of the LGBT Equality Bill, which also added gender identity to the city's nondiscrimination ordinance and offered tax credits to companies that expanded their employee benefits to include coverage of transgender-specific health care and health benefits for same-sex domestic partners. In May 2014, a federal district court judge ruled that the state's ban on same-sex marriage was unconstitutional. The following year, in June 2015, the United States Supreme Court invalidated similar state-level prohibitions, clearing the way for same-sex marriage across the country.

The twenty-first century also brought a greater focus on the rights of transgender people. In 2009, Philadelphia activists formed Riders Against Gender Exclusion (RAGE) with the goal of eliminating gender identification stickers from Southeastern Pennsylvania Transportation Authority (SEPTA) TransPasses. RAGE members argued that the stickers opened a risk of embarrassment and harassment of people whose outward gender expression did not match the stickers on their cards. Over the course of a three-year campaign, the group collected stories of harassment from transgender and gender nonconforming SEPTA riders, staged a protest drag show inside a SEPTA station, and interrupted a public SEPTA hearing to present officials with a six-foot-long "RAGE Rider's Bill of Rights" outlining their demands. On July 1, 2013, for the first time in thirty-two years, SEPTA riders were able to use TransPass cards without the gender identification stickers.

Beginning in the late 1980s, Philadelphia LGBT activists and their allies also worked to add sexual orientation and gender identity to existing hate-crime laws. The PLGTF made anti-gay violence a political issue as early as 1986, and in 1990 state representative Babette Josephs introduced an unsuccessful bill that would have extended the state's hate-crime law to cover sexual orientation. The 1998 killing of University of Wyoming student Matthew Shepard, which became a national news story, revived local interest in the issue. Weeks after Shepard's death, the PLGTF organized a protest at the Liberty Bell to call for a state-level hate-crime law covering sexual orientation. In 2002, after the brutal beating in Middleburg, Pennsylvania, of a man who was perceived to be gay, the state legislature finally passed a bill that expanded Pennsylvania's Ethnic Intimidation Act to include sexuality and gender identity. However, the state supreme court struck down the 2002 expansion of the law in 2008.

Following a highly publicized attack on two gay men in Center City in September 2014, the Philadelphia City Council passed its own hate-crime bill. Pennsylvania lawmakers also introduced, but never voted on, hate-crime legislation covering sexual orientation and gender identity at the state level. In contrast, New Jersey added sexual orientation to its hate-crime statute in 1990 and did the same for gender identity in 2008. Wilmington, Delaware, added a provision for hate crimes based on sexual orientation to its City Code in 1992. The state of Delaware added sexual identity to its own hate-crime statute in 1998, followed by gender identity in 2013.

Pennsylvania similarly lagged behind its neighbors in guaranteeing LGBT civil rights. Although Pennsylvania became the first state to ban sexual-orientation discrimination in state employment, under a 1975 executive order by Governor Milton Shapp, as of July 2023, Pennsylvania had no law barring discrimination against LGBT people in housing, employment, and public accommodations. In contrast, New Jersey's Law Against Discrimination included provisions for sexual orientation beginning in 1991 and for gender identity and expression beginning in 2006. Delaware passed legislation barring discrimination based on sexual orientation in 2009 and a similar law against discrimination based on gender identity and expression in 2013. In Pennsylvania, state legislators in 2023 continued to press for legislation against discrimination based on sexual orientation and gender identity or expression.

The struggle for LGBT civil rights in Philadelphia after World War II yielded important gains for people who had been vulnerable to discrimination and harassment on account of their sexual and gender identities. Activists also won recognition for same-sex couples, first in Philadelphia, then in Pennsylvania, and, finally, nationwide. In so doing, they challenged prevailing ideas of sexual citizenship and laid claim to both symbolic and material forms of belonging in American society. At the same time, the periodic failures and reversals suffered by activists exposed the extent to which LGBT Philadelphians were impacted by local, state, and federal policies—and the work that remained to be done.

Civil Rights (Persons with Disabilities)

Charlene Mires

Philadelphia-area people with disabilities and their allies joined the nationwide escalation of activism for civil rights during the second half of the twentieth century. Their protests and legal actions forced substandard institutions to close and liberate their residents. They also held local authorities accountable for implementing landmark federal legislation to improve accessibility, especially on public transportation, and to secure equal opportunity for work and education. Into the twenty-first century, individuals with disabilities and their allies remained vigilant to prevent the erosion of hard-won victories.

The disability rights movement of the twentieth century challenged decades of social and legal restrictions placed on persons with disabilities by states and localities. During the nineteenth century, these included barring people perceived as impaired from casting ballots; New Jersey and Delaware were among the states whose early constitutions banned any "idiot or insane person" from voting. Almshouses, asylums, hospitals, and other institutions confined many physically and mentally disabled people, effectively incarcerating them for life. Across the nation, cities enacted ordinances later known as "ugly laws" to outlaw people considered "deformed" from being seen in public. By the late nineteenth century, the pseudoscience of eugenics sought to prevent future generations of "defectives" through laws to ban marriages and require sterilizations, including statutes enacted in New Jersey and Delaware (but not Pennsylvania).

The disability rights movement emerged from a combination of factors in the decades following World War II. Wounded veterans from two world wars, together with survivors of recent epidemics of polio, expanded the population of people with disabilities who needed public and private support. Meanwhile, the emphasis on individual freedom and human rights voiced by the federal government during the war and subsequently by the United Nations provided a vocabulary for pursuing civil rights on many fronts. People with disabilities, their families, and allies embraced this framework and embarked on strategies similar to those deployed by African Americans, women, and other groups seeking their full rights as citizens. Activists in the preceding movements at times worked in tandem with the quest for disability rights.

Parents of children with disabilities were among the earliest to organize to advocate for equal access to education and quality of care in residential treatment facilities. Local chapters of national organizations focusing on specific conditions, such as cerebral palsy, formed throughout the Greater Philadelphia region to raise awareness and funding. During the 1950s, a time of idealization of family life, parents called attention to disability as an experience that could affect any family. Author Pearl S. Buck, living in Bucks County, Pennsylvania, encouraged parents across the nation to share their stories when she published *The Child Who Never Grew* (1950) about seeking care for her daughter, Carol, at the Training School at Vineland, New Jersey. Buck later chaired the Governor's Committee on Handicapped Children formed in Pennsylvania in 1958. Parental concern led another Pennsylvania governor, Richard L. Thornburgh, to become an early advocate for disability rights after one of his sons suffered a brain injury. Later, as U.S. attorney general, Thornburgh helped secure passage of the 1990 Americans with Disabilities Act.

Parent advocacy groups based in Philadelphia included the Pennsylvania Association for Retarded Children (PARC), organized in 1949. A member of PARC triggered a chain of events with national implications in 1968 by encouraging local television reporter Bill Baldini to expose horrendous conditions at the Pennhurst State School and Hospital in Chester County, Pennsylvania. A subsequent class-action lawsuit, *PARC v. Pennsylvania*, resulted in a consent decree ordering the state to provide access to free public education to "retarded" children. The case, argued by the Public Interest Law Center of Philadelphia, provoked similar lawsuits that culminated with the federal Education for All Handicapped Children Act, passed in 1975.

Years of additional litigation on behalf of Pennhurst residents, including *Halderman v. Pennhurst* (filed 1974)

FIGURE 65. Disability rights patriots, 1989, photograph by Tom Olin. Activists from the disability rights group ADAPT proceeded from Independence Hall to the Liberty Bell on the eve of a federal court case heard in Philadelphia to challenge regulatory limits on accessible public transportation. Their choice of this historic setting called attention to the irony of limits placed on their independence and civil rights. TOM OLIN COLLECTION.

and *Youngberg v. Romeo* (filed 1976), culminated with closing the institution in 1987. Other institutions across the nation shut down as the Public Interest Law Center trained attorneys in other states to apply their strategies. In 2002 the Law Center filed a class action in Delaware that led to a settlement for greater access to community services for people with developmental disabilities housed in the Stockley Center in Sussex County. Individuals with developmental disabilities also organized to speak on their own behalf with the group Speaking For Ourselves, which originated in Montgomery County in 1982 and expanded with chapters elsewhere in the region.

Legal actions for equal opportunity in education further included the 1993 case *Oberti v. Board of Education of the Borough of Clementon (New Jersey)*, which secured classroom support for a student with Down syndrome. In Pennsylvania, the class action *Gaskin v. Commonwealth* in 1994 called attention to needs for greater compliance with the federal Individuals with Disabilities Education Act (IDEA).

In pursuit of accessibility and independent living, adults with disabilities mobilized from the 1960s through the end of the century to insist that federal laws such as the Architectural Barriers Act of 1968 were fully implemented. In Philadelphia and South Jersey, activists pressed SEPTA (the Southeastern Pennsylvania Transportation Authority) and PATCO (the Port Authority Transit Corporation) to make trains, buses, and subways fully accessible. In Philadelphia, the long campaign of attending meetings, staging protests, and filing lawsuits was led by the Pennsylvania chapter of

Disabled in Action, an advocacy group founded in New York in 1970 by Philadelphia-born Judith E. Heumann. A survivor of childhood polio and wheelchair user, raised in Brooklyn, Heumann waged a highly publicized and successful battle to gain a teaching license in New York City. She remained a prominent leader of the disability rights movement throughout her life, including an appointment as assistant secretary of the Office of Special Education and Rehabilitation Services at the U.S. Department of Education during the Clinton administration.

Philadelphia attorney Stephen F. Gold represented individuals, Disabled in Action, and the organization known as ADAPT (American Disabled for Accessible Public Transit) in lawsuits over accessibility and equal opportunity. A New York–based group founded by veterans with spinal cord injuries, the Eastern Paralyzed Veterans Association, included Philadelphia and South Jersey in a series of 1988 lawsuits to secure greater elevator access to subway stations. The organization prevailed in seeking installation of an elevator in the transportation center then under construction in downtown Camden, where the PATCO Speedline ran underground. Similarly, the U.S. District Court found that SEPTA discriminated against persons with disabilities by failing to comply with federal laws and regulations when renovating subway facilities.

Following passage of the federal Americans with Disabilities Act of 1990, Disabled in Action and twelve individuals with disabilities filed a lawsuit in 1992 to require the City of Philadelphia to install curb ramps (curb cuts) as part of any street resurfacing project. The successful suit, argued by Gold, set a precedent for other cities across the country. Curb ramps remained a decades-long issue in Philadelphia, leading to another lawsuit by Disabled in Action and others in 2019. The resulting settlement agreement, approved in 2023, ordered the City of Philadelphia to install or repair at least ten thousand curb cuts over the next fifteen years.

The disability rights movement in Greater Philadelphia unfolded through the efforts of multiple organizations and individuals, often setting nationally significant precedents. Throughout the region, vigilance by local activists remained necessary into the twenty-first century to secure and expand the civil rights of persons with disabilities.

American Civil Liberties Union

Will Caverly

The American Civil Liberties Union (ACLU), a national legal organization dedicated to the defense and preservation of civil liberties in the United States, has been organized in the Philadelphia region since 1951, when chapters formed in Pennsylvania and New Jersey as part of a move toward establishing branches throughout the nation. Both chapters played a role in the civil liberties history of the region.

The national ACLU grew out of curtailments of civil liberties during and after World War I. The organization's activity in the Philadelphia region began even before formation of the local chapter, most notably when it protested bans of the film *Birth of a Nation* (1915) as it continued to be shown in Philadelphia, Newark, Jersey City, and Detroit in 1921. This, along with the ACLU's support for the free speech rights of the Ku Klux Klan, drew criticism from the National Association for the Advancement of Colored People (NAACP) in its attempts to ban the film's premiere and protect critics of the film.

The Greater Philadelphia chapter of the ACLU originated when the Citizens' Council on Democratic Rights, a Philadelphia group devoted to the protection of individual civic freedoms, voted to affiliate with the national ACLU in late 1951. The Citizens' Council on Democratic Rights had been involved with the controversial Loyalty Review Boards that were part of President Harry S. Truman's probes into the loyalty of government employees, hosting lawyers from the national ACLU for open meetings on the subject as late as 1950. Having made the transition to ACLU affiliate status, the newly minted chapter focused on advocacy, public education, and litigation to preserve and enhance civil liberties.

Under Spencer Coxe's tenure as the first full-time director, the organization's litigator and board president Henry Sawyer represented the family of Edward Schempp before the Supreme Court in *Abington School District v. Schempp* (1963). The Schempp family disputed whether the Abington School District could require their children to read and recite the Bible in a public school setting. The Supreme Court ruled in favor of the Schempp family and affirmed the separation of church and state in public schools, making the case the organization's first significant victory. The decision resulted in changes in how education was carried out across the country, with reports of policy confusion among superintendents becoming common as they struggled with the implications of the decision.

As the ACLU presence in Pennsylvania grew, the Philadelphia office worked in conjunction with other offices in the state. The Philadelphia chapter, despite opposition from community groups, was vociferous in opposing mandatory minimum sentencing for repeat offenders and for individuals who committed violent crimes on public transportation. The Philadelphia chapter's stances on issues such as these in the early 1980s were consistent with the broader goals of the ACLU, which advocated alternatives to incarceration.

The ACLU's positions at times placed it at odds with city and state officials and governments. During the Newark riots of 1967, for example, the New Jersey chapter documented police abuses. In 1985 the Philadelphia ACLU, in conjunction with the wider state organization, sued the City of Philadelphia for the closure of its largest homeless shelter. In *Committee for Dignity and Fairness for the Homeless et al. v. Pernsley* the City of Philadelphia entered into a settlement, agreeing to house the homeless in compliance with the Pennsylvania State Department of Welfare's regulations regarding their care.

More recently, the New Jersey ACLU challenged the state's abortion laws, overturning a ban on late term abortion in 1998 and laws requiring the consent of parents for a minor's abortion procedure in 2000. In 2012, the organization represented residents of Newark in their case against their city's alleged nondisclosure of plans for $100 million donated by Facebook CEO Mark Zuckerberg for use in the city's public schools.

The Pennsylvania and New Jersey chapters have continued to represent citizens in cases with potential for lasting impact on civil liberties. These cases include disputes over freedom of speech, the press, expression, and religion, as well as cases involving police misconduct, racial discrimination, reproductive freedom, and children's, immigrant, and women's rights. The branches operate with both staff and volunteer legal assistance and are 501(c)(3) nonprofit organizations.

Gray Panthers

Emily Krichbaum

In 1970, Philadelphian Maggie Kuhn, a white middle-class woman and frustrated victim of mandatory retirement at age sixty-five, formed an anti-ageist organization called the Gray Panthers. From challenging mandatory retirement to critiquing ageist media depictions of older Americans, the Gray Panthers fought to recreate the image, expectations, and roles of middle-class retirees in American society. Inspired by social movements of the 1960s, emboldened by their own lengthy activist backgrounds, and frustrated by the absence of an anti-ageist movement, these Gray Panther activists remained politically and socially active by fighting against ageism in their retirement years.

After being subjected to mandatory retirement in 1970, months before her sixty-fifth birthday, Kuhn along with five other older, professional women facing retirement founded the Consultation of Older Persons, later named the Gray Panthers. A janitor's broom closet in the Tabernacle Church in West Philadelphia served as their first office, and retirees volunteered their time to organize local events. These women believed that older persons were "a great national resource which has largely been unrecognized, undervalued and unused" and that retirees should remain politically and socially "involved in new and significant ways." The movement quickly gained overwhelming support as thousands, both young and old, joined the Gray Panthers to fight against ageism.

In 1972, Kuhn, by then sixty-seven and nationally recognized, addressed reporters and introduced the radical Gray Panthers to the nation as a new liberation movement to motivate seniors to "get out of their rocking chairs and into public affairs." This movement was unlike the economic-driven struggles during the 1930s and the membership organizations for retirees founded during the 1950s and 1960s. Distinctly, Kuhn mobilized the elderly toward social activism. The Gray Panthers was an organization of the aged acting on behalf of the aged. Kuhn and the Gray Panthers encouraged grassroots organization and emboldened older, retired Americans to be vocal and active in society and address political issues that both applied to their specific age-based concerns and transcended age.

FIGURE 66. Maggie Kuhn, by Bachrach Photographers, ca. 1984. SPECIAL COLLECTIONS RESEARCH CENTER, TEMPLE UNIVERSITY LIBRARIES.

The organization's greatest accomplishments included a role in changing mandatory retirement laws, reforming nursing homes, critiquing media depictions of older Americans, and raising public awareness to the vulnerability of older people. Gray Panther members regularly testified before the United States Congress, served on the White House Council on Aging, and helped found the Older Women's League, the Black Caucus for the Aged, the National Shared Housing Resource Center, and the National Citizens' Coalition for Nursing Home Reform. At one point, the Gray Panthers recorded over seventy-five thousand members and 122 networks in forty-three states throughout the nation.

In one example of their activist activity, during the 1976 Christmas season, the Gray Panthers picketed businesses in Philadelphia and Chicago. After being informed that all John Wanamaker department store employees over the age of sixty-five would be let go on Christmas Eve, the Gray Panthers networks in Philadelphia and South Jersey staged a two-hour demonstration at the stores, handing out over three thousand pink slips to shoppers "telling the story of Scrooge Reincarnated." That same week in Chicago, Gray Panthers in Santa Claus suits picketed the department store Carson, Pirie, Scott for its mandatory retirement policies. Standing on State Street, Panthers held signs that read, "Santa Claus is too old to work for Carson, Pirie, Scott." The protesting Santa Clauses sang Christmas carols such as "Deck the Halls" and abruptly stopped and pulled enormous white handkerchiefs to cry into. Both events were well covered by local news and radio stations.

The Gray Panther networks served as gatherings where older, predominantly white middle-class Americans came together to critique social, economic, and cultural expectations of the aged, redefine old age, and be empowered. Indeed, older Americans challenged the social and cultural expectations of older people in various spheres, eschewed images of the aged as static, traditional, and sedentary individuals, and fought to create a new image of older Americans as dynamic, productive, and a necessary component of American society.

The Gray Panthers continued to be active in the early decades of the twenty-first century, though on a much smaller scale. Their national office moved to Washington, D.C., and networks existed in many states—some more active than others. Their primary concerns focused on universal health care, protecting the environment, promoting peace, civil rights and liberties, as well as jobs and economic security, extending the legacy of the Philadelphia-born Gray Panthers.

Occupy Philadelphia

John E. Smith III

For fifty-six days between October 6 and November 30, 2011, local activists participated in Occupy Philadelphia—a leaderless, decentralized movement against social and economic inequality. Their action joined an international wave of dissent against political and economic corruption that ranged from anti-austerity protests in Europe to the Arab Spring demonstrations throughout North Africa and the Middle East. Occupy movements in cities across the globe united protesters and inspired change.

In Philadelphia, the Occupy movement unofficially began on September 29, 2011, when a general assembly of activists gathered at the Arch Street United Methodist Church. A few days later, on October 4, a second meeting attracted an even larger crowd to plan a protest similar to the ongoing, nearly month-long Occupy Wall Street demonstration in New York City's Zuccotti Park. At the meeting, the group determined where and when to begin the occupation of a public space in Philadelphia. Possible locations included Love Park, Rittenhouse Square, Independence Hall, and the Benjamin Franklin Parkway. After much discussion, the group agreed to begin the demonstration on October 6 at Dilworth Plaza adjacent to Philadelphia City Hall—the epicenter of Philadelphia's political bureaucracy.

Occupy Philadelphia transcended age, race, religion, and political affiliation. This diversity generated incoherent messages, as some protested against corporate greed, bank bailouts, big money's influence on elections, and other economic injustices, while others protested police brutality, foreign wars, and social conservatism. Although people joined the movement for vastly different reasons, collectively the group identified as "the 99 percent." They argued that a disproportionate 1 percent of the population controlled the majority of political power and wealth. While some opponents criticized the group's lack of specific goals, members emphasized the movement's ability to unite dissimilar political factions and rally around a broader message.

A city of tents occupied Dilworth Plaza on the west side of City Hall for eight weeks as Occupy Philadelphia activists executed their public protest with no anticipated end date. The camp included a first-aid station, library and education center, food station, and meeting areas for various subcommittees. Over time, the camp attracted the participation of many of the city's houseless population and raised public concern regarding crime and sanitation.

Throughout the occupation, demonstrators practiced peaceful, nonviolent protest methods including chanting slogans, raising signs, and practicing civil disobedience. Many felt empowered to join the movement because of support from the American Civil Liberties Union and the National Lawyers Guild, who led "Know Your Rights" trainings during the early days of the occupation. Occupy Philadelphia organized several marches across the city to parade their strength in numbers to locations including to the Liberty Bell, Wells Fargo Bank, the Comcast Center, and Rittenhouse Hotel where Republican presidential candidate Mitt Romney held a fundraising event. On October 21, U.S. House majority leader Eric Cantor of Virginia canceled a scheduled talk at the University of Pennsylvania when protesters announced plans to rally outside Penn's Huntsman Hall in an event dubbed "Occupy Cantor."

Occupy Philadelphia attracted the attention of both local and national progressive leaders who spoke in support of the movement. Visitors to the encampment included scholar-activist and author Angela Davis, City University of New York professor Frances Fox Piven, and civil rights activist Jesse Jackson. Philadelphia mayor Michael Nutter (who was up for reelection on November 8, 2011) expressed support throughout the occupation, stating that he too identified as the 99 percent. Despite the endorsement, many Occupy protesters questioned whether the mayor served as a genuine ally or simply offered his sympathies to avoid becoming a target. Opponents criticized the mayor's legislative track record and suggested his policies did not align with his public statements. They pointed specifically to Nutter's cuts to education and public services like libraries, pools, recreation centers, and the Fire Department.

On November 16, city officials posted public notices throughout the encampment ordering protesters to evacuate Dilworth Plaza so a previously planned $50 million renovation project could commence. Unsure of when the police would raid the camp, anticipation grew and many of the occupiers dispersed. Two weeks later, in the early morning hours of November 30, Philadelphia police evacuated the Occupy Philadelphia encampment using heavy equipment to remove the remaining debris. Lingering protesters trekked around Center City until 5 a.m., when police arrested around fifty people on charges including obstruction of a highway, failure to disperse, and conspiracy (most were later acquitted on all charges). At 7 a.m., Nutter spoke with the media and declared the occupation "over."

Although Occupy Philadelphia failed to produce direct legislation, it helped introduce economic inequality into a broader political discourse. The widening gap between rich and poor became a major talking point during the 2012 presidential election. Locally, the 2011 Occupy Philadelphia movement mobilized progressive activists and prepared them for future protests, including demonstrations following the 2016 presidential election and the 2018 Occupy ICE protest at the Immigration and Customs Enforcement Agency's office in Philadelphia. Occupy Philadelphia may have lasted only for a few weeks in the fall of 2011, but the movement's ideas and messages remained relevant in shaping Philadelphia's image as a progressive American city.

Black Lives Matter

Gwendolyn Fowler

Black Lives Matter (BLM) as an organization and a movement came to public attention after the deaths of two young Black men, Trayvon Martin in Sanford, Florida, and Mike Brown in Ferguson, Missouri. A Philadelphia chapter of the decentralized, nonhierarchical movement officially formed in May 2015. With direct ties to earlier civil rights era organizations, the movement has continued the Black freedom struggle against systemic racism and anti-Black violence, and its manifesto echoed the politics of Black feminist groups like the Combahee River Collective and the Third World Women's Alliance. Within a decade, Black Lives Matter grew from a social media hashtag to a movement estimated to include between fifteen million and twenty-six million people in the United States alone by 2020, when worldwide protests responded to the murder of another Black man, George Floyd, in Minneapolis, Minnesota.

The movement began in 2013 in response to the acquittal of George Zimmerman, a white vigilante, for the killing of Trayvon Martin. Three Black women, Alicia Garza, Patrisse Cullors, and Opal Tometi, originated the hashtag #BlackLivesMatter on social media. The hashtag initiated protests the next year following the killings of Mike Brown in Ferguson, Missouri, and Eric Garner in New York City at the hands of police officers. Subsequently, between 2014 and 2016 Black Lives Matter exploded into a national network of organizations, including the Black Lives Matter Global Network, the Dream Defenders, and the Ella Baker Center for Human Rights, among many others. In August 2014 organizers in St. Louis issued a call for Black activists to take part in the Black Life Matters Freedom Ride. Started by Cullors, this ride took place on August 28 when about thirty activists from New York, Philadelphia, and New Jersey traveled by bus from New York City to Ferguson, Missouri, and attended ongoing protests there.

Philadelphia's chapter of Black Lives Matter formed in 2015 through the work of community activists Azsherae Gary and Taylor Johnson-Gordon. The first meeting, in May, focused on the initiatives of abolition of police and educational justice. The local group also supported the #AiyanasDreams annual campaign, named after seven-year-old Aiyana Stanley-Jones, who died at the hands of the Detroit Police Department Special Response Team on May 16, 2010. The campaign emphasized that although Black women and girls constituted only 13 percent of the population, they made up a third of police killings of all women.

In 2020, in the wake of the killing of George Floyd, the Philadelphia chapter of BLM led mass protests that resulted in multiple clashes with police and numerous arrests. Philadelphia police, often clad in riot gear, arrested over two hundred people on May 30, the majority for breaking a city-imposed curfew or failing to disperse. On June 1, police responded to marchers on the Vine Street Expressway with pepper spray and tear gas. Similar to protests in New York City and Portland, Oregon, officials in the city brought in the National Guard to quell protests. In June 2020, BLM Philly and eleven other organizations in the Black Philly Radical Collective announced thirteen demands to the City of Philadelphia. They wanted police departments defunded and abolished, the release of political prisoners, and economic justice, among other demands. The American Civil Liberties Union of Pennsylvania later criticized the police response in Philadelphia as "overwhelming, racially-targeted, and excessive," and subsequent lawsuits cost the city settlements totaling $9.25 million.

BLM protests during the summer of 2020 also sparked calls to remove statues in several American cities on the basis that the monuments represented an erasure of the harm done by white supremacy. In Philadelphia, protesters tried to topple the statue of former mayor Frank Rizzo. A former police commissioner, to many Rizzo represented a legacy of racial intolerance and oppression tied to past police violence, his call for Philadelphians to "vote white" in the 1970s, and the 1978 police standoff with the Black liberation group MOVE. Efforts to remove the Rizzo statue began in 2017, but it was not taken down until June 2020. Black Lives Matter actions that year also included murals painted in cities with historic Black communities. In Camden, New Jersey, a mural painted on Broadway covered four blocks of the city. The momentum from the summer of protests also hastened placement of a marker at Cooper Poynt in northwestern Camden commemorating a site where enslaved Africans were bought and sold.

While BLM Philly protested in their city and were met by police in riot gear, in Camden Police Chief Joseph Wysocki marched with protesters over the murder of George Floyd. This reflected changed police-community relations forged in Camden during the previous decade. The city had a long history of community organizing amid an ineffective relationship with police. In 1967, Charles "Poppy" Sharp founded the Black People's Unity Movement, which tackled the power structure and police brutality in the city. Elmer Winston helped found and run the Camden Neighborhood Renaissance Organization. Camden residents, many of them elderly, formed block patrols, challenged drug dealers, and improved their community on their terms. In 2012, when murder rates were eighteen times the national average and scores of excessive-force complaints were lodged against police, the residents, city council, and mayor joined together to dissolve the Camden Police Department and replace it in 2013 with a countywide department. Homicides decreased from sixty-seven in 2012 to twenty-five in 2019, with only three excessive-force complaints in 2020.

The results of Camden's new policing system predated the Black Lives Matter movement but came to the forefront during BLM protests in 2020 amid calls to defund the police. Camden showcased an example of how community-led policing could change a city's trajectory in the wake of a worldwide reckoning with police brutality and anti-Blackness.

FIGURE 67. Fanny Jackson Coppin, a teacher and principal at the Institute for Colored Youth (later Cheyney University) in the late nineteenth century. In 2022, the school community at Twelfth and Federal Streets, Philadelphia, honored her by renaming their elementary school in her honor, dropping the name of Andrew Jackson. Undated photograph published in Levi Jenkins Coppin, *Unwritten History* (A. M. E. Book Concern, 1919). LIBRARY OF CONGRESS.

EXPLORE MORE

Exploring the struggles for equality, freedom, and power in the Philadelphia region and the nation could begin at the beginning, at Independence National Historical Park and adjacent museums dedicated to the nation's early history. The *Great Essentials* exhibit in the West Wing of Independence Hall, on Chestnut Street between Fifth and Sixth Streets, displays original printed copies of the Declaration of Independence, the Articles of Confederation, and the U.S. Constitution. The National Constitution Center, 525 Arch Street, offers exhibits, programs, and online resources that trace the unfolding history of constitutional rights and contemporary issues. For overview histories, see *The Story of American Freedom*, by Eric Foner (W. W. Norton, 1998); Jill Lepore, *These Truths: A History of the United States* (W. W. Norton, 2018); and Kermit Roosevelt III, *The Nation That Never Was: Reconstructing America's Story* (University of Chicago Press, 2022).

Classic and more recent books on the ideals forged in Philadelphia include Pauline Maier, *American Scripture: Making the Declaration of Independence* (Alfred A. Knopf, 1997); Charlene Mires, *Independence Hall in American Memory* (University of Pennsylvania Press, 2002); Gary B. Nash, *Forging Freedom: The Formation of Philadelphia's Black Community, 1720–1840* (Harvard University Press, 1988); Thomas J. Sugrue, *Sweet Land of Liberty: The Forgotten Struggle for Civil Rights in the North* (Random House, 2008). The embrace of the language of the Declaration of Independence in calls for social justice is the subject of Philip S. Foner's *We, the Other People: Alternative Declarations of Independence by Labor Groups, Farmers, Woman's Rights Activists, Socialists, and Blacks, 1829–1975* (University of Illinois Press, 1976). For the rhetoric of African American protest, see *Pamphlets of Protest: An Anthology of Early African American Protest Literature, 1790–1860* (Routledge, 2000), edited by Richard Newman, Patrick Rael, and Phillip Lapsansky.

For the Bank War of the 1830s, visit the second Bank of the United States building, 420 Chestnut Street, Philadelphia, and Andalusia, the home of the bank's president, Nicholas Biddle, in Bucks County. For more on Philadelphia's nationally significant history in banking, see Robert E. Wright, *The First Wall Street: Chestnut Street, Philadelphia, and the Birth of American Finance* (University of Chicago Press, 2005). The Historical Society of Pennsylvania, 1300 Locust Street, Philadelphia, holds the Bank of the United States Papers, Biddle and Craig Family Papers, Biddle Family Papers, and John Sergeant Papers.

Urban disorder of the 1830s and 1840s is the subject of *The Turbulent Era: Riot and Disorder in Jacksonian America*, by Michael Feldman (Oxford University Press, 1980), and the Philadelphia nativist riots of 1844 are examined closely by Zachary M. Schrag in *The Fires of Philadelphia: Citizen-Soldiers, Nativists, and the 1844 Riots over the Soul of a Nation* (Pegasus Books, 2021). Historical markers aid in following the trail of nineteenth-century social conflict and violence, among them: the Lombard Street race riot, marker at the southeast corner of Sixth and Lombard Streets; St. Augustine's Roman Catholic Church, marker and church surviving from the nativist riots of 1844, Fourth and Vine Streets; and the site of the murder of Octavius Catto, 812 South Street. A monument to Catto stands on the south side of Philadelphia City Hall. For additional national and local context, see Daniel Walker Howe, *What Hath God Wrought: The Transformation of America, 1815–1848* (Oxford University Press, 2007); Bruce Laurie, *Working People of Philadelphia, 1800–1850* (Temple University Press, 1980); and Andrew Heath, *In Union There Is Strength: Philadelphia in the Age of Urban Consolidation* (University of Pennsylvania Press, 2019).

The Philadelphia region's association with the American Revolution often overshadows its role in the Civil War, but scholars and public historians have documented this history and made it accessible. Histories include J. Matthew Gallman, *Mastering Wartime: A Social History of Philadelphia During the Civil War* (Cambridge University Press, 1990); Judith Giesberg, *Keystone State in Crisis: The Civil War in Pennsylvania* (Pennsylvania Historical Association, 2013); Alan A. Siegel, *Beneath the Starry Flag: New Jersey's Civil War Experience* (Rutgers University Press, 2001); Michael Morgan, *Civil War Delaware: The First State Divided* (History Press, 2012); and Daniel R. Biddle and Murray Dubin, *Tasting Freedom:*

Octavius Catto and the Battle for Equality in Civil War America (Temple University Press, 2010). The National Constitution Center's exhibits encompass the Civil War and Reconstruction, and other places to visit include the Grand Army of the Republic Museum and Library, 8110 Frankford Avenue; Fort Delaware State Park, reached by ferry from Delaware City, Del.; and Gettysburg National Military Park Museum, 1195 Baltimore Pike, Gettysburg, Pa. Programs and exhibits are also offered by the Union League Legacy Foundation in the Heritage Center of the league's headquarters, 140 S. Broad Street. Relevant sites for the United States Colored Troops, in addition to the Octavius Catto monument at Philadelphia City Hall, include Camp William Penn, La Mott Historic District, Cheltenham Township, Pa., and the Philadelphia National Cemetery, 6909 Limekiln Pike, where a wayside marker identifies USCT gravesites. For the story of Camp William Penn, see Donald Scott Sr.'s *Camp William Penn* (Arcadia Publishing, 2008). Explore the experiences of Black soldiers further in Joseph T. Glatthaar, *Forged in Battle: The Civil War Alliance of Black Soldiers and White Officers* (Louisiana State University Press, 1990); and Holly A. Pinheiro Jr., *The Families' Civil War: Black Soldiers and the Fight for Racial Justice* (University of Georgia Press, 2022).

For the Lenape people in the Delaware Valley, visit the LNPA Cultural Center and Trading Post, 169 Northampton Street, Easton, Pa.; Penn Treaty Park, North Delaware Avenue and Beach Street; Penn Museum, 3260 South Street, Philadelphia; and Nanticoke Lenni-Lenape Headquarters, 18 E. Commerce Street, Bridgeton, N.J. Also see John Norwood, *We Are Still Here! The Tribal Saga of New Jersey's Nanticoke and Lenape Indians* (Native New Jersey Publications, 2007).

Important places in the history of civil rights movements include the African American Museum in Philadelphia, 701 Arch Street; Girard College, 2101 S. College Avenue; the Church of the Advocate, 1801 W. Diamond Street; MOVE Bombing historical marker, Osage Avenue and Cobbs Creek Parkway; and the Black Student Walkouts historical marker near Twenty-First and Winter Streets. In Camden, Wiggins Waterfront Park is named for physician and nationally prominent civil rights activist Ulysses S. Wiggins; South Jersey's civil rights history is within the scope of the African American Heritage Museum of Southern New Jersey at the Noyes Arts Garage of Stockton College, Atlantic City. Significant locations in LGBT civil rights include Sixth and Chestnut Street, site of a historical marker for the Annual Reminder demonstrations of the 1960s; the site of the Dewey's Lunch Counter sit-in, 219 S. Seventeenth Street; and William Way LGBT Community Center, 1315 Spruce Street, Philadelphia. An icon of the woman suffrage movement, the Justice Bell, is on display at Washington Memorial Chapel, Valley Forge National Historical Park; the home of suffrage leader Alice Paul is a National Historic Site and center for girls' leadership development in Mount Laurel Township, N.J. Series of historical markers, including sites important to civil rights, make up women's history trails in New Jersey and Pennsylvania; in Delaware, demonstrations for suffrage took place on Dover Green at the Old State House, a site in First State National Historical Park.

Among many works on the Philadelphia region and civil rights in the twentieth and early twenty-first centuries are Stanley Arnold, *Building the Beloved Community: Philadelphia's Interracial Civil Rights Organizations and Race Relations, 1930–1970* (University Press of Mississippi, 2014); Matthew Countryman, *Up South: Civil Rights and Black Power in Philadelphia* (University of Pennsylvania Press, 2006); Lisa Levenstein, *A Movement Without Marches: African American Women and the Politics of Poverty in Postwar Philadelphia* (University of North Carolina Press, 2009); Abigail Perkiss, *Making Good Neighbors: Civil Rights, Liberalism, and Integration in Postwar Philadelphia* (Cornell University Press, 2014); James Wolfinger, *Philadelphia Divided: Race and Politics in the City of Brotherly Love* (University of North Carolina Press, 2007); John D'Emilio, *Sexual Politics, Sexual Communities: The Making of a Homosexual Minority in the United States*, second edition (University of Chicago Press, 1998); Marc Stein, *City of Sisterly and Brotherly Loves: Lesbian and Gay Philadelphia, 1945–1972* (University of Chicago

Press, 2000); Roger Sanjek, *Gray Panthers* (University of Pennsylvania Press, 2009); Howard Gillette Jr., *Camden After the Fall: Decline and Renewal in a Post-Industrial City* (University of Pennsylvania Press, 2005); and Christopher J. Lebron, *The Making of Black Lives Matter: A Brief History of an Idea* (Oxford University Press, updated edition, 2023).

Women's rights histories include studies centered on the lives and activism of local leaders, for example Carol Faulkner, *Lucretia Mott's Heresy: Abolition and Women's Rights in Nineteenth-Century America* (University of Pennsylvania Press, 2011), and Katherine H. Adams and Michael L. Keene, *Alice Paul and the American Suffrage Campaign* (University of Illinois Press, 2008). To trace legal aspects, see Linda K. Kerber, *No Constitutional Right to be Ladies: Women and the Obligations of Citizenship* (Hill and Wang, 1998). On disability rights, see Dennis B. Downey and James W. Conroy, eds., *Pennhurst and the Struggle for Disability Rights* (Pennsylvania State University Press, 2020); Doris Z. Fleischer and Frieda Zames, *The Disability Rights Movement: From Charity to Confrontation* (Temple University Press, updated edition, 2011); and Judith Heumann, *Being Heumann: An Unrepentant Memoir of a Disability Rights Activist* (Beacon Press, 2020).

Archival collections are also rich with the history of civil rights. The Special Collections Research Center, Temple University Libraries, Philadelphia, holds many relevant manuscript and records collections, including Occupy Philadelphia records, Maggie Kuhn and the Gray Panthers papers, Evening Bulletin Clippings Collection, Fellowship Commission Papers, Philadelphia Branch of the National Association for the Advancement of Colored People Records, Philadelphia Urban League Records, and Philadelphia Lesbian and Gay Task Force Records and Scott Wilds Collection. See also the Maggie Kuhn Papers, Presbyterian Historical Society, 425 Lombard Street; and ephemera files and periodicals collection, William Way LGBT Community Center, 1315 Spruce Street, Philadelphia.

Demonstrations for freedom, equality, and justice regularly take place across the region, although permits are required for prime locations. Visit locations such as Independence National Historical Park, Philadelphia City Hall, LOVE Park, and the Benjamin Franklin Parkway to witness and join the ongoing, living history of contesting and expanding the nation.

Jim Crow
Must GO
NAACP
STOP!
SEGREGATION
AT
Girard College
NAACP

Chapter 9

DEFENDING THE NATION

Introduction

Although the Greater Philadelphia region has not been an active theater of war since the era of the American Revolution, connections with the military resonate deeply in local people, places, and historical memory. Thousands of veterans recall their service in conflicts from the Second World War through the war in Afghanistan; thousands more serve in reserves and the National Guard. Respect for service is activated annually through the rituals of Memorial Day and Veterans Day, and daily as military hospitals and other support services for veterans carry out their missions. The region's active military bases contribute not only to the nation's defense but also to the region's economy, despite reductions of installations in the late twentieth and early twenty-first centuries. In all these ways, local and national interests have been entwined through military infrastructure and service.

Such deep engagement with military matters surely would have surprised the English Quaker settlers who dominated the region's colonial-era history. They brought with them pacifist principles that proved difficult to uphold in a location open to invasion by sea or attack from their western frontier. Fortifying Philadelphia against attack required action by non-Quaker leaders including Benjamin Franklin, who in the 1740s conceived of a private lottery to raise funds for a battery and militia. The tension between pacifism and governance came to a head in 1756, when Quaker members of the Pennsylvania Provincial Assembly resigned their seats rather than vote for military defenses for the province. The issue brought an end to Quaker dominance of the Pennsylvania legislature. Many remained personally committed to pacifism, however, and the Philadelphia Yearly Meeting enforced the principle. During the American Revolution, with Philadelphia at the center of the War of Independence, many pacifist Quakers paid the price of scorn or banishment. Some migrated to Canada after the war rather than adhere to a new nation conceived in violence.

During and after the American Revolution, Philadelphia's geography played a role in its expanding array of local military installations. Because so much of Philadelphia's commerce depended on the sea, accessed by the Delaware River, defending the city required forts on islands and on both riverfronts spanning Pennsylvania, New Jersey, and Delaware. The river had enabled Philadelphia to become a shipbuilding center, which made the city a logical choice when the federal government sought a site for a new naval shipyard in 1801. Later in the nineteenth century, Philadelphia's position as a railroad hub and as the northern metropolitan center closest to the South gave it a strategic position during the Civil War, prompting new uses for the old forts and the addition of new facilities such as camps, recruiting stations, and hospitals. Still a port city into the twentieth century, Philadelphia served as a point of embarkation for troops during World War

I, a factor in locating Fort Dix in nearby Burlington County, New Jersey.

Military activity shaped the region's population, economy, and built environment. Communities grew around the bases in New Jersey, Pennsylvania, and Delaware, and businesses relied heavily on patronage by soldiers and their families. The bases also provided civilian employment, which surged during wartime to tens of thousands of jobs. During World War II, the Philadelphia Navy Yard alone employed nearly fifty thousand people. As a component of the nation's military infrastructure, the region acquired both assets and risks. A significant sector of the local economy, directly or indirectly tied to military activity and needs, could swing with federal decision-making about budgets and defense policies. The risk of this local-national interdependence became especially clear during the post-Vietnam era as installations downsized, closed, or merged. Federal decisions left local people jobless and localities scrambling for new purposes for sizable physical plants like the Frankford Arsenal and the Navy Yard.

In many ways, service to the nation begins and ends at home. In times of national emergency, local residents have mobilized to mount home-front defenses. They joined and supported militia units and the National Guard, they bought Liberty bonds, and they served as air raid wardens. They built fallout shelters. They honored veterans on Memorial Day and Veterans Day, and they extended aid to the wounded. But they also did not hesitate to speak out against weapons or warfare they considered unjust. Currents of pacifism persisted in the Delaware Valley, which in that way would still be recognizable to its Quaker founders.

Civil Defense

Sarah E. Robey

Because of Greater Philadelphia's position as a political, cultural, and economic hub, the region's residents have often found their daily lives deeply affected by times of national crisis. Civil defense, generally defined as local voluntary programs designed to protect civilian life and property during times of conflict, has taken many forms: militia, home defense, civilian defense, civil defense, and emergency response. As the nature of conflicts changed, so too did residents' roles in home-front defense, from colonial-era militiamen to the sandbaggers who confronted coastal storms.

In the earliest days of European settlement in the Delaware Valley, colonists formed militias of able-bodied men to guard their settlements against other imperial powers, Native Americans, and pirates. However, by the time of Pennsylvania's colonial charter in 1681, militia practices ran counter to the pacifist tenets of the region's Quaker leadership, and militias mostly disbanded. Neighboring New Jersey and the Lower Counties of Delaware, however, continued to maintain permanent volunteer militias to be at the ready in times of crisis. By the middle of the eighteenth century, noting Pennsylvania's inability to protect itself, Benjamin Franklin was instrumental in mobilizing Philadelphians to join "associated companies," local voluntary defense groups. When the Revolutionary War broke out, Philadelphia's associated companies and the Delaware Valley's regional militias proved difficult to integrate into the Continental army. In the first years of the war, state legislatures—including that of the formerly pacifist-minded Pennsylvania—passed legislation making militia service compulsory for all white men of fighting age, thereby streamlining military organization.

Like other states and cities in the eighteenth and nineteenth centuries, the Philadelphia region relied on local militias to preserve public safety during both peace and war. Often, the urgency of emergencies blurred the distinction between militia volunteers, police forces, and those enlisted or drafted into the armed services. As such, civil defense and active defense—or military defense—were often one and the same. In addition to participating in the Revolutionary War, Philadelphia-area militias played an integral role in smaller conflicts in the early republic, including the Whiskey Rebellion (1791–94), Fries Rebellion (1799–1800), the War of 1812, and the nativist riots in the Kensington and Southwark sections of Philadelphia (1844). However, in the relative peace of the antebellum years, militias also were important civic and social organizations, with individual companies frequently composed of men belonging to a particular trade, ethnicity, religion, or political party. Muster days—events held for roll call and training—often included parades, games, and patriotic celebrations.

During the Civil War, Philadelphia became central to the Union's production effort, but invasion threatened the city only briefly when the Confederate army led by Robert E. Lee entered Pennsylvania in June 1863. Fearful that Lee would march to Philadelphia, volunteer groups rushed to construct physical barriers to defend the city. However, the works projects did not last long; the Union's victory at Gettysburg ended the immediate threat to Philadelphia. Still, throughout the war, Philadelphia civic organizations such as the Union League called for participation in home guards and home defense groups as part of Philadelphians' patriotic duty. Generally, these all-male brigades and regiments assumed similar functions to past militias. Women and families contributed to the war effort through charitable efforts such as Philadelphia's 1864 Sanitary Fair or women's auxiliaries.

The United States' early twentieth-century conflicts placed the Delaware Valley in an integral position in war industry and national transportation networks. As the Philadelphia home front became deeply involved in both World Wars I and II, the changing nature of war made new demands on Philadelphia's civilian defense. New military technologies from both wars, including airplanes, submarines, and missiles, expanded the reach of a potential enemy attack to include the American mainland, beyond the geographic boundaries that once offered Philadelphia protection during ground or naval war. As modern war increasingly threatened the homeland, many Philadelphians grew concerned that the region could be a target.

During World War I, some Philadelphian civilians joined antisabotage programs designed to maintain a watchful eye on suspicious activity, especially in military industrial plants. But civilian defense during the Great War was primarily a mobilization effort to support the military, including bond drives for liberty loans and draft rallies. Echoing Civil War home guards, citizens enlisted in organizations such as the Philadelphia Home Defense Reserve to assist local officials in the event of a home-front crisis. But the United States' brief involvement in the war cut short the tenure of civilian defense activities, and most programs were dismantled shortly after the war concluded.

After the United States entered World War II, however, the region revived and strengthened many of its earlier civilian defense programs. While residents of the Delaware Valley once again participated in bond rallies, food rationing, and antisabotage campaigns, the preparations for an attack took on a more militarized focus. The Philadelphia city government, newspapers, and civic organizations printed millions of informational pamphlets that included air-raid information, instructions for building shelters, and basic first aid techniques. Periodic blackout drills required residents to turn off outdoor lighting, cover building windows with dark curtains, and dim automobile lights to disguise the city from potential attacking aircraft. Citizens across the region learned to identify enemy planes, and along the region's rivers and coastlines residents volunteered to take shifts as submarine spotters.

After the end of World War II, the region's civilian defense underwent another transformation. Nuclear weapons, used by the United States against Japan at the end of the war and soon after acquired by the Soviet Union, presented a new threat to public safety. The power of nuclear weapons exceeded the destructive capabilities of earlier weapons of war by several orders of magnitude, endangering more civilians in civil defense than ever before. Because of the Philadelphia area's importance in industrial production, its critical transportation infrastructure, and its large metropolitan population, the region rushed to find ways to prepare and defend itself from attack. While postwar Americans looked to civilian defense methods from earlier eras, many saw activities such as victory gardens and bond rallies as anachronistic and ineffective for the Atomic Age. In Philadelphia and across the country, Cold War civilian defense became known as "civil defense" in part to distance new strategies from the legacy of outmoded programs.

As in many threatened American cities, Philadelphia's leadership took an early active role in local civil defense planning. In 1951, Mayor Bernard Samuel established the Philadelphia County Civil Defense Council, responsible for hosting educational programs and organizing a military-style chain of command to connect city residents with block wardens, neighborhood coordinators, city offices, and civil defense officials. Throughout the 1950s, the council ran citywide drills designed to give civilians an idea of the kind of destruction they could expect and the actions they would need to take should a real attack occur. Notably, during

FIGURE 68. Call for civil defense volunteers, ca. 1941–43. The Philadelphia Council of Defense, with the Liberty Bell in its logo (lower right), urgently recruited air raid wardens and first responders with this poster created by federal Works Progress Administration artists. LIBRARY OF CONGRESS.

1954's Operation SCRAM (Survival of our Citizens depends on Cooperation, Alertness, and Mobility), more than twenty-five thousand Philadelphians evacuated the blocks closest to city hall to a muster point on the Benjamin Franklin Parkway. With the assistance of federal civil defense funds, cities, counties, and states built a system of fallout shelters—identified by ubiquitous yellow and black signage—in many buildings, including Philadelphia's city hall and public schools.

One of the most challenging aspects of the Philadelphia area's Cold War civil defense efforts, however, was the relationship between its cities and surrounding towns and counties. Should an attack occur, the entire Delaware Valley region would need to mobilize to deliver supplies and transport millions of evacuees. Successful civil defense plans thus relied on coordination among the cities of Philadelphia; Trenton and Camden, New Jersey; and Wilmington, Delaware, as well as hundreds of towns and several counties. Because every municipality had different civil defense needs, and every state had its own civil defense legislation, regional and interstate coordination was a logistical problem that officials never fully resolved.

In the end, Philadelphia's Cold War–era civil defense fell victim to the changing city politics of the postwar period. The Civil Defense Council had difficulty defending its budget and usefulness to reform Democrats, especially as nuclear weapons technology advanced well beyond the capacity of civil defense strategies. Moreover, civil defense was a hard sell to Philadelphians, who balked at rehearsing for such catastrophic war in a time of peace. By the late 1960s, facing significant public apathy and ridicule from critics, the region's civil defense activities had declined drastically, and emergency planning energy was redirected toward preparation for peacetime crises. In 1972, Philadelphia's Civil Defense Council merged with the Fire Department to become the Office of Emergency Preparedness (OEP). The OEP relied on regional volunteers and local relief organizations during extreme weather, industrial accidents, and other disasters to assist in preparation and recovery efforts.

Throughout its history, Greater Philadelphia has relied upon its citizens to help keep the region safe. Whether compulsory or voluntary, popular or unpopular, civil defense has shaped the region's politics and culture. Although the nature of crises and war has changed significantly since the seventeenth century, civil defense has remained a consistent part of civic life in the Philadelphia area.

Veterans and Veterans' Organizations

Robert J. Kodosky

Military veterans began organizing in the Philadelphia area during the waning days of the Revolutionary War. Veterans emerged from this tumult as an integral factor in the region's identity and have remained prominent in the nation's veteran affairs. While creating organizations that served local communities, Philadelphia-area veterans effectively raised their voices to address issues of concern to their peers, regionally and nationally. Often they provided models of reintegration for their nation's other veterans to follow.

In the era of the American Revolution, Americans expected veterans to follow the ideal of a citizen soldier embodied by the tradition of Lucius Quinctius Cincinnatus, a consul in ancient Rome. When summoned, he set down his plow to command an army against invaders. Sixteen days later, Cincinnatus returned to his fields. He shunned all honors. Among veterans of the American Revolution, however, many who took up arms cared less about glory than they did in collecting their promised pay and bounties. This became evident in the streets of Philadelphia.

On October 4, 1779, more than a year after the British army ended its 1777–78 occupation of Philadelphia, a large group of militiamen gathered at Burns Tavern on N. Tenth Street. The tradesmen serving in the city's militia shifted their disdain from the British to Philadelphia's merchants, whom they accused of profiteering while avoiding service. They forcibly marched four prominent merchants through town in an attempt at public humiliation. Then they stormed the house of James Wilson, a prominent political ally of the merchants. This attack on "Fort Wilson" resulted in at least six dead and seventeen wounded. Authorities soon arrested several of the militiamen, but then pardoned them to alleviate the heightened class tension that their captivity had produced.

Continental army veterans shared the financial concerns expressed by the militia. In January 1781, the 2,400 veterans of the Pennsylvania Line mutinied, disgruntled about their coerced reenlistment, lack of pay, and poor conditions. Authorities responded quickly. Joseph Reed, president of Pennsylvania's Supreme Executive Council, met with representatives from the disgruntled line at its camp in Princeton, New Jersey. He addressed their grievances by granting discharges to those who sought them and by offering more favorable terms to those who chose to reenlist.

Two years later, their war won against Great Britain, veterans unified once more. Rather than going home as ordered, units from York, Carlisle, and Lancaster Counties in Pennsylvania joined with veterans from Maryland in Philadelphia to demand their promised pay. Congress deemed this a mutiny and relocated to Princeton. The protest collapsed when veterans received word that General Robert Howe commanded an army marching toward the city with orders to quell the uprising. This incident ultimately resulted in the constitutional provision granting the U.S. Congress exclusive jurisdiction over the nation's capital.

While the Continental army's soldiers took to Philadelphia's streets, its officers retired to the city's back rooms. They created the State Society of the Cincinnati of Pennsylvania on October 4, 1783, at the City Tavern, months before the General Society held its first meeting there. This rendered the Pennsylvania society as the ninth of fourteen constituent societies to comprise the General Society of the Cincinnati, an organization proposed by Major General Henry Knox at the Continental army's encampment at Newburgh, New York, in May 1783. The society's founding document, the Institution, acknowledged the subordination of the military to civilian rule. It created a fraternal organization for former officers as a vehicle to advocate for a number of issues, including promised pay. In addition to Pennsylvania, constituent societies included New Jersey and Delaware (together with the rest of the thirteen states) and France, America's wartime ally against England.

Philadelphia remained central to veterans' organizations following the nation's nineteenth-century conflicts as those who served sought to preserve the camaraderie experienced in wartime. At Congress Hall on January 9, 1854, more than 1,500 War of 1812 veterans created the Society of the War of 1812, a fraternal group for former officers. The Aztec Club, formed for officers who served in the Mexican-American War, also congregated in Philadelphia. Members met annually at the mansion of Robert Patterson, their longtime president, at Thirteenth and Locust Streets (later the site for a new building to house the Historical Society of Pennsylvania).

Philadelphia also became the site for the first national home for veterans. In 1826 the U.S. Navy acquired 20.7 acres at Grays Ferry Avenue from prominent Philadelphia Quaker Timothy Abbott and appointed Philadelphia architect William Strickland as superintendent to build a permanent facility for disabled sailors. The U.S. Naval Asylum (renamed as the U.S. Naval Home in 1889) housed retired sailors until replaced by a new facility in Gulfport, Mississippi, in 1976.

Following the assassination of President Abraham Lincoln, veterans in Philadelphia held a mass meeting at Independence Hall to pledge renewed allegiance to the Union. This resulted in the creation of the Military Order of the Loyal Legion of the United States, or the Loyal Legion. Philadelphian George Cadwalader, a major general in the Union army, served as the legion's first commander-in-chief. As with previous veterans' organization, the legion welcomed only officers. It deviated, however, by moving toward advocacy on behalf of the general welfare of the Union, its soldiers, and their widows. In this way, the Loyal Legion bridged the earlier veterans' organizations, which remained exclusive and fraternal, with groups that later proved more inclusive and activist. Its members contributed to preserving the war's history by gathering its artifacts.

A year after the Loyal Legion's creation, the Grand Army of the Republic (GAR) formed in Decatur, Illinois, to advocate on behalf of all Civil War veterans. Beginning in 1868, local GAR posts throughout the Philadelphia region meticulously executed parades and services to honor the Civil War dead each May on Memorial Day. In Philadelphia, GAR Post 2, one of the largest and most influential in the United States, collected books, artifacts, and memorabilia to educate the public about the war. The post's headquarters at 4278 Griscom Street became the Grand Army of the Republic Museum and Library.

The GAR established a model for American veterans of ensuing wars who formed the Veterans of Foreign Wars (1914), the American Legion (1919), Vietnam Veterans of America (1978), and Iraq and Afghanistan Veterans of America (2004). Each new generation of veterans established a presence in the Philadelphia area through service to their communities. For example, the Bridesburg-Lawton Veterans of Foreign Wars Post 2 (4638 Richmond Street), whose members first mustered on July 24, 1902, remained active in community service for more than a century. The post's original leader, Robert S. Hansbury, organized the American Veterans of Philippine and China Wars, a forerunner to both the regional American Veterans of Foreign Services and the national Veterans of Foreign Wars created in 1914. Members of the Bridesburg-Lawton post contributed to the inaugural Philadelphia Veterans Parade (2015) by sending its motorcycle "Riders Group," the oldest in Philadelphia.

Posts often remained segregated by race. Initially, policy dictated this. Unable to join Post 2 of the Grand Army of the Republic, in 1867 Philadelphia's African American veterans of the Civil War chartered Charles Sumner Post 103. Although the military desegregated in 1953, local veterans' posts continued to reflect the region's residential segregation patterns. For example, in 1954, an influx of many Puerto Rican World War II and Korean War veterans in Philadelphia resulted in the creation of Latin American Legion Post 840 of the American Legion.

In the suburbs, the Veterans of Foreign Wars granted separate Black and white posts to Coatesville and Kennett Square. In West Chester, veterans created two American Legion posts within three months of one another in 1919. The Bernhard F. Schlegel Post 134 began with fifteen members, all white, while fifteen African American veterans created Nathan Holmes Post 362. Still, the two posts worked closely with one another. They jointly orchestrated activities and parades, occupied seats on the county's veteran council, and sent delegations to the funerals of each other's members. Their members also joined the same local Veterans of Foreign Wars post. The activist spirit promoted by veterans' organizations became embraced by individuals such as Philadelphian John Alferi, a World War I veteran and member of the James J. Cochran Veterans of Foreign Wars Post 251. On December 14, 1931, Alferi led a "Veterans' Bonus Brigade" of fifty veterans on a four-day protest march from Philadelphia to the nation's capital to call for early payment of bonuses promised by Congress. Although this march attracted little public attention, it inspired an army of veterans who came to call Alferi "Mr. Bonus Army." The 1931 action inspired the better-known "Bonus Army" march on Washington by thousands of veterans during the summer of 1932.

The region's activist veterans also included Smedley D. Butler, a native of West Chester, Pennsylvania, the most decorated marine in American history at the time of his death. Butler, twice awarded the Medal of Honor, wrote an exposé of war profiteering entitled *War Is a Racket* (1935). Butler supported veterans' lobbying and visited the Bonus Army to encourage its marchers during their encampment in Washington. He toured the country in 1933 to recruit members for the Veterans of Foreign Wars.

Years later, over Labor Day weekend in 1970, veterans staged another protest march when 150

FIGURE 69. Veterans of Foreign Wars, 1954. With military bearing, VFW leaders in Philadelphia for a national convention marched to a city hall ceremony between lines formed by the Audubon (N.J.) All-Girl Drum and Bugle Corps. SPECIAL COLLECTIONS RESEARCH CENTER, TEMPLE UNIVERSITY LIBRARIES.

members of Vietnam Veterans Against the War walked from Morristown, New Jersey, to Doylestown, Pennsylvania, and on to Valley Forge, drawing on the area's Revolutionary-era symbolism. Aided by the Philadelphia Guerrilla Theater Company, the group dramatized its allegations of the American military's misconduct in Vietnam, analogous to many acts allegedly perpetuated by the Redcoats in colonial America. At Valley Forge the veterans, joined by over a thousand protesters, conducted a peace rally that featured antiwar speeches delivered by veterans, political leaders, and celebrities.

While the Vietnam War divided the country, Greater Philadelphia's veterans' groups projected unity in lobbying to honor veterans in the naming of the city's new sports arena completed in 1971. Veterans Stadium served as the home field for the Philadelphia Phillies and the Eagles until its demolition in 2004.

The unity of Philadelphia area veterans also led to the creation of the Philadelphia Veterans House (4108 Baltimore Avenue) in 1994. Initially a facility to provide short-term housing and meals for veterans commuting for treatment at the Philadelphia Veterans Affairs Medical Center, in 2012 Philadelphia Veterans House began to provide shelter to veterans experiencing homelessness. Mayor Michael A. Nutter cited this initiative as essential to his announcement in December 2015 that Philadelphia had effectively ended homelessness among the city's veterans.

The activist spirit persisted. This was exemplified

by the mural *Communion Between a Rock and a Hard Place*, dedicated in 2012 at 4129 Woodland Avenue near the Veterans Affairs Medical Center. A product of the Philadelphia-based Warrior Writers organization and the city of Philadelphia's Mural Arts program, it depicted parallel worlds of Baghdad and Philadelphia: the spheres of soldier and citizen. Philadelphia-area veterans worked to bridge these realms from the beginning. The history of Greater Philadelphia's veterans, characterized by organization and activism, offered a model for the nation.

Forts and Fortifications

Jeffery M. Dorwart

Constructed from the seventeenth through the mid-twentieth century, defensive fortifications along the lower Delaware River and Bay guarded the region during times of international and sectional upheaval. As important structures with such long histories, forts help to explain the political, economic, and social history of the Greater Philadelphia region.

The earliest fortifications in the lower Delaware region resulted from the intense economic colonial rivalries and wars of the early seventeenth century. Dutch, Swedish, and English Protestant capitalist states battled Spanish, Portuguese, and French Catholic kingdoms for control of the North American and West Indian trade and settlement. Their rivalry led to construction of Fort Nassau, built in 1626 by the Dutch West India Company on the east bank of the Delaware (the future site of Gloucester City, New Jersey), and Fort Christina, built in 1638 by the New Sweden Company at the confluence of the Christina River and Brandywine Creek (the future site of Wilmington, Delaware). Both fortifications served as centers for fur trading, and Fort Christina also developed as an agricultural settlement. When Lieutenant Colonel Johan Björnsson Printz, a veteran of the Thirty Years' War (1618–48), became governor of New Sweden in 1643 he further fortified the colony with Fort Nya Elfsborg (Elsinboro, Salem County, New Jersey) and Fort New Gothenburg (Tinicum Island, Pennsylvania).

The Dutch West India Company, responding to New Sweden's threat to New Netherland's commercial monopoly on the South River, strengthened Fort Nassau by building a number of small, fortified trading posts across the river and erecting Fort Casimir where the river met the Delaware Bay (later the site of New Castle, Delaware). The new fort stood well below the Swedish forts and promised to stop Swedish ships entering the bay and river. New Sweden soon seized Fort Casimir but had neither the resources nor manpower to construct and hold such a fort. New Netherland director general Peter Stuyvesant aggressively sent an expedition up the Delaware in 1655 to retake the defensive works and bring an end to New Sweden.

The regained Dutch influence on the Delaware River was short-lived. In 1664, after the Dutch surrendered New Netherland to the British, they quietly abandoned their forts on the Delaware. Without major threats to control and naval supremacy in the bay and nearby Atlantic coast, the British decided not to garrison fortifications on the Delaware. Spending money on forts or defense also did not interest the Quaker provincial government of Pennsylvania, created by land grant to William Penn in 1681. By the mid-eighteenth century, though, the need for fortifications in the Delaware Valley increased as Britain became locked in a century of colonial warfare with France and Spain.

Greater defenses became an issue by the 1740s as French soldiers and their Native American allies came south from Canada into western and central Pennsylvania to block English westward settlement, while French and Spanish naval forces—particularly privateers from the West Indies—came up the coast and plundered several Delaware Bay and river settlements. Local residents constructed a fortified redoubt in 1748 near Wilmington, but the Quaker assembly in Philadelphia refused to raise money for the city's fortification. When the French and Spanish threatened Philadelphia's trade and business, more militant Quaker merchants joined with a non-Quaker political faction that included Benjamin Franklin to fund defensive measures. During King George's War (1744–48) Franklin used the sale of lottery tickets to fund the construction in 1747–48 of the Grand (Association) Battery, a great twenty-seven-gun stone wall along the South Philadelphia (Southwark) riverfront, and a smaller Society Hill battery upriver. Fortifying the lower Delaware and Philadelphia became more urgent during the French and Indian War (1754–63), particularly after the British were driven from Fort Duquesne in western Pennsylvania and moved eastward toward Philadelphia. In response, Franklin oversaw construction of fortifications in the Lehigh Valley, where he personally directed the building of Fort Allen (Weissport, Carbon County) in 1755.

The British government, overtaxed by continual warfare against the French in Europe, the Caribbean, Atlantic Ocean, and North America, expected the Pennsylvania Provincial Assembly to bear the burden of arming the Delaware Valley, particularly fortifying the Delaware River approaches to Philadelphia. To this end the British army dispatched military engineer Captain John Montresor to fortify Mud Island (also called Fort Island) on the Delaware riverfront near the mouth of the Schuylkill River. Montresor designed a small stone fort and began construction of a southern and eastern wall of Mud Fort (later Fort Mifflin). Worsening relations between England and her North American colonies interrupted construction until 1775, as the Continental Congress met in Philadelphia and increasingly protested British taxation and trade policies.

Months of debate over whether Pennsylvania, Philadelphia, or the Continental Congress should select sites and pay for defensive works along the river reached a critical stage after the Declaration of Independence. On July 5, 1776, the Continental Congress purchased a site for a fort in Billingsport (Paulsboro), New Jersey. General George Washington asked Colonel Thaddeus Kosciuszko, a highly skilled French-trained Polish-Lithuanian military engineer, to design the fort, and the Continental Congress hired French military engineer Philippe du Coudray to build it as an anchor for a chain of frames of large iron-tipped logs known as *cheveaux-de-frise* to be spread across the river channels to prevent British warships coming upriver to attack Philadelphia. Congress also authorized construction of Fort Mercer on a high bluff known as Red Bank, Gloucester County, New Jersey.

The British attack on Philadelphia in late summer and fall of 1777 forced completion and garrisoning of the three Delaware River forts. Fort Billings, defended by local militia, was the first to fall to the British army, then British naval vessels breached the *chevaux-de-frise* and slowly moved upriver toward the Mud Island (Fort Mifflin) and Red Bank (Fort Mercer) fortifications. British naval bombardment of Mud Island, reportedly the heaviest cannon fire of the Revolutionary War, reduced the Mud Fort (Fort Mifflin) to rubble. Forts Mercer and Mifflin were abandoned on November 15, and the British army occupied Philadelphia.

The Revolutionary War marked the last time that forts in the Philadelphia region defended against an enemy force. Nevertheless, fortifications became important while Philadelphia served from 1790 until 1800 as the national capital. President Washington and his secretary of the Treasury, Alexander Hamilton, pressed for rebuilding Fort Mifflin and constructing river defenses, particularly with the growing threat of French and British naval incursions in the Delaware during the wars of the French Revolution. The federal government hired civil engineer Major Pierre Charles L'Enfant to redesign Fort Mifflin and military engineer Ann Louis de Tousard to build the bastion. Tousard used government funds to buy material from Philadelphia merchants and hire local German, Irish, and English carpenters and bricklayers. Enslaved African Americans, many owned by Tousard, supplied additional labor. The fort was named Fort Mifflin in 1795 after Washington's wartime adjutant general, Thomas Mifflin of Philadelphia.

Work ceased on Fort Mifflin when the national capital left Philadelphia in 1800 for the Potomac River. Some construction resumed during the War of 1812, but Jeffersonian Republicans preferred to spend money on several temporary batteries of twenty-four-pounder cannon on islands in the Delaware River and use small gunboats to protect the city. Moreover, it seemed that the region should be defended with a fort farther downriver because Fort Mifflin stood too close to Philadelphia to provide adequate defense against increasingly long-range naval armament. The U.S. government began to look at sites near New Castle, Delaware, and Pea Patch Island, a large island in the middle of the Delaware River channel where the river met the bay. Work began on a Pea Patch Island fort soon after the War of 1812. Fire destroyed the partially built fort in 1831, but construction resumed in 1833 on a large stone fortification called Fort Delaware.

Defense of the region became necessary once again with the advent of the Civil War. After the Confederate capture of Fort Sumter in the Charleston, South Carolina, harbor in 1861, the United States and

A SKETCH OF FORT ISLAND
THE PENNSYLVAN
Kingsess Creek
Boons Creek
Carpenters
Bow Creek
Hog Isla
Derby Creek
Crum Creek
Ridley's Creek
CHESTER
Billings Island
Tinicum Island
Tinicum Channel
the Spit
Main or Ship Channel
Billing's Point or Bill ngport
Cooper's Point
Thompson's Point
THE
Two Miles

FIGURE 70. Delaware River fortifications, 1777. To aid British troops, the map depicted the river between Philadelphia and Chester and defensive works erected by Americans. MAP BY WILLIAM FADEN, LIBRARY OF CONGRESS.

Pennsylvania governments demanded the arming of Fort Delaware. They worried that a nearby secessionist movement in the state of Delaware and southern counties of New Jersey threatened the security of Philadelphia, Chester, and Wilmington, which were rapidly emerging as centers of munitions manufacturing, gun casting, and ironclad shipbuilding. Railroads carrying troops and matériel to meet the rebel forces also passed through these cities. Rumored construction of a huge Confederate navy ironclad warship disturbed the region, and Fort Delaware needed to mount heavy smoothbore guns and floating mines to stop enemy ironclads from attacking Philadelphia. The federal government began to build a great ten-gun battery on the Delaware City riverfront (Fort DuPont) to protect Pea Patch Island. Fort Delaware and to a lesser extent Fort Mifflin served as prisoner-of-war prison camps throughout the Civil War. Fort Delaware held more than thirty thousand Confederate prisoners and local Southern sympathizers in the extremely unhealthy, disease-ridden Pea Patch Island facility.

The last decades of the nineteenth century became the golden age of American coastal fort building as the United States entered into imperial rivalries with Germany, Russia, England, France, Japan, and particularly Spain, which seemed a threat to American interests in Cuba and the Philippine Islands. As the federal government moved to modernize and strengthen American seacoast defenses, the Philadelphia region gained additional fortification in the 1870s with construction of a battery on Finn's Point, Pennsville, Salem County, New Jersey. Named Fort Mott after New Jersey Civil War and National Guard commander Brigadier General Gershom Mott, the new fort created a defensive triangle with Forts Delaware and DuPont to stop any enemy fleet before it could reach the great manufacturing centers upriver at Wilmington, Chester, and Philadelphia.

Delaware Valley forts played no fighting role during the Spanish-American War, but U.S. entry into the First World War in 1917 brought the prospect of a greater need for defending the region as it continued to be a center for naval and merchant shipbuilding, munitions making, and other war goods. Moreover, the region became a mobilization nexus for troops to be shipped to the European fronts. Forts Mott and DuPont were garrisoned by artillery units. Fort DuPont built more barracks, a hospital, and warehouses to train and equip draftees and house troops and matériel destined for the Great War. However, the region faced no real threat from enemy forces other than sabotage of defense industries by German agents in New Jersey.

The threat to the region became greater by the time of the Second World War, when the Japanese attack on Pearl Harbor in December 1941 raised the possibility of long-distance aerial attack. Older, obsolete forts gained new purposes as sites for antiaircraft batteries, including Fort Mifflin, manned by the first African American Coast Artillery unit. It soon became apparent, though, that the greatest threat to the region during the Second World War came from powerful German U-boats that torpedoed merchant ships and oil tankers off the New Jersey and Delaware coasts and lurked just off the Delaware Bay and capes to intercept ships coming out of the Delaware Bay. In response, the United States moved all Delaware River and Bay defenses to the seacoast, erecting Fort Miles on Cape Henlopen, near Lewes, Delaware. Fort Miles featured giant, long-range, sixteen-inch guns and 90 mm antiaircraft batteries. Round concrete observation and fire control towers were constructed along the New Jersey coast as far north as Sandy Hook and down the Delaware coast to Ocean City, Maryland.

Locating coastal defenses ever farther away from Philadelphia and the Delaware River during World War II attested to the increasing spatial dimensions of modern warfare and long-range capabilities of new weapons. It suggested the increasing obsolescence of the Greater Philadelphia region's historic forts as well. All Delaware River forts were declared war surplus after World War II, and remaining guns or other military matériel were removed. Forts Mott, DuPont, and Delaware were given to New Jersey and Delaware and became parts of historic districts and state park systems. Fort DuPont retained a National Guard armory. Fort Mifflin was eventually obtained by the City of Philadelphia and supported by a private Fort Mifflin Society to preserve one of the most historic forts in American history. The U.S. Army Corps of Engineers retained a presence on site. None of the early seventeenth-century forts remained, but plaques and monuments marked the original sites of Forts Elfsborg,

Billings, Mercer, Casimir, and Christina. The surviving structures and monuments and plaques served as reminders of the central role forts played in the earliest history of the Greater Philadelphia area.

Military Bases

Melissa Ziobro

For centuries, the American military valued Philadelphia because of its size, manufacturing capability, and location. Bases and other military facilities in the region contributed to the United States' national defense while also serving as economic engines for surrounding areas, creating jobs not just on the installations but also in surrounding communities. Closures, conversely, led to job losses, unless redevelopment filled the void.

The region's early military facilities, such as Fort Mifflin on Mud Island near the junction of the Delaware and Schuylkill Rivers and Fort Mercer, New Jersey, physically impeded enemy advancements. After the Revolution, the new nation sought to establish itself as a military force. Toward that end, the government began construction of the Schuylkill Arsenal in Philadelphia in 1800, assumed control of a shipyard in the Southwark district in 1801 (the first Philadelphia Navy Yard), and established the Frankford Arsenal in northeast Philadelphia in 1816. These facilities proved critical to national defense and the local economy.

During the Civil War, the Naval Shipyard employed at least three thousand men whose work included producing eleven warships. The Frankford Arsenal employed about one thousand and churned out munitions, while the Schuylkill Arsenal, as the Union army's primary depot for clothing, put thousands of seamstresses to work making uniforms. Philadelphia also hosted two of the largest military hospitals in the United States in the Civil War era: Satterlee Hospital in West Philadelphia and Mower Hospital in Chestnut Hill. These institutions closed with the war's end, but the arsenals and the shipyard survived (with reduced workloads). In 1867, Congress passed legislation to enlarge and relocate the shipyard to the southern tip of Philadelphia, surrounded on three sides by the Schuylkill and Delaware Rivers. It ultimately encompassed approximately 1,200 acres. During World War I, employment at the shipyard soared to around twelve thousand. The Schuylkill Arsenal employed close to ten thousand civilians at the peak of its operations in 1918, while the Frankford Arsenal employed just over six thousand that same year. Women comprised a significant portion of these employees, as they did in factories across the country during this conflict and World War II.

World War I also led the military to establish Camp Dix near Wrightstown, New Jersey, a site that offered proximity to major ports of embarkation (including Philadelphia, thirty-two miles away) and supply routes, including the Pennsylvania Railroad. Opened in June 1917, the camp was named for Major General John Adams Dix, a veteran of the War of 1812 and the Civil War who also served as a U.S. senator, secretary of treasury, and governor of New York. During the war, Camp Dix trained and staged the Seventy-Eighth, Eighty-Seventh, and Thirty-Fourth Divisions, and following the armistice, it became a demobilization center.

The interwar period saw employment at sites like the arsenals and the shipyard fall off dramatically. The Schuylkill Arsenal survived (renamed the Philadelphia Quartermaster Depot) and moved from its original site at Grays Ferry Avenue and Washington Avenue to W. Oregon Avenue and Twenty-Second Street. Growth also occurred, however, as Congress in 1931 authorized construction of the Philadelphia Naval Hospital. The hospital complex, on a twenty-two-acre tract north of League Island Park and the Navy Yard, included an impressive art deco main hospital building for 650 patients and associated facilities such as a nurses' home, corpsmen's quarters, four officers' quarters, a garage, a film-storage building, and a greenhouse.

During the World War II era, new military installations opened and existing sites expanded, easing the deprivations of the Great Depression for Philadelphia and the surrounding region. The workforce of the Philadelphia Naval Shipyard, for example, climbed to forty-seven thousand, by one count. Coastal defense fortification Fort Miles, with its sixteen-inch guns and 90 mm antiaircraft batteries, began operations in 1941 in Delaware to protect Philadelphia and its environs. That same year, the military opened Fort Dix

Army Air Force Base in New Jersey and took over the municipal airport in Dover, Delaware, converting it to a U.S. Army Air Corps airfield. In 1942, the United States Navy purchased land in Horsham, Pennsylvania (north of Philadelphia in Montgomery County), for the U.S. Naval Air Station Willow Grove. These acquisitions indicated the increased importance of aerial warfare during the period.

When the American military demobilized following World War II, the numbers employed by military bases in the Philadelphia region decreased correspondingly, as they had following World War I. A few bases closed, while others gained new purposes for the emerging Cold War era. Fort Miles, for example, closed as advancements in aerial warfare rendered its coastal artillery obsolete. On the other hand, the Fort Dix Army Air Force Base, though mothballed briefly, reopened in 1948 as McGuire Air Force Base. The name memorialized Medal of Honor recipient Major Thomas B. McGuire Jr., who died in action during World War II. Naval Air Station Willow Grove became a Naval Air Reserve training station, and in 1957 the Department of Defense purchased additional land, bringing the air station to a total of 1,100 acres. The Philadelphia Naval Hospital grew as well. By the Vietnam War era, it could accommodate up to 1,100 patients. In later years, the hospital became a renowned training and research facility.

The United States' protracted involvement in Southeast Asia did not produce the level of wartime mobilization that had yielded economic benefits for the Philadelphia region during earlier conflicts. The shipyard, for example, gradually outsourced new construction and focused on repairs and maintenance. The last ship it constructed was the USS *Blue Ridge*, commissioned in 1970. As the Vietnam War wound down, the American military continued to curb spending and divest property and missions that could be streamlined or outsourced to private industry. This mindset contributed to the 1976 decision to close the Frankford Arsenal, which had opened in 1816 and still employed about two thousand people at the time of its closing in 1977.

As the Cold War diminished, Philadelphia-area facilities severely curtailed operations or closed following recommendations by the federal Base Realignment and Closure (BRAC) Commission, a board of civilian appointees created by Congress in 1988 to identify excess military property, subject to approval by Congress and the president. The BRAC commission sought to ensure, among other things, that bases were not shuttered for purely political reasons (although congressional districts impacted by base closures still often cried foul).

In 1988, the BRAC Commission deemed the Philadelphia Naval Hospital "unsafe and inadequate to support modern health care" and recommended closure. The hospital employed about eight hundred personnel at that time and provided medical care for about 130,000 active-duty navy personnel, retirees, and dependents in southeastern Pennsylvania, New Jersey, and Delaware. By 1993, the government vacated the property. The main hospital building was demolished in 2001; some of the other buildings were repurposed as housing and office space.

At a time when the region also was losing large numbers of industrial jobs due to ongoing shifts in the American economy, in 1991 the BRAC Commission also recommended closing the Philadelphia Naval Shipyard because of a reduced need for ship repairs. A 1993 Coopers & Lybrand study for the Pennsylvania Economy League found that in addition to its seven thousand employees, the shipyard was directly and indirectly responsible for 36,400 regional jobs, $326.2 million in direct income, and $113 million in annual state and local tax revenues. Closing the naval installation provoked an outcry from the local community and politicians, culminating in *Dalton v. Specter*, 511 U.S. 462 (1994). This Supreme Court case ultimately decreed that an executive order to shut down the Philadelphia naval base could not be overturned because the decision was outside the purview of the court (a decision some legal scholars called "puzzling").

In 1993 the government closed the quartermaster's textile factory (with its roots in the Schuylkill Arsenal) and moved the remaining part of the South Philadelphia operation to the Naval Support Station in Northeast Philadelphia, a facility later renamed the Defense Supply Center Philadelphia in 1998 and the Defense Logistics Agency Troop Support in 2010.

In 2005, BRAC Commission recommendations led to merging the contiguous McGuire Air Force Base, Fort Dix, and the Lakehurst Naval Air Station (in Ocean County, New Jersey) into Joint Base McGuire-Dix-

FIGURE 71. Joint Base McGuire-Dix-Lakehurst, 2016. In a training exercise, reservists of the 404th Civil Affairs Battalion provided cover against simulated enemy fire. PHOTOGRAPH BY MATT HECHT, U.S. DEPARTMENT OF DEFENSE.

Lakehurst and shifting about one hundred personnel from Walter Reed Medical Center in Washington, D.C., to Dover Air Force Base. The commission's recommendations also closed the World War II–era Willow Grove Naval Air Station in 2011, with a loss of three thousand jobs.

Despite the loss of thousands of government jobs in the region as a result of government consolidations and attempts at cost saving, the military maintained an active (if reduced) presence in the Philadelphia region into the twenty-first century. Active military installations within approximately fifty miles of Philadelphia included the Naval Support Activity-Philadelphia (at 700 Robbins Avenue, Philadelphia, with its Philadelphia Naval Yard Annex at 5001 S. Broad Street). A portion of the former site of Naval Air Station Joint Reserve Base Willow Grove (renamed the Biddle Air National Guard Station) remained in use by the 111th Attack Wing (ATKW) of the Pennsylvania Air National Guard as a control center for the MQ-9 remotely piloted aircraft (or drones). In Delaware, the Dover Air Force Base served as home to the U.S. Air Force's 436th Airlift "Eagle Wing" and the U.S. Air Force Reserve's 512th Airlift "Liberty Wing." The base became perhaps best known, however, as the site for the return of soldiers killed in action overseas. In New Jersey, the massive Joint Base McGuire-Dix-Lakehurst had more than forty-four thousand civilian employees, active-duty personnel, and their family members living and working on and around the base and contributing to its economic impact on the region.

From the Revolutionary War to the global war on terror and beyond, military bases and other facilities in the Greater Philadelphia region protected the homeland and trained, equipped, and otherwise served military personnel. Despite the loss of thousands of government jobs in Philadelphia and the surrounding region in the late twentieth and early twenty-first centuries, the military maintained an active presence that supported overseas contingency operations and contributed to local economies.

Philadelphia Navy Yard

Jim Saksa

The history of the Philadelphia Navy Yard has been one of constant struggle, repeatedly staring down imminent closure only to be saved at the last second by stalwart local politicians or a timely military conflict. Although fondly remembered as the outfitter of the first American fleet, builder of the first warship under the Constitution, launcher of the largest U.S. battleships, and a frontrunner in aviation experimentation, the Navy Yard served as a secondary naval facility throughout

FIGURE 72. Navy Yard at Hog Island, ca. 1917. During World War I, the shipyard expanded and modernized. LIBRARY COMPANY OF PHILADELPHIA.

most of its active life. After closing as an active yard and base in 1996, the Navy Yard rebounded in the twenty-first century as an office park employing thousands of people, but far less than its peak of nearly fifty thousand workers during the Second World War.

The federal government established the Philadelphia Navy Yard in 1801 in Southwark, then south of the city limits, on the site of a shore battery built toward the end of King George's War (1744–48). Just nine years after it opened, the Southwark Navy Yard faced its first shutdown scare when Congress debated closure. British naval aggression, which soon led to the War of 1812, saved the nascent facility. The war's end brought renewed worries about imminent closure, held at bay only by the continued construction of the 74-gun *Franklin*, the Navy Yard's first major warship, which launched before fifty thousand onlookers on August 21, 1815. The Southwark yard laid keel on another ship-of-the-line, the *Pennsylvania*, in 1821, but budget cuts delayed its launch until 1837. Redesigned into a 136-gun, four-deck behemoth, the *Pennsylvania* was the U.S. Navy's largest sailing warship.

The cramped Southwark site lacked space for the machine shops required to build state-of-the-art steam-powered and ironclad warships in use by the time of the Civil War (1861–65). Fearing again that the navy would leave the city, Philadelphians offered a new site at League Island, at the confluence of the Schuylkill and Delaware Rivers, which they proposed to sell to the federal government for a single dollar in 1862. Politics delayed the deal's consummation for six years while New England congressmen sought to bring more shipbuilding jobs to their constituents.

League Island's development benefited from the

largesse of Camden, New Jersey, lawyer George Maxwell Robeson, who became secretary of the navy in 1869. The Republican bigwig showered his shipbuilding friends along the Delaware with government contracts. For League Island, he ordered construction of a freshwater basin, new machine shops, foundries, and other more mundane improvements like roads and residences. Blueprints for the yard's development drafted in 1871 guided construction for the next 125 years. Over eight years, the navy slowly shifted outfitting and repair work to League Island from the Southwark yard, which closed with great fanfare during the nation's centennial year in 1876.

Although a corruption scandal involving falsified payment records raised another threat of closure in 1883, a naval renaissance of building and expanding the American fleet kept the yard busy between 1881 and 1891. Still, the lack of a modern industrial plant, machine tools, shipbuilding ways, and dry docks at League Island meant that contracts for new steel warships went to private shipbuilders along the Delaware. The Philadelphia Navy Yard assumed the role that became its primary purpose for most of its active life: an outfitting station and reserve fleet storage facility.

The Spanish-American War (1898) fueled expansion, including dredging of the back channel and construction of officers' quarters and modern shops for steel shipbuilding. But Philadelphia lacked a facility large enough for modern battleships until the completion of Dry Dock 2 in 1907. A string of accidents and frequent groundings caused by the narrow channels and cramped waterways around League Island landed Philadelphia's Navy Yard back on a closure list. A group of naval officers stationed on League Island averted that prospect by raising objections with Secretary of the Navy George von Lengerke Meyer. Meyer not only kept the yard open but also authorized some of the most extensive improvements in its history.

The Navy Yard gained many of the buildings that defined its modern character during the period of the First World War (1914–18). Shipbuilding Ways No. 1 opened in June 1915 and went into work immediately to build a marine transport ship, the *Henderson*. Wartime expansion effectively divided League Island in two: On the western side, the "new" naval shipyard with new dry docks, expanded shipbuilding ways, steel shops, a new foundry, and a 350-ton hammerhead crane, then the world's largest; on the eastern side, a navy base with a new receiving station, training center, and Marine Corps Reservation. Despite the improvements, Philadelphia Navy Yard launched just two ships before the armistice of November 11, 1918.

After the war, the Reserve Basin once again filled with a mothball flotilla, and the workforce shrank from more than twelve thousand to roughly five thousand. By this time League Island also had an aviation presence, which began in 1910 when the Aero Club of Pennsylvania built a hangar and airfield on the island's eastern end. Seven years later, the navy added a new hangar plus an aircraft factory that focused mainly on seaplanes.

The Navy Yard benefited from the Depression-era New Deal programs of President Franklin D. Roosevelt, which financed physical plant improvements. Roosevelt, a former undersecretary of the navy, also lavished funds on new warships, with a dozen turned out in Philadelphia between 1934 and 1938. It took the German invasion of Poland in 1939, however, to put sudden steel in the spines of navy leadership and turn Philadelphia into a first-class shipbuilding facility. Dry Docks 4 and 5 opened in 1941 and 1942. In 1940, work began on the battleship *New Jersey*, which served with distinction in World War II, the Korean War, and the Vietnam War, plus U.S. intervention in the Lebanese civil war, making it the most decorated battleship in U.S. history.

During World War II (1941–45), the Philadelphia Navy Yard became a self-contained community, replete with sports leagues, bands, and a newspaper. By far the Navy Yard's most prolific period, the war saw shipyard workers build 48 new warships, convert 41 more, repair and overhaul 574, complete and dry-dock 650, and outfit 600. The Naval Aircraft Factory built 500 planes and the Receiving Station processed 70,000 navy recruits. During 1941, the workforce rose from 24,000 to 33,000. In 1944 it hit 47,695 full-time civilian employees; adding military officers and high school students in the summer, employment topped 60,000.

Unbeknownst to nearly all who worked there, the Navy Yard played a role in experiments instrumental to building the atomic bomb. In 1944, a wooden building storing uranium for the Manhattan Project exploded, killing two and burning nine. At the time, few noticed—industrial mishaps were common at the yard, given the frenetic pace of construction and thousands of hastily trained workmen. The Naval Boiler and Turbine Laboratory at the yard were being used to separate U-235 isotopes from uranium ore to produce nuclear fuel. "Little Boy," dropped by the *Enola Gay* on Hiroshima on August 6, 1945, most likely used fissile material produced in Philadelphia.

The deadly accident, plus the Navy Yard's proximity to Philadelphia's large population, meant the base would never become a nuclear naval facility. Still, a small atomic plant at the Navy Yard operated until September 1945, and some of the research conducted at the yard guided the construction of the U.S. Navy's first atomic-powered submarine. These activities, plus rocket technology experiments and degaussing operations (demagnetizing ship hulls to protect against magnetic mines), may have inspired the urban myth of a "Philadelphia Experiment" to render a ship invisible.

After World War II, the renamed Philadelphia Navy Base and Naval Shipyard entered the Cold War era in its more traditional role as a port where ships were mothballed and overhauled. The workforce fell to nine thousand by July 1946. Minor surges of activity during the Korean and Vietnam Wars were short-lived. In 1967, a congressional mandate to move new ship construction to private yards made the *Blue Ridge*, a command ship launched in 1969, the last U.S. naval vessel built at the Philadelphia Navy Yard.

The Navy Yard entered the slow, ebbing decline that led to its eventual closing in 1996. The Marine Corps Reservation closed in 1977, ending the Marines' almost continuous 250-year presence in Philadelphia. Periodically, the Navy Yard faced closure, only to be saved by the efforts of the Delaware Valley's congressional delegations. Programs to upgrade older warships with state-of-the-art weapons systems kept the Navy Yard somewhat busy during the 1980s and 1990s, first with destroyers and cruisers in the Fleet Rehabilitation and Modernization Program, and later with the aircraft carrier Service Life Extension Program.

Despite the best efforts of local politicians—including a lawsuit by Senator Arlen Specter that Specter himself argued before U.S. Supreme Court—the base closed on September 26, 1996. For a time, the navy continued to operate the Propeller Manufacturing Center, the Inactive Ship Maintenance Facility, and the Philadelphia Naval Ship Systems Engineering Station. Area politicians scrambled to recruit shipbuilding companies to use the Navy Yard's large dry docks. Mayor Edward G. Rendell pursued a deal with German shipbuilder Meyer Werft that fell through in 1995 after Governor Tom Ridge rebuffed the proposal's $167 million in government incentives as "pure fantasy." Ironically, two years later, Ridge supported a more expensive deal to bring Norway's Kværner (which later merged with Aker, adopting the latter's name) to Philadelphia.

In 2000, the Philadelphia Industrial Development Corporation (PIDC) acquired control of the Navy Yard's remaining twelve hundred acres and drafted plans to develop it into an office park. Following a master plan adopted in 2004, PIDC spent $150 million to improve the Navy Yard's infrastructure. More than 150 companies opened offices at the Navy Yard, spending $750 million on private development—much of it to renovate historically significant naval buildings. By 2022, fifteen thousand employees worked at the Navy Yard, exceeding employment during any other point in the Navy Yard's history except for World War II.

National Guard

William V. Bartleson

The roots of the National Guard can be traced to Philadelphia and congressional action during the city's decade as the nation's capital. The contributions and shortcomings of the colonial militia during the War of Independence, combined with cultural and political mistrust of standing military forces, spurred Congress to define how the United States would defend itself from foreign and domestic aggression. The resulting Militia Act of 1792 standardized regulations for militia companies throughout the states. This act was the first in a series of developments that gradually led to the creation of the modern National Guard.

Volunteer militias formed and disbanded in the Philadelphia region throughout the nineteenth century as needed for domestic unrest and major military conflicts, including the War of 1812 and Mexican-American War. Following the Civil War, in 1870, the Pennsylvania militia companies formally changed their name to "The National Guard of Pennsylvania," almost fifty years before the federal government adopted the term. Several prominent Philadelphia military organizations with lineages dating back to the Revolution became part of the statewide body, including the First Troop Philadelphia City Cavalry, Washington Grays of Philadelphia, and the Philadelphia Associators.

Similarly, New Jersey militia companies consolidated into state regiments that eventually folded into U.S. Army divisions. The 1st New Jersey Regiment, originally mustered for the Continental army and revived during the Civil War, in 1869 became the "New Jersey National Guard," which also encompassed the 3rd New Jersey Regiment from Burlington and Camden Counties. Delaware, despite the state's small geographic size and population, had 564 organized militia companies in 1891, many with long lineages dating to the Revolutionary War and the War of 1812.

The first major mobilization of the Pennsylvania National Guard resulted not from trouble abroad but from trouble at home and resulted in tragedy. In 1877, the Great Railroad Strike caused a massive labor stoppage, and protests engulfed several major cities, including Philadelphia and Pittsburgh. After the Pittsburgh militia proved insubordinate to state orders to quell the unrest, Governor John F. Hartranft ordered troops of the First Division of National Guard from Philadelphia to disperse a large crowd of protesters at Pittsburgh's Pennsylvania Railroad Depot. The outnumbered troops faced more than twelve thousand strikers and sympathizers, and the situation quickly deteriorated. As the guardsmen advanced, the crowd did not back down, troops fired into the fray, and the violent clash killed twenty people. A full-scale riot ensued and drove the Philadelphians from the yard. It took the U.S. Army to finally restore order.

Philadelphia and the surrounding counties contributed several National Guard regiments to the U.S. Army during the Spanish-American War, the first major conflict in which the Pennsylvania, New Jersey, and Delaware National Guards were mustered for federal service. Fourteen regiments formed, including six from the Philadelphia area. The First Troop Philadelphia City Cavalry—once the personal guard for General George Washington and the oldest unit in the National Guard—re-formed and joined two Philadelphia Volunteer Artillery Batteries and the Volunteer Infantry Regiments at camp near Lebanon, Pennsylvania. The majority remained stateside, but the 4th Pennsylvania Infantry saw action during the Puerto Rican campaign near Guayama in August 1898. Their only combat action was cut short by the announcement of the armistice on the same day.

Four New Jersey National Guard regiments raised during the Spanish-American War were sent to camps in Florida, Georgia, and South Carolina to prepare for deployment in the Caribbean. Delaware also raised about five hundred troops in ten companies. The New Jersey and Delaware National Guard did not leave the United States but nevertheless lost dozens of men to disease and accidents while encamped in southern states.

By the time of the Great War (1914–18), the federal Efficiency in Militia Act had created the modern National Guard system. Drawing upon prior militia legislation, the 1903 act sought to improve the efficiency, standardization, and armament of the National Guard; formalized the circumstances in which the National Guard could be federalized and deployed; and established the Corp of Reserve Officers.

Under the new law, National Guard units of New Jersey, Pennsylvania, and Delaware were called into federal service several times during the twentieth century. During the First World War, which gave the National Guard its first experience in intense direct combat, Philadelphia units consisting of the 111th Infantry Regiment (the "Associators"), the 104th Cavalry Regiment (the 1st Troop City Cavalry), and the 108th Field Artillery joined units from the Pittsburgh region to form the 28th Infantry Division. This division remained the designated unit for the Pennsylvania National Guard while under federal service throughout the twentieth century.

Modern warfare drastically reshaped roles on the battlefield for Philadelphia units with Revolutionary lineages. They created machine-gun battalions, and the famed 1st Troop of the Philadelphia City Cavalry dismounted and joined the 103rd Trench Mortar Battery. The 28th Division, known as the "Keystone" division, arrived on the western front in France on

May 31, 1918, and was quickly thrust into the Battle of Château-Thierry. After the Pennsylvanians repelled a German attack while suffering heavy losses, General John Pershing referred to them as his "iron division." Unlike the Spanish-American War, the National Guard was not held in reserve and saw combat in the Meuse-Argonne, Champagne, and Marne campaigns. The 28th Division spent 102 days on the front line and suffered fourteen thousand casualties.

New Jersey National Guard regiments, along with elements from the Delaware National Guard, were assigned to the 29th Infantry Division. The 1st New Jersey Infantry and the 5th Delaware Infantry comprised the 114th Infantry Regiment and participated in the Meuse-Argonne Offensive in September 1918. Despite their relatively short time at the front, intense combat inflicted heavy casualties: 5,570 men, more than 30 percent of the division, were killed or wounded.

In keeping with the complex and expansive evolution of the United States military following the First World War, the National Guard continued to modernize and reorganize. Infantry regiments of the Pennsylvania National Guard were reassigned to engineering battalions and coastal artillery batteries, and New Jersey transferred several regiments into military police and reconnaissance. In 1933, the Pennsylvania National Guard headquarters transferred from Philadelphia, its home since 1776, to the state capital in Harrisburg.

During World War II, National Guard units from the Delaware Valley returned to the fields of France. In Philadelphia, the 28th Infantry Division re-formed and deployed to the European Theater, and several Philadelphia-based regiments returned to the Keystone Division, including the 108th Field Artillery Battalion. The 104th Cavalry Regiment, pulling troops from the 1st Troop of the Philadelphia City Cavalry, initially served stateside to provide security for the critical industrial areas around the Delaware River. Similarly, the 111th Infantry Regiment of "Ben Franklin Associators" detached from the 28th Infantry Division to guard port facilities along the Eastern Seaboard.

Once deployed, the 28th Infantry Division fought in some of the most ferocious battles in France, including the breakout of Allied forces from Normandy. During the liberation of Paris in 1944, elements of the division famously paraded down the Champs Élysées. This revelry preceded the most vicious combat the Pennsylvania National Guard experienced, in the Battle of the Hurtgen Forest, where the 28th Division earned the nickname "the bloody bucket" in reference to its keystone shaped insignia and heavy losses. After participating in the Battle of the Bulge and the Rhineland campaign, the division was pulled off the line after forty-one months in combat. Following the surrender of German forces, the division was deactivated from federal service in Harrisburg on November 20, 1945.

New Jersey National Guard regiments were assigned to the 44th Infantry Division during the Second World War. Originally conceived in 1920, the 44th Infantry Division was designed to receive New Jersey, Delaware, and New York National Guard regiments, but Delaware guardsmen were never incorporated. The New Jersey 57th Infantry Brigade, consisting of the 114th and 113th Infantry Regiments, joined the 112th Field Artillery Regiment at Fort Dix and initially deployed to the Delaware River after the Japanese attack on Pearl Harbor. In September 1944, the 44th Infantry Division deployed to Europe, serving 190 days in combat and participating in campaigns in central and northern France, the Ardennes, and the Rhineland. The 44th suffered 6,111 battlefield casualties, earned three distinguished unit citations, and accepted the surrender of famed rocket scientist Werner Von Braun.

With the exception of single regiments and battalions, the Pennsylvania, New Jersey, and Delaware National Guard were not federalized during the Korean or Vietnam Wars. During the Persian Gulf War, Philadelphians from the 121st Transportation Company deployed to the Middle East, but the majority of Philadelphia regiments remained inactive on a federal level. The September 11, 2001, attacks and the invasion of Iraq in 2003 brought the Keystone Division back into combat as regiments and combat brigades deployed in support of Operation Iraqi Freedom and Operation Enduring Freedom. Two of the oldest Philadelphian units, Ben Franklin's "Associators" of the 111th Infantry Regiment and the 1st Troop Philadelphia City Cavalry of the 104th Cavalry Regiment, deployed to Kuwait and Iraq as part of the Pennsylvania National Guard.

The 50th Combat Brigade of the New Jersey National Guard, under the 42nd Infantry Division,

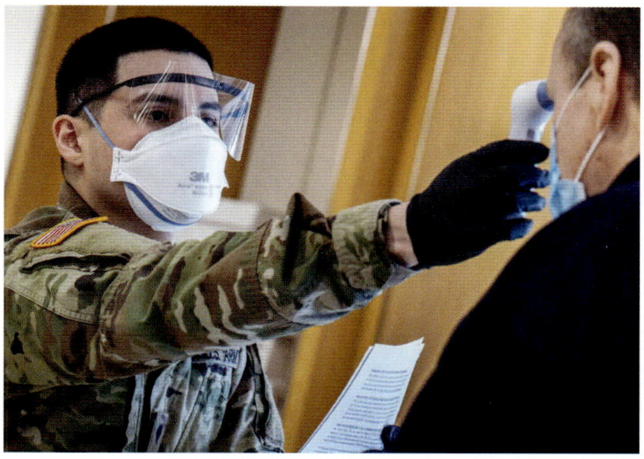

FIGURE 73. On COVID duty, 2021. In Moorestown, N.J., the New Jersey National Guard assisted with temperature screening at a vaccination site during the COVID-19 pandemic. PHOTOGRAPH BY MARK C. OLSEN, U.S. DEPARTMENT OF DEFENSE.

deployed as part of the occupation of Iraq in 2008. From 2003 to 2013, the Delaware Army National Guard deployed several units in support of U.S. forces in Iraq and Afghanistan. In conjunction with the National Guard State Partnership Program, units from the Delaware Valley participate in joint training exercises and general ambassadorship in countries including Lithuania, Albania, Trinidad and Tobago, Jordan, Kuwait, and the United Arab Emirates.

National Guard units from the tristate area deployed stateside after major snowstorms, Hurricane Katrina, Hurricane Ivan, and Superstorm Sandy. The 114th Regiment of the New Jersey National Guard and the 112th Regiment of the Pennsylvania National Guard provided security for personnel of the Federal Emergency Management Agency (FEMA) in New Orleans in 2005. In February 2010, Delaware National Guard soldiers participated in "Operation Arctic Vengeance" and aided emergency management, fire, and police agencies during a blizzard. In the aftermath of Superstorm Sandy, New Jersey National Guard units aided in the rescue, evacuation, and resupply of devastated areas across the region.

In the early decades of the twenty-first century, thousands of men and women in Pennsylvania, New Jersey, and Delaware continued the tradition of citizen service. The National Guard of the Delaware Valley remained a vital organization in international conflicts and local disaster relief and recovery.

Armories

Jean-Pierre Beugoms

Armories served as military training and recruiting sites, arms depots, headquarters, and social clubs for the nation's citizen soldiers. Early armories in Philadelphia were simply rented spaces in commercial buildings. After the Civil War, permanent structures for the exclusive use of the Pennsylvania National Guard supplanted these ad hoc armories as business interests responded to labor unrest by funding an armory construction boom. In the twentieth century, government-funded armories evolved into community centers as well as military sites. Armory design reflected these changes in purpose, patronage, and function.

During the eighteenth and early nineteenth centuries, Philadelphia and other cities lacked permanent armories. Militia units such as the First Troop, Philadelphia City Cavalry, the Second Troop of Light Horse, and the State Fencibles met in hotel rooms and taverns and drilled in public parks and squares, riding schools, and circuses. For drill, these units often rented floors in multistory commercial buildings, including the Union Building at Eighth and Chestnut Streets, the cast-iron Swain Building at 503–7 Chestnut Street, and a restaurant in the Northern Liberties neighborhood known as Military Hall. However, these facilities were not structurally strong enough to support drills by large units or secure enough to protect arms and equipment from theft.

In 1857, Philadelphia became one of the first cities with a permanent armory when the Infantry Corps, National Guards, purchased ground opposite Independence Hall and built the three-story National Guards Hall. In addition to quarters, storage, and meeting rooms, the building contained a drill hall on the second floor that could support an entire regiment.

The First Troop constructed its first armory, a two-story structure, in 1863. In 1874, the troop commissioned the architectural firm Furness & Hewitt to design a new armory, to be built at Twenty-First and

Ash Streets with funds from wealthy members. Frank Furness designed a compact three-story structure with a drill hall annex in the style of a medieval castle. The building was one of the nation's first castellated armories, which were distinctive for their thick walls topped with battlements, narrow windows, and bartizans. Industrialists and National Guard officials favored this style because it provided greater security in times of labor unrest. Architects embraced it because it unified form and function.

In an era of labor unrest, fundraising for armory construction in Philadelphia accelerated as wealthy private donors increasingly came to view the Pennsylvania National Guard as a strikebreaking force. In the wake of the nationwide Great Railroad Strike of 1877, Philadelphia gained new armories for the First Regiment, Second Regiment, and First Troop. James H. Windrim designed the First Regiment Armory (built in 1884), located at Broad and Cherry Streets until it was demolished in 1979. The Second Regiment Armory (1895–97), designed by the firm Rankin & Kellogg, stood at Broad Street and Susquehanna Avenue. The First Troop's third armory (1901), at Twenty-Third and Chestnut Streets, replaced the Furness armory, which suffered a collapsed roof in 1899 following a snowstorm. The local firm Newman, Woodman, & Harris designed the new armory, which continued to be used by the First Troop into the twenty-first century. All three castellated armories limited access to the interior with raised windows and single entranceways. As a cavalry armory, the First Troop Armory's interior contained a spacious central hall with a dirt floor to serve as a riding ring (later paved to accommodate motor vehicles). These buildings received funding almost entirely from private donors. For example, the patrons of the First Regiment Armory included the Pennsylvania Railroad, merchant John Wanamaker, and Edwin Benson, an ex-National Guard officer and future president of the Union League.

By the end of the nineteenth century, Philadelphia boasted six permanent armories. In New Jersey, meanwhile, officers of New Jersey's Sixth Regiment successfully lobbied the state legislature to approve construction of a new armory in Camden to replace the old one at Bridge and West Streets (which remained standing until destroyed by fire in 1906). A Philadelphia contractor completed the building in 1897, and it remained in use as an armory, and after 1953 as a convention center, until its demolition in 1977 to create a site for a Veterans Administration hospital. For state officials and guardsmen, the army primarily served to protect the men and stores from attack by a mob. Toward that end, architect Charles A. Gifford designed the Camden Armory on Haddon Avenue to look like a fortress, and a line of railroad tracks alongside the structure allowed for safe transport of troops out of the city. In the early twentieth century, Camden gained an additional armory on Wright Avenue to serve as the headquarters of a field artillery unit.

Unlike Pennsylvania, New Jersey built its armories mostly from public funds. The state legislature passed armory appropriations bills—five in the span of a decade—and established a state armory board that supervised the construction of new facilities. Pennsylvania followed suit when that state's legislature created its armory board in 1905. The influx of this new source of funding led to a surge in construction in the Philadelphia suburbs, with armories sprouting in Media (1908), West Chester (1916), Reading (1919), and Norristown (1928). Delaware also shifted from private to public funding of armories. Troop B, First Delaware Cavalry, was able to raise money from private sources to build its home at the Wilmington Armory, located on Twelfth and Orange Streets. From 1890 to 1925, this "State Arsenal" served as quarters for all of the city's National Guard units. When guardsmen complained that the space was too cramped, the Delaware legislature authorized a State Armory Commission to build a new armory and appropriated $250,000 for that purpose.

As the perceived threat of a revolution by labor subsided and the federal Militia Act of 1903 transformed state militias from industrial police forces to reserve forces for the regular army, the purpose and form of armories changed. With armories no longer considered targets of attack, governments hired architects to design new armories with civilian functions in mind and adapted existing armories for public use. Armories in a diversity of architectural styles superseded the fortresses of the late nineteenth century. In Philadelphia, Windrim designed the Third Regiment Armory (1898), Broad and Wharton Streets, in the Romanesque style typical of the day but also included the features of a medieval castle, such as crenellations. The armory became the site for circuses, prizefights, and fraternal club meetings and was converted into loft apartments in 2003. Philip H. Johnson designed two armories in the Classical Revival style: a three-story cavalry armory (1916) resembling a railroad station at Thirty-Second and Lancaster, later adapted into a gymnasium by Drexel University, and the two-story General Thomas J. Stewart Memorial Armory (1928) in Norristown. Delaware architect Edward Canby May chose an Egyptian Revival style for his design of the Wilmington Armory (1928), located on Tenth and DuPont Streets.

During the 1930s, the armory construction program of the Works Progress Administration and Public Works Administration continued this process toward civilian-oriented armory functions and design. To save taxpayer money, economy of design became the watchword, in stark contrast to the monumental privately funded armories of the nineteenth century. Armories typically followed standardized designs with T-shaped or I-shaped plans in art deco or art moderne style. The New Deal dramatically increased the amount of federal funds disbursed by the states for armory construction. As a result, armories proliferated across the region, especially in towns and suburbs. Examples include the Hamburg Armory (1937) in Berks County and the Special Troops Armory in the Ogontz neighborhood (1938–39) of Philadelphia and company-sized armories in Milford (ca. 1938) and New Castle (ca. 1934–35?), Delaware.

At the turn of the twenty-first century, a few of these suburban and small-town armories were turned over to local communities to use as they saw fit. For example, the Borough of Media redeveloped the Media Armory as a home for the Pennsylvania Veterans Museum and a grocery store, and the West Chester Armory became a theater for the performing arts.

National Guard armories in the region developed in tandem with architectural fashion, the mission of the citizen soldier, and the role of government in the social life of the nation. The ornate castellated armories of Philadelphia, Camden, and Wilmington provide physical evidence of domestic turmoil and close links between the National Guard and their wealthy patrons during the post–Civil War era. Guardsmen's reliance on private funding for armory construction not only helped turn state militias into a police force for industry, but also enabled local architects to develop a distinctive style for a building type that had never had one. The shift to public funding in the twentieth-century armories meant that armories were often the product of pork barrel legislation or took the form of government make-work projects. States responded to the public desire for more civic spaces by expanding construction to small towns and suburban neighborhoods. Architects, in turn, embraced contemporary styles and the armories lost much of their aesthetic distinctiveness.

Arsenals

Jean-Pierre Beugoms

For much of the nation's history Philadelphia held a preeminent position as the provider of logistical support to the U.S. Army, and federal arsenals played a considerable role in the economic life of the city. The Schuylkill Arsenal and Frankford Arsenal were, respectively, the largest manufacturers of uniforms and small-arms ammunition in the country, often employing more workers than private industry. The Frankford Arsenal was also the site of innovations in mass production and munitions development.

The Schuylkill Arsenal, established by an act of Congress on April 2, 1794, occupied an eight-acre site between the east bank of the Schuylkill River and Grays Ferry Road. Constructed between 1802 and 1806, in its early years the arsenal operated as a storage depot for gunpowder, arms, and other supplies. (In 1803, the arsenal issued clothing, blankets, tents, and equipment to the Lewis and Clark Expedition.) The functions of the arsenal changed after the War of 1812 and the opening of a new arsenal in Frankford in 1816. While Frankford superseded the Schuylkill Arsenal as an ordnance depot, the older site evolved into a clothing arsenal because of its proximity to textile mills. It ceased storing arms in the 1830s, and in 1842, after the Quartermaster Department acquired the site from a defunct supply agency, the Schuylkill Arsenal became a center for manufacturing, procuring, and distributing clothing, footwear, and camp equipage.

The Schuylkill Arsenal provided the army with supplies either by contracting out requisitions to private firms or, when the contract system proved deficient, by manufacturing goods onsite. The arsenal's facilities for making bootees (ankle-length boots) and tents, in particular, produced items superior to those acquired by contract. The arsenal also employed a large female workforce, which varied from four hundred to ten thousand depending on military demand. While the men worked as packers, cutters, tailors, and laborers, women found jobs as seamstresses. Working from home, the seamstresses sewed cut textiles provided to them by the arsenal, returned with finished uniforms, and received wages on a per-piece basis. Seamstresses hired by contractors, on the other hand, often worked in crowded sweatshops and received a fraction of what the public employees earned.

The low wages of seamstresses in Philadelphia and other cities drew criticism in 1833 from Philadelphia economist and publisher Mathew Carey, who argued that the women made too little to support themselves or their children. Seamstresses also began forming trade unions, organizing strikes, and writing petitions to improve their lot. In 1835, seamstresses and women employed in other trades organized the Female Improvement Society to protest inadequate wages. During the Civil War, arsenal seamstresses petitioned the War Department to set a minimum wage for both public and private sector workers and called for an end to the army's use of contractors. Although the petitioners met with President Abraham Lincoln and government workers received a pay raise, the practice of subcontracting continued.

By the time of the First World War, the Schuylkill Arsenal's site had become too small to meet the demands of outfitting the American Expeditionary Forces. The arsenal, renamed the Philadelphia Quartermaster Depot, moved in 1918 to a new location on Twenty-First Street and Oregon Avenue. From 1921 to 1941, the depot housed a quartermaster training school for commissioned officers, officer candidates, and enlisted personnel. It lost this function, however, when rapidly increasing enrollment during World War II resulted in the school's removal to Fort Lee, Virginia. The arsenal served as a storage site until its closing in 1958.

Philadelphia's second arsenal, in Frankford, served different purposes. Established by the Ordnance Department on May 27, 1816, the arsenal occupied twenty-two acres on the north bank of the Frankford Creek, near its confluence with the Delaware River. Equipped with a wharf, the site provided waterborne access to the Worrell gunpowder mills. Initially, the arsenal included four stone buildings arranged around a parade ground, and open land in the surrounding area offered the possibility of future expansion.

In the decades prior to the Civil War, the Frankford Arsenal functioned as a depot for storing, repairing, and cleaning military equipment and weapons. On a small scale, the arsenal also manufactured ordnance, including paper cartridges, percussion caps, and musket balls. Arsenal commanders also awarded contracts to private firms such as the DuPont Company, whose gunpowder they inspected before shipping it to other posts.

In the 1830s, the site began to develop into a bustling industrial and scientific complex. In 1835, the secretary of war made the arsenal the Ordnance Department's only proving ground for gunpowder, and the site nearly doubled in size with the purchase of adjacent land in 1836 and 1850. Previously manned by about twenty-five soldiers plus a temporary civilian workforce, the arsenal expanded to employ hundreds of civilian workers.

During the Philadelphia nativist riots of 1844, the Frankford Arsenal faced the only threat to its security in its 161-year history. On May 8 in neighboring Kensington, mobs destroyed St. Michael's Roman Catholic Church and several homes belonging to Irish immigrants. Smoke could be seen from the arsenal, whose commander sent arms and ammunition to Philadelphia County sheriff Morton McMichael. Rumors of an impending attack on the arsenal and a nearby church prompted the War Department to deploy reinforcements from a unit based in Fort Columbus, New York. Nothing came of the rumors, however.

In the ensuing years, commanders expanded the arsenal with a rolling mill, a laboratory for conducting experiments in ballistics and explosives, and a factory that produced more than one million percussion caps a month by 1853. Steam-powered machinery, introduced in 1852, hastened the transition from hand craftsmanship to industrial production. By 1864, the arsenal had become a manufacturing center that employed 1,226 civilian laborers and artisans, many of them from the neighboring community of Bridesburg.

Given the Frankford Arsenal's role as a scientific testing ground, fires and explosions were common. In 1861, an explosion at one of the laboratories resulted in

FIGURE 74. Loading bullets at Frankford Arsenal, ca. 1914–18. Women often worked in the region's arsenals. LIBRARY OF CONGRESS.

two fatalities and, in 1862, another destroyed part of the percussion cap factory. Arsenal commander Major Theodore T. S. Laidley responded to events such as these by constructing new buildings with wrought-iron frames, an innovation that allowed the beams and columns to withstand explosions even if the roofs collapsed and the walls blew out.

Throughout the late nineteenth and twentieth centuries, the Ordnance Department purchased more land and added an array of buildings, including an optical shop for developing instruments and munitions. Engineers and scientists contributed to the arsenal's already substantial catalogue of innovations by developing the Gatling gun, smokeless powder, 75 mm and 105 mm recoilless rifles, rocket-powered pilot ejection seat, and laser rangefinder, to name a few. Production of munitions increased dramatically during the Spanish-American War, the two world wars, and the Korean War. At its peak, in 1942, the arsenal employed twenty-two thousand workers and produced nearly all of the nation's wartime supply of small-arms ammunition for that year.

In November 1974, the Department of Defense announced that the Frankford Arsenal would be closed. The move, part of a nationwide base reduction and consolidation process, drew criticism from residents and local politicians and became a bone of contention during the 1976 presidential election campaign. On the eve of Election Day, vice presidential candidate Walter Mondale visited the arsenal and promised to keep it open if the voters elected Jimmy Carter president. The site had grown to more than two hundred buildings on 110 acres of land and maintained a workforce of two thousand people. The arsenal closed in the fall of 1977, but it later reopened as a business park.

The Schuylkill Arsenal and Frankford Arsenal played critical roles in U.S. military supply system during times of war and peace. They also contributed to Philadelphia's status as one of the nation's principal manufacturing and commercial cities.

EXPLORE MORE

To delve into the history of Philadelphia-area military defenses, see works by Jeffery M. Dorwart, including: *Invasion and Insurrection: Security, Defense, and War in the Delaware Valley, 1621–1815* (University of Delaware Press, 2008), *Fort Mifflin of Philadelphia: An Illustrated History* (University of Pennsylvania Press, 1998), and *The Philadelphia Navy Yard: From the Birth of the U.S. Navy to the Nuclear Age* (University of Pennsylvania Press, 2001). Books that expand on the experiences of veterans include Wallace E. Davies, *Patriotism on Parade: The Story of Veterans' and Hereditary Organizations in America, 1793–1900* (Harvard University Press, 1955); Richard H. Taylor, *Homeward Bound: American Veterans Return from War* (Praeger, 2007); and Paul Dickson and Thomas B. Allen, *The Bonus Army: An American Epic* (Walker & Company, 2004). Also see John K. Mahon, *History of the Militia and the National Guard* (Macmillan, 1983). For more on Quaker principles, see Peter Brock, *Pioneers of a Peaceable Kingdom: The Quaker Peace Testimony from the Colonial Era to the First World War* (Princeton University Press, 1968) and explore the Peace Collection at Swarthmore College in Swarthmore, Pa.

Museums and public events offer limited access to the region's active military installations. Joint Base McGuire-Dix-Lakehurst in New Jersey offers group tours by appointment and invites the public to the annual "Power in the Pines Air & Space Open House." Also in New Jersey, the Navy Lakehurst Historical Society offers walking tours of historic sites of Naval Air Station Lakehurst. In Delaware, Dover Air Force Base is the site of the Air Mobility Command Museum, which includes an outdoor airpark as well as exhibits housed in a restored World War II hangar. In Horsham, Pa., adjacent to the Biddle Air National Guard Station is the volunteer-run Harold F. Pitcairn Wings of Freedom Aviation Museum. Additional museums across the region, including local historical societies, feature exhibits on military topics. The Independence Seaport Museum, 211 S. Columbus Boulevard, Philadelphia, encompasses naval and maritime history and is home to two historic ships, the cruiser *Olympia* and submarine *Becuna*. On the opposite side of the Delaware River in Camden, N.J., is the Battleship New Jersey Museum and Memorial, a ship that became the most decorated in U.S. history after launching from the Philadelphia Navy Yard during World War II. In Media, Pa., the former Media Armory at 12 E. State Street is home to the Pennsylvania Veterans Museum. Farther afield are the Vietnam Veterans Memorial and Museum and the National Guard Museum of New Jersey in Monmouth County; the Pennsylvania National Guard Military Museum at Fort Indiantown Gap in Lebanon County, Pa.; and the Delaware Military Museum in Wilmington, Del.

Representing the ongoing service of citizen soldiers, the First Troop Philadelphia City Cavalry Twenty-Third Street Armory remains active at 22 S. Twenty-Third Street, Philadelphia. Some of the region's armories have been adapted for other purposes; for example, the Uptown Knauer Performing Arts Center occupies the former armory at 226 N. High Street, West Chester, Pa. On the community presence of armories, see Robert M. Fogelson, *America's Armories: Architecture, Society, and Public Order* (Harvard University Press, 1989).

Other former military installations put to new purposes include the former Frankford Arsenal, 2275 Bridge Street in Philadelphia, rebranded the Arsenal for its new life as an office and production center. Its history is told by James J. Farley in *Making Arms in the Machine Age: Philadelphia's Frankford Arsenal, 1816–1870* (Pennsylvania State University Press, 1994). The Philadelphia Navy Yard, 4747 S. Broad Street, is an evolving waterfront community in South Philadelphia. Many of its historic structures have been restored, preserved, or adapted to new purposes, including a World War II–era navy chapel that became home to the Chapel of the Four Chaplains, formerly located at Temple University, in 2001. The chapel is named for the four chaplains—a rabbi, a Roman Catholic priest, and two Protestant ministers—who lost their lives while ministering to soldiers during the sinking of the troop ship *Dorchester* in the North Atlantic in 1943. The ongoing redevelopment of the Navy Yard has added distinctive new commercial buildings to the historic landscape. The Navy Yard is also a certified arboretum with twenty acres of parks and a program of public art.

The service of military veterans is recalled by monuments throughout the region, among them the Tomb of the Unknown Revolutionary War Soldier in Washington Square and the All Wars Memorial to Colored Soldiers and Sailors, Logan Square and Benjamin Franklin Parkway, in Philadelphia. Sealing the relationship between local individuals and service to the nation are the region's national cemeteries: the Philadelphia National Cemetery, Haines Street and Limekiln Pike, Philadelphia; Washington Crossing National Cemetery, 830 Highland Road, Newtown, Pa.; soldiers' and naval plots in Mount Moriah Cemetery, Sixty-Second Street and Kingsessing Avenue, Philadelphia; Beverly National Cemetery, 916 Bridgeboro Road, Beverly, N.J.; and Finn's Point National Cemetery, Pennsville, N.J.

H.B.C.
REGULAR CLERKS
Mailing Section
TIME CARDS
338
334
320
318
319
306
312
313
314
307
308
309
295
303
287
294
288
289
290
282
283
284
277
278
276
271
272

Chapter 10

The Region's Reach to the Nation

Introduction

More than simply a place on a map, Greater Philadelphia is a dynamic participant in complex and always-evolving interactions with the rest of the nation and beyond. From the colonial period to the present, the region's energies in politics, financial industries, publishing, transportation, communications systems, and more have helped to weave together the many interests and cultures that comprise the United States. Such numerous pathways for interaction have made it possible for Americans to see—or at least imagine—themselves as living in common community despite the vast geographic expanse of the nation. By joining political parties, taking out insurance policies, subscribing to magazines, riding the rails or using the mails, placing telephone calls, or tuning in to radio or television, individual Americans have forged connections with each other while also tapping into the influences of Greater Philadelphia.

The Philadelphia region's reach has emanated in large part from entrepreneurship. Benjamin Franklin looms large as the prototypical networker whose interests extended beyond the city limits. He arrived in Philadelphia in 1723 as a runaway printing apprentice from Boston, bringing into his new home city the experience of that intercolonial journey. As he established his print shop in Philadelphia, he extended the business through partnerships across the British North American colonies. As a postmaster general, he oversaw delivery routes that spanned the Atlantic Seaboard from Florida to Maine and parts of Canada. Long before the American Revolution, Franklin's intercolonial outlook spawned his proposal for a more unified plan of government for the colonies—adopted in 1754 by seven colonies meeting in Albany, New York, but not ultimately enacted.

Philadelphia's role as a commercial and governmental center during the eighteenth century produced financial and political networks that reached beyond the city. The nation's first insurance companies, the Insurance Company of North America and the Philadelphia Contributionship (another Franklin initiative), formed in Philadelphia. Banking in the United States also traces its roots to Philadelphia as the home of the first commercial bank in the country (the Bank of North America, chartered in 1781). Philadelphia's service as capital of the United States during the 1790s enhanced its role in banking by making the city the site of the first Bank of the United States, and currency for the new nation flowed from the United States Mint. During that critical decade of the nation's history, Philadelphia not only hosted the federal government but also fanned the partisanship that produced the nation's first political parties. Like banking and insurance, the shape and scope of political parties changed over time but remained a constant link between the Philadelphia region and the nation.

Transportation and communication networks extended the region's reach as the nation expanded.

During the 1790s, Philadelphia-based publishers spread news from the nation's capital to a national readership in newspapers sent by mail, delivered by riders on horseback or by drivers of stagecoaches. Beginning in the 1830s, railroads not only made the mail move faster but also linked the Philadelphia region's residents and commerce with increasingly distant points across the continent. Telegraph lines followed the railroads, establishing similar connectivity for communication as newer cities like Cincinnati, St. Louis, and Chicago arose in the interior. The next leap in communication technology, the telephone, came to public attention in 1876, when Alexander Graham Bell demonstrated his invention at the Centennial Exhibition held in Philadelphia's Fairmount Park. By the turn of the twentieth century, the advent of wireless communication set the stage for Philadelphia to become an influential hub in national networks for radio and television.

Print and broadcast media allowed mass audiences to form around books, periodicals, and, later, radio and television programs produced in the Philadelphia region. *Godey's Lady's Book* became a national trendsetter from the 1830s through the 1860s under the editorship of Sarah Josepha Hale. Women in the middle class, or those who aspired to be, turned to Hale's periodical for fashion plates, news, and literary fiction. In the 1860s, Hale led a successful campaign to make Thanksgiving a national holiday. Later in the decade, Cyrus H. K. Curtis launched the *Ladies' Home Journal* and transformed the *Saturday Evening Post* into the nation's most popular magazine. As mass media moved to the airwaves in the twentieth century, local radio and television stations joined national networks, most based in New York. Programming flowed into the region but also outward through Philadelphia-based programs such as *The Atwater Kent Hour* on radio and *American Bandstand* and *The Mike Douglas Show* on television. Because of Philadelphia's centrality in broadcasting, in 1948 the city hosted three national conventions of political parties eager to reach the nationwide television audience.

By the late twentieth century, the nation's population began to shift toward Sun Belt cities like Los Angeles, which surpassed Philadelphia in the U.S. census of 1960, and Houston, which topped Philadelphia by 1990 (see Table 1). Although the Philadelphia region lost much of its preeminence in arenas such as finance and publishing by the twenty-first century, it nevertheless remained enmeshed in complex webs of connectivity with the rest of the nation. Look no farther than the Philadelphia skyline and the two towering skyscrapers of Comcast—once merely one of four cable television franchisees in Philadelphia—to see that the city remains home to communications and technology networks with immense impact. The invisible tentacles of the Internet reach into the region and outward, igniting connections with the potential to unite as well as divide. Headquarters of banks, insurance companies, and publishing houses—whether still operating or displaced by other uses when their occupants closed or left town—stand as reminders of the region's legacy. And even in the twenty-first century, coins bearing the imprint "P" pour from Philadelphia's U.S. Mint to replenish cash drawers and jangle in American pockets.

Postal Services

Charlene Mires

Philadelphia played a significant role in establishing and innovating postal services in the British colonies in North America and across the expanding United States. In Philadelphia, actions by the Second Continental Congress, the Constitutional Convention, and the U.S. Congress made mail delivery a function of American government. Important innovations occurred during the postmasterships of Philadelphians Benjamin Franklin and John Wanamaker. As delivery of mail extended across the continent with riders on horseback and drivers of stagecoaches, and later by steamboats, railroads, airplanes, and motor vehicles, the Philadelphia region's reach extended across an increasingly complex and far-flung network of communication.

The region's earliest-known mail carriers were indigenous Lenape runners, whom Dutch colonizers hired in the mid-seventeenth century to carry letters between settlements on the lower Delaware River (later Delaware) and the island of Manhattan. Lenape mail runners became fewer as English colonizers displaced the Dutch and set up post offices, where private couriers could pick up and deliver mail. William Penn established a post office in Philadelphia in 1683 to facilitate mail between the Falls of Delaware (Trenton, New Jersey) and

Maryland. After 1691, when the Crown established a private monopoly post office to serve all English colonies in America, absentee owner Thomas Neale appointed New Jersey governor Andrew Hamilton to head the enterprise. Post offices established in Burlington (1693) and Perth Amboy (1692), New Jersey, enabled mail between Philadelphia and New York, and weekly deliveries served major towns in the middle colonies and New England.

Benjamin Franklin entered postal service history in 1737, thirty years after the British government purchased control of the North American postal services from its earlier proprietors. Appointed local postmaster for Philadelphia, Franklin ran the post office with his wife, Deborah, from his successful print shop on High (Market) Street near Second Street. Newspaper publishers like Franklin often served as postmasters, which gave them advantages for circulating their publications and gaining access to news. But Franklin's interest in the mail also aligned with his other expanding intercolonial activities, such as scientific exchanges among members of the American Philosophical Society (which he founded in 1743). In 1753, Franklin successfully lobbied to be appointed postmaster general for the colonies, a position he held jointly with his friend and fellow printer William Hunter, the postmaster of Williamsburg, Virginia.

Franklin retained his royal appointment until his sympathies with the rebellion brewing in the British North American colonies led to his dismissal in 1774. Although he spent long periods of time in England, where he served as agent for Pennsylvania and other British colonies, Franklin has been credited with introducing innovations that enabled faster, more reliable communication along the Atlantic Seaboard. The number of post offices between Philadelphia and New York expanded to seven, and the speed of delivery between the two port cities increased with the addition of nighttime post riders. Franklin inspected post offices throughout the northern colonies and surveyed new routes to reorganize the system. American post roads (the routes for carrying mail) extended south to Florida and north to Maine and parts of Canada. Franklin also instituted new accounting methods, and for the first time the American postal service turned a profit. The innovation of the "penny post" allowed recipients to pay for their mail to be home delivered from the post office.

Franklin's reputation led the Second Continental Congress to appoint him the first postmaster of the new United States. By November 1776, however, he turned the work over to his son-in-law, Richard Bache, who served until 1782. Mail delivery remained a power of government under the Articles of Confederation and in Article I of the U.S. Constitution, heeding arguments by Philadelphia physician Benjamin Rush and others that a postal system would serve the vital purpose of uniting a growing, informed citizenry. As the new nation came to fruition, new post roads connected Philadelphia westward as far as Pittsburgh. While Philadelphia served as the nation's capital during the 1790s, Congress passed the Postal Act of 1792, which set special low rates for mailing newspapers, a boost for the circulation of local papers covering the federal government but also a benefit for countryside editors who reprinted news from exchange papers they received. The 1792 law also prohibited public officials from conducting surveillance of mail and gave Congress authority to designate postal routes, an important power for shaping the nation's further expansion.

Administration of the postal service moved to Washington, D.C., with the rest of the federal government in 1800, but Philadelphia and the surrounding region continued to benefit from expansion of the system. Innovations in transportation added to the reach and speed of mail. The government contracted with stagecoaches to carry mail as early as 1785, and stagecoach "express routes" continued into the early nineteenth century. Stagecoach operator James Reeside, based in Philadelphia starting in 1820, instituted a line of speedy, flashy red coaches between Philadelphia and New York and then expanded to Pittsburgh and beyond to become the largest mail contractor in the country. Steamboats also moved mail to the South and West, and a greater leap of speed came with railroads beginning in the 1830s. Early contracts for railroad transportation of mail included a route between Philadelphia and West Chester in 1832 and between Philadelphia and Mauch Chunk, Pennsylvania, in 1836; in New Jersey, the Camden and Amboy Railroad began to carry mail in 1834. Over the next four decades, postal service spanned the continent by means of overland stagecoaches, pony express riders, and finally the transcontinental railroad completed in 1869.

FIGURE 75. Post roads (map detail), 1796. Designated routes for mail delivery connected Philadelphia with points north, south, and west. MAP BY ABRAHAM BRADLEY JR., LIBRARY OF CONGRESS.

Nationwide postal service required a vast federal bureaucracy, which created equally vast opportunities for political patronage. Philadelphia's next noteworthy postmaster general, department store innovator John Wanamaker, gained the position in 1889 as a reward for fundraising for President Benjamin Harrison. Wanamaker brought his flair for modern marketing to the task, for example introducing commemorative stamps, which became wildly popular. He also proposed parcel post and rural free delivery, although these services did not come to fruition until after his term. Wanamaker's religious convictions shaped some of his actions, for example ending deliveries on Sundays and banning lottery tickets from the mail.

As in his department stores, Wanamaker sought to deploy modern technologies. With Philadelphia as one of the trial cities, Wanamaker introduced pneumatic tubes to speed mail between urban post office locations. The system involved six-inch pipes, buried underground, which hurtled canisters full of mail at high speed by force of air pressure. Wanamaker inaugurated Philadelphia's first tube in 1893 by sending a Bible wrapped in an American flag from a substation near Fourth and Chestnut Streets to the main post office then located at Ninth and Chestnut. The delivery took sixty-two seconds. Philadelphia's tube system subsequently expanded to more than nineteen miles connecting the main post office with business locations like the Bourse, other substations, and the city's primary railroad stations. Congress perennially questioned post office expenditures on the tube systems, however, and government-funded tubes ceased operation in Philadelphia and elsewhere in 1918.

In the early decades of the twentieth century, postal delivery innovations turned to the air, with Philadelphia playing a literally pivotal role due to its location between Washington, D.C., and New York City. Federal postal authorities chose a site in Bustleton, Northeast Philadelphia, for an airfield where planes carrying mail simultaneously from New York and Washington would land and hand off their mail bags to fresh planes and pilots for the rest of the route. Experienced army pilots carried out the experimental service between May and August 1918. The Post Office Department then took over the service and by 1919 extended airmail delivery across the continent, initially with a series of short connecting flights reaching from New York to San Francisco (stopping not in Philadelphia, but in central Pennsylvania in Bellefonte, Centre County). Transatlantic airmail began in 1939, but again originating from New York.

Largely out of the national spotlight for the rest of the twentieth and early twenty-first centuries, the Philadelphia region's mail delivery benefited and suffered from continuing changes in technology and management of the nation's vast postal network. Capacity and speed increased with automated sorting and zip codes (introduced in 1963), and trucks and airplanes moved more of the mail as railroads declined. Motorized routes served the expanding suburbs. But mounting debts and inefficiencies plagued the system, leading to the Postal Reorganization Act of 1970, which ended the federal Post Office Department and transferred its functions to the United States Postal Service, a government-owned corporation. By the early twenty-first century, the system continued to struggle as electronic communication drastically cut the volume of physical mail and private carriers like UPS competed effectively to deliver packages. Cost-cutting measures led to closures of many local post offices in communities across the region. Mail-sorting operations in Philadelphia moved in 2006 from the main post office at Thirtieth and Market Streets (opened in 1935) to a new facility near Philadelphia International Airport.

Regardless of continuing changes in technology and mail habits, Philadelphia maintained at least one distinctive place in the nation's mail service: the place where stamps are affixed to the corners of envelopes. Symbols of Philadelphia appeared on postage stamps beginning with the first American stamps issued in 1847, which depicted Benjamin Franklin as well as George Washington. In 2007, when the postal service issued the first "forever" stamp without a printed postage rate, the stamp bore a picture of the Liberty Bell. Chosen for its apparent timelessness as a national symbol, the iconic bell also connected the latest postal service innovation with Philadelphia and its longstanding role in mail delivery in the United States.

FIGURE 76. Christmas at the post office, 1951. Holiday mail that poured into the Philadelphia post office required sorting by hand in the era before automation. SPECIAL COLLECTIONS RESEARCH CENTER, TEMPLE UNIVERSITY LIBRARIES.

TABLE 1. Philadelphia Population Trends Relative to Other American Cities

Populations enumerated by the U.S. Census Bureau. Prior to the 1854 consolidation of Philadelphia City and County, census rankings included outlying districts of Philadelphia County (Northern Liberties, Southwark, Spring Garden).

1790	
1. New York, N.Y.	33,131
2. Philadelphia, Pa.	**28,522**
3. Boston town, Mass.	18,320
4. Charleston, S.C.	16,359
5. Baltimore town, Md.	13,503
6. Northern Liberties township, Pa.	**9,913**
7. Salem town, Mass.	7,921
8. Newport town, R.I.	6,716
9. Providence town, R.I.	6,380
10 (tie). Marblehead town, Mass.	
Southwark district, Pa.	**5,661**

1800	
1. New York, N.Y.	60,515
2. Philadelphia, Pa.	**41,220**
3. Baltimore, Md.	26,514
4. Boston town, Mass.	24,937
5. Charleston, S.C.	18,824
6. Northern Liberties township, Pa.	**10,718**
7. Southwark district, Pa.	**9,621**
8. Salem town, Mass.	9,457
9. Providence town, R.I.	7,614
10. Norfolk borough, Va.	6,926

1810	
1. New York, N.Y.	96,373
2. Philadelphia, Pa.	**53,722**
3. Baltimore, Md.	46,555
4. Boston town, Mass.	33,787
5. Charleston, S.C.	24,711
6. Northern Liberties township, Pa.	**19,874**
7. New Orleans, La.	17,242
8. Southwark district, Pa.	**13,707**
9. Salem town, Mass.	12,613
10. Albany, N.Y.	10,762

1820	
1. New York, N.Y.	123,706
2. Philadelphia, Pa.	**63,802**
3. Baltimore, Md.	62,738
4. Boston town, Mass.	43,298
5. New Orleans, La.	27,176
6. Charleston, S.C.	24,780
7. Northern Liberties township, Pa.	**19,678**
8. Southwark district, Pa.	**14,713**
9. Washington, D.C.	13,247
10. Salem town, Mass.	12,731

1830	
1. New York, N.Y.	202,589
2. Baltimore, Md.	80,620
3. Philadelphia, Pa.	**80,462**
4. Boston town, Mass.	61,392
5. New Orleans, La.	46,082
6. Charleston, S.C.	30,289
7. Northern Liberties township, Pa.	**28,872**
8. Cincinnati, Ohio	24,831
9. Albany, N.Y.	24,209
10. Southwark district, Pa.	**20,581**

1840	
1. New York, N.Y.	312,710
2. Baltimore, Md.	102,313
3. New Orleans, La.	102,193
4. Philadelphia, Pa.	**93,665**
5. Boston, Mass.	93,383
6. Cincinnati, Ohio	46,338
7. Brooklyn, N.Y.	36,233
8. Northern Liberties district, Pa.	**34,474**
9. Albany, N.Y.	33,721
10. Charleston, S.C.	29,261

1850	
1. New York, N.Y.	515,547
2. Baltimore, Md.	169,054
3. Boston, Mass.	136,181
4. Philadelphia, Pa.	**121,376**
5. New Orleans, La.	116,375
6. Cincinnati, Ohio	115,435
7. Brooklyn, N.Y.	96,838
8. St. Louis, Mo.	77,860
9. Spring Garden district, Pa.	**58,894**
10. Albany, N.Y.	50,763

1860	
1. New York, N.Y.	813,669
2. Philadelphia, Pa.	**565,529**
3. Brooklyn, N.Y.	266,661
4. Baltimore, Md.	212,418
5. Boston, Mass.	177,840
6. New Orleans, La.	168,675
7. Cincinnati, Ohio	161,044
8. St. Louis, Mo.	160,773
9. Chicago, Ill.	112,172
10. Buffalo, N.Y.	81,129

1870	
1. New York, N.Y.	942,292
2. Philadelphia, Pa.	**674,022**
3. Brooklyn, N.Y.	396,099
4. St. Louis, Mo.	310,864
5. Chicago, Ill.	298,977
6. Baltimore, Md.	267,354
7. Boston, Mass.	250,526
8. Cincinnati, Ohio	216,239
9. New Orleans, La.	191,148
10. San Francisco, Calif.	149,473

1880	
1. New York, N.Y.	1,206,299
2. Philadelphia, Pa.	**847,170**
3. Brooklyn, N.Y.	566,663
4. Chicago, Ill.	503,185
5. Boston, Mass.	362,839
6. St. Louis, Mo.	350,518
7. Baltimore, Md.	332,313
8. Cincinnati, Ohio	255,139
9. San Francisco, Calif.	233,959
10. New Orleans, La.	216,090

1890	
1. New York, N.Y.	1,515,301
2. Chicago, Ill.	1,099,850
3. Philadelphia, Pa.	**1,046,964**
4. Brooklyn, N.Y.	806,343
5. St. Louis, Mo.	451,770
6. Boston, Mass.	448,477
7. Baltimore, Md.	434,439
8. San Francisco, Calif.	298,997
9. Cincinnati, Ohio	296,908
10. Cleveland, Ohio	291,353

1900	
1. New York, N.Y.	3,437,202
2. Chicago, Ill.	1,698,575
3. Philadelphia, Pa.	**1,293,697**
4. St. Louis, Mo.	575,238
5. Boston, Mass.	560,892
6. Baltimore, Md.	508,957
7. Cleveland, Ohio	381,768
8. Buffalo, N.Y.	352,387
9. San Francisco, Calif.	342,782
10. Cincinnati, Ohio	325,902

1910	
1. New York, N.Y.	4,766,883
2. Chicago, Ill.	2,185,283
3. Philadelphia, Pa.	**1,549,008**
4. St. Louis, Mo.	687,029
5. Boston, Mass.	670,585
6. Cleveland, Ohio	560,663
7. Baltimore, Md.	558,485
8. Pittsburgh, Pa.	533,905
9. Detroit, Mich.	465,766
10. Buffalo, N.Y.	423,715
1920	
1. New York N.Y.	5,620,048
2. Chicago, Ill.	2,701,705
3. Philadelphia, Pa.	**1,823,779**
4. Detroit, Mich.	993,078
5. Cleveland, Ohio	796,841
6. St. Louis, Mo.	772,897
7. Boston, Mass.	748,060
8. Baltimore, Md.	733,826
9. Pittsburgh, Pa.	588,343
10. Los Angeles, Calif.	576,673
1930	
1. New York, N.Y.	6,930,446
2. Chicago, Ill.	3,376,438
3. Philadelphia, Pa.	**1,950,961**
4. Detroit, Mich.	1,568,662
5. Los Angeles, Calif.	1,238,048
6. Cleveland, Ohio	900,429
7. St. Louis, Mo.	821,960
8. Baltimore, Md.	804,874
9. Boston, Mass.	781,188
10. Pittsburgh, Pa.	669,817

1940	
1. New York, N.Y.	7,454,995
2. Chicago, Ill.	3,396,808
3. Philadelphia, Pa.	**1,931,334**
4. Detroit, Mich.	1,623,452
5. Los Angeles, Calif.	1,504,277
6. Cleveland, Ohio	878,336
7. Baltimore, Md.	859,100
8. St. Louis, Mo.	816,048
9. Boston, Mass.	770,816
10. Pittsburgh, Pa.	671,659
1950	
1. New York, N.Y.	7,891,957
2. Chicago, Ill.	3,620,962
3. Philadelphia, Pa.	**2,071,605**
4. Los Angeles, Calif.	1,970,358
5. Detroit, Mich.	1,849,568
6. Baltimore, Md.	949,708
7. Cleveland, Ohio	914,808
8. St. Louis, Mo.	856,796
9. Washington, D.C.	802,178
10. Boston, Mass.	801,444
1960	
1. New York, N.Y.	7,781,984
2. Chicago, Ill.	3,550,404
3. Los Angeles, Calif.	2,479,015
4. Philadelphia, Pa.	**2,002,512**
5. Detroit, Mich.	1,670,144
6. Baltimore, Md.	939,024
7. Houston, Tex.	938,219
8. Cleveland, Ohio	876,050
9. Washington, D.C.	763,956
10. St. Louis, Mo.	750,026

1970	
1. New York, N.Y.	7,894,862
2. Chicago, Ill.	3,366,957
3. Los Angeles, Calif.	2,816,061
4. Philadelphia, Pa.	**1,948,609**
5. Detroit, Mich.	1,511,482
6. Houston, Tex.	1,232,802
7. Baltimore, Md.	905,759
8. Dallas, Tex.	844,401
9. Washington, D.C.	756,510
10. Cleveland, Ohio	750,903

1980	
1. New York, N.Y.	7,071,639
2. Chicago, Ill.	3,005,072
3. Los Angeles, Calif.	2,966,850
4. Philadelphia, Pa.	**1,688,210**
5. Houston, Tex.	1,595,138
6. Detroit, Mich.	1,203,339
7. Dallas, Tex.	904,078
8. San Diego, Calif.	875,538
9. Phoenix, Ariz.	789,704
10. Baltimore, Md.	786,775

1990	
1. New York, N.Y.	7,322,564
2. Los Angeles, Calif.	3,485,398
3. Chicago, Ill.	2,783,726
4. Houston, Tex.	1,630,553
5. Philadelphia, Pa.	**1,585,577**
6. San Diego, Calif.	1,110,549
7. Detroit, Mich.	1,027,974
8. Dallas, Tex.	1,006,877
9. Phoenix, Ariz.	983,403
10. San Antonio, Tex.	935,933

2000	
1. New York, N.Y.	8,008,278
2. Los Angeles, Calif.	3,694,820
3. Chicago, Ill.	2,896,016
4. Houston, Tex.	1,953,631
5. Philadelphia, Pa.	**1,517,550**
6. Phoenix, Ariz.	1,321,045
7. San Diego, Calif.	1,223,400
8. Dallas, Tex.	1,188,580
9. San Antonio, Tex.	1,144,646
10. Detroit, Mich.	951,270

2010	
1. New York, N.Y.	8,175,133
2. Los Angeles, Calif.	3,792,621
3. Chicago, Ill.	2,695,598
4. Houston, Tex.	2,099,451
5. Philadelphia, Pa.	**1,526,006**
6. Phoenix, Ariz.	1,445,632
7. San Antonio, Tex.	1,327,407
8. San Diego, Calif.	1,307,402
9. Dallas, Tex.	1,197,816
10. San Jose, Calif.	945,942

2020	
1. New York, N.Y.	8,804,190
2. Los Angeles, Calif.	3,898,747
3. Chicago, Ill.	2,746,388
4. Houston, Tex.	2,304,580
5. Phoenix, Ariz.	1,608,139
6. Philadelphia, Pa.	**1,603,797**
7. San Antonio, Tex.	1,434,625
8. San Diego, Calif.	1,386,932
9. Dallas, Tex.	1,304,379
10. San Jose, Calif.	1,013,240

SOURCE: U.S. Census Bureau; Campbell Gibson, "Population of the 100 Largest Cities and Other Urban Places in the United States: 1790 to 1990" (U.S. Census Bureau Working Paper, June 1998), https://www.census.gov/library/working-papers/1998/demo/POP-twps0027.html.

Political Party Origins

Brian Hendricks

Philadelphia, long considered the "Cradle of Liberty" in America, also became a "cradle of political parties" during the 1790s, when the city served as the fledgling nation's capital. A decade that began with George Washington as the unanimous choice for first president of the United States ended with partisan rancor over issues such as the economic policies of Alexander Hamilton, tensions in the United States' relationship with France, and the controversial Jay's Treaty with England. With Philadelphia as the epicenter of a political earthquake, Americans divided into two distinct political parties that had little, if anything, in common.

Partisan fighting at the national level exacerbated local factions and rivalries that had existed for many years. In Pennsylvania, disaffected "have-nots" had waged political war with the "haves" since the 1750s and 1760s, when Benjamin Franklin allied with many Quakers against the proprietorship of the Penn family—a family they blamed for exploiting the province for revenue. Later, a quasi-party system of "Constitutionalists" and "Republicans" developed in the aftermath of ratification of the 1776 Pennsylvania Constitution, a radically democratic document replaced by a more conservative constitution in 1790. Similar divides over state issues existed in New Jersey and Delaware. Throughout the region, state-level politics interacted with emerging national parties, and vice versa.

Across the new nation, battles over ratification of the 1787 United States Constitution produced two distinct factions: "Federalists" who supported the document and "Anti-Federalists" who opposed it. During the first federal Congress, which convened in New York in 1789 before moving to Philadelphia in 1790, representatives from both factions reached agreement on the Bill of Rights and the establishment of cabinet departments. But schisms erupted over proposals by Secretary of the Treasury Alexander Hamilton, including his plan for state war debts to be assumed by the federal government. This plan angered states that had already paid off a large portion of their debts. Virginia congressman James Madison, Hamilton's coauthor for many of the Federalist Papers that had promoted ratification of the Constitution, sternly opposed Hamilton's measures. Pennsylvania denounced the "funding scheme," especially when speculators who became aware of the plan galloped across the countryside and bought up debt certificates from unsuspecting Pennsylvania veterans.

When Hamilton later proposed the creation of a national bank, Secretary of State Thomas Jefferson joined Madison in alarm over the growth and encroachment of the new central government and the bank's questionable constitutionality. Hamilton's plan for a mixed economy including the bank, assumption of debts, tariffs, and excise taxes passed Congress but became a touchstone for political position. By 1792, those opposed to Hamilton's programs had coalesced into an opposition party, known at first as the Republican Party (also styled as "Jeffersonians"). In the elections in that year, the nascent party gained a majority in the U.S. House of Representatives.

The Washington administration's foreign policy widened the gap between the solidifying parties, as Hamilton's Federalists favored closer ties with the British while the Jeffersonians favored France. When the two European superpowers went to war against each other in 1793, the Republicans advocated honoring the alliance with France that had been forged during the American Revolution. Washington, hoping to avoid a war the country could ill afford, sided with Hamilton and implemented a policy of neutrality, which many Republicans interpreted as favoring Britain. Republicans also accused Washington and Vice President John Adams of having monarchical tendencies, further associating them with England.

Opposition to the Federalists also prompted Democratic societies to form across the country. One of the most prominent of these groups, the Pennsylvania Democratic Society, began in Philadelphia under the leadership of such prominent citizens as Alexander Dallas, who later served in Madison's cabinet. The societies extolled the virtues of the French Revolution and drew inspiration from "Citizen" Edmond-Charles Genêt, an emissary from the new French republic to the United States. Domestic issues also fostered growth among the societies. In 1794 the Pennsylvania Democratic Society vehemently opposed Hamilton's excise tax on whiskey, which impacted many farmers in

FIGURE 77. *Congressional Pugilists*, 1798. Capturing the rancor of early national politics, this cartoon depicted a fight on the floor of Congress between Representatives Matthew Lyon of Vermont (a Democratic-Republican) and Roger Griswold of Connecticut (a Federalist). LIBRARY OF CONGRESS.

western Pennsylvania, and sought to elect candidates to office to repeal it.

Three events soon damaged the credibility of the societies. The French Revolution became more violent, culminating in the beheading of King Louis XVI. Genêt alienated Washington by belligerently outfitting American privateers to engage in combat with British ships. And farmers in western Pennsylvania resorted to violence (the "Whiskey Rebellion") to oppose the excise tax. After Washington denounced the societies as disruptive and unrepublican, they rapidly declined. Nevertheless, they served as a framework for the continuing emergence of the opposition party.

The increasing partisanship of the 1790s was mirrored in the press as Federalists and Republicans waged political war in the pages of the country's newspapers. Hamilton and Jefferson both hired editors to publish partisan newspapers. John Fenno did the Federalists' bidding in the *Gazette of the United States*, which originated in New York in 1789 and moved with the government to Philadelphia one year later. The Republicans countered with the *National Gazette* of Philip Freneau and the *Aurora*, edited by Benjamin Franklin's grandson, Benjamin Franklin Bache.

The differences between the parties widened further with Jay's Treaty, signed between the United States and Britain in 1794 and ratified by the U.S. Senate in 1795. While the treaty prevented war with Britain, Republicans severely criticized it as a capitulation to England. The treaty did not address certain grievances, particularly the British practice of seizing American ships and the impressment of American seamen. But as a result of the treaty, along with the seeds planted by the Democratic societies shortly beforehand, Republicans made major gains in Pennsylvania. By the middle of the decade, moderate Republicans led by Thomas McKean, a signer of the Declaration of Independence and former Federalist, took control of the reins of Pennsylvania's government. In New Jersey, the opposition party gained support amid widespread protests against the Alien and Sedition Acts (1798), a Federalist-backed measure to suppress dissent. In Delaware, the state divided between Republican sympathies in northernmost New Castle County and the Federalist-leaning southern counties. Vitriolic party politics on both sides defined opponents as enemies of the republic, leaving no room for compromise.

The presidential elections of 1796 and 1800 made clear that the nation's politics had become a contest between two political parties, the Federalists and the

Republicans (who adopted the label Democratic-Republicans in 1798). With the presidency at that time decided by electors appointed by state legislatures, in 1796 the Federalist John Adams prevailed by three electoral votes over Thomas Jefferson (whose second-place finish made him vice president, in keeping with electoral provisions of the 1787 Constitution). In 1800, the Democratic-Republican candidates Jefferson and Aaron Burr attracted the most electoral votes, but a tie between them threw the choice to the Federalist-controlled House of Representatives. After thirty-six ballots, Jefferson became the first Democratic-Republican president of the United States. Although contentious, the election resulted in a peaceful transfer of power, a historic achievement for the young nation.

By the time of Jefferson's election, the federal government had moved from Philadelphia to the new District of Columbia. But the politics of the 1790s, emanating from Philadelphia, had produced for the nation a two-party system with lasting consequences. Acceptance of legitimate opposition, as demonstrated by the 1800 election, laid a foundation for political parties to continue in American history. While the Federalists faded from power in the early nineteenth century, the Democratic-Republicans held the presidency for more than two decades, through two terms under Jefferson, two terms under Madison, and two more under James Monroe. That dominance, however, produced factions that became a second two-party system for the United States by the 1830s: the Democratic-Republicans, known simply as Democrats beginning in 1844, and their opposition, the Whig Party. In 1854, a new Republican Party supplanted the Whigs, and thereafter the Democratic and Republican parties dominated. Despite periodic forays by third parties, the system of two-party competition born during Philadelphia's decade as capital of the United States continued to be the driving force in American politics.

Political Conventions

Daniel T. Kirsch

Philadelphia has hosted national political conventions from the time of the American Revolution to the modern era. The Pennsylvania State House, later known as Independence Hall, was the site of both the signing of the Declaration of Independence in 1776 and the Constitutional Convention in 1787. In the mid-nineteenth century, as national party conventions became the norm, politicians often returned to Philadelphia to nominate candidates in the city most closely associated with the nation's founding ideals. Between 1848 and 2012, nearly one of every four major national political party conventions met in Philadelphia, drawing visitors to the city and reinforcing its place as an important center of national politics.

In June 1848, thousands of Whig Party supporters (although only three hundred delegates) convened in Philadelphia, a city convenient to the still-underdeveloped national capital of Washington, D.C., and accessible by rail from New York City and from the South. The Whig convention met at Ninth and Sansom Streets in the lower saloon of the Philadelphia Museum Building, also called the Chinese Museum. On the fourth ballot, the delegates nominated General Zachary Taylor, a hero of the Mexican-American War supported by the southern "Cotton Whigs," over the candidate favored by northern antislavery "Conscience Whigs," perennial presidential candidate and party leader Henry Clay. In the general election Taylor carried Philadelphia by more than ten thousand votes. The convention adopted no platform, but Whigs stood for a protective tariff (high tax on imported goods), a national bank, and internal infrastructure improvements such as roads, canals, and railroads.

Philadelphia hosted two conventions in 1856, first the American or "Know-Nothing" Party and then the first national nominating convention of the new Republican Party. The anti-immigrant Know-Nothings were so called because of their origins as a secret society whose members denied knowledge of their party when asked. Their Philadelphia convention, attended by fewer than two hundred delegates, nominated former president Millard Fillmore of Buffalo, New York, and adopted a platform that called for a twenty-one-year waiting period for immigrant naturalization, preference for native-born citizens in public office, and prohibition of convicted criminals from entering the United States. On slavery, the convention called for popular sovereignty in the territories, which caused antislavery delegates to quit the convention, weakening the impact of the party.

The newly formed Republican Party met at Musical Fund Hall, 808 Locust Street. For a party committed to combating the evil of slavery, Philadelphia offered symbolic resonance as the birthplace of liberty. Many Philadelphia residents, however, were wary of what they perceived as the antislavery radicalism of the new party. Nevertheless, on the eleventh ballot more than six hundred delegates nominated Senator John C. Frémont of California, known as "The Pathfinder" because of his pioneering expeditions to map the Oregon Trail and his exploits in the Mexican-American War. The party platform endorsed the admission of Kansas as a state that prohibited enslavement as well as massive "internal improvements" in the form of river and harbor expansion and construction and federal funding of a transcontinental railroad.

In 1872, Republicans returned to Philadelphia with eight hundred delegates and nominated the incumbent president Ulysses S. Grant for a second term. They met at the Academy of Music on Broad Street, then the largest musical and convention venue in the city. Their platform endorsed Grant's Reconstruction policy in the South, the Homestead Act to encourage western settlement, and more tariffs to both raise revenue and protect domestic trade for American businesses. Republicans also called for an extension of women's rights and equal rights for all races, in keeping with their roots as an antislavery party.

When Republicans returned to Philadelphia in 1900, the party sent more than nine hundred delegates to nominate incumbent president William McKinley, whom they credited with improving business conditions throughout the country. Delegates and visitors to the convention streamed into the city to pay tribute to both McKinley's Republican Party and Philadelphia's historic associations. Large parades made their way down Broad Street on the Saturday before the convention, and thousands visited attractions such as Wanamaker's department store. A brand new, white-marble Exposition Auditorium (so named to host the National Export Exposition of 1899) near Thirty-Fourth and Spruce Streets served as the backdrop for the Republicans' quadrennial gala. The only rival for McKinley's popularity was New York governor Theodore Roosevelt, the Rough Rider of San Juan Hill, who accepted the nomination for the vice presidency even though he had said he would do so "under no circumstances."

Democrats met in Philadelphia for the first time in 1936, at the newly christened Municipal Auditorium and Convention Hall, built in 1931 adjacent to the old Exposition Auditorium. To woo the party to the city, Philadelphia leaders had raised more than $200,000 and suspended blue laws against drinking on Sundays. The Democratic convention of more than one thousand delegates largely endorsed continuing President Franklin D. Roosevelt's New Deal and its aggressive government spending to combat the Great Depression. No floor votes were counted, only voice votes, and the president was renominated by acclamation. At Roosevelt's urging, the party abandoned its two-thirds supermajority rule for nominating candidates and passing floor resolutions, a requirement that had made the party disproportionately beholden to southern white interests. Roosevelt also broke with tradition by accepting the nomination in person in both 1932 and 1936. At the University of Pennsylvania's Franklin Field in 1936, Roosevelt spoke to a crowd of perhaps one hundred thousand people in accepting his renomination, proclaiming to a Depression-weary United States that Americans had "a rendezvous with destiny." The party's platform, a brief one, largely accepted and advocated more New Deal policies.

Four years later, in 1940, more than one thousand Republicans met in Philadelphia once again, this time at the Municipal Auditorium and Convention Hall. Republicans nominated businessman and vocal New Deal opponent Wendell Willkie of Indiana for president on the sixth nominating ballot to oppose Roosevelt. They endorsed a platform that neither opposed involvement in the ongoing World War II nor advocated for intervention. The party also did not argue against the concept of relief for the poor during the Great Depression but called for state administration of those programs. The convention of more than two thousand delegates and alternates generally opposed government spending and called for cuts. An "American-Patriotism

Session" held at Independence Hall called attention to ways the New Deal was spoiling the freedoms and rights the founders had intended.

The summer of 1948, the first presidential election year after World War II, was truly the summer of national political party conventions in Philadelphia. Following $600,000 in renovations, the Municipal Auditorium and Convention Hall hosted conventions of three parties: Republicans, Democrats, and the new Progressive Party. Republicans and their eleven hundred delegates met June 21–25 and nominated New York governor Thomas E. Dewey, their 1944 nominee, on the third ballot, to oppose incumbent Democratic president Harry S. Truman. Republicans stressed an internationalist foreign policy. The party's central substantive plank (and disagreement with Democrats) endorsed the anti-labor Taft-Hartley Act, which had been passed over Truman's veto by a Republican-dominated Congress. The Republican platform also called for ending poll taxes and segregation in the South and favored a federal anti-lynching law, which Roosevelt and Truman had failed to pass through Congress, as well as a law prohibiting employment discrimination on the basis of sex.

A major southern revolt rocked the Democratic Party when twelve hundred delegates gathered July 12–15 to nominate Truman at the Municipal Auditorium and Convention Hall. Southerners initially supported their own candidate, Senator Richard Russell of Georgia, until Truman soundly defeated all challengers on the first ballot. When Minneapolis mayor Hubert Humphrey of Minnesota made a floor speech endorsing the first-ever civil rights plank in the party's platform, southern delegates walked out and later formed the "States Rights Democratic Party," more popularly known as the Dixiecrats. The Democrats in Philadelphia called for repealing the Taft-Hartley Act (a structural impediment to labor union growth), extending Social Security, raising the minimum wage, and establishing a national health insurance program. The temperature in the convention reached more than one hundred degrees as delegates attempted to finish their business of passing rules, nominating candidates, and approving the platform. To celebrate convention-goers, Philadelphia's police and fire department bands paraded down Broad Street to sing and play music for them at the Ritz-Carlton Hotel. The party endorsed Truman's foreign policies, calling for expansion of the United Nations and diplomacy to handle the new threat of the atomic bomb. Truman accepted the nomination before a crowd of sixteen thousand at the auditorium.

The Progressive Party of more than three thousand delegates met July 23–25 and nominated for the presidency former vice president Henry Wallace, who made his acceptance speech before more than thirty-two thousand spectators at Shibe Park, home to the Philadelphia Athletics baseball team. The party's platform denounced the U.S.-led rebuilding of Europe known as the Marshall Plan and favored national health insurance, an end to the military draft, an agricultural policy that favored small farmers, and a rethinking of the concept of national sovereignty worldwide. Like both of the major parties, the Progressives also endorsed equal rights for women and racial minorities.

Fifty-two years passed before a major party held another national convention in Philadelphia. In the interim, the Republican Party attempted to alternate between major cities in the Midwest, West, and South, and the Democrats held the majority of their conventions in New York, Los Angeles, and Chicago. For the Republicans in 2000, Philadelphia spent $66 million putting on a weeklong extravaganza, which also was marked by dissent by labor unions supporting striking municipal workers and demonstrations calling attention to social causes. Almost four hundred protesters were arrested.

On July 31, 2000, more than two thousand Republican delegates unanimously nominated Texas governor George W. Bush as their presidential candidate. Unlike earlier Philadelphia conventions,

FIGURES 78, 79, 80. Three conventions, one city, 1948. Philadelphia's television capabilities drew three national political conventions to the city in 1948: the Democrats, who nominated Harry S. Truman; the Republicans, shown demonstrating their enthusiasm for Robert A. Taft (who lost the nomination to Thomas Dewey); and the Progressives, shown here during an address by Paul Robeson at Shibe Park. HARRY S. TRUMAN LIBRARY; SPECIAL COLLECTIONS RESEARCH CENTER, TEMPLE UNIVERSITY LIBRARIES.

LOUISIANA
PENNA
ALWAYS
ARKANSAS
WIN WITH

FOUNDING
CONVENTION
OF THE

the nomination was a foregone conclusion. The party avoided a floor fight on the issue of abortion and settled another matter of conflict, the primary election calendar, without radical changes that would have disadvantaged early nominating states such as Iowa and New Hampshire. Former president Gerald Ford, in attendance, was taken to the hospital—at first suffering from an earache, for which he was treated and released, but later readmitted and diagnosed with a minor stroke. He remained at Hahnemann University Hospital for several weeks after the convention.

Philadelphia's union and business leaders joined forces to lure the Democratic National Convention in 2016, prevailing over competing bids from Columbus, Ohio, and a New York City site in Brooklyn. The competition for the 2016 convention and the strength of Democratic allies in the labor movement signaled that Philadelphia continued to be a wellspring of American political activity, laying claim to a heritage as host to more national political party conventions than any other city in the United States. At the convention, held July 25–28, 2016, Hillary Clinton—the first female in American history to be a major party's nominee for president—invoked the legacy of the nation's founders as she accepted the nomination. The Declaration of Independence and the Constitution, both drafted and adopted in Philadelphia, were only the beginning of Philadelphia's role as a battleground of American politics.

Insurance

Hannah Farber

Insurance has sometimes been called an "invisible" element of commerce, but in the Philadelphia region it has never been far from view. From the eighteenth century through the twenty-first, Philadelphia's leadership in the field of insurance has enhanced the city's preeminence in many commercial and communal endeavors. Insurance in Philadelphia, over the years, has meant everything from disability insurance funds managed by immigrants, to "factory mutuals" protecting industrial manufacturers against the risk of fire, to enormous capitalist ventures in marine and property/casualty insurance. As the business of insurance grew and evolved, it established Philadelphia within global commercial networks, regional zones of economic activity, and statewide legal regimes.

From the eighteenth through the early nineteenth centuries, Philadelphia's leadership in insurance grew from its deep involvement in global, national, and local projects. Perhaps counterintuitively, the city's global insurance ventures began first. The first marine insurance brokerage established in Philadelphia in 1721 demonstrated that the city had become a significant player in world trade. At a brokerage, a Philadelphia merchant seeking to insure a ship or cargo could fill out a detailed policy. Others, usually fellow merchants, would take on a portion of the voyage's risk by underwriting it—literally writing their names underneath the policy's text. If an insured ship was lost or property was damaged in transit, the underwriters paid in proportion to the amount for which they had pledged themselves responsible. If the voyage ended successfully, the underwriters shared the premium that had been paid to the broker for the insurance. The appearance of a reliable group of local underwriters created some financial independence for Philadelphia merchants involved in the global marketplace. Insuring locally meant they would not have to spend months negotiating with overseas insurers or tracking down far-flung underwriters reluctant to pay their shares of a claim.

Insurance brokerages were numerous in Philadelphia by the mid-eighteenth century; the continent's largest port city had become the principal provider of financial services for the region's merchants. Brokers clustered together near the wharves, where they thrived on the constant influx of commercial information from ports around the world. Commerce and finance linked marine insurers far more closely to their peers in London, Bordeaux, and the West Indies than to local inhabitants of nearby towns or rural hinterlands. The extent of Philadelphia's regional dominance in insurance is evident in the degree to which its commercial newspapers—in which marine insurers advertised their services—dominated the region. Since the printing of Philadelphia's first newspaper in 1719, the city's printers had competed with one another in ever-greater numbers. In New Jersey and Delaware, by contrast, not a single newspaper was printed before the American Revolution.

Despite Philadelphia's relative prosperity, the city remained a relatively peripheral provider of financial services in the context of Atlantic trade. Even after the Revolution, American merchants generally preferred to acquire insurance in London or other European cities where all kinds of financial transactions were cheaper and more widely available. A structural transformation in American marine insurance began only after the funding of the debt of the United States in 1790. As Philadelphia became the financial capital of the new republic, enthusiastic investors poured money into public and private projects, including the first marine insurance company in the United States, the Insurance Company of North America (INA). While facilitating Philadelphians' ocean commerce, INA embedded itself in local and national financial networks by investing heavily in the shares of Philadelphia banks and in federal bonds.

The success of INA inspired other speculators to charter corporations along similar lines. While Philadelphia's marine insurers remained overwhelmingly dominant in the mid-Atlantic states, capitalists in smaller towns also took advantage of the wealth-generating possibilities of insurance companies. In Trenton and New Brunswick, New Jersey, for example, two new financial corporations received state permission to engage in both the banking and insurance businesses. In this fashion, the new companies could spread the risks they took with their invested capital across two intertwined and complementary types of business.

Marine insurance companies enhanced Philadelphians' ability to engage in commercial transactions spanning continents, but other types of new insurance groups provided them with security at home. Fire insurance associations and mutual aid societies eased the distribution of aid among neighbors in times of personal and communal catastrophe. Benjamin Franklin organized Philadelphia's first fire insurance society—North America's second—in 1752. Dues-paying subscribers to the Philadelphia Contributionship and its imitators affixed "fire marks"—usually symbols of peace, amity, or patriotism—to the fronts of their buildings to prove their membership. Fire insurance developed in tandem with organized techniques of fire prevention: members of the Contributionship were required to "keep always in good order . . . a certain number of leather buckets," and by 1808, a London visitor noted forty operative fire engines in the city. Inhabitants of cities from Boston to Charleston followed Philadelphia's lead, creating Contributionship-style societies that benefited subscribers as well as joint-stock companies that sold fire insurance for profit. By 1806, Philadelphia boasted eight chartered insurance companies, which did the majority of their business in marine insurance and a smaller portion in fire. Through correspondence with insurers in Wilmington and Baltimore, the Philadelphia marine insurance companies brought insurance prices around the Middle Atlantic into closer alignment. Although insurance remained principally an urban—and maritime—commercial practice, the establishment of the Lancaster and Susquehanna Insurance Company in 1807 testified to Philadelphia's deepening connections with its backcountry.

While fire and marine insurers protected the capital of the city's property holders, scores of mutual aid societies provided security to Philadelphia's more vulnerable residents. In 1787, Absalom Jones and Richard Allen formed the Free African Society. Members paid one shilling per month and were eligible to receive three shillings and nine pence per week in times of need. By 1838, Black Philadelphians had founded 119 mutual aid societies with more than seven thousand members. European immigrants began similar projects: Philadelphia's German immigrants formed at least fifty-six mutual aid societies in the 1830s and 1840s. Fraternal orders and tradesmen's associations also provided crisis insurance to members and their families well into the twentieth century.

As the city grew, the size and concentration of its industrial neighborhoods encouraged manufacturers to join "factory mutuals," through which they insured themselves against catastrophic losses from factory fires. A group of Rhode Island cotton mill owners created the first factory mutual, which rapidly became associated with New England manufacturing, but Philadelphian factory owners rapidly adopted the practice, and it grew apace with the city's manufacturing over the following century. By the 1930s the amount of factory insurance in force in Pennsylvania was $266 million, second only to New York. New Jersey's factory insurance, $150 million, was also a substantial portion of the national total.

The hazards of industrialization taught Philadelphia fire insurers the advantages of doing business outside of

FIGURE 81. Philadelphia Contributionship fire mark, 1802. Affixed to the homes of policyholders, fire marks advertised insurance companies and let volunteer firefighters know that properties were insured. NATIONAL MUSEUM OF AMERICAN HISTORY, SMITHSONIAN INSTITUTION.

their immediate neighborhoods. After the Great Fire of New York bankrupted several New York insurance companies in 1835, Philadelphia insurers pioneered the practice of enrolling customers in other cities using full-time remote agents. This forged stronger financial links between Philadelphia corporations and inhabitants of other American cities.

Fire insurance companies also physically shaped Philadelphia and other cities. The companies' judgments on the safety of different building materials and layouts guided urban architecture, for example. The detailed maps they generated as surveyors and assessors of urban property became new ways of understanding the cities' built environments.

The growing scale of insurance in Philadelphia did not simply transform insurance companies into depersonalized vehicles of capital; rather, insurers maintained and even deepened their intimate relationships with urban spaces and their inhabitants. This was as true in the field of life insurance as it was in fire. America's first life insurance company originated in Philadelphia in 1809. This company and its imitators targeted the hopes and fears of the emerging middle class. Life insurance was particularly appealing to urban male office workers, who feared their deaths would leave their families indigent, and who appreciated the way insurance companies addressed them as intelligent investors. Imposing life insurance buildings, brick-and-mortar advertisements of corporate stability, became Philadelphia landmarks.

The new fields of auto and health insurance emerged very rapidly in the early twentieth century. Both were defined more by state regulations than they were by the demands of port cities. Pennsylvania, a populous state with large numbers of factories and far-flung farms, laid claim to 7 percent of the nation's cars, but accounted for 14 percent of its traffic deaths. Alarmed by these statistics, state legislators imposed strict regulations on vehicles and drivers in the 1920s, and automobile owners increasingly found auto insurance an appealing option. While most companies in the established lines of insurance hesitated to enter the auto market, new companies grew quickly. The Erie Insurance Exchange, based in western Pennsylvania, reached $1 million in annual sales by 1946. The success of new corporations such as the Erie Insurance Exchange signaled two important changes in the insurance business: The wealthy Philadelphia insurance companies of the nineteenth century could not count on retaining their dominance in the twentieth as new lines of insurance emerged. Secondly, state laws and regulations increasingly defined and controlled insurance practices. Insurance in the twentieth century became articulated more by state boundaries than by global networks of maritime commerce or regional zones of industry.

Health insurance, like auto insurance, was a twentieth-century phenomenon shaped by the states rather than metropolitan regions. Across the country, advances in technology and the systematic accreditation of doctors spurred demand for ever-more-costly medical services, and more Americans grew interested in acquiring health insurance. Health insurance projects such as Blue Cross and Blue Shield were promoted by national organizations, and like auto insurers, they were regulated on the state level.

State regulation even made its mark on the old, established lines of insurance. Soon after 1900, many states started setting fire insurance rates directly, while others began supervising rates set by industry associations. Mutual aid societies run by immigrants, voluntary groups, and trade associations peaked after the immigration boom of the early twentieth century, but during the Great Depression they were superseded by state and federal aid projects.

The increased influence of the states on the insurance business created divergent experiences for corporations situated in neighboring states. State legislatures in each of the mid-Atlantic states took their own course. Delaware, for example, became a national financial center when it passed a series of laws friendly to the banking and finance industries in 1981. These laws established a new corporate constituency in Wilmington and set that city on a course dramatically different from Philadelphia.

Philadelphia maintained its prominence in insurance through education and innovation. The Wharton School at the University of Pennsylvania offered the country's first collegiate-level class on insurance economics in 1904, and in 1941 Wharton partnered with industry leaders to form a foundation for insurance research and education. The Insurance Company of North America revolutionized homeowners insurance at midcentury by bundling insurance against fire, theft, flooding, and other hazards into single policies that quickly became standard.

During the latter half of the twentieth century, corporate mergers transformed some of Philadelphia's oldest insurance companies. INA, founded in 1792, merged with the Connecticut General Life Insurance Company to form CIGNA in 1982. The resulting entity was purchased by ACE Group, an international company with more than $87 billion in assets, in the 1990s. INA, linked through its corporate successor with offices in Tokyo, London, Zurich, and Santiago, had made its name more than two centuries earlier by insuring merchant ventures to Amsterdam, Port au Prince, St. Petersburg, and Jakarta. Over nearly three centuries, insurance has forged connections between Philadelphians and their neighbors, their fellow citizens, and their business partners around the world.

Banking

Michael A. Martorelli

Greater Philadelphia's banking roots go deeper than those of any region in the country. Philadelphia was the home of the first commercial bank (1782), the first national bank (1791), the first savings bank (1816), and the first savings and loan association (1831). Until the mid-1980s, celebrated local institutions such as First Pennsylvania, Girard, and Provident dominated the region. By the late twentieth century, however, historic regulatory changes led to acquisitions by out-of-town giants and changed the face of the banking industry locally and nationally.

The region's prominence in banking began with the Bank of North America, created in 1781 when Philadelphia was the largest and most important city in North America. Even as the War of Independence still raged, the Continental Congress granted approval for Robert Morris, its superintendent of finance and one of the city's best-known businessmen, to establish the first commercial bank in the country. Although it was difficult to attract capital at first, by early 1782 the Bank of North America opened for business. The bank loaned money to the federal and state governments as well as to many of the city's businesses, thereby facilitating commerce among the colonies and between the United States and other countries.

Soon after ratification of the Constitution of the United States in summer 1788, commercial banks sprouted in more than a dozen other cities. The Bank of Pennsylvania (1793) was the second founded in Philadelphia, and the Delaware legislature chartered the Wilmington-based Bank of Delaware in 1795. Meanwhile, in 1791, Secretary of the Treasury Alexander Hamilton followed through on his long-standing idea for a national bank whose main purposes would be to collect taxes, hold government funds, and make loans to the government and other worthy borrowers. While it would be a private institution with a twenty-year charter from Congress, the Bank of the United States would be more national than local in scope. In 1797, it moved to Third and Chestnut Streets, where a new Greek Revival building with a Roman portico and Corinthian columns suggested solidity and stability.

Adding to the earlier institutions that largely served the needs of governments, upper-class merchants, lawyers, and influential businessmen, during the first decade of the nineteenth century the Philadelphia Bank (1803), Farmers' and Mechanics' Bank (1809), Commercial Bank of Pennsylvania (1810), and Mechanics Bank of the City and County of Philadelphia (1810) were formed by and for artisans, farmers, mechanics, and manufacturers. In 1810, the leaders of the District of Northern Liberties, just north of Vine Street but not served by the Philadelphia banks, formed the National Bank of the Northern Liberties. Another innovation occurred in 1816 when a group of businessmen, inspired by the success of savings institutions in England and Scotland, established the Philadelphia Saving Fund Society (PSFS) to cater to small depositors not targeted by commercial banks. The depositors owned this "mutual" savings bank and shared in its profits.

In the first decade of the nineteenth century, Delaware authorized the Farmers Bank of the State of Delaware in 1807 and established its headquarters in Georgetown, where it served farming communities in the state's southern townships. During the following ten years, Delaware authorized three more banks in Wilmington. New Jersey established its first banks in Newark and Trenton in 1804. In 1812, it chartered six more banks, including the State Bank at Camden, the first in southern New Jersey.

Although Philadelphia did not serve as the nation's capital after 1800, the presence of the Bank of the United States kept the city at the center of controversies about the nation's finances. In 1811, anti-banking forces in Congress refused to extend its charter. Republicans believed the bank to be unconstitutional and benefiting only the moneyed class at the expense of all others. Local merchant and trader Stephen Girard acquired its building and fixed assets, then used his own capital to establish the Bank of Stephen Girard as the country's first private bank, a bank with no publicly traded shares and no mandated service to customers.

Philadelphia became home to a national bank once again in 1816, following the wreckage to the economy caused by the War of 1812. Congress realized the need for another national bank to help regulate the supply of credit and expedite financial dealings of the federal government. Philadelphia was still a leading financial center, so it was no surprise when Congress decided to locate the second national Bank of the United States among the other banks on Chestnut Street. The bank operated from Carpenters' Hall for five years, and then opened in 1824 in its new Greek Revival structure modeled on the Parthenon, a symbol of strength and permanence.

Banking in Pennsylvania expanded after the commonwealth's Omnibus Banking Act of 1814 divided the state into twenty-seven banking districts and approved charters for forty-one banks. Citizens quickly organized banks in Bristol, Chester, Germantown, Norristown, and West Chester. Within a few years, more than 40 percent of the new banks in Pennsylvania failed, however, as they could not maintain money supplies adequate for their lending practices.

Philadelphia's long-established banks survived, and they became important cogs in Pennsylvania's attempts to battle New York and Baltimore for commercial supremacy. Throughout the 1830s, banks seeking renewals of their charters were compelled by law to loan funds to the state for a program of transportation connections between Philadelphia and inland areas to the north and west. Although the state got its canals and turnpikes, most were unprofitable because they could not prevent lucrative commercial traffic from using other transportation corridors to the ports of New York and Baltimore. Pennsylvania's revenue decreased even as its debt level ballooned. Bank creditors forced to finance those construction projects throughout the 1820s and 1830s suffered financially when the state suspended interest payments on its debt in 1841 and then demanded that the banks extend even more loans.

In Philadelphia, meanwhile, the second Bank of the United States became the flashpoint for the national political conflict known as the "Bank War." Soon after his election as president in 1828, Andrew Jackson made clear his displeasure with banks in general and the Bank of the United States in particular. In his view a large central bank, controlled and operated by the moneyed class, limited the growth of state banks. Bank president Nicholas Biddle sought to blunt Jackson's campaign by applying for a new charter in 1832, some four years before the first charter expired. Congress passed this recharter bill but could not override Jackson's

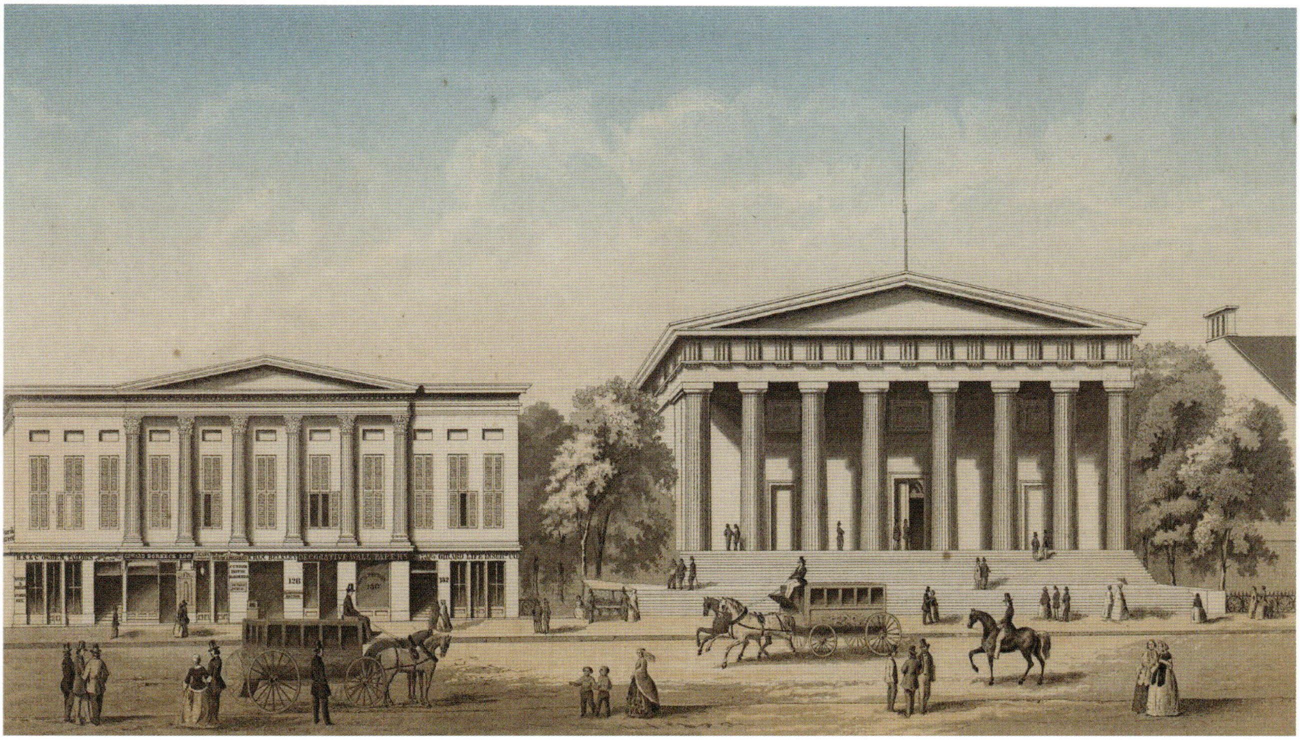

FIGURE 82. Chestnut Street banks, 1856. A panorama of financial institutions included (at right) the second Bank of the United States. CHROMOLITHOGRAPH BY EDWARD COLLINS AND CHARLES M. AUTENRIETH, LIBRARY COMPANY OF PHILADELPHIA.

veto. Jackson, reelected in 1832, then emasculated the bank by transferring government funds to other banks and convincing his allies in Congress to refuse another charter. As the bank wound down its affairs, the contraction of loans, discounts, exchanges, and deposits led to severe economic dislocations. Following its 1836 closing, the Commonwealth of Pennsylvania immediately granted a state charter to a successor bank that promised both to loan the state additional sums and to pay a bonus for the privilege of operating. Working under such onerous restrictions, the new United States Bank of Pennsylvania failed only five years later and took six other Philadelphia banks with it.

Philadelphia's banks suffered proportionately in the financial panics that gripped the nation in 1837 and 1857. Yet, throughout the period, entrepreneurs continued to establish new banks. Most of the action occurred in outlying districts of the city such as Kensington, Moyamensing, Southwark, and Spring Garden. Political lending became less important as most of the city's institutions sought to finance the growing number of railroads and manufacturers. After the Panic of 1873, mergers enabled those institutions to continue to serve the needs of local and national firms. A handful of these acquisitive institutions evolved into such stalwarts of the twentieth century as Fidelity, Girard, and Provident, joining the successors of the Philadelphia Bank (Philadelphia National) and the Bank of North America (the Pennsylvania Company, later First Pennsylvania) as market leaders. After the turn of the twentieth century, many of the region's banks further expanded their business to a nationwide clientele. Their appetite for acquisitions remained strong; through mergers, the number of banks in Philadelphia declined between 1900 and 1914.

After World War I, banking broadened to involve still more businesses and citizens. Corporations (such as Gimbel Brothers), unions (such as the Brotherhood of

Locomotive Engineers), and the community leaders of various minority, ethnic, and religious groups established commercial banks, mutual savings banks, and trust companies. The largest commercial banks continued their merger and acquisition sprees, and they supplied capital that funded the growth of utility and industrial companies.

The Great Depression devastated the banking community, particularly in the working-class neighborhoods. One-third of Philadelphia's banks failed, including such high-profile institutions as Bankers Trust, with more than one hundred thousand depositors. Institutions in North and South Philadelphia, areas with high percentages of immigrant and working-class customers, collectively lost as much as 45 percent of their deposits. Losses were closer to 15 percent for banks in Northwest Philadelphia or Center City. One prominent survivor was the Citizens and Southern Bank in South Philadelphia, at Nineteenth and South Streets, founded in 1921 by the civil rights advocate and entrepreneur Richard R. "Major" Wright Sr. as the only African American–owned bank in the North. His conservative lending policies helped the bank become one of the first to reopen after the 1933 bank holiday declared by President Franklin D. Roosevelt. Market leaders such as Fidelity, Girard, and Provident also survived the Depression but made few acquisitions. As a result, a smaller but more stable banking community emerged by the 1940s.

Philadelphia's banks prospered along with the city in the first two decades after World War II. Regulations constrained competition among the institutions that served Philadelphia and its contiguous counties by limiting branch banking and prohibiting interstate banking. But in the 1970s, firms such as American Express, General Motors, Merrill Lynch, and Sears Roebuck began offering loan and deposit services that made such longstanding banking restrictions less relevant. Competition became even more intense during the early 1980s, when Pennsylvania, New Jersey, and Delaware joined other states in allowing statewide branching and then intrastate mergers. In 1994, Congress passed the Riegle Neal Act, removing all restrictions on interstate banking. Finally, in 1999 President Bill Clinton signed the Gramm-Leach-Bliley Act, which removed all remaining barriers between commercial banks, savings banks, investment banks, and other types of lending and depository institutions, thus remaking the landscape of the financial services industry.

From 1983 to 1998, seven of the eight largest locally based institutions succumbed to acquisitive initiatives by larger so-called "super-regional" organizations. Those transactions robbed Philadelphia of its place as a headquarters city for prominent commercial banks. Philadelphia National Bank (PNB) emerged as the only locally based super-regional. It adopted the name CoreStates Financial and acquired banks in Lancaster, Reading, Trenton, and Philadelphia. (In 1998, Charlotte's First Union Corporation acquired CoreStates, but a decade later First Union became part of Wells Fargo, headquartered in San Francisco.)

Among the dozens of institutions providing banking services to consumers and businesses in Greater Philadelphia, by 2010 only WSFS Bank in Wilmington could trace its founding as far back as 1832, when it was established as the Wilmington Savings Fund Society. Philadelphia's Beneficial Bank, formed as a mutual savings bank, was established in 1853; and two other institutions headquartered in Philadelphia's suburbs had legacies dating to the 1870s (Univest and National Penn Bancshares). Some newer organizations (including United Bank of Philadelphia) were reminiscent of the limited-audience banks of the 1920s. However, the number of branch offices and the amount of deposits had become highly concentrated among national and international nameplates. In the twenty-first century, former banking headquarters buildings survived as the last traces of their original tenants and the history of banking in Philadelphia.

United States Mint (Philadelphia)

Stephen Burciaga

Coins have been minted in Philadelphia for as long as the federal government has produced legal tender coins. First authorized by Congress in 1792, the U.S. Mint's Philadelphia facility (commonly known as the Philadelphia mint) in the early twenty-first century remained the nation's largest producer of coins. Its history has been intertwined with the complicated history of the American currency system.

Following the Revolutionary War, virtually all coins circulating in the United States were foreign. Because these coins reflected several dissimilar coinage systems, they could be difficult to use in everyday transactions. To create a simple, uniquely American coinage system, Congress passed the Coinage Act in 1792. This groundbreaking legislation authorized creating a mint to manufacture coins representing American denominations (dollars and cents). The site chosen for this mint was Philadelphia, then the capital of the United States.

The first Philadelphia mint, founded in 1792, operated in a multibuilding facility on Seventh Street between Arch and Filbert Streets. Guarded by the newly established United States Mint Police, the first mint produced copper half-cent and one-cent pieces, silver half dimes (the precursor to the modern nickel), dimes, quarters, half dollars, and dollars, as well as gold two-and-a-half-dollar, five-dollar, and ten-dollar coins. Dependent upon the power of men and horses, production of the nation's first coins was slow and laborious. As the United States grew, the small, increasingly outdated mint could not keep up with the demand for coins. Consequently, in 1833 the mint moved to a new, larger building at Juniper and Chestnut Streets. In 1911, the last surviving building from the first Philadelphia mint facility was demolished.

FIGURE 83. Workers in the smelting room of the Philadelphia Mint, 1888 PHOTOGRAPH BY FRANCES B. JOHNSTON, LIBRARY OF CONGRESS.

At the second Philadelphia mint, advanced metal-refining methods and state-of-the-art, steam-powered coin presses increased the output of coins. Following gold rushes in North Carolina, Georgia, and California during the 1830s and 1840s, the Philadelphia mint converted vast quantities of newfound gold into millions of circulating gold coins. To alleviate frequent coin shortages, the second Philadelphia mint briefly produced several unusual denominations, including bronze two-cent pieces, silver three-cent pieces, and gold three-dollar coins. To ease pressure on the Philadelphia mint and reduce transportation costs, the United States government established several other mints around the nation, but none surpassed Philadelphia in overall production.

Toward the end of the nineteenth century, as the United States took its place as a global power, the Philadelphia mint began producing coins for other nations. Eventually, the Philadelphia mint struck coins for dozens of countries, including Panama, the Philippines, and Cuba. To increase output and improve efficiency, the mint moved in 1901 to an even larger facility at 1700 Spring Garden Street. The building that housed the second Philadelphia mint was demolished shortly after being sold in 1902.

Located near the United States Smelting Company, several machine shops, and Reading Railroad tracks, the third Philadelphia mint had an ideal location for receiving raw supplies and transporting finished coins. The massive building occupied nearly a full city block and quickly became one of the most productive coin manufacturing facilities in the world. The highly productive mint responded to the fluctuating demands of the American economy, ensuring that the nation's coin supply remained plentiful.

External political changes altered the metal compositions of the coins produced by the Philadelphia mint. In 1933, the mint ceased production of circulating gold pieces after the federal government abandoned the gold standard. During World War II, the mint produced coins with reduced quantities of nickel and copper (metals vital to the production of arms and munitions), including the 1943 steel penny. At the end of 1964, the mint ended production of circulating silver coins as the federal government went off the silver standard.

Despite the impressive productivity of the third Philadelphia mint, over time its equipment became outdated and its production processes grew increasingly inefficient. To improve efficiency, in 1969 the Philadelphia mint moved once again to a larger, more technologically sophisticated facility on Independence Mall. After the opening of the fourth mint, the building that once housed the third mint became part of the Community College of Philadelphia's main campus.

Since opening in 1969, the fourth Philadelphia mint has been the United States' premiere producer of circulating coins. Beginning in the 1980s, the mint diversified its output by producing collectable bullion and commemorative coins and medals. One of the most productive manufacturing facilities in the city, the Philadelphia mint could produce more than one million coins within a twenty-four-hour period. Identified easily by a "P" mintmark or, in the case of pennies and older coins, the absence of a mintmark, coins manufactured at the Philadelphia mint have been among the most readily available in the United States. Evidence of the Philadelphia mint's impact on the nation's money supply can be found in pockets, piggy banks, and cash drawers throughout the nation.

Printing and Publishing

James J. Wyatt

From the late seventeenth century to the mid-twentieth century, Philadelphia's printing and publishing industry was a central component of the city's evolution. Growing from small do-it-all shops into large fully mechanized publishing houses, Philadelphia's printers and publishers capitalized on the broad social, political, and economic changes that reshaped the region and nation between the Revolutionary and industrial periods. Men such as Benjamin Franklin, Mathew Carey, William M. Swain, and Cyrus H. K. Curtis pioneered new sales and marketing techniques and adopted technologically advanced printing methods while founding some of the nation's largest publishing companies and establishing Philadelphia as one of America's most historically significant publishing centers. However, during the post–World War II era, publishers experienced an extended period of upheaval that resulted in the sale or closing of several of the most famous and venerable companies.

As Philadelphia evolved into America's largest port city during the eighteenth century, its printer-publishers increased from one in 1683, to nine in 1740, and eventually to fifty-one in 1785. Philadelphia's colonial printers generally located their shops close to highly trafficked commercial streets and squares, and most cobbled together a living by performing multiple tasks. Virtually all found their bread and butter in fee-based print jobs for clients. Colonial printers published almanacs, pamphlets, and newspapers, and they often sold supplies and imported books.

Of the many printers who utilized this business model, none was more successful than Benjamin Franklin. Franklin understood that the key to success lay in finding steady revenue streams and new markets. Shortly after establishing his print shop, Franklin purchased a newspaper and acquired a lucrative government printing contract. He shrewdly renamed the paper the *Pennsylvania Gazette* and changed its format to include more news and entertainment, thereby making it one of the more popular publications in the city and a continuing source of advertising revenue. Franklin used his profits to finance one of the first printing networks in the American colonies by training a coterie of apprentices and helping them establish their own print shops in outlying parts of the region. The network of printers enabled Franklin to sell periodicals and books that he published to a larger audience, and through it, works like the annual *Poor Richard's Almanack* became widely popular. Franklin's far-reaching, multifaceted, and enormously successful business served as the prototype for building a lasting printing and publishing company in the American colonies.

Do-it-all print shops of this sort predominated in Philadelphia until the early nineteenth century, when market changes separated the city's printers and publishers into two distinct groups. Philadelphia's role as the nation's capital during the 1790s sparked this transition, as several local printer-publishers dedicated themselves to producing crusading, politically partisan newspapers. Most of these papers, with the exception of the *Philadelphia Aurora* (1789–1824) published by Benjamin Franklin Bache, did not last much past 1800. However, in the ensuing decades, a second group of entrepreneurs like Mathew Carey built publishing companies that specialized in works for specific segments of the American marketplace.

Carey took advantage of the growing demand for religious reading materials by focusing on producing Bibles. He correctly theorized that producing a small assortment of easily printed works for a growing segment of the market would reduce risk and provide consistent profits. Carey also pioneered the use of traveling salesmen and book peddlers to carry his products far beyond the Philadelphia region. These initial successes made Carey wealthy and helped prove that publishing, by itself, could be lucrative. In later years, denominational publishers, including the Baptist General Tract Society (1826) and the Lutheran Publication Society (1855), among others, helped make Philadelphia a hub of religious publishing.

Technological innovation facilitated the further development of Philadelphia's print-based industries. During the 1820s, printers and publishers began experimenting with steam-powered presses and stereotyping, a printing process using metal plates cast from molds of set type. Early steam-powered presses tripled and quadrupled print speeds while reducing manpower costs, thereby increasing profits. Steam-powered presses enabled newspaper publishers to reduce the price of their papers to a penny, a price affordable to a much wider reading public.

Philadelphia became one of the first cities in America to boast a penny paper when Dr. Christopher Columbus Conwell published the *Cent* in 1830. Conwell's paper was short-lived, but by 1836 William M. Swain founded the *Public Ledger*. Like most penny papers of the 1830s, the *Public Ledger* played to working-class readers by including sensational headlines and titillating reports, local news and human-interest stories, and entertainment features. Within two years, the *Public Ledger*'s daily circulation exceeded twenty thousand readers. Swain added a two-cylinder press, which tripled his printing capacity. Less than a decade later, with the *Public Ledger* among the most read papers in America, Swain installed the first type-revolving press. By the 1850s, the publisher had the capacity to produce more than twenty thousand *Public Ledgers* per hour.

Advanced printing technologies also facilitated a nascent magazine publishing industry in Philadelphia during the 1830s. Publishers like Louis A. Godey utilized powered steam presses and stereotypes to produce high-quality monthly publications. *Godey's Lady's Book* (1830–78) targeted rising numbers of middle-class women, and high subscription rates ensured the periodical's exclusivity. Following the 1837 appointment of Sarah Josepha Hale as editor, the magazine emerged as a taste-making, trendsetting journal with national appeal. *Godey's* became required reading for many women claiming or aspiring to middle-class status. Its circulation surpassed 150,000 in the 1850s.

By the mid-nineteenth century, Philadelphia had grown into one of America's foremost printing and publishing centers, surpassed only by New York City and rivaled only by Boston. In the latter half of the century, as the city matured into a densely populated industrial metropolis, these industries continued to succeed and expand. The emergence of large downtown department stores such as Wanamaker's brought increased advertising revenue. Ever more technologically advanced printing presses and methodologies enabled publishers to produce larger newspapers faster while keeping costs down. By the 1890s, Philadelphia supported thirteen daily newspapers whose cumulative daily circulation exceeded eight hundred thousand. Among the papers competing with the *Public Ledger* for morning readers were the *Record*, *Inquirer*, and *North American*. Evening dailies, printed in the afternoon to service the working class, included the *Item*, *Call*, *Herald*, *Telegraph*, and *Evening Bulletin*. They varied in size and tone, and some, like the *Inquirer*—then widely recognized as a mouthpiece for Philadelphia's Republican machine—gained notoriety for their political positions.

Philadelphia's newspaper industry was bolstered by the emergence of numerous ethnic presses during the late nineteenth and early twentieth centuries. Publications such as the Italian *Voce Della Colonia* (1893–1918), the Polish *Patryota* (1889–1955), and German *Philadelphia Tageblatt* (1877–1944) gained popularity by serving as the voices of their communities. They translated important information for non-English-speaking readers, carried news of the homeland, and helped establish community bonds by promoting ethnic events and organizations. Some, like the Jewish paper *Idishe Welt* (1914–42), were considered radical or revolutionary. During this period, the *Philadelphia Tribune* (established 1884) was founded to perform similar functions for Philadelphia's African American community.

Also taking advantage of changes wrought by industrialization were the city's magazine publishers. Among the industrial era's most successful publishers, Cyrus H. K. Curtis kept subscription rates low and interest high by selling enormous amounts of advertising and incorporating helpful and informative content. The *Ladies' Home Journal* (established 1883) frequently blended columns addressing fashion, cooking, and homemaking with articles penned by social reformers such as Jane Addams. Under the guidance of famed editor Edward Bok and Curtis's wife, Louisa Knapp Curtis, the *Journal* became the first magazine to achieve a circulation of one million copies per issue in 1904. Curtis used the profits to purchase the *Saturday Evening Post* in 1897 and transform it into the nation's most popular magazine. The *Post* attracted readers and advertisers with a little something for everyone, including poetry, short stories, and news. By 1910, its circulation exceeded one million and its annual advertising revenue topped $5 million.

Flush with success, Philadelphia's publishers upgraded their presses and facilities during the first half of the twentieth century. Curtis opened an enormous Georgian Revival headquarters at Sixth and Walnut Streets in 1910. Along with the neighboring J.B. Lippincott Company and Lea & Febiger, the Curtis Building helped anchor Philadelphia's publishers' row for decades. During the same period, newspaper publishers James Elverson Jr. and William L. McLean moved the *Inquirer* and *Evening Bulletin* into gleaming new homes that enabled centralized operations and faster production.

Philadelphia's printing and publishing industries continued to prosper well into the 1950s. Competition and market changes reduced the number of daily newspapers in the city from thirteen to three by midcentury, but the *Evening Bulletin* thrived and consistently ranked among the nation's most widely read papers with a daily circulation often exceeding seven hundred thousand. In 1955, the Bulletin Company opened one of the most technologically advanced newspaper plants in the world, near Thirtieth and Market Streets, with presses capable of producing nearly one million newspapers an hour. In 1946, *Inquirer* publisher Walter Annenberg founded Triangle Publications, Inc. and began branching into magazine publishing and broadcast media. By the late 1950s, Triangle's stable of publications included the *Inquirer*, the afternoon tabloid *Daily News*, *Seventeen* magazine, and *TV Guide*, which grew into the nation's largest weekly periodical by the 1970s. Annenberg built Triangle into one of the nation's largest and most profitable multimedia corporations.

Other Philadelphia publishing stalwarts continuing their successes into the postwar era included the Curtis Publishing Company, which broke ground in 1946 on an enormous new production facility in Sharon Hill, Pennsylvania. The facility, with capacity to produce more than a million magazines a day, introduced the first successful four-color "perfecting" presses capable of printing rolls of paper on both sides simultaneously. Specialized book publishing, particularly in the areas of science, medicine, education, and religion, also thrived.

Beginning in the 1960s and carrying forward into the early twenty-first century, however, suburbanization and new communications mediums contributed to a prolonged wave of consolidations and closings among book, magazine, and newspaper publishing companies across the nation. Philadelphia felt these shifts acutely. A diverse array of suburban daily and weekly newspapers siphoned circulation and advertising from their urban counterparts. Outside corporate ownership also increased during the postwar period. In the 1960s, the Gannett newspaper chain purchased several daily and weekly newspapers in southern New Jersey. In 1969, Annenberg sold the *Inquirer* and *Daily News* to Knight Newspapers, and in 1978 Harper & Row, Publishers acquired book publisher J.B. Lippincott. The company sold to Wolters Kluwer, a Dutch company, in 1990 for $250 million.

FIGURE 84. Curtis Publishing Company presses, ca. 1910. The *Ladies' Home Journal*, the *Saturday Evening Post*, and other publications circulated to the nation from Curtis headquarters in Philadelphia. FREE LIBRARY OF PHILADELPHIA.

Many Philadelphia publishers and publications did not survive this shifting landscape. During the 1960s, changing reader tastes and increased competition from pictorial magazines like *Life* and *Look* as well as television contributed to the rapid decline of Curtis Publishing's periodicals. A series of poor management decisions compounded the company's dwindling profits and led to its collapse. In 1969, the *Saturday Evening Post* ceased publication and the *Ladies' Home Journal* was sold. Among the city's remaining newspapers, the *Evening Bulletin* experienced a prolonged slide in the face of increased competition from the Knight-backed *Inquirer* and thriving suburban daily and weekly newspapers. In 1982, after the McLean family sold the paper to Charter Company, the *Evening Bulletin* folded, which left the city without a large independently-owned daily newspaper. In 1990, Lea & Febiger, a prominent Philadelphia publisher of scientific books with historic roots extending to Mathew Carey's publishing company, ceased operations after being purchased by Waverly Press of Baltimore.

The closings and corporate takeovers of the late twentieth century rocked Philadelphia's printing and publishing industry, but they did not fully cripple it. The shifting market conditions created opportunities for some established publications to expand and for new companies and publications to emerge. While many of Philadelphia's established ethnic and religious newspapers failed to survive past the 1950s, some, like the *Jewish Exponent* (established 1887), grew into regional publications. The *Philadelphia Gay News* began publishing in 1976, and two free alternative weeklies, *Philadelphia Weekly* (established as the Welcomat in 1971) and the *City Paper* (1981–2015) quickly gained popularity. Additionally, the influx of new immigrant groups into the region fostered development of new ethnic newspapers. *Al Día*, a free tabloid serving Latino communities, began publishing in 1992, and *Metro Chinese Weekly* appeared in 2007 to serve Asian Americans.

Digital communication presented existential challenges, however. Newspapers, long a mainstay of Philadelphia's publishing industry, struggled as massive numbers of readers and advertisers migrated to the Internet in the late twentieth and early twenty-first centuries. After multiple changes in ownership and a decades-long series of staff reductions, ownership of the *Inquirer* and *Daily News* transferred in 2016 to a nonprofit organization, the Lenfest Institute for Journalism. In 2021, the *Inquirer* closed its massive Montgomery County printing plant, which had been operating only since 1992. The company outsourced printing of the *Inquirer* and *Daily News* to a Gannett Company–owned facility in Cherry Hill, New Jersey. In the early twenty-first century, the region's printing and publishing industry no longer maintained the lofty status it once enjoyed as one of the nation's foremost centers for the printed word.

Almanacs

Kelli Billings

Almanacs, annual publications containing calendars, recipes, humor, and references to medicine and other resources, played an important role in disseminating useful information and in developing the publishing business in the British North American colonies and during the early republic. English settlers brought the almanac format to the North American colonies, including to Pennsylvania shortly after its founding. By the mid-eighteenth century, Philadelphia emerged as a central location for their production, and its printers issued some of the era's most popular almanacs. Almanac publishing continued into the twenty-first century, but the emergence of daily newspapers and, later, ready access to information from Internet sources led to their general decline.

During the colonial period and into the era of the early republic, these short publications, usually numbering fewer than fifty pages, were smart investments for printers. Relatively simple to produce, they did not require time-consuming illustrations or excessive amounts of paper. Printers often compiled their contents, which they generally tailored to the local audiences to ensure relevance and interest. Printers adjusted print runs each year to meet demand. Almanacs were extremely popular; after the Bible and other religious works, they were the most widely purchased books in America.

Before the proliferation of newspapers in the early nineteenth century, almanacs were among the only sources of standardized timekeeping. Calendars included information about eclipses, the tides, and the phases of the moon. Reference sections might include weather forecasts, currency conversions, and the dates of local court sessions. To make their publications stand out in a competitive market, some almanac makers eventually included lighthearted additions such as recipes, jokes, and short stories.

William Bradford published Pennsylvania's first almanac, the *Kalendarium Pennsilvaniense*, in 1686. Titan Leeds compiled *The American Almanack* starting in 1715. Germantown printer Christopher Saur produced a German-language almanac beginning in 1738 to serve Pennsylvania's significant German-speaking population. Women also engaged in the trade; Cornelia Bradford took over her husband's Front Street print shop upon his death and printed almanacs written by many prominent figures in the business.

The most successful publisher of almanacs was Benjamin Franklin. His *Poor Richard's Almanack* ranked among the best-selling almanacs in the region, with Franklin at its helm from 1732 through 1758. Adopting the witty persona of "Richard Saunders," Franklin proffered his unique brand of prophecy, proverbs, poetry, puzzles, and practical advice on all manner of subjects. He also ran serial stories to hold readers' attention over the years and occasionally used his almanac to advocate for public issues, most famously his effort to promote paper currency in the colonies. *Poor Richard's* became so popular (and profitable) that Franklin expanded its coverage and production, sometimes printing as many as ten thousand copies a year and selling hundreds of copies to printers as far away as Boston and Charleston.

Across the Philadelphia region other printers produced almanacs to meet local interests. Readers in

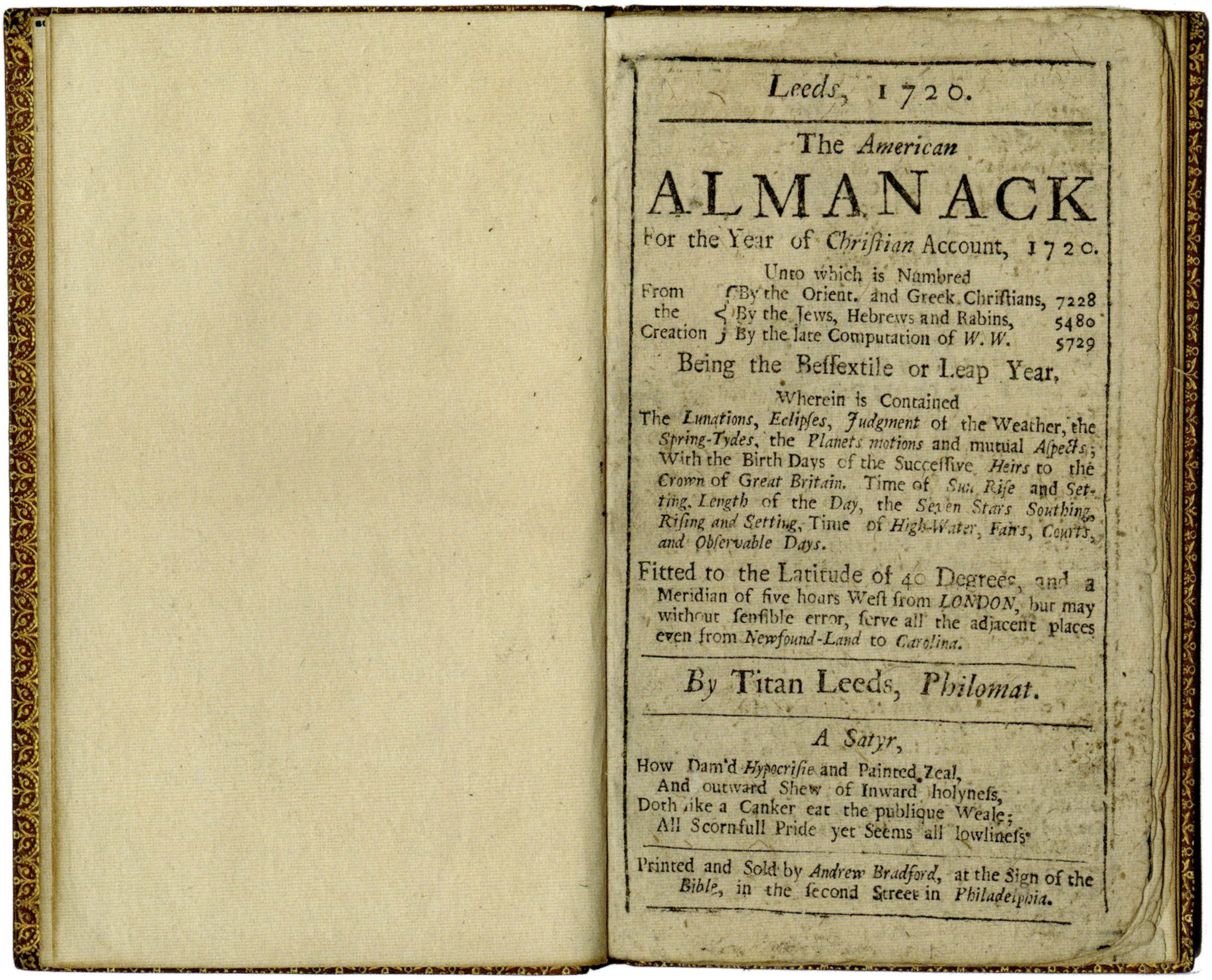

Leeds, 1720.

The *American*

ALMANACK

For the Year of *Chriſtian* Account, 1720.

Unto which is Numbred

From the Creation { By the Orient. and Greek Chriſtians, 7228 | By the Jews, Hebrews and Rabins, 5480 | By the late Computation of *W. W.* 5729

Being the Beſſextile or Leap Year,

Wherein is Contained

The *Lunations*, *Eclipſes*, *Judgment* of the Weather, the *Spring-Tydes*, the *Planets motions* and mutual *Aſpects*; With the Birth Days of the Succeſſive *Heirs* to the *Crown* of *Great Britain*. Time of *Sun Riſe* and *Setting*, *Length* of the *Day*, the *Seven Stars Southing*, *Riſing and Setting*, Time of *High-Water*, *Fairs*, *Courts*, and *Obſervable Days*.

Fitted to the Latitude of 40 Degrees, and a Meridian of five hours Weſt from *LONDON*, but may without ſenſible error, ſerve all the adjacent places even from *Newfound-Land* to *Carolina*.

By Titan Leeds, *Philomat.*

A Satyr,

How Dam'd *Hypocriſie* and Painted Zeal,
And outward Shew of Inward holyneſs,
Doth like a Canker eat the publique Weale;
All Scornfull Pride yet Seems all lowlineſs.

Printed and Sold by *Andrew Bradford*, at the Sign of the *Bible*, in the ſecond Street in *Philadelphia*.

FIGURE 85. *The American Almanack*, printed and sold by Andrew Bradford on Second Street, Philadelphia, 1720. COLLECTION OF THE HISTORICAL SOCIETY OF PENNSYLVANIA.

agricultural areas looked to them for weather forecasts and other information useful for planning plantings and maintaining various crops and animals. Almanacs held a unique significance to Lancaster County, Pennsylvania's most important agricultural region. Lancaster printer John Baer debuted the *Lancaster Agricultural Almanac* in 1825. An excellent example of the utility and tradition an almanac can provide to a community, it remained in print in the twenty-first century, with readership across the mid-Atlantic region and into Ohio. Other almanacs linked Greater Philadelphia with surrounding areas. *The New Jersey and Pennsylvania Almanac* was published regularly in Trenton from the early 1790s through the 1820s. Serving an even larger area, Samuel Adams printed and sold *The New Jersey, Pennsylvania, Delaware, Maryland, and Virginia Almanac* (1790–1810) from his Philadelphia shop on Market Street.

Almanac production waned in the nineteenth century as increasing numbers of daily newspapers dispensed information previously the province of almanacs. Still, some area printers continued to produce almanacs, including Philadelphia's *Farmers Almanac*, printed by Jacob Hollowbush in the 1850s—not to be confused with the famous and longer-lasting *Farmers' Almanac* founded in Morristown, New Jersey, in 1818 and later relocated to Maine (available in an online edition since 1997). John Baer's *Agricultural Almanac* embodied the changes in almanacs during the nineteenth and twentieth centuries. As industrialization pulled workers into the cities, content transitioned from farming advice to gardening tips, trivia, and folklore, in addition to the standard calendar and weather forecasts.

Significant transformations in mass media and technology occurred throughout the twentieth century, but the Philadelphia almanac tradition persisted. The city's *Evening Bulletin* newspaper published the annual *Bulletin Almanac* from 1924 to 1976. In lieu of the standard calendar as the focal point, this almanac provided useful information about the governments, laws, and municipal services of Pennsylvania, New Jersey, and Delaware. It did, however, retain such traditional almanac elements as recipes, tables of weights and measures, and proverbs. Kenneth Finkel revived this handbook style of almanac in the late twentieth century, publishing the *Philadelphia Almanac and Citizens' Manual* for the Library Company of Philadelphia in 1994 and 1995.

Despite their ephemeral nature and heavy use, many almanacs survived as valuable resources for historical inquiry. Their contents have provided historians and others with meteorological and astronomical data unavailable elsewhere, as well as insights into the histories of food preparation, moral advice, and humor. These unassuming but important books provide revealing snapshots of daily life and interests in the Greater Philadelphia region.

Book Publishing and Publishers

Ann K. Johnson

Between 1750 and 1800, Philadelphia became the center for book printing and publishing in the United States, surpassing New York and Boston. Although Philadelphia lost that primacy in the nineteenth century, firms specializing in medical and religious publishing continued to do well. By the mid to late twentieth century, however, as the publishing industry consolidated, few independent Philadelphia book publishers remained.

In the late seventeenth century, William Bradford established the first printing press in Philadelphia. For many years, he was the only printer in the city. In colonial America, printers often acted as booksellers and sometimes as publishers of broadsides, pamphlets, newspapers, and almanacs. Book publishing was far less common during this period because it was so risky. Printing and binding books was expensive, and would-be publishers had no guarantee that they would be able to recoup their investment through sales. Instead, printers preferred to import books from Great Britain.

Nonetheless, a few enterprising printers in the Philadelphia region published books during the eighteenth century. Perhaps the most famous was Benjamin Franklin. Over the course of his career, Franklin printed and financed sixteen books, including Samuel Richardson's *Pamela* (1742–44) and Philadelphia politician and scholar James Logan's translation of *Cato Major* (1744) by Marcus Tullius Cicero. One of Franklin's contemporaries, Christopher Saur, set up shop in Germantown and printed and published German-language materials to serve a growing population of immigrants. Delaware-born Isaac Collins got his start in Philadelphia as an apprentice before moving to Burlington and, later, Trenton, New Jersey. Collins mostly published religious texts as well as a few schoolbooks.

Scottish-born printer Thomas Dobson took on perhaps the most ambitious printing and publishing project during this period: the first American edition of the *Encyclopaedia Britannica* (1789–98). To finance this expensive multivolume work, Dobson gathered subscribers from across the country, including George Washington and Thomas Jefferson. Still, Dobson had trouble finding enough support for the project, and the *Britannica* was not a financial success.

In the second half of the eighteenth century the number of printers began to grow substantially. Printers gravitated to Philadelphia because of its large, cosmopolitan population and its high concentration of learned organizations, from the American Philosophical Society to the University of Pennsylvania. Philadelphia's proximity to important rivers and roads also meant that printed materials could more easily reach markets in the South and West. With the opening of the Erie

Canal in 1825, however, New York possessed superior waterways and several of its large general publishing firms proved to be tough competition. By the late 1830s, Philadelphia's growth slowed.

By the nineteenth century, the market for print had expanded considerably. More Americans could read than ever before, and there was a growing sense that an educated society was crucial to a thriving democracy. These changes, along with a booming economy, made printers more willing to take risks and publish books. Also during this period, the line between printer and publisher became more defined. Irish-born Mathew Carey, generally considered Philadelphia's first modern publisher, got his start as a printer but soon focused his attention solely on publishing and bookselling. He found success publishing British novels, such as Susanna Rowson's *Charlotte Temple* (first published by Carey in 1794). Carey also pioneered new methods in marketing and distribution.

In the 1820s, Carey asked his oldest son, Henry Charles Carey, and his son-in-law, Isaac Lea, to take over the firm under the new name Carey & Lea. The firm went on to publish a wide variety of books, including popular novels by Washington Irving and James Fenimore Cooper. Eventually, fierce competition from the growing Harper Brothers in New York helped convince the firm to shift its focus to medical publishing. The specialization suited Carey & Lea's location in Philadelphia, home to a growing medical community with two medical schools. Over the years, the firm changed names several times, becoming known as Lea & Febiger by the twentieth century.

Another important nineteenth-century Philadelphia publishing firm, J.B. Lippincott & Company, got its start publishing religious books in 1836. Founded by New Jersey–born Joshua B. Lippincott, the firm began to focus on medical publications and gift books by the 1850s. While Lippincott was known as a publisher, the firm did considerable work as a jobber, helping to distribute books published by other firms to retail stores in the South. Lippincott also operated a large factory for printing and bookbinding at 715 Market Street. By the end of the nineteenth century the company was printing around two thousand books per year.

Religious publishers thrived in Philadelphia during the nineteenth century. These organizations, financed largely by donations, sold some of their publications but mostly gave books away for free. The Philadelphia Bible Society, founded in 1809, published Bibles and New Testaments. The American Sunday School Union got its start in Philadelphia in 1824 and soon became one of the largest national religious publishing societies in the United States. The group aimed to establish Sunday schools across the country and to supply each school with religious books appropriate for children. In addition to noncommercial publishers, by the mid-nineteenth century many general publishers partnered with specific denominations to supply religious works. J.B. Lippincott & Company, for example, allied with the Protestant Episcopal Church.

Another distinctive aspect of the book trade in Philadelphia was its focus on subscription publishing. Subscription books were sold door to door by agents, instead of through a bookstore. Many types of books were sold by subscription, including novels, histories, and reference works. Mathew Carey was one of the earliest American publishers to rely on a book peddler to sell his books. After the Civil War, a number of publishing firms specializing in subscription books formed in Philadelphia, and even general publishers like J.B. Lippincott & Company maintained a subscription book department. Most subscription publishers eventually went bankrupt during the early twentieth century, when the practice of selling books door to door largely ended.

Despite the many book publishers in Philadelphia during the eighteenth and nineteenth centuries, few were women. Two of the city's earliest female publishers were Jane Aitken and Lydia Bailey. Although they were printers first and foremost (Lydia Bailey did printing work for Mathew Carey, among others), Aitken and Bailey occasionally acted as publishers. Aitken, for example, published the first American translation of the Bible in 1808. By the late nineteenth century, although more women were entering other areas of the book trade, the number of women book publishers did not increase. In 1880, Florence I. Duncan and Mary R. Heygate Hall formed Duncan & Hall. The firm published at least one book, *Ye Last Sweet Thing in Corners* (1880), which was written by Duncan. Another woman publisher, Louise C. Boname, taught French in the city together with writing and publishing French language books for students beginning in 1896.

By the early twentieth century, a few well-established firms, including Lea & Febiger and J.B. Lippincott Company, dominated book publishing in Philadelphia. In 1901, Lippincott moved to new offices at 227 S. Sixth Street, overlooking Washington Square. W.B. Saunders, Lea & Febiger, David McKay, and others eventually moved to the area as well, making it a center for publishing. Perhaps the best-known book Lippincott published during this period was Harper Lee's *To Kill a Mockingbird* (1960). Lippincott was sold to Harper & Row in 1978, and then to the Dutch company Wolters Kluwer in 1990. The imprint became Lippincott Williams & Wilkins. Lea & Febiger was sold to Baltimore-based Waverly Inc. in 1990. Waverly, bought by Wolters Kluwer in 1998, became part of Lippincott Williams & Wilkins.

Only a handful of new publishing firms formed in Philadelphia during the twentieth century. One of the most important was Running Press, founded in 1972 by brothers Stuart and Larry Teacher to publish nonfiction, children's literature, and miniature books. Although acquired in 2002 by New York's Perseus Book Group, a firm bought by Hachette Book Group in 2016, Running Press remained headquartered in Philadelphia.

While commercial publishing declined, universities became the major publishers of books in the Philadelphia region. University presses got their start publishing faculty scholarship, but soon expanded to publishing the work of other scholars. The University of Pennsylvania Press, established in 1890, began to regularly publish books in 1927, when Phelps Soule was brought in from Yale University Press to act as a full-time editor. Under Soule, the press grew substantially, publishing books on a wide variety of topics from finance to medicine to bibliography to history. Other presses soon followed. The University of Delaware Press was founded in 1922, Rutgers University Press was founded in 1936, and Temple University Press began publishing in 1969. Saint Joseph's University Press, primarily a publisher of books on Catholic history and culture, was founded in 1997.

Book publishing is one of Philadelphia's oldest industries. Early on, Philadelphia printers like Benjamin Franklin and Mathew Carey understood the importance of books to a new nation. Especially during the first half of the nineteenth century, Philadelphia publishers played a crucial role in producing books for readers in remote areas across the United States. As the book trade grew, Philadelphia publishers successfully adapted to a changing market. Ultimately, Philadelphia's book publishers became part of a national and international industry.

Railroad Industry

John Hepp

The history of the railroad industry in the United States and the growth of the Greater Philadelphia region are inextricably linked. Philadelphia money and engineering built the national network and, from the middle of the nineteenth century to the middle of the twentieth, railroads helped make and maintain Philadelphia as a "Workshop of the World," the nation's largest and most diverse manufacturing center. Throughout the twentieth century one of the nation's wealthiest and most powerful transportation companies, the Pennsylvania Railroad, was headquartered in the city.

The region's first rail freight carrier, Thomas Leiper's railroad, began service in Delaware County in 1810. Built by Leiper to link his quarry with a stream so that the stone could be more easily transported to Philadelphia, the horse-drawn tramway was replaced by a canal in 1828. This small line reflected trends common in Europe and the United States in the first few decades of the nineteenth century: railroads initially were short-distance solutions for carrying bulk freight like stone and coal when canals were impractical or too expensive. Beginning with the Stockton and Darlington Railway in 1825, however, British industrialists began to build railways to haul both freight and passengers over longer distances. This new concept was quickly imported by American capitalists. The first of these new railroads in the United States, the Baltimore and Ohio (the B&O), was chartered by Maryland in 1827 to link the growing port of Baltimore with the Ohio River.

The B&O spurred most of the other major Atlantic Seaboard cities to develop similar railroads. In 1830, New Jersey authorized a route between Philadelphia and New York City. The next year, Pennsylvania granted charters to a number of railroads, including the Philadelphia and Columbia (a line that formed part of a rail and canal system between the Quaker City and Pittsburgh that competed with the B&O), and other more local lines like the Philadelphia and Delaware County (the start of a route to Baltimore) and the Philadelphia, Germantown & Norristown (PGN) (serving Philadelphia County). Through the 1840s, most railroad companies operated a single route, often accurately reflected by the locations in its name. Some were mostly passenger lines, like the PGN, while others were more focused on freight, such as the Philadelphia and Reading (the Reading), which was chartered in 1833 and transported anthracite between those cities.

A new vision for railroads came to the region in 1846 with the founding of the Pennsylvania Railroad (the PRR), an integrated system headquartered in Philadelphia that planned to replace the canal route to Pittsburgh with a direct rail line. During the second half of the nineteenth century, the PRR acquired and built lines that linked New York with Washington (the region later known as the Northeast Corridor) and extended west from Pittsburgh to Detroit, St. Louis, and Chicago. Although the PRR was a trunk line railroad that hauled passengers and general freight, the majority of its revenue came from carrying bulk commodities like bituminous coal and iron ore to industrial cities. The self-proclaimed "Standard Railroad of the World" built a four-track main line from New York to Chicago known as the "Broad Way" by the early twentieth century. In 1912, the company named its premier passenger train between New York and Chicago (via Philadelphia) The Broadway Limited, a moniker that continued to be used by the PRR and its successors until 1995.

On a national scale, the PRR competed in the late nineteenth and early twentieth centuries with the B&O and two other carriers based in New York City: the Erie and the New York Central. These four companies made up the major freight and passenger carriers in the middle Atlantic and midwestern regions when those areas were the nation's industrial heartland. Like most American railroads, all four of these carriers hauled far more freight than passenger traffic. Philadelphia, like New York and Baltimore, was a major international port where shipping lines interchanged cargo from Europe and the Americas with the railroads. The PRR's main competitor in the Greater Philadelphia area, however, was the Reading. The Reading, through its alliances with the B&O, New York Central, and other regional lines, played a key role in the national system far greater in importance than its small size would suggest.

Like other railroads, both the PRR and the Reading exercised great political power throughout the region and, to a lesser extent, the nation. For most of the second half of the nineteenth century, the PRR effectively controlled the Pennsylvania legislature in Harrisburg. Franklin Gowen, while president of the Reading, had himself appointed a special prosecutor of the Molly Maguires (who had allegedly acted against the railroad's coal-mining subsidiary). In a nation known for corruption, the railroads were very wealthy corporations willing to spend as needed to obtain what they wanted. By the early twentieth century, broad public disgust with corporate excess and corruption led to Progressive Era reforms that limited railroad power and earnings.

Change, both regulatory and technological, threatened railroads nationwide. As the country's first large-scale private enterprises, railroads caused safety and financial concerns that led the industry to be regulated on both the state and national levels beginning in the late nineteenth century. Initially the railroads successfully fought many of these regulations but slowly accepted them. By the early twentieth century, power slowly shifted from the railroads to the government. Federal and state agencies issued regulations that affected safety and pricing, and these rules often limited corporate earnings.

Around the same time that regulation began, technological changes created increased competition. First came electric trolleys, which carried passengers, some freight, and even mail in cities and the surrounding countryside starting in the 1880s. After World War I, automobiles, buses, and trucks operating on taxpayer-paved streets and highways began to compete more effectively with the railways for a wide variety of traffic. To fight this competition, railroads experimented with electrifying some of their lines. The PRR was a leader in this effort, experimenting with a trolley-like line in 1895 and mainline electrification of a secondary route between Camden and Atlantic City in 1906. By the 1930s, the PRR operated the United States' busiest system of electric passenger and freight trains between New York, Washington, and Harrisburg. Nationally,

WASHINGTON
OREGON
MONTANA
DAKOTA
WYOMING
NEBRASKA
COLORADO
KANSAS
UTAH
ARIZONA
NEW MEXICO
TEXAS
PUBLIC LAND
MEXICO
SAN FRANCISCO
SACRAMENTO

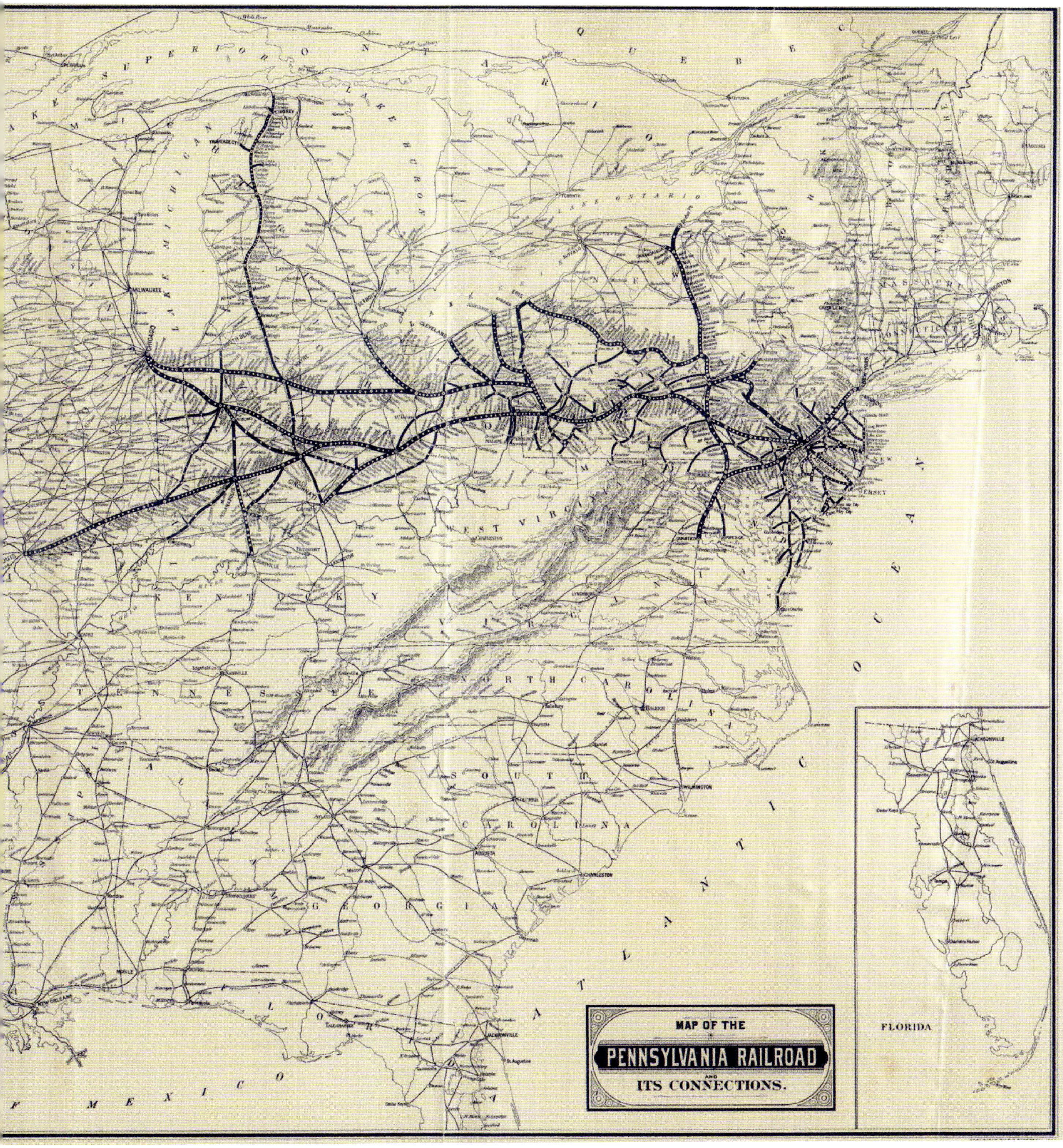

FIGURE 86. The Pennsylvania Railroad and its connections, 1889. The dark lines extending from Philadelphia in all directions show the Pennsylvania Railroad connecting with a nationwide rail network. LIBRARY OF CONGRESS.

however, traffic continued to decline in the 1920s and 1930s. World War II reversed this trend temporarily, but after the war these declines resumed. The 1950s also saw the expansion of the airline industry, which adversely affected the railroads' long-distance passenger and mail traffic. As losses mounted, more trains were abandoned and all railways accelerated their conversion from steam to less-expensive-to-operate diesel locomotives.

In 1968, the PRR merged with its longtime competitor the New York Central to form the Penn Central, headquartered in Philadelphia. Just two years later, the Penn Central declared bankruptcy. At the time, it was the nation's largest railroad, and its bankruptcy was the largest in American history. One consequence of the Penn Central debacle was that many other struggling mid-Atlantic railways became insolvent (including the Reading). The federal government intervened and created the National Railroad Passenger Corporation (Amtrak) in 1971 and the Consolidated Rail Corporation (Conrail) in 1976. Amtrak took over most intercity passenger trains nationwide, while Conrail operated freight trains and initially commuter trains in New England, the Middle Atlantic, and the Midwest. Conrail's headquarters was in Philadelphia and Amtrak maintained a key operational hub in the city.

Philadelphia's decline as a national railroad center began in 1998 when Conrail was purchased by its two main competitors: CSX (a corporate successor to the B&O) and Norfolk Southern. Although Conrail continued to operate in certain areas (including Greater Philadelphia) as a jointly owned switching line, for the first time since the 1830s no major railroad company was headquartered in the city.

At the start of the twenty-first century, a wide variety of railroad operations continued to serve the Philadelphia region. Although Philadelphia remained an important regional transportation hub for passengers and freight, the city was no longer a center of national importance to the railway industry.

Telegraphy

Lucy Davis

Telegraphy transformed communication in the nineteenth century, allowing information to travel nearly instantly across the nation and the world. Developing alongside railroad transportation, the telegraph bridged the distance between Philadelphia and cities around the globe.

The earliest telegraph systems were devised in the 1790s in France and consisted of a line of towers on which an operator could broadcast signals, similar to flag semaphore. The short range and great expense of constructing and operating these optical telegraphs limited their application to major government projects. Many people worked on the development of the electric telegraph, but the cumbersome systems found little support until Samuel Morse devised a "bi-signal" system of long and short current bursts to represent individual characters, along with a receiver that recorded the transmission automatically on paper tape to allow translation. Morse code became the de facto cypher used in telegraphic communications. Morse and a partner, Alfred Vail, built their first experimental telegraph device at the Speedwell Ironworks in Morristown, New Jersey. On February 8, 1838, the pair demonstrated the system to a scientific committee at the Franklin Institute in Philadelphia.

Philadelphia's location between other major cities on the Eastern Seaboard made it a prime location for an early telegraph system. Service began in June 1846, when the Magnetic Telegraph Company connected the city to New York City and later to Baltimore and Washington, D.C. Publisher William M. Swain of the *Philadelphia Public Ledger* and the *Baltimore Sun*, realizing the utility of the device for transmitting news quickly, raised over a third of the $10,000 capital required for the southern line. This line allowed the *Ledger* and the *Sun* to report dispatches from the Mexican-American War. During the Civil War, Philadelphia newspapers used the telegraph to provide same-day updates on the Battle of Gettysburg. The technology also proved invaluable for emergency services. By 1856, Philadelphia had installed a municipal services telegraph system connecting police and fire stations across the city to create a rapid response network.

Telegraph lines often paralleled new railroad lines, which expanded rapidly during the same period. The two services allowed both people and information to be transported rapidly across the vast expanses of the nation. When the transcontinental railroad connected the West to the existing rail network in the East in 1869, a telegraph line was built along it. A transatlantic line—the third attempt at connecting Europe and North America—began operation in 1866, allowing news and messages to be transmitted across the western world. Consolidation followed as small regional networks were purchased by large companies like Western Union, which held a near-monopoly in the United States by the turn of the twentieth century.

Wireless telegraphy eliminated the need for expensive cables by transmitting messages using radio waves. The first wireless telegraphy company in the nation, the American Wireless Telephone and Telegraph Company, transmitted its first message in 1900 between Camden, New Jersey, and Philadelphia. As proof of the technology's ability to traverse much greater distances, the De Forest Wireless Telegraph Company built a wireless telegraphy station within the headquarters of the Philadelphia-based *North American* at 121 S. Broad Street. The newspaper almost instantly received and published the March 1905 inaugural address of President Theodore Roosevelt. Wireless telegraphy became an invaluable tool during World War I by allowing instantaneous communication with troops in the field, the air, and the sea, but its use declined soon after.

The introduction of the telephone at the 1876 Centennial Exhibition heralded the decline of telegraphy, as the new technology gradually replaced text-based messaging for many daily uses. During World War II, the military used telegraphs to inform next of kin of war deaths. Telegraphy remained in limited use due to the high cost of long-distance telephone calls until the Internet and satellite communications rendered the format obsolete in the late 1990s. Although amateur radio operators kept wireless telegraphy alive into the twenty-first century, the communication medium otherwise came to an end in 2006, when Western Union carried the last telegram in the United States.

Telephones

Lucy Davis

The telephone, which debuted to the public at the Centennial Exhibition of 1876, surpassed communication by telegraph by allowing sound to be transmitted instantly to nearly anywhere in the world. Philadelphia became home to many of telephony's milestones and a center of telephone innovation, promoted by pioneers and supporters including inventor Alexander Graham Bell and retail magnate John Wanamaker. The city continued to serve a unique role in telecommunications through the twentieth century with the introduction of the first wireless telephone and the first computer-regulated commercial wireless system.

The telegraph, invented in 1844 by Samuel Morse, had been popular and effective but not without problems. In addition to requiring operators fluent in Morse code to quickly transcribe messages, only one message could be sent over a single wire at a time. This flaw could delay urgent messages, and several inventors in the latter half of the nineteenth century sought a solution.

Among the inventors seeking to improve the telegraph, Elisha Gray, an Ohio-based electrical engineer, also discovered a method of transmitting voice over wire using a liquid transmitter. On February 14, 1876, Gray filed a caveat (a legal notice of intent to patent) for his device. Coincidentally, just hours before, Scottish-born teacher for the deaf Alexander Graham Bell filed a patent for a remarkably similar invention.

Bell's invention made its public debut in Philadelphia at the 1876 Centennial Exhibition, where prototypes were installed at opposite ends of Machinery Hall. After much adjustment, Bell demonstrated the device by reciting lines from *Hamlet*. Among the many to be amazed by this new technology, Emperor Dom Pedro II of Brazil reportedly exclaimed, "My God! It talks!" Less impressed was Elisha Gray, who took Bell and his assistants to court over purported patent violations. No technology similar to the liquid transmitter used in Bell's functioning prototype existed in his notes until March 1876, after Gray filed his caveat. Nonetheless, Bell was awarded the patent and continued to improve his device and protect it from would-be competitors.

FIGURE 87. Bell Telephone operators, 1965. New switchboards with buttons relieved operators of manually plugging in cords to make connections. SPECIAL COLLECTIONS RESEARCH CENTER, TEMPLE UNIVERSITY LIBRARIES.

Philadelphia gained its first private telephone line for practical use in 1877, when Thomas E. Cornish, an electronics supply dealer, founded the Telephone Company of Philadelphia at the request of Pennsylvania Railroad president Thomas A. Scott, who wanted a telephone line installed directly between his home and office. The company and the line were both quickly purchased by Bell. The renamed Bell Telephone Company of Philadelphia established its first headquarters at Fourth and Chestnut Streets.

The first fully functioning switchboard was installed at 1111 Chestnut Street that same year. By then, the telephone was sufficiently developed to allow intercity phone calls, the first of which was made between Philadelphia and New York City. Even more extraordinary, the sound transmitted was not speech but music. Listeners in New York's Steinway Hall heard a pianist performing in the Philadelphia headquarters of Western Union at Tenth and Chestnut Streets.

The relationship between Bell and Western Union quickly soured, however. Shortly after Bell filed his patents, he offered them for $100,000 to Western Union, which held a monopoly on telegraph transmission in the United States. Western Union declined the offer, failing to see the commercial viability of such a device. When Bell's invention proved popular and Bell was unwilling to sell, Western Union hired Thomas Edison to circumvent Bell's patent by making slight adjustments to the telephone. Bell sued Western Union for patent infringement, and in 1879 Western Union conceded the patent rights to Bell, creating a monopoly on the telephone industry that lasted for more than a decade.

Retail magnate John Wanamaker, a prominent early adopter of the new communication device, had a telephone installed in his "Grand Depot" at Thirteenth and Chestnut Streets as early as 1879. By 1906, the store had a telephone ordering system, the first of its kind to allow customers to call in orders. Wanamaker's system distinguished itself from competitors by allowing customers to order items from the New York City Wanamaker's store and have them delivered to the Philadelphia location. The service was initially only available to residents of Philadelphia and its suburbs. On December 30, 1911, a special long-distance telephone device allowed customers in the New York Wanamaker's to hear the grand opening ceremonies for the new Philadelphia store, including a performance of the "Triumphal March" from the opera *Aida* on the famed Wanamaker organ.

Other early adopters of the telephone included businessmen, physicians, and druggists, who valued the instantaneous nature of telephone transactions. But home and personal use remained low until well into the twentieth century. Many people failed to see the purpose in using the device for social calls, and most advertisements were directed toward business owners. In Philadelphia, Bell began with only 15 customers in 1877 and had only 3,300 in 1890. But the practical use of the telephone soon proved it indispensable. By 1917, Bell Telephone had 175,000 subscribers and 450,000 miles of telephone wire spanned Philadelphia.

When Bell's patent on his telephone system ended in 1894, competitors quickly emerged. In 1900, a U.S. congressman from Pennsylvania, Robert H. Foerderer, founded the Keystone Telephone Company, launching a rivalry that spanned nearly fifty years. Keystone never approached Bell in size, but it used this to its advantage in marketing its service to consumers. Keystone operated only seven telephone exchanges at its peak and could assign one number to each exchange. As a result, Keystone telephone numbers were only five digits long, one for the exchange and four for the extension, as opposed to the more common seven-digit numbers used by Bell. Print advertisements highlighted this feature, billing Keystone's as "the fastest telephone in Philadelphia." Keystone telephones had exchange numbers printed on their rotary dials to further facilitate speedy dialing.

Bell and Keystone competed for the market across the Delaware River as well. In 1902, the Eastern Telephone and Telegraph Company completed a cable under the Delaware River connecting its lines to Keystone's system in Philadelphia. Keystone later bought out Eastern as well as a number of smaller communications companies. The first interstate automatic telephone exchange was introduced in Philadelphia in 1943, but this service was not extended to South Jersey customers. Philadelphians wishing to reach Camden residents from Keystone lines were still instructed to speak to operators at manual exchanges.

The two companies continued to compete fiercely, even building exchanges across the street from one another, until Bell bought Keystone in 1944. Keystone service ended on September 17, 1945. At the time, Philadelphia was the only major American city with two competing telephone service companies. In the Wilmington, Delaware, area, service originally provided by the Atlantic & Delaware Telegraph Company was

FIGURE 88. Telephone booths at Suburban Station, 1977. PHOTOGRAPH BY RICHARD ROSENBERG, SPECIAL COLLECTIONS RESEARCH CENTER, TEMPLE UNIVERSITY LIBRARIES.

purchased by Diamond State Telephone Company, a subsidiary of Bell. Bell again effectively created a monopoly on telecommunications in the United States that remained in place until January 1, 1984, when the Bell System was broken into seven "Baby Bell" companies. Philadelphia customers came under the control of Bell Atlantic, which merged with Connecticut-based GTE Corporation in 2000 to form Verizon Communications.

Philadelphia was home to some of the early milestones of mobile telephony. In 1919, William W. MacFarlane of Elkins Park, Montgomery County, invented a portable wireless telephone in his home workshop. Weighing twelve pounds and with a range of just one-quarter mile, the device was hardly practical and just barely portable. Nevertheless, MacFarlane's invention generated interest among hobbyists when he demonstrated it by taking reporters for a ride in his automobile, then calling his wife at home.

MacFarlane envisioned that mobile telephony would soon be in use on railroads. It would be another fifty years, however, before this prediction came true. In January 1969, the first commercial cellular radio system was designed by the Bell System for Penn Central's high-speed *Metroliner* service between New York City and Washington, D.C. The system was managed by a computerized control center located in Philadelphia's Thirtieth Street Station.

The first consumer mobile phone did not enter the market until 1983, when Motorola released its DynaTAC, colloquially known as the "brick phone." As with telephone service in its early days, the mobile phone initially succeeded only among business owners and professionals, but later became almost universal. In 2015, a Pew Research Center survey found that 92 percent of U.S. adults owned a cellular telephone.

Philadelphia continued to play an important role in telecommunications in the twenty-first century. Although Bell left the city in 1997, Philadelphia became the home of Comcast, one of the largest providers of telephone landlines. Once a novelty, the telephone became an almost indispensable technology for both business and social communication. The telephone companies that called the region home helped the Philadelphia area become a center for telecommunications businesses and innovation.

Radio

Vibiana Bowman Cvetkovic

From radio's inception to contemporary times, Philadelphia-area innovators, performers, and manufacturers contributed to shaping the industry. Like its technological forerunner, the telegraph, radio made possible the direct, real-time transmission of information. The immediacy and intimacy of radio waves arriving directly into listeners' homes made radio revolutionary. The medium quickly became not only a technology for news and information but also a source for education and entertainment.

Inventors and engineers began to experiment with wireless transmission in the last part of the nineteenth century. Soon after, Philadelphia companies joined in manufacturing and distributing components for the emerging industry. Amateur radio enthusiasts in the early twentieth century constructed home sets from kits and listened to the limited broadcasts available (news, weather, sports, and ship-to-shore messages).

By the 1920s, commercial broadcasting and the increasing popularity of the medium created a market for assembled radio receivers. In North Philadelphia, the Atwater Kent Company became the largest manufacturer of radios in the United States from 1926 to 1929, and Philco reigned as the top-selling radio brand in the country from 1930 until the 1950s. Radio manufacturing came to Camden, New Jersey, in 1929, when the Radio Corporation of America (RCA) bought the Victor Talking Machine Company and became a manufacturing powerhouse.

In addition to manufacturing the sets, the radio industry had to create an audience. This required establishing broadcasting networks, programming, and business models. In the early 1920s, large department stores across the United States started radio stations to pique consumer interest in the new technology. Philadelphia department stores joined this trend in 1922, one year after Hamburgers in Los Angeles established the first department store radio station in the United States. The Federal Radio Commission issued radio broadcasting licenses to Wanamaker's station WOO, Strawbridge & Clothier's WFI, and Gimbels, WIP. In 1924, Lit Brothers received its license to operate WLIT.

(Wanamaker's ceased broadcasting in 1929, and WFI and WLIT consolidated in 1935 to become WFIL.) In Camden, WCAM, founded in 1926 as the city's first radio station, played a notable role in the region's broadcast history as a home for emerging talent.

The era from the late 1920s through to the start of World War II is regarded by media historians as the golden age of radio, when the medium's impact reached all aspects of popular culture. New York–based networks linked Philadelphia listeners in an emerging mass audience. WFI and WLIT carried programming from the National Broadcasting Network (NBC) "Red Network," which began regular broadcasting from New York to major East Coast cities in 1926. Philadelphia's WCAU affiliated with the Columbia Broadcasting System (CBS), inaugurated in 1927. At times, the networks featured Philadelphia programming, such as *The Atwater Kent Radio Hour*, a classical music concert show carried on both NBC and CBS from 1925 to 1934. On NBC in 1929, the Philadelphia Orchestra performed the first commercially sponsored radio broadcast of a symphony orchestra in the United States.

The broadcasting industry created a template later duplicated by television, including sponsored programming and commercials performed by the shows' stars and announcers; genres such as "soap operas" and situation comedies; segmentation of the broadcast day to appeal to different sectors of the audience (adult/child; male/female); and ratings systems. Serials became extraordinarily popular. Local affiliates tended to produce cost-effective shows (news, music, talk, and sports) that required less staff and talent than radio comedies and dramas, but they also produced long-running shows that drew large audiences. *The Horn and Hardart Children's Hour*, launched in Philadelphia in 1927 and later broadcast from New York, had a second incarnation as a television series and achieved a record as broadcasting's longest-running talent show by the time it ended in 1957.

As radio began permeating the consumer market, station owners and broadcasters took note of untapped potential audiences, including burgeoning immigrant and African American communities in urban markets. Foreign-language news and music shows for the Jewish, Polish, and Italian communities (to name a few) became prominent in the 1920s and 1930s. In Philadelphia, Dannenbaum and Steppacher (cloth retailers) launched WDAS, featuring shows in Yiddish and Polish. The long-lasting and influential *Irish Hour* hosted by Patrick Stanton began on WDAS's predecessor, WELK. Italian American radio programs emanated from the studios of Angelo and Rose Fiorani in Scranton and Reading. Philadelphia gained an African American–focused station when Lenning Brothers, a radio supply company at 827 Spring Garden Street, obtained a license for WNAT ("We Never Are Tired") and began broadcasting in 1922. In 1929 the call letters changed to WHAT, a station that grew into an important African American voice in subsequent decades. WHAT produced *Standard Theater's Kiddies Radio Revue*, sponsored by the *Philadelphia Tribune*, and an African American history program.

Local radio personalities became celebrities. They included the much-beloved "Uncle WIP" (Philadelphia-born Christopher Graham), who read children's stories on WIP; Taylor Grant, whose career as a reporter and analyst spanned decades; and newscaster Alan Scott, who went on to be a successful local television personality. Nationally, politicians and activists recognized the power of the medium. President Franklin D. Roosevelt reached millions of Americans with his "fireside chats." Philadelphians listened to radio evangelists such as Aimee Semple McPherson and political personalities such as Father Charles Coughlin, who established wide followings. In the Philadelphia area, Rev. Carl McIntire, founder of the Bible Presbyterian Church (Collingswood, New Jersey), became a nationally known fundamentalist preacher. Firmly anti-Communist, during the Cold War era of the 1950s and 1960s McIntire achieved prominence through his syndicated radio show advocating Christian fundamentalism and a radical right political agenda.

After World War II, as television found a foothold with American home audiences, radio broadcasters began looking for ways to reinvigorate the flagging industry. Music soon became the default programming of choice, and disc jockeys developed into hitmakers with the power to promote artists, singles, and styles of music. Changes in radio technology, programming, and demographics made Philadelphia an epicenter of a new genre of music: rock and roll, the music of 1950s American teen culture. Japanese-made transistors and car radios made broadcasts more portable, and local

FIGURE 89. Listening to war news, 1944. Passersby gathered around a car radio at Seventeenth and Market Streets, Philadelphia, to listen to reports of the Allied assault on Europe. SPECIAL COLLECTIONS RESEARCH CENTER, TEMPLE UNIVERSITY LIBRARIES.

radio stations promoted homegrown performers like teen idols Frankie Avalon, Fabian Forte, and Bobby Rydell. Philadelphia stations also furthered the nationally known "Sound of Philadelphia," a form of rock infused with smooth jazz and orchestrated with the lush sound of strings and horns.

Some of the best-regarded rock DJs of the era worked in Philadelphia AM radio. At WIBG, the area's top rock station from the late 1950s through the late 1960s, star DJs included Hy (Hyman) Lit, Joe Niagara, and Bill Wright Sr. In 1966 WFIL challenged the supremacy of WIBG with "The Pop Explosion," a new format with a shorter, research-driven playlist and fewer commercials per hour. Its DJs ("the boss jocks") included Jim Nettleton, George Michael, and Dave Parks.

This era of radio renaissance also provided new opportunities for African American voices to be heard on-air and for a large audience of white teens to experience "race music": rhythm and blues, juke-joint music, and gospel. Philadelphia had two of the country's most successful African American radio stations, WDAS and WHAT. During the 1940s, under the ownership of William Banks and the directorship of his sister Dolly Banks, WHAT cultivated Philadelphia's increasing population of African Americans as an audience. In the early 1950s the station began to carry National Negro Network programming and became an important media outlet for African American civil rights leaders. WDAS-FM, launched in 1959, featured Black music and Black artists.

Until the 1960s AM (amplitude modulation) broadcasting dominated commercial radio. FM (frequency modulation) technology had been available since the mid-1930s, and the country's first commercially licensed FM station, WFIL-FM, went on-air in Philadelphia in 1941. The Philadelphia classical music station WFLN-FM, one of the country's first FM stations with an all-classical format, began broadcasting in 1949 (its AM sister station came on air in 1958). In 1954 the region gained WHYY ("Wider Horizons for You and Yours"), an educational radio station founded by a partnership of community leaders including Dr. W. Laurence LePage, president of the Franklin Institute. In 1956, Philadelphia's WHAT-FM became the first twenty-four-hour jazz station in the United States. Sid Mark, one of the station's first DJs, in 1957 introduced *Friday with Frank*, his decades-long series featuring Frank Sinatra.

FM broadcasting became more commercially viable by the mid-1960s after two rulings by the Federal Communications Commission (FCC) loosened restrictions on FM licenses. By 1960, Philadelphia had at least 15 of the 741 FM stations operating in the United States. After the FCC required FM stations to produce original programs rather than merely simulcasting with the affiliated AM stations in 1964, FM stations looked for ways to differentiate themselves from their AM counterparts and attract new audiences. David Kurtz, a Philco engineer, inaugurated WDVR-FM, which featured adult-oriented "beautiful music" ("easy listening" instrumental and soft pop music) as an alternative to hit-based FM stations. Since FM disc jockeys were not locked into the "top hits" lists of AM formats, they had more freedom to showcase progressive rock, emerging artists, and alternative music. By 1968 Philadelphia boasted three progressive rock FM stations: WDAS, WIFI, and WMMR. Early pioneers of this format in Philadelphia included Gene Shay, Ed Sciaky, Michael Tearson, and Lyn Kratz.

On both AM and FM, from the 1960s through the 1990s Philadelphia radio stations sought new niches by departing from music to feature news, sports, and call-in programs. KYW (1060 AM), one of the first all-news stations in the United States, launched on September 21, 1965. In 1975 WWDB became the first all-talk radio station in the country, and from the 1980s through 2007 WHAT moved to a talk-show format and became known as the "Voice of the African American Community." Philadelphia's historic WIP 610-AM adopted an all-sports format in 1988, one year after WFAN-FM in New York became the nation's first twenty-four-hour all-sports radio station. In the 1980s and 1990s, commercial radio also targeted "drive-time" commuters with "shock jocks" like New York–based Howard Stern and humorous "morning zoo" shows, including locally produced *John DeBella Show* (WMGK) and *The Preston and Steve Show* (WMMR).

Other Philadelphia stations catered to less commercially oriented musical formats such as classical, jazz, folk, and world music. WXPN of the University of Pennsylvania, granted a full college radio license in 1957, became known for critically acclaimed programs such as *Kid's Corner* and *World Cafe*. Temple University's radio station, WRTI ("Radio Training Institute"), began as an AM station in 1948, obtained an FM license in 1953, and became a public radio station specializing in jazz and classical music. At the same time, many local stations relied on syndicated programming, and some dropped longtime formats, particularly classical music.

In the early twenty-first century, radio broadcasters faced competition from subscription and satellite services such as XM and Sirius, but digital services such as iHeartRadio and TuneIn Radio also made Philadelphia programs and stations available to vast audiences beyond the reach of traditional airwaves. Radio not only survived but thrived. In 2015, according to *Forbes* magazine, 91 percent of all Americans listened to radio at least one hour a week. Radio held the appeal of being free, simple, and straightforward to use, and widely available in the car, at home, and at work. In the Philadelphia area, listeners could choose from more than eighty AM and FM stations offering a range of formats and music, including a half-dozen Spanish-language and multicultural stations.

With changes in tastes and technologies, radio continued to reinvent and remain financially solvent, as it had for nearly a century. Philadelphia's radio industry, long a technological leader and popular culture trailblazer, continued to develop nationally recognized shows and personalities and consistently ranked as one of the top ten radio markets in the United States.

Television

Vibiana Bowman Cvetkovic

The Philadelphia region had a key role in the ascent of television, from the manufacturing of television sets to the production of innovative programming. Technicians, researchers, and creative talents in the region produced many of the "firsts" that propelled television to success as a new mass medium in the twentieth century.

Philadelphia's role in developing television began in the 1930s, when inventors and corporations began to investigate the possibility of transmitting moving images over the air to a home receiver. Two figures widely credited with developing the modern electronic television set—Philo T. Farnsworth and Vladimir Zworykin—had close ties to the Philadelphia region. Zworykin served as associate director of the fledgling electronics research lab at the Radio Corporation of America (RCA) in Camden, New Jersey. In the early 1930s he and his team performed field tests for television transmissions. In 1933, they successfully transmitted an image of Mickey Mouse to a test site in nearby Collingswood, New Jersey.

Meanwhile, in 1932 Farnsworth relocated from California to Wyndmoor, Pennsylvania, to pursue his research under contract with Philco Radio Corporation (founded in Philadelphia in 1892 as Helios Electric Company). In 1932, Philco established an experimental station, W3XE, at its manufacturing plant at C and Tioga Streets. Farnsworth and Philco parted ways in 1933, but Farnsworth continued research under the auspices of the University of Pennsylvania until he left the region in 1938.

The television industry developed slowly during the 1930s. By 1941 approximately seven thousand television sets in the United States had access to fifty hours a week of national and local programming. Production of television sets ceased for the most part during World War II, although limited program broadcasting continued. At war's end, commercial production began anew. With the rise of postwar consumerism in the 1950s, the television industry hit its stride. By the end of the decade almost 90 percent of American households had at least one receiver and the average person watched approximately five hours of television each day. A new and powerful medium was born.

In the early days of commercial television in Philadelphia, from the mid-1940s through the late 1960s, national programming was limited, for the most part, to the three broadcasting systems—ABC (American Broadcasting Company), CBS (Columbia Broadcasting System), and NBC (National Broadcasting System). The DuMont Network also had a presence in Philadelphia from 1946 until the network's demise in 1956. Because the networks did not broadcast shows until the evening, the bulk of the broadcast day consisted of locally produced programming. Thus, the experimental "golden age of television" emanated largely from local affiliates of the national networks.

During the first decade of commercial television, the Philadelphia viewing area represented the fourth-largest market as measured by advertising revenue. Local stations Channels 3, 6, and 10 developed innovative, nationally trendsetting programs. They also pioneered and refined techniques such as color broadcasting, "green screen" special effects, and on-location remote broadcasts. From the late 1940s until the early 1960s these three original VHF (Very High Frequency) band stations provided the only television programming for most of the Delaware Valley. Educational/public television station WHYY, inaugurated in 1957 as an experimental UHF (Ultra High Frequency) station, did not receive its VHF designation as Channel 12 until 1963.

Channel 3 (WPTZ-TV, later WRCV-TV, KYW-TV, and CBS 3), which began as Philco's experimental station in 1932, is one of the oldest television stations in the world. When the station received a commercial license from the FCC in 1941, it became WPTZ-Channel 3. An affiliate of NBC, whose parent company RCA was developing commercial color television technology for the consumer market, the station stood in the forefront of color broadcasting. In 1947, RCA researchers debuted the company's simultaneous color system before the scientific community at the Franklin Institute. Research and development continued throughout the early 1950s.

Channel 3 broadcast one of the nation's earliest color-programming events on December 18, 1953: *Skinner's Spotlight*, an interview show starring local host George Skinner. During the 1950s, the station changed hands from Philco to Westinghouse. In 1956, NBC gained control. At that point the station's call letters became WRCV-TV (for RCA-Victor). In 1965, after lengthy legal negotiations, the station again became part of

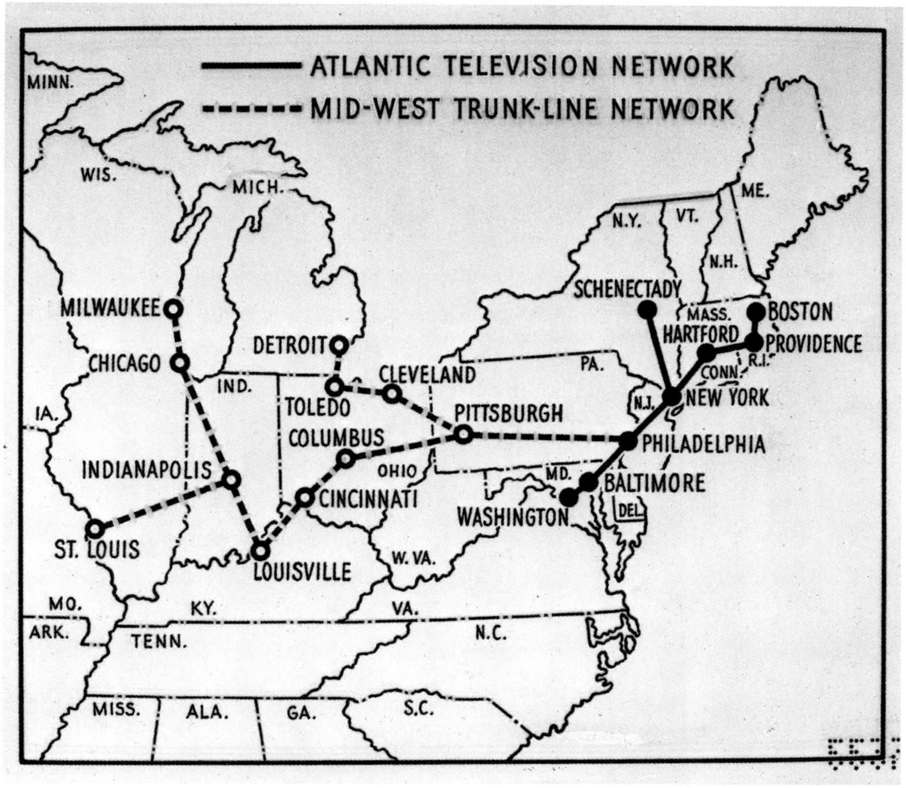

FIGURE 90. Television networks, 1943. The new medium connected Philadelphia with other major cities through networks based in New York. HAGLEY MUSEUM AND LIBRARY.

Westinghouse's broadcasting division and the call letters changed to KYW-TV, although the station retained its affiliation with NBC until 1995, when a multistation deal shifted it to CBS. Its ownership also changed later to Viacom (2000) and the CBS Corporation (2006).

During the industry's early era, a number of important shows and personalities made their home at Channel 3. In 1940, the station broadcast the entirety of the Republican National Convention held in Philadelphia. This on-site political reporting represented a television first. Ernie Kovacs, a comedic genius, began his television career at the station and had other shows from 1950 through 1952, when he left for WCBS-TV in New York. Channel 3 also produced much-beloved children's shows such as *Lunchtime with Uncle Pete*, which ran in various incarnations during the 1950s and starred "Uncle" Pete Boyle. *Bertie the Bunyip* ran from 1953 to 1960 under the creative helm of Lee Dexter. The award-winning *Mike Douglas Show* aired from Philadelphia from its debut in 1965 until it moved to Los Angeles in 1978.

Channel 6 (WFIL-TV, later WPVI-TV and 6ABC) originated with the merger of two radio stations that had been owned since the 1920s by Philadelphia department stores. When purchased in 1947 by Triangle Publications (owned by publisher and philanthropist Walter Annenberg), the station affiliated with the DuMont television network for one year, then became the first affiliate of ABC. Channel 6 showcased groundbreaking shows and performers in the new medium. Arguably one of the most influential was *American Bandstand*, which helped to define post–World War II American teen culture. The show, called *Bandstand* before it went national in 1957, broadcast from Philadelphia from 1952 to 1964. The station also developed programs with local celebrities who became pioneers in developing the format of the hosted children's show. Channel 6's lineup included one of the few female hosts with her own show (Sally Starr) and the only children's show host in the region who was an ethnic minority—Chief Traynor Ora Halftown, a member of the Seneca nation, who was on Channel 6 from 1950 until 1999.

Channel 10 (WCAU-TV, later NBC10), the region's third television station, came online in 1948 as a CBS affiliate owned by the *Philadelphia Bulletin* newspaper.

CBS bought the station in 1958; from 1965 through to 1986, it was the only network-owned station in Philadelphia. During the late 1950s and throughout the 1960s the station produced memorable children's shows including *Pixanne*, *Cartoon Corners*, *The Gene London Show*, and an early 1960s puppet show, *Tottle*. The station also gained notice during this era for its news department. As an affiliate of CBS, the "Tiffany Network," Channel 10 brought legendary journalists Edward R. Murrow and Walter Cronkite to local television viewers, and the highly respected local anchor John Facenda helped make the station a ratings leader. Channel 10 remained with CBS until 1995, then affiliated with NBC.

The 1970s and 1980s brought dramatic changes to television and local affiliates. Competition for advertising dollars and audience share increased with the inauguration of commercially successful UHF stations and cable networks. Three new UHF stations launched in the Philadelphia market: Channel 17 (WPCA, later WPHL) in 1960; Channel 29 (WIBF, later WTXF) in 1965; and Channel 48 (WKBS, later WGTW) in 1965.

Cable television, which originated in the 1940s primarily as a means of providing programming through coaxial cables to areas beyond the reach of broadcast signals, found major new markets by the 1980s. In Philadelphia, in 1983 city council awarded three cable franchises: Comcast, Cablevision Systems Philadelphia Corp., and Philadelphia Inner City Cable (a minority-owned business). Wade Cablevision (also a minority-owned company) received the fourth franchise in 1987. Of these four, Comcast rose to become an industry leader (it acquired Cablevision Systems, by then known as Greater Philadelphia Cablevision, in 1999; Time Warner acquired Wade in 1995 and Inner City in 2005). Founded in Tupelo, Mississippi, in 1962 and incorporated in Pennsylvania in 1969, Comcast grew exponentially through acquisitions that spanned the nation and new products such as cellular telephone and Internet services. The company acquired NBCUniversal in 2013, and three years later Comcast NBCUniversal completed a $3.8 billion acquisition of DreamWorks Animation. Expanding its business far beyond television, Comcast became a global media and technology company headquartered in Philadelphia's two tallest skyscrapers.

The Philadelphia region produced influential cable programming as well. PRISM (Philadelphia Regional In-Home Sports and Movies), a regional cable service, operated as a premium channel from 1976 to 1997. Its main offerings were televised sporting events of Philadelphia's major franchises (as well as college Big 5 basketball and World Wrestling Federation events held at the Spectrum) and first-run movies. QVC ("Quality, Value, Convenience"), a "shop-at-home" cable network, opened in West Chester, Pennsylvania, in 1986. Founded by Philadelphia-area entrepreneur Joseph Segel, QVC, with its international affiliates and a strong digital presence, became one of the world's largest retailers.

News departments became a staple for local stations, with Channel 10's local newscast leading the ratings from the late 1940s through the mid-1960s. From 1948 through 1973, under the leadership of John Facenda (nicknamed "The Voice of God" for his elegant delivery), the news team's innovations included a late-night (11 p.m.) newscast introduced in 1948; the hiring of an African American woman news reporter, Edie Huggins, in 1966; and the region's first African American news anchor, Jack Jones, in 1971. Facenda is also credited with bringing the thirty-minute newscast format to Philadelphia: news, sports, weather, sign-off.

In the mid-1960s, Channel 10 lost its top spot to Channel 3, where news director Al Primo had pioneered the *Eyewitness News* format featuring personality-based, on-site reporting. Although critics dismissed *Eyewitness News* as too sensational, it became a ratings success and the format spread throughout the United States and Europe. Locally, Channel 6 news director Mel Kampmann responded in 1970 with *Action News*, which took the *Eyewitness News* style to the next level by tightening the pace of the segments, expanding suburban coverage, and featuring young talent. Like *Eyewitness News*, *Action News* quickly spread nationwide to other stations. Arguably a factor in its success was the theme song "Move Closer to Your World," written by composer Al Ham and introduced in 1972. Longtime anchorman Jim Gardner joined Channel 6 in 1976 and became the station's main anchor in 1977, the year the station became the top-rated local newscast.

In the era of twenty-four-hour-news networks and digital delivery of the news, weather and sports gained new prominence for local television stations.

Allowing for specialization and target marketing, severe weather and sports-related stories often led the news. Digital applications for computers and smartphones added immediacy and interactivity for viewers. Local meteorologists became active on social media and encouraged viewers to participate in broadcasts by sending photos and videos of the weather.

In the first decades of the twenty-first century, new technologies and new platforms for delivering "television" programs radically changed viewer expectations for interactivity and control over viewing schedules and options. VCRs, DVR technology, video on demand, and streaming video freed viewers from broadcast schedules. Cable and the Internet broke the monopoly on programming choices once held by legacy broadcast networks.

EXPLORE MORE

The region's reach to the nation has often begun with individual initiative, whether through commerce, technology, politics, public service, or other means. As an exemplar of networking on many fronts, Benjamin Franklin is abundantly accessible in the form of monuments, historic sites, publications, and websites. Franklin Court, a unit of Independence National Historical Park facing Market Street between Third and Fourth Streets, includes a museum, a printing shop, and the B. Free Franklin Post Office. Among the many editions of *Benjamin Franklin's Autobiography*, see the Norton critical edition published in 1986, edited by J. A. Leo Lemay and P. M. Zall, for related documents, criticism, and a map tracing Franklin's first walk through Philadelphia in 1723. Among biographies, see Esmond Wright's *Franklin of Philadelphia* (Belknap Press of Harvard University Press, 1986) for emphasis on Franklin's intercolonial outlook. Also see Ralph Frasca, *Benjamin Franklin's Printing Network: Disseminating Virtue in Early America* (University of Missouri Press, 2006). Franklin's papers are available in both printed and digital form (https://franklinpapers.org/) through the efforts of teams at Yale University and the American Philosophical Society. A digital project at the Philosophical Society explores colonial correspondence networks through the ledgers of Franklin's post office (https://diglib.amphilsoc.org/franklindata/).

The U.S. Postal Service regularly updates a detailed narrative of its history, *The United States Postal Service: An American History* (2020). Also see Richard R. John, *Spreading the News: The American Postal System from Franklin to Morse* (Harvard University Press, 1995) and Winifred Gallagher, *How the Post Office Created America: A History* (Penguin Press, 2016). For entry points to the history of printing and publishing, see Rosalind Remer, *Printers and Men of Capital: Philadelphia Book Publishers in the New Republic* (University of Pennsylvania Press, 1996) and Edwin Wolf II, *The Book Culture of a Colonial American City: Philadelphia Books, Bookmen, and Booksellers* (Clarendon Press, 1988). Follow the history of book publishing further through *A History of the Book in America* (five volumes, University of North Carolina Press, 2014). The longtime editor of *Godey's Lady's Book* is the subject of Melanie Kirkpatrick's *Lady Editor: Sarah Josepha Hale and the Making of the Modern Woman* (Encounter Books, 2021). Works that trace the histories of Philadelphia newspapers include James Tagg, *Benjamin Franklin Bache and the Philadelphia* Aurora (University of Pennsylvania Press, 1991) and Peter Binzen, *Nearly Everybody Read It: Snapshots of the* Philadelphia Bulletin (Camino Books, 1998). Extensive clippings and photographs from the *Philadelphia Bulletin, Daily News,* and *Inquirer* are housed in the Special Collections Research Center, Temple University Libraries, which also holds collections of regional Jewish publications. Many Philadelphia-area publications, including the *Philadelphia Tribune,* are available in digital form through databases accessible through the Free Library of Philadelphia and other public and university libraries.

Chestnut Street in the Old City section of Philadelphia is the starting point for exploring the emergence of political and financial systems of the early United States. Congress Hall, Sixth and Chestnut Streets, is preserved as a setting of government and politics of the 1790s, when Philadelphia served as the nation's capital. Read about the emergence of political parties in Harry Tinkcom, *The Republicans and Federalists in Pennsylvania, 1790–1801: A Study in National Stimulus and Local Response* (Pennsylvania Historical and Museum Commission, 1950), and Saul Cornell, *The Other Founders: Anti-Federalism and the Dissenting Tradition in America, 1788–1828* (University of North Carolina Press, 1999), and follow the story of political conventions forward in R. Craig Sautter, *Philadelphia Presidential Conventions* (December Press, 2000).

A stroll on Chestnut Street eastward from Congress Hall passes bank buildings from Philadelphia's period as "America's first Wall Street," including the second Bank of the United States and, near Third and Chestnut, the first national Bank of the United States. Nearby, the Federal Reserve Bank of Philadelphia offers a *Money in Motion* exhibit at Seventh and Arch Streets, and the U.S Mint is open for public tours at Fifth and Arch Streets. Books about banking and insurance include Robert E.

Wright, *The First Wall Street: Chestnut Street, Philadelphia and the Birth of American Finance* (University of Chicago Press, 2005); Hannah Farber, *Underwriters of the United States: How Insurance Shaped the American Founding* (University of North Carolina Press, 2021); and John A. Fowler, *History of Insurance in Philadelphia for Two Centuries (1683–1882)* (Review Publishing and Printing Company, 1888). For a pictorial history of coin production in Philadelphia, see Joshua McMorrow-Hernandez, *The United States Mint in Philadelphia* (Arcadia Publishing, 2018).

To contemplate the region's transportation history, seek out the *Spirit of Transportation* (1895), a massive relief sculpture by Karl Bitter, in the north waiting area of Philadelphia's William H. Gray III Thirtieth Street Station. Books about the dominant railroad companies of the nineteenth century include Albert J. Churella, *The Pennsylvania Railroad: Building an Empire, 1846–1917* (University of Pennsylvania Press, 2012), and James L. Holton, *The Reading Railroad: History of a Coal Age Empire* (two volumes, Garrigues House, 1989 and 1992). The communications networks that linked Greater Philadelphia with the nation are the subject of Menahem Blondheim, *News Over the Wires: The Telegraph and the Flow of Public Information in America, 1844–1897* (Harvard University Press, 1994); Tom Standage, *The Victorian Internet: The Remarkable Story of the Telegraph and the Nineteenth Century's Online Pioneers* (Walker and Company, 1998); and Claude S. Fischer, *America Calling: A Social History of the Telephone to 1940* (University of California Press, 1992).

A membership organization, the Broadcast Pioneers of Philadelphia, collects the history of local radio and television and makes selections of photographs, videos, and oral histories available digitally (https://broadcastpioneers.com/). The Special Collections Research Center, Temple University Libraries, has news footage from Channels 3 and 6. To explore the history of RCA in the Philadelphia region, visit the RCA Heritage Program Museum at Rowan University, 201 Mullica Hill Road, Glassboro, N.J.; also see *Capital Moves: RCA's Seventy-Year Quest for Cheap Labor*, by Jefferson Cowie (Cornell University Press, 1999). Read more about radio and television in Alan Boris, *Philadelphia Radio* (Arcadia Publishing, 2011); Gleason L. Archer, *History of Radio to 1926* (Arno Press, 1971); Richard Butsch, *The Making of American Audiences: From Stage to Television, 1750–1990* (Cambridge University Press, 2000); and Lynn Spigel, *Make Room for TV: Television and the Family Ideal in Postwar America* (University of Chicago Press, 1992). Joseph N. DiStefano's *Comcasted: How Ralph and Brian Roberts Took over America's TV, One Deal at a Time* (Camino Books, 2005) demonstrates the continuing impact of entrepreneurial individuals in extending the reach of the Greater Philadelphia region.

Chapter 11

PHILADELPHIA IN AMERICAN POPULAR CULTURE

Introduction

IN AN AGE OF MASS MEDIA, POPULAR CULTURE shapes perceptions of Philadelphia that may linger long in public memory, for better or worse. Impressions of Philadelphia have formed from the region's music, through movies and television, from broadcasts of nationally competitive sports teams, and more. Snippets of lyrics, iconic scenes, freeze-frames from championship moments, and memorable characters and storylines spin a web of fact and fiction—an extended series of partial quotations from the region's lived experience. Delivered as entertainment to the nation and beyond, popular culture contributes to the region's reputation and appeal. But the "Philadelphia" of popular culture is not simply a mirror held up to reality. This imagined place, coexisting and mixing with the real thing, results from interactions of cultural trends, technology, the intentions of creators, and the reception of audiences.

The kernel of truth in the popular culture image of Philadelphia lies to a large degree with creators with Philadelphia ties. W. C. Fields had a Philadelphia native's knowledge of the city and adjacent counties when he quipped, "On the whole, I'd rather be in Philadelphia." As his career arced from local vaudeville stages into the movies, he made Philadelphia a punchline for widening audiences. The expanding movie, television, and music industries of the twentieth century provided multiple avenues for locally connected creators to project interpretations of Philadelphia in many dimensions, even if they did their work on sound stages or in studios across the country. Philadelphians also created local footholds in these industries. From television studios on Market Street, *American Bandstand*'s local teenage stars popularized dances and styles that set national trends. At Philadelphia International Records on Broad Street, Kenny Gamble and Leon Huff elevated local artists and produced "The Sound of Philadelphia" brand of Philly Soul, building a reputation that attracted other artists to the city to record. The movies of M. Night Shyamalan brought audiences to the region time and again, and the Greater Philadelphia Film Office promoted the many characteristics of the city and its countryside as production sets.

For much of the twentieth century, the city and its toniest suburbs served to illustrate the divide between American social classes. The theme of social stratification drove the action in the movies *The Philadelphia Story* (1940, based on the 1939 play of the same name), *Kitty Foyle* (1940, based on the 1939 novel by Christopher Morley), *The Young Philadelphians* (1959), and *Trading Places* (1983). On television, the long-running daytime drama *All My Children* (1970–2011) situated its wealthy protagonists in mythical "Pine Valley" outside Philadelphia and rendered "Center City" as the seedier world of have-nots and dive bars. West Philadelphia provided the fictional backstory and the start of the catchy theme music for Will Smith's more privileged life as *The Fresh Prince of Bel-Air* (1990–96). In the movies and on television, characters who ventured out of their customary social positions found themselves in unfamiliar and often precarious territory, whether played for drama or comic effect.

Portrayals of Philadelphia could be grim when rendering the city as a symbol of danger or urban struggle. But themes of camaraderie and perseverance also abound. In cartoon form, *Fat Albert and the Cosby Kids* (1972–85) on Saturday mornings taught life lessons through the animated antics of a group of young friends in North Philadelphia. The television drama *Thirtysomething* followed the Philadelphia-centered lives of a tight-knit group of couples and singles. Another fictional friend group assembled for the long-running *It's Always Sunny in Philadelphia* (debuted 2005), and a workplace family weathered the challenges of teaching in an underfunded public school in *Abbott Elementary* (debuted 2021). In these fictional worlds, Philadelphia could be a challenging place but not isolating or hopeless.

Viewed as popular culture, sports have occupied a place of prominence in both fiction and in the lived experience of Philadelphia fans. The fictional boxer Rocky, who like the city itself battled adversity in the 1970s, became a Philadelphia icon with lasting appeal that extended into the twenty-first century. Dedication to the Philadelphia Eagles ran deep in the movie *Invincible* (2006), based on the true story of player Vince Papale, and through the fictional family at the center of *Silver Linings Playbook* (2012). The region's professional sports teams, while undeniably big businesses with immense power and economic impact, generate indelible moments of joy and heartbreak that feed into the region's popular image. Broadcast to the nation on game days, the fans and their teams, their mascots and fight songs, add up to a portrait of Philadelphia reinforced by announcers who invoke "the City of Brotherly Love" while displaying aerial views of local landmarks like LOVE Park, Independence Hall, and the South Philadelphia sports complex.

Along with glimpses of familiar landmarks, popular culture creates a fictional geography with potential to enhance local pride of place and attract attention. Imagination overlays reality. We can stand in the footsteps of Rocky atop the steps of the Philadelphia Museum of Art or whisper "I see dead people" inside one of the historic buildings seen in *The Sixth Sense*. We can hang out at the bar that inspired *It's Always Sunny in Philadelphia*. Popular culture has given us a place-based soundtrack that echoes across time: "South Street," "The Bristol Stomp," "MotownPhilly," "Philadelphia Freedom," "Fly, Eagles Fly." As these glimpses of Philadelphia reach mass audiences, they allow impressions of the region to form across the nation and beyond.

"I'd Rather Be in Philadelphia"

Charlene Mires

The expression "I'd rather be in Philadelphia" is derived from a fictional epitaph that locally born entertainer W. C. Fields proposed for himself in *Vanity Fair* magazine in 1925: "Here lies W. C. Fields. I would rather be living in Philadelphia." By implying that Philadelphia would be slightly preferable to the grave, the joke tapped a vein of critical commentary about the city in the nineteenth and twentieth centuries. Variations of the witticism persisted in popular culture, but it did not ultimately appear on the entertainer's tomb.

Fields often lampooned Philadelphia, the boyhood hometown that he left to follow a career in show business. Born in Darby, Delaware County, with the given name William Claude Dunkenfield (or Claude William, according to some sources), Fields grew up in a succession of rented row houses in West and North Philadelphia. After only a few years of school, he picked up odd jobs available to boys of his era: assisting in a cigar shop, hawking newspapers, delivering ice, shucking oysters, racking balls in billiard halls, peddling produce, and carrying cash between departments in the Strawbridge & Clothier store on Market Street. Frequently at odds with his father, he left home for at least a few months of his youth—a period he later embellished into tall tales of life on the streets as a vagabond.

Fields found his calling as an entertainer in Philadelphia's theater district, which at the time thrived on N. Eighth Street between Race and Vine. Captivated by the vaudeville shows of the 1890s, he taught himself to juggle and developed an act as "tramp juggler," a silent hobo character who could adeptly toss cigar boxes, which became a hallmark of his act. After getting his start in venues like Natatorium Hall at Broad Street and

FIGURE 91. W. C. Fields, 1938. PHOTOGRAPH BY HARRY WARNECKE AND LEE ELKINS, NATIONAL PORTRAIT GALLERY, SMITHSONIAN INSTITUTION.

Columbia Avenue, Plymouth Park near Norristown, and Fortescue's Pier in Atlantic City, he attracted the notice of promoters of touring burlesque and vaudeville shows. With them, he performed nationally and internationally, gaining the skill and acclaim that led him to Broadway and the famed Ziegfeld Follies. The stage name he adopted, "W. C. Fields," became his legal name in 1908.

By the 1920s, when *Vanity Fair* published his imagined epitaph, Fields was transitioning from pantomime juggler to character actor, comedian, and storyteller, not only on stage but in the emerging mediums of radio and the movies. Barbs about Philadelphia became a common part of the act. "I once spent a year in Philadelphia," he said. "I think it was on a Sunday." Or, "Anyone found smiling after the curfew rang was liable to be arrested." In a later feature film, *My Little Chickadee* (1940), a character played by Fields described his last wish: "I'd like to see Paris before I die. Philadelphia will do." His humor struck a chord among audiences accustomed to thinking of Philadelphia as sedate, old-fashioned, and corrupt—a perception that had been nurtured by such commentators as Charles Dickens, who described the city as "rather dull and out of spirits"; Lincoln Steffens, who identified Philadelphia as "the most corrupt and the most contented" of cities; and Henry James, who referred to its "bourgeois blankness."

In later years, place-marketing and tourism promotion campaigns worked vigorously to counteract the image of Philadelphia embedded in Fields's comedy. Still, variations of "I would rather be living in Philadelphia" persisted. While hospitalized in Washington after the 1981 assassination attempt on his life, President Ronald Reagan scribbled on a note, "All in all, I'd rather be in Philadelphia." Similar phrases cropped up in dialogue in the movie *Die Hard* (1988) and the television series *Lois and Clark: The New Adventures of Superman* (1993). "I'd Rather Be in Philadelphia" served as a title for a 1983 compilation rock album, a 1993 mystery novel by Gillian Roberts, and a 2007 episode of the television series *Gilmore Girls*. On the Internet in the early decades of the twenty-first century, the expression appeared frequently as a touchstone for bloggers and as the title for a Twitter feed.

The comedy of W. C. Fields, while not flattering to Philadelphia, contributed to the city's place in American popular culture even after the entertainer left the city behind. After his death, the marker on his vault at Forest Lawn Memorial Park in Glendale, California, bore the simple inscription: "W. C. Fields, 1880–1946."

Philadelphia in Popular Music

Jack McCarthy

Philadelphia has been a key center in popular music—music appealing to popular tastes—since the late eighteenth century and at several points in history has been recognized as a world leader in the genre. Shaped by the rich musical traditions of its numerous ethnic and religious groups, the city produced many widely popular and influential artists and styles.

Music in early Philadelphia developed slowly because the city's founders, members of the Religious Society of Friends (Quakers), shunned all music, but by the mid-eighteenth century a public musical life began to emerge.

Most popular music in early Philadelphia derived from English musical theater and popular and folk songs from the British Isles.

The first Philadelphian to contribute significantly to popular music was Francis Hopkinson, whose song "My Days Have Been So Wondrous Free" (1759) is generally considered the first secular song composed by a native-born American (never published, the song exists only in manuscript form at the Library of Congress). In 1788 Hopkinson published *Seven Songs for the Harpsichord or Forte Piano*, the first set of secular songs published in the new United States.

In the federal period, European immigrant musicians dominated Philadelphia musical life. Alexander Reinagle, born in England, settled in Philadelphia in 1786 and became a leading musical figure, composing "serious" works and theater music but also writing and arranging popular songs, marches, and dance pieces. From 1793 to 1803, Reinagle served as musical director for Philadelphia's Chestnut Street Theatre, America's premier popular entertainment venue. London-born Benjamin Carr, who settled in Philadelphia in 1793, became an important musician and music publisher. One of the best-known songwriters of federal-period America, Carr wrote both sophisticated art songs and simpler songs for popular tastes. He also composed and published songs setting the words of famous poets and playwrights to music.

The most widely known song to come out of federal-period Philadelphia was "Hail, Columbia." Joseph Hopkinson, a prominent Philadelphian (and son of Francis Hopkinson), wrote the words, set to the tune of "The President's March," a patriotic instrumental piece by Philip Phile, a German immigrant musician active in Philadelphia in the 1780s and 1790s. Premiered at the Chestnut Street Theatre on April 25, 1798, "Hail, Columbia" became an instant hit, widely disseminated in sheet music form throughout the nation.

FIGURE 92. Frank Johnson, 1846. The popular bandleader, composer, and musician played concerts throughout the region and toured with his ensemble in Europe. Lithograph. COLLECTION OF THE HISTORICAL SOCIETY OF PENNSYLVANIA.

MUSIC PUBLISHERS AND POPULAR MUSICIANS

Philadelphia was the center of the American music publishing industry from the late eighteenth through mid-nineteenth century. Thousands of popular songs issued from the presses of Benjamin Carr's Musical Repository on High (later Market) Street, G. Willig's Musical Magazine on Chestnut Street, and other publishers. German-born George Willig, who immigrated to Philadelphia in 1794, took over an earlier music publishing business and built it into one of the largest in the nation. In 1843, the firm Lee & Walker, founded by former Willig employees, published the popular patriotic song "Columbia, the Gem of the Ocean."

In 1818 Willig published *A Collection of New Cotillions*, written by African American bandleader and composer Francis Johnson. Johnson, the favored bandleader for the balls of Philadelphia's social elite, led wind and brass ensembles for major military companies and concertized throughout the Philadelphia region and beyond. His *Collection of New Cotillions* was the first music by an African American to be published, and Johnson became the first American, Black or white, to lead a musical ensemble on a tour of Europe in 1837. Local publishers issued some three hundred Johnson compositions, mostly marches and dance pieces but also some ballads and songs.

MINSTRELSY

A new type of popular music with African American roots developed in the antebellum period: blackface minstrelsy, which grew out of white performers "blacking up" their faces with burnt cork and performing derogatory songs and dances supposedly based on those of enslaved Black people. By the mid-nineteenth century, such performances had evolved into the enormously popular minstrel show. After the Civil War, Black entertainers, who faced limited professional opportunities otherwise, entered minstrelsy as well.

The presence of well-known minstrel performers and prominent minstrel theaters and publishing houses in Philadelphia made it an important center of the genre. Popular minstrel performers Edward Pierce "E. P." Christy and Samuel S. Sanford, who were white, and James Bland, who was Black, had important ties to Philadelphia. Bland, dubbed the "World's Greatest Minstrel Man," lived in Philadelphia briefly when he was young and purportedly fell in love with the banjo after hearing a local Black street musician play the instrument. He later spent his final years in the city. His prolific songwriting output included "Oh, Dem Golden Slippers," the unofficial theme song of the Philadelphia mummers, and longtime standards "Carry Me Back to Old Virginny" and "In the Evening by the Moonlight."

SONGWRITERS AND VENUES

Philadelphia's preeminence in music publishing yielded to New York City by the mid-nineteenth century, but local publishing houses still turned out a wide range of popular music. Sentimental ballads were especially popular. Philadelphia songwriter, publisher, and businessman Septimus Winner wrote several well-known sentimental songs, including the hugely successful "Listen to the Mocking Bird," which sold millions of copies of sheet music and remained perennially popular. In 1869, Winner's brother, songwriter and music publisher Joseph Eastburn Winner, wrote and published "The Little Brown Jug," which also had a long period of popularity.

At the turn of the twentieth century, before recordings and radio came into widespread use, songs reached audiences through sheet music or live performances. Outdoor band concerts attracted enthusiastic audiences. John Philip Sousa, America's "March King," first came to Philadelphia in 1876 to perform in an orchestra as part of the U.S. Centennial festivities and remained for several years, playing in theater pit orchestras. By the early twentieth century, Sousa reigned as the nation's most popular bandleader and renowned composer of march tunes that long remained an important part of the American popular music canon. From 1901 to 1926, Sousa's outdoor concerts at Willow Grove Park in Montgomery County, Pennsylvania, were a major attraction.

In addition to concerts, local vaudeville houses, theaters, and opera houses presented variety shows, operettas, and musical comedies that featured popular songs of the day. Philadelphia served as one of the main tryout cities for Broadway musicals before they headed to New York City, so local audiences heard popular songs before they became well known.

CHANGING CULTURES AND TECHNOLOGIES

Recordings and radio revolutionized popular music in the early twentieth century, allowing music to be disseminated much more broadly and rapidly. The Berliner Gramophone Company of Philadelphia began recording popular singers and bands in the mid-1890s. Its successor in the gramophone business, the Victor Talking Machine Company, formed in 1901 and moved its recording studio from Philadelphia to its manufacturing complex in Camden, New Jersey, in 1907. The company produced and sold popular recordings that reached the homes of millions. Commercial radio broadcasting, which began in Philadelphia in 1922, became an important outlet for popular music, with many local stations sponsoring in-house bands and vocalists.

Popular music in Philadelphia absorbed the influences of the waves of newcomers who settled in the city in the late nineteenth and early twentieth centuries, both immigrants from eastern and southern Europe and Black migrants from the southern United States. Molly Picon (Malka Opiekun), born to Polish Jewish immigrants, grew up in Philadelphia Jewish neighborhoods and became immersed in local Yiddish theater. Ethel Waters, born in Chester, Delaware County, and raised partly there and partly in Black neighborhoods of South Philadelphia, grew up surrounded by her community's vibrant music scene. Pearl Bailey, born in Newport News, Virginia, moved to Philadelphia with her family in the early 1930s and in 1933 won an amateur contest at the Pearl Theatre on Ridge Avenue in North Philadelphia. Mario Lanza (Alfredo Arnold Cocozza), born in South Philadelphia to Italian immigrants, had early training in the Italian opera tradition. All went on to become major singing stars across many media—stage, screen, recordings, radio, and, later, television.

Singers Nelson Eddy and Jeanette MacDonald emerged from the Philadelphia entertainment world in the early twentieth century and became forever linked in American popular culture. MacDonald was born and raised in Philadelphia; Eddy moved to the city with his family as an adolescent. Eddy began in opera and operetta, MacDonald as a dancer-turned-singer. Each went on to great individual success, while their starring roles as romantic partners in 1930s and 1940s Hollywood film musicals endeared them to millions.

ROCK AND ROLL

In the years following World War II, Philadelphia produced several singers who succeeded in mainstream popular music geared toward adult audiences, including Katie "Kitty" Kallen, Armondo Joseph "Buddy" Greco, Al Martino (Jasper Cini), Edwin Jack "Eddie" Fisher, and the Four Aces, led by Al Alberts (Al Albertini). However, in the mid-1950s this market was overtaken by rock and roll, the high-energy, youth-oriented music that went on to dominate popular music for decades.

Rock and roll emerged from Black rhythm and blues, which flourished in Philadelphia in the 1940s and 1950s as local groups played Black dance halls and clubs and produced records that became hits on the R&B charts that tracked Black music sales. White musicians began incorporating elements of rhythm and blues into their music, including country and western bandleader William John Clifton "Bill" Haley, based in Boothwyn, Delaware County. His group, Bill Haley and His Comets, had hit records in the early 1950s with their blended country and western/rhythm and blues style and then massive success in 1955 with "Rock Around the Clock," the first megahit in the new rock and roll style, which sold millions of records worldwide and helped usher in the rock and roll era.

LOCAL MUSIC, NATIONAL STAGE

Philadelphia emerged as a key center of rock and roll on the strength of successful local record labels and the enormous influence of *American Bandstand*, the teen music and dance television show broadcast nationally from Philadelphia from 1957 to 1964. Hosted by Richard Wagstaff "Dick" Clark and featuring teenagers dancing to the latest records along with live appearances by popular recording artists, *Bandstand* reached millions of teenagers nationwide and set major trends in popular music.

Philadelphia-based independent record labels Cameo-Parkway and Chancellor became hit-making machines, with primarily homegrown artists who specialized in teenybopper dance tunes and romantic ballads. Cameo-Parkway had singer/guitarist Charlie Gracie (Charlie Graci), vocal groups the Orlons and the Tymes, and singers Bobby Rydell (Robert Ridarelli), Dee Dee Sharp (Dione LaRue), and Chubby Checker (Ernest Evans). Checker's "The Twist," a huge hit, started an enduring dance craze. Chancellor Records had teen idol singers Frankie Avalon (Francis Avallone) and Fabian (Fabiano Forte).

Philadelphia also produced popular doo-wop groups, who sang in the close-harmony vocal style created by young people singing on street corners and in school hallways. Black groups the Silhouettes and Lee Andrews (Arthur Lee Andrew Thompson) and the Hearts and white groups Danny & the Juniors and the Dovells had big doo-wop hits in the late 1950s and early 1960s.

PHILLY SOUL

In the mid-1960s, a new Black popular style, "Philly Soul," began to emerge from the city's gospel and rhythm and blues traditions. Singer Barbara Mason had the first big hit in the distinctive Philly Soul style in 1965 with "Yes, I'm Ready." Three songwriter/producers became the chief architects of the Philly Soul style beginning in the late 1960s: Kenneth "Kenny" Gamble, Leon Huff, and Thomas "Thom" Bell. Gamble was

FIGURE 93. The Roots Picnic, 2019. The influential group, led by graduates of Philadelphia High School for the Performing Arts, drew fans to their annual picnic in Philadelphia and played as house band on *The Tonight Show Starring Jimmy Fallon*. PHOTOGRAPH BY J. FUSCO FOR VISIT PHILADELPHIA.

born in Philadelphia, Huff in Camden, New Jersey, and Bell in Kingston, Jamaica, but raised in Philadelphia. Thom Bell scored a number of hits in the late 1960s and early 1970s with Philadelphia vocal groups the Delfonics and Stylistics and with the Spinners, who were from Detroit but recorded in Philadelphia under Bell.

Gamble and Huff, after succeeding as producer/songwriters for other labels—their first number one hit was "Expressway to Your Heart" by the Soul Survivors in 1967—formed Philadelphia International Records, billed as the "Sound of Philadelphia," in 1971. Black owned and managed and featuring primarily Black artists, Philadelphia International released dozens of gold and platinum records from the early 1970s to early 1980s. Its roster included local singers and groups that had come up in the city's rich Black music scene—the Intruders, Harold Melvin and the Blue Notes, Theodore "Teddy" Pendergrass, Billy Paul (Paul Williams), Patti LaBelle (Patricia Holte) and the Bluebelles, and others—as well as out-of-town artists who came to Philadelphia to capture the city's distinctive soul sound, including Lou Rawls, the Jackson Five, and the O'Jays. After a decade of success, Philadelphia International Records went into decline in the early 1980s, as the Philly Soul style fell out of favor.

Philadelphia continued to produce popular white rock and roll artists, including Todd Rundgren, who came into prominence in the late 1960s; Hall & Oates (Daryl Hohl and John Oates), who had the first of their many hits in the late 1970s and became the most successful rock duo of all time; and the Hooters, who became popular in the mid-1980s. By then, rock had become big business, with Philadelphia a major stop on the rock touring circuit. Electric Factory Concerts, founded in the late 1960s by Philadelphia club owners the Spivack brothers and promoter Larry Magid, became one of the nation's premier rock concert promotion companies.

NEO SOUL AND RAP

Philadelphia again became an important center of Black popular music around the turn of the twenty-first

FIGURE 94. Lubin Film Studios, undated. With a studio complex at Twentieth and Indiana Streets, Siegmund Lubin made Philadelphia an early leader of the silent motion picture industry. FREE LIBRARY OF PHILADELPHIA.

century with the emergence of "Neo Soul," a style that built on the legacy of soul but incorporated modern elements. Philadelphia-based Neo Soul artists include vocal group Boyz II Men and singers Jill Scott, Musiq Soulchild (Taalib Hassan Johnson), Bilal (Bilal Sayeed Oliver), and Jazmine Sullivan.

Philadelphia was also important in the development of rap. In 1985, Schooly D (Jesse Bonds Weaver Jr.) released "P.S.K. (What Does It Mean?)," generally considered the first gangsta rap song. (The title references the Parkside Killers, a gang from Philadelphia's Parkside neighborhood.) Other local rappers popular in the late twentieth and early twenty-first centuries included the duo DJ Jazzy Jeff and the Fresh Prince (Jeffrey Allen Townes and Willard Carroll "Will" Smith II), Beanie Siegel (Dwight Equan Grant), and Meek Mill (Robert Rihmeek Williams).

The most popular and influential Philadelphia African American group in this period was the Roots, led by drummer/producer Ahmir "Questlove" Thompson (the son of Lee Andrews), and vocalist/rapper Black Thought (Tarik Luqmaan Trotter). The Roots had success with albums, concerts, and festivals, and gained broad national exposure as house band for the TV show *Late Night with Jimmy Fallon* and subsequently *The Tonight Show*, where Fallon routinely introduced them as "The Roots from Philadelphia, Pennsylvania."

From mainstream popular song to groundbreaking new styles, by the early twenty-first century Philadelphia could boast over 250 years as an important center for popular music.

Feature Films

Jake Blumgart

Philadelphia's association with the film industry dates to the industry's beginning, when the city's Lubin Manufacturing Company created and distributed many of the first generation of silent films. But after the company's early collapse, the city never again attained a prominent role in the nation's filmmaking. After Lubin, Philadelphia served as a setting for telling stories set outside the national centers of power in New York and Washington, D.C., and far away from Los Angeles, the kind of urban stories that needed local color and a unique backdrop.

Siegmund "Pop" Lubin, an eyeglasses salesman-turned-industrialist, got his start shooting homemade movies in his backyard and then founded the Lubin Manufacturing Company in 1902. Between 1896 and his film company's demise in 1916, Lubin produced more than three thousand movies, but Philadelphia did not play a prominent role beyond the image of the Liberty Bell that served as the company's imprint.

After Lubin's brief reign at the top of the motion picture industry, the city and its environs appeared periodically in movies, usually playing one of three roles. In the mid-twentieth century, visions of haughty, manner-bound Main Line society dominated depictions of Philadelphia. As deindustrialization began in earnest, in the 1970s, attention began to shift to the city itself, especially its rotting manufacturing infrastructure and working-class row house neighborhoods. Subsequently, Philadelphia served either as a distinctive backdrop for a few recurring directors, notably M. Night Shyamalan and David O. Russell, or more often as an archetypal urban area. The frequency of the city's anonymous appearances greatly expanded with the multimillion-dollar tax credits that Pennsylvania began offering to film studios in 2004. New Jersey enacted tax credits for film and digital media productions in 2022.

The Main Line suburbs dominated depictions of Philadelphia in many midcentury films, which represented the city—or at least its upper crust—as a bastion of old money and rigid, almost European, class distinctions. The most famous, and highest quality, of these pictures, *The Philadelphia Story* (1940), managed to squeeze three of Hollywood's most indelible stars onto one screen: Katharine Hepburn, Jimmy Stewart, and Cary Grant. Hepburn's heiress, based on real-life socialite Helen Hope Montgomery Scott, must choose between the affections of three men. The city itself is never seen and is mentioned only in passing when Grant promises to pick up Stewart's visiting journalist at a train station in North Philadelphia.

Largely forgotten, *Kitty Foyle* (1940), based on a novel by Philadelphia journalist Christopher Morley, tells the story of a working-class girl who dreams of ascending into the city's ossified elite class. She comes close to succeeding when she falls into a romance with a scion of a prominent banking family, only to be frozen out and nearly destroyed by the massed forces of snobbery and inherited wealth. In her early life, Rogers's character haunts the Bellevue-Stratford Hotel, depicted as the city's citadel of privilege. Nearly twenty years later, Paul Newman's *The Young Philadelphians* (1959) explored similar tropes, again focusing on the city's elites depicted as WASP blue bloods obsessed with class distinctions. To drive home the point, the film's posters featured the slogan "When you rip the upper crust off any city, you'll find raw flesh underneath."

The Philadelphia Story was much more forgiving of the American aristocracy, depicting Hepburn's up-by-the-bootstraps fiancé as the heel, not Grant's absurdly wealthy dilettante. However, the stultified and oppressive depictions of the city's social hierarchy in *Kitty Foyle* and *The Young Philadelphians* proved to have far greater longevity. As the twentieth century wore on, films focusing on the Main Line or Rittenhouse Square set became rarer, although the unflattering depictions of the city's old-school elite as cruel, prejudiced, and capricious appeared again in the Oscar-winning HIV/AIDS morality film *Philadelphia* (1993). In a lighter, though similarly damning vein, the comedy *Trading Places* sent up Philadelphia's elite. But that 1983 film unknowingly highlighted one of the reasons for the decline of old, glamorous, rigid Philadelphia society: In the 1980s, old-money families were being supplanted by those winning fortunes in the newly financialized economy, focused on New York and leaving little for Philadelphia's sclerotic stock market.

Philadelphia's most indelible cinematic scenes emerged from the gritty, bleak, and oppressive movies of the 1970s and 1980s. As industrial capital escaped the city in the 1970s, countless abandoned factories and warehouses were left looming over impoverished working-class neighborhoods. Similar vistas of deindustrialization captured the imaginations of filmmakers in New York and Detroit, but Philadelphia more than held its own in this grim competition.

The most famous film of postindustrial grit was, inarguably, 1976's *Rocky*. After the parade of cheerier sequels, each seemingly more motivational than the last, it is easy to forget the darkness—literally and figuratively—of the first film starring the "Italian Stallion." A pall of soot and ash seems to hang over the movie, choking Rocky's row house neighborhood in Kensington. Sylvester Stallone's iconic character works as an enforcer for a loan shark and is painfully awkward in his interactions with Adrienne (who, in turn, works in a shabby little pet store). Everyone seems angry, alienated, and hopelessly stuck in place.

A similar atmosphere pervades the industrial wasteland of David Lynch's 1977 movie *Eraserhead*, although here the existential dread and grotesquery is ramped up to an almost unbearable degree. The story, such as it is, focuses on a bizarrely coiffed factory worker, Henry Spencer, who works, lives, and courts women in a space dominated by factories and ex-factories. The movie cannot be properly said to have a narrative but is instead obsessed with the products of an impoverished, deindustrializing landscape. Factories are still operative in the movie, as mysterious mechanical sounds, clanking and shrilling, adding to the unease of Lynch's film. Meanwhile the absurd grotesques who populate the landscape are nightmarish caricatures of the characters the filmmaker met while living in an impoverished, violent, dirty corner of the city in the 1960s and 1970s. While *Eraserhead* was filmed in Los Angeles a few years after Lynch had moved away from Philadelphia, the vistas of the film are avowedly formed by his experiences in Philadelphia, where he lived in Callowhill and Fairmount, when both of those neighborhoods were more violent and sootier than they became when they later gentrified.

Other classic movies of the era reflected the rising crime wave that threatened to swamp the city, along with much of urban America, and pervasive paranoiac views of authority. In both 1985's *Witness* and 1981's *Blow Out*, people are murdered horribly in the bathroom of Thirtieth Street Station by figures of supposed law and order (a police officer and a government assassin, respectively). When 1995's *12 Monkeys* is not depicting a postapocalyptic city ruled by animals released from the zoo, it is flashing back to pre-Armageddon days of the city as a dingy and dangerous streetscape scarred by graffiti and abandonment.

Unlike the glitzier Philadelphia films of earlier years, these gritty masterpieces were anchored in the city itself. Although Center City claimed the spotlight most often, with its array of distinctive landmarks and monuments, these movies also exposed less-seen aspects of Philadelphia. *Blow Out* even featured a mummers troupe marching in a Fourth of July parade, while *Rocky* and, to a lesser extent, *Witness* showed the old row house blocks that have long housed such a large portion of the city's poor and working-class residents.

Later years witnessed movies that offered a new window on the city and its suburbs, with neither old money glitz nor postindustrial grime. *Silver Linings Playbook* (2012) was largely set in white working-class suburbs of Delaware County, including locations in Ridley Park, Upper Darby, Ridley Township, and Lansdowne. David Russell's follow up, *American Hustle*, focused on the Abscam scandal that took down several prominent Philadelphia-area politicians, but it focused on the New Jersey angle instead. M. Night Shyamalan's movies often took place in the tonier sections of Center City: Rittenhouse Square, Society Hill, Old City, or in the city's stable northwestern neighborhoods. Like almost all Philadelphia movies, the city's iconic Center City sights featured prominently while neighborhoods like West Philadelphia, Kensington, South Philadelphia, or the Northeast were absent. There were a few exceptions, like 2010's *Night Catches Us*, set in 1976 and focusing on an ex-Black Panther's return to his old neighborhood and the dangers and temptations that awaited him there.

But the city's distinctive presence in the films of Russell and Shyamalan did not become the norm in the latest era of Philadelphia movies. Instead, the industry increasingly used the city or its environs to stand in for "Anywhere U.S.A." That practice dated back at least to 1958 creature feature *The Blob*, shot in Chester County and Downingtown, but it could have been anywhere. That practice remained the exception, however, until the mid-1980s, with the creation of the Greater Philadelphia

Film Office, which generated economic returns for the city by promoting it as a backdrop for filmmakers.

Further benefits followed Governor Edward G. Rendell's establishment of a $75 million Pennsylvania tax credit for filmmakers. In 2009, eleven movies and television shows shot in Philadelphia, resulting in $270 million in direct spending in the region. But few of these movies—*Transformers: Revenge of the Fallen* (2009), *The Best and the Brightest* (2010), *Shooter* (2007), *Unstoppable* (2010), *Paranoia* (2013)—actually used the city as a setting, instead using it as a stand-in for New York or some other vague metropolis. When the tax credits were reduced under Governor Tom Corbett to $60 million and then $42 million in fiscal year 2009–10, movies that had planned to use Philadelphia moved elsewhere.

Although the tax credits recovered from their postrecession decline, their fruits were spread across the state, and Philadelphia was not guaranteed a prime position. While Philadelphia managed to retain some role in film into the twenty-first century, its position remained a pale shadow of its promising beginnings.

The Philadelphia Story

Joanna Kolendo

The Philadelphia Story, a comedy of manners, originated in 1939 as a three-act play set in a magnificent mansion in Philadelphia's western Main Line suburbs, a location of wealth and exclusivity. Written by Philip Barry, a prolific dramatic and comic playwright, the play became a movie in 1940 and inspired a second film adaptation, *High Society*, in 1956.

The Philadelphia Story centers on an upper-class Philadelphia family, the Lords. The main protagonist, Tracy Lord, was inspired by Philadelphia socialite Helen Hope Montgomery Scott, whom Barry knew from his acquaintance during college at Harvard with her husband Edgar Scott, heir to the Pennsylvania Railroad fortune. Barry wrote *The Philadelphia Story* with actress Katharine Hepburn in mind after observing her falling star in Hollywood in the summer of 1938. Before completing the play, he met with Hepburn, studied her mannerisms, and obtained her input. With a background similar to the Tracy Lord character—she was brought up in an affluent household in Hartford, Connecticut, and graduated from Bryn Mawr College on the Main Line—Hepburn was ideal for the play.

FIGURE 95. The Philadelphia Story on stage, 1939. Katharine Hepburn (standing) also played the lead in the 1940 film of the same name. PHOTO BY VANDAMM STUDIO ©THE NEW YORK PUBLIC LIBRARY FOR THE PERFORMING ARTS.

Produced by the Theatre Guild, the original Broadway show, which premiered at the Shubert Theatre in March 1939 and continued until March 1940, ran for 417 performances. The show continued on the road for an additional two years. Besides Hepburn, the original play starred Joseph Cotten as C. K. Dexter Haven, Van Heflin as reporter Macauly (Mike) Connor, Frank Fenton as George Kittredge, and Shirley Booth as Elizabeth Imbrie.

Set during preparations for Tracy Lord's upcoming wedding, the play centers on Tracy, her family, and her fiancé, George Kittredge, a self-made millionaire attempting to be accepted into high society. The action occurs when Tracy's younger sister, Dinah, invites

C. K. Dexter Haven, Tracy's ex-husband who is still in love with Tracy, to the nuptials, and Tracy's estranged father arrives uninvited. Additional conflict arises as the Lord family discovers that *Destiny* magazine is in the process of running an article about patriarch Seth Lord's adultery. Tracy's brother Sandy Lord, editor of the *Saturday Evening Post*, solves the situation, not wholly to Tracy's satisfaction, by inviting the Philadelphia-based magazine to cover the wedding instead. Eventually, Tracy becomes infatuated with one of the *Post*'s reporters, Mike Connor, and he fancies himself in love with her. The two are from different worlds but connect on a human level as he, unlike Kittredge, sees her as a human being and not as someone to worship or to help raise his position in society. Tracy's infatuation leads to her skinny-dipping with Mike and being discovered in a compromising situation by both her fiancé and her ex-husband. Ultimately, Tracy and Kittredge break off their engagement and Tracy remarries her ex-husband.

Tracy is presented as a character full of prejudices. Both her father and ex-husband confront her about her intolerance of others' weaknesses. Her estranged father blames Tracy for being unforgiving and too critical of people, revealing the roots of the strained father-daughter relationship. Tracy's confrontation with Dexter reveals the reason behind their divorce. During their marriage, Dexter struggled with alcoholism, and he claims that Tracy did not support him, as she is unable to forgive people's flaws. Only after Tracy sees her own human weakness through her drunken actions with Mike does she forgive failure in the man she still loves.

The play also comments on the tension between social classes, demonstrates cultural distinctions between the city (represented by the character of Mike) and the country (exemplified by the Lords), and provides a dose of negative commentary on social climbers. The Main Line as represented in *The Philadelphia Story* is synonymous with wealth and old aristocracy, which in turn is associated with fashion, Old World manners and morals, debutante balls, cricket clubs, and, above all, exclusivity. In the play, the disdain of the upper crust of society toward the lower classes can be seen in Tracy and her family's dislike of reporters, whom they view as insensitive and lacking manners. On the other hand, Mike's initial attitude toward the Lords shows prejudice and dislike on the part of working-class intellectuals, who think of the rich as useless fools and parasites. Although Mike is presented as a good person, he and George are middle-class working men and as such, they cannot marry Tracy. Tracy, who must marry within her own social class, chooses Dexter, an insider born into wealth. In this, Barry shows the powerful hold of the status quo.

In addition to theater productions, *The Philadelphia Story* became a movie, also starring Hepburn. Hepburn owned the rights to the play, and as part of the agreement with MGM she played the lead and approved the director and costars. Released in 1940, the movie version of *The Philadelphia Story*, directed by George Cukor, met with great success. Joining Hepburn on the movie set were Cary Grant as C. K. Dexter Haven, James Stewart as Mike Connor, and John Howard as George Kittredge. Stewart won an Academy Award for his performance, and Donald Ogden Stewart won the Oscar for his screenplay.

The popular movie led to a second movie adaptation, the 1956 musical *High Society*. With a setting shifted from Philadelphia to Newport, Rhode Island, *High Society* featured Grace Kelly, an actual Philadelphia socialite, and, thus, a great fit for the role of Tracy Lord. This version of the film was adapted into a Broadway stage musical in 1998 but proved unsuccessful and quickly closed.

Whether in play or film format, the popularity of *The Philadelphia Story* helped Katharine Hepburn regain her stardom. Additionally, the play cemented Barry's status as a playwright of note, as a few of his earlier plays were not well received. Ultimately *The Philadelphia Story* provided audiences with a glimpse into the exclusive and aristocratic world of Philadelphia's Main Line society, a world that many would never otherwise experience.

Television Shows About Philadelphia

Megan C. McGee Yinger

The Philadelphia area has provided a backdrop for numerous television programs, including shows by creators from the region. Although the programs often were shot in other places, like New York or Los Angeles, the Philadelphia setting provided important references and details. From posh suburbs to gritty urban settings, the depictions were not always flattering, but they created an image of the city and its suburbs that reached viewers across the country.

In the early days of television, most shows were set in New York City, then the center of the television industry. It took some time for shows to be set outside New York. One of the first national programs to be broadcast from Philadelphia, *American Bandstand* (WFIL, 1952–57; ABC, 1957–87; USA, 1989), started as a local program in 1952 and went national in 1957. The legacy of *American Bandstand* continued with the 2002 drama *American Dreams* (NBC, 2002–5), which examined life in Philadelphia in the early 1960s.

Philadelphia's suburbs became a favorite setting for the intrigue and scandal of daytime soap operas. The Main Line suburbs west of Philadelphia had a reputation as a place of wealth, enhanced by *The Philadelphia Story*, the 1939 play that became a 1940 film and later the 1956 movie musical *High Society* starring Philadelphia's Grace Kelly. In combination with the nearby city, suburban neighborhoods also provided a setting of socioeconomic diversity. Two long-running soap operas, *All My Children* (ABC, 1970–2011) and *One Life to Live* (ABC, 1968–2013), operated in the same soap opera universe but took place in different suburbs. *All My Children* was set in fictional "Pine Valley," modeled on Rosemont on the Main Line. *One Life to Live*'s "Llanview," a nod to the area's Welsh background, took inspiration from Chestnut Hill in Northwest Philadelphia. The creator of both shows, Agnes Nixon, a longtime resident of the Main Line, grew up in Tennessee and provided her shows with an outsider's view of a world she came to know well. Nixon created a world that illustrated the socioeconomic diversity of the area and did not seek to whitewash the setting.

The 1980s renaissance of television drama found Philadelphia and its suburbs in the spotlight again, primarily with *Thirtysomething* (ABC, 1987–91). This program followed a group of friends through the stresses of children, career, and marriage. The "prestige drama" had a relatively small audience, but those viewers gained a new perspective of Philadelphia. Cocreator Marshall Herskovitz, a Philadelphia native, gave his characters careers at city hall and alma maters like the University of Pennsylvania and Princeton. The show depicted Philadelphia as a city with a vibrant, educated, and creative upper-middle class through characters who worked in a fictional Philadelphia advertising agency. Through the death of a main character in a car crash, *Thirtysomething* also reinforced the reputation of the Schuylkill Expressway as a dangerous place to drive.

During the 1990s, Philadelphia and its suburbs also served as settings for family sitcoms. *Boy Meets World* (ABC, 1993–2000) made references to Philadelphia sports teams, landmarks, and universities, although the city remained largely unseen and unimportant to the action. In contrast, *The Goldbergs* (ABC, 2013–23) relied on its setting of Jenkintown and its proximity to the city to tell stories. In addition to the family's love for the Philadelphia Flyers and Phillies, the show represented the city's Jewish population. Based on the childhood of creator and Jenkintown native Adam F. Goldberg, the stories required specific local institutions and landmarks, such as Veterans Stadium and the Spectrum.

Philadelphia-centered programs increasingly depicted a broader spectrum of race and class. In 1972, Bill Cosby created the cartoon *Fat Albert and the Cosby Kids* (CBS, 1972–85), which took place in the projects of North Philadelphia. In the 1990s, *The Fresh Prince of Bel-Air* (NBC, 1990–96) confronted juxtapositions of class and race as its main character, an African American teenager played by Philadelphia-born Will Smith, went to live with family in the wealthy Los Angeles suburb of Bel-Air. The show's catchy opening theme song ("In West Philadelphia born and raised . . .") established a close association with Philadelphia. In the wake of riots in Los Angeles in 1992, the show confronted issues of race in major cities in the early 1990s.

The issues of race and class continued to be analyzed on *Abbott Elementary* (ABC, debuted 2021), a mockumentary-style sitcom depicting the challenges of working in a Philadelphia public elementary school. Creator and Philadelphia native Quinta Brunson, inspired by her mother's career as a teacher, brought attention to such issues as public versus charter schools in Philadelphia and the universal challenges faced by educators. *Abbott Elementary* frequently featured places and things closely associated with Philadelphia, including the Franklin Institute, the Philadelphia Zoo balloon, and the Flyers' mascot, Gritty.

The city's gritty reputation from the 1970s and 1980s contributed to making it a backdrop for crime procedurals and dramas in the early twenty-first century. *Hack* (CBS, 2002–4) shot primarily on location in Philadelphia, but others including *Body of Proof* (ABC, 2011–13) and *Cold Case* (CBS, 2003–10) filmed elsewhere and used the city as a setting perceived to have a high crime rate. *How to Get Away with Murder* (ABC, 2014–20) used University City as its setting and created the fictional Middleton University as a composite of Philadelphia's many elite schools. The show also featured a diverse cast, reflecting the heterogeneous professional class in Philadelphia. The miniseries *Mare of Easttown* (HBO, 2021) used the Philadelphia suburbs as the backdrop for a murder investigation and drew praise for its accurate rendition of the Philadelphia-area accent.

Philadelphia-area natives who became show creators found success in highlighting their hometowns, even if the depiction was not always kind. The creator of *It's Always Sunny in Philadelphia* (FX / FXX, debuted 2005), Rob McElhenney, was born and raised in Philadelphia and attended St. Joseph's Preparatory School. The show often referred to major landmarks and institutions, such as the University of Pennsylvania and South Street. The show tended to depict the city as dirty and populated by shifty, undereducated eccentrics. This vision of Philadelphia was played to comic effect, however, and McElhenney's charity work and restaurants in the city demonstrated his affection for his hometown.

The proliferation of reality programming starting in the early 2000s also placed Philadelphia at center stage, albeit in an extensively edited way. *The Real World* (MTV, debuted 1992), which cast diverse twentysomethings to live and work together, set up in Philadelphia in a former bank building at Third and Arch Streets in 2004. As cameras recorded typical young adult angst and problems in the house, *The Real World: Philadelphia* cast worked for the Philadelphia Soul arena football team and performed charity work for the Northern Home for Children. As with many *Real World* casts, controversy followed throughout the show's filming, and an altercation between a Philadelphia police officer providing security and some off-duty officers cast the city in a negative light. *Parking Wars* (A&E, 2008–12) followed the Philadelphia Parking Authority on its daily rounds as officers wrote tickets, booted vehicles, and dealt with angry drivers. While the show also filmed in Providence, Rhode Island, and Detroit, Michigan, Philadelphia became the city most commonly associated with the program. *Cops* (Fox/Spike, 1989–2020, revived by Fox Nation 2021) and *The First 48* (A&E, debuted 2004) also shot episodes in Philadelphia.

The region's diverse depictions on television often created realistic representations of the city and reflected dominant characteristics of its people, but some programs also reinforced problematic stereotypes. Often with guidance from creators with local ties, Philadelphia became, in effect, another character on the shows set in the city and its suburbs. These depictions, in turn, attracted fans seeking to visit sites and neighborhoods from their favorite programs, leading to increased tourism and demonstrating the impact of Philadelphia's longstanding and continuing presence on television.

American Bandstand

Jordan McClain and Amanda McClain

American Bandstand (1952–89) was a massively popular music television program with strong Philadelphia roots, storied national success, and the power to shape the music industry and society. The show epitomized many important aspects of ever-evolving American popular culture: mass communication, popular music, youth culture, dance and fashion trends, as well as race and gender relationships. Particularly during the show's prime Philadelphia years (1952–63), Philadelphia youth culture became American culture through *American Bandstand*.

First called *Bandstand*, the program premiered October 6, 1952, hosted by Philadelphia radio DJ Bob Horn. Shot live from Studio B at Forty-Sixth and Market Streets, the two-and-a-half-hour show broadcasted regionally on WFIL-TV Channel 6. Via this network, which advertised itself as "WFIL-adelphia," the show reached almost six million viewers in the Delaware Valley, the nation's third-largest market at the time. Pennants from local high schools lined the walls of the production studio, emphasizing the show's local orientation to viewers and advertisers.

Dick Clark replaced Horn as host in 1956, just before the show was renamed *American Bandstand*, shortened to ninety minutes, and expanded to a national ABC audience on August 5, 1957. The show then aired at 3 p.m., Monday through Friday, corresponding with the typical school day's end. An immediate success, *American Bandstand* attracted an audience estimated at twenty million viewers.

From its earliest days, the show featured young people dancing to a rock and roll soundtrack or other popular genres of the day. Their dancing included the bop, the twist, the jitterbug, and the stroll. The show also incorporated appearances by acts like Paul Anka, Frankie Avalon, and Connie Francis, who would lip-synch performances. Being featured on the show all but guaranteed a spike in popularity and demand for a new group or single. Another component of the show was its Rate-a-Record segment—where people evaluated a record on a scale of thirty-five to ninety-eight—which originated the saying, "It's got a good beat and you can dance to it." For this era's music industry, *American Bandstand* was arguably the most significant television venue in the country.

FIGURE 96. *American Bandstand*, 1957. Dick Clark (center) hosted the trendsetting program from a studio on Market Street, Philadelphia. SPECIAL COLLECTIONS RESEARCH CENTER, TEMPLE UNIVERSITY LIBRARIES.

Throughout its Philadelphia years, the show transformed local-area teens into national celebrities. On each broadcast day the line of teens hoping to appear on the show snaked around the block. To help establish a clean-cut image, the show required teens to dress in "good taste," for example ties with suit jackets or sweaters or high-cut blouses with dresses or skirts. Clark felt such conventions helped boost the perception of rock and roll, which in the 1950s was a controversial genre often disliked by older generations.

Several teens belonged to a select group of tastemaking gatekeepers who helped monitor dress code and admission. Clark and producer Tony Mammorella dubbed this group "The Committee," led from 1954 to 1956 by future DJ Jerry Blavat. Many subsequently became celebrities (albeit temporarily), appearing in other media, receiving fan mail, and starting fashion trends. Peter Pan collars worn by many of the show's dancers—a feature of their Catholic girls' school uniforms—at one point sparked a nationwide trend imitating the look.

Arguably, *American Bandstand* both contributed to racial integration and supported segregation. The show's producers allegedly practiced discriminatory policies that excluded or limited appearances by Black teen dancers, presumably to appease advertisers. In the early years of *American Bandstand*, non-white people were rarely seen on television. However, musicians such as Chuck Berry, Bo Diddley, and Sam Cooke all made national appearances on *American Bandstand* during the late 1950s, potentially promoting racial equality and intercultural understanding.

Over the decades, *American Bandstand*'s location, air days, duration, and content changed. The program moved production in 1964 from Philadelphia to Hollywood, months after it began airing once per week. In its later years the show was challenged by the diversifying tastes of fragmented audiences. As music styles evolved, *American Bandstand* incorporated more emerging genres. Throughout its run the show featured various types of popular music, such as rock and roll,

FIGURE 97. *It's Always Sunny in Philadelphia* cast at Comic Con International in San Diego, Calif., 2013. PHOTOGRAPH BY GAGE SKIDMORE, WIKIMEDIA COMMONS.

R&B, Motown, British rock, psychedelic rock, disco, new wave, and more.

Despite changes over the years, *American Bandstand* continued to embody and represent evolutions in American music, fashion, dance, and other sociocultural norms. Its Philadelphia years were long recalled with impassioned nostalgia. Emphasizing this sentiment, Philadelphian John Oates (of musical duo Hall & Oates) said, "The show had such an impact on the music business, it set the tone and the pace for teenage style and attitude and everything else across America."

It's Always Sunny in Philadelphia

Cody Schreck

It's Always Sunny in Philadelphia, a comedy series that premiered on the FX cable television channel in August 2005, introduced a group of five friends who engaged in narcissistic and questionable schemes from their Irish bar, Paddy's Pub, fictionally located at Dickinson and Third Streets in South Philadelphia. Created by executive producer Rob McElhenney, a Philadelphia native, the show brought area landmarks and cultural references to its national audience with every episode.

McElhenney and his friends Charlie Day and Glenn Howerton shot the pilot for *It's Always Sunny* in 2005 for less than $200 with their own recording equipment. After pitching the show to FX executives and earning the support of the network, they began writing and producing the series, and together with actress Kaitlin Olson they portrayed the friends running Paddy's Pub. The dive bar, located in a fictional run-down neighborhood in South Philly, served as home base for "the gang" whose greed and narcissism fueled their schemes, which generally devolved into shenanigans for the entertainment of viewers.

Along with its local focus, the series' first season included societal commentary about issues such as racism, abortion, and gun rights. Initial reviews of the show were scathing. One critic from *USA Today* wrote in 2005, following the series premiere, that *It's Always Sunny in Philadelphia* handled issues of race and homophobia clumsily and simply was not funny. The show failed to capture a wide audience in its first season. Low viewership threatened its longevity heading into the second season, until Danny DeVito joined the cast and increased the audience. The show rose in popularity and continued to satirize sensitive topics, including the Great Recession, class discrimination, conflicts in the Middle East, the welfare system, and drug addiction. Tackling polarizing subjects head-on became the show's greatest strength. *It's Always Sunny in Philadelphia* earned four People's Choice Awards nominations and three Primetime Emmy Awards nominations. The popularity of the show even made the bar that inspired the show's

FIGURE 98. Super Bowl celebration, 2018. Flag-waving fans joined the procession up Broad Street and the Benjamin Franklin Parkway. PHOTOGRAPH BY J. FUSCO FOR VISIT PHILADELPHIA.

setting, Paddy's Old City Pub at 228 Race Street, an international destination for fans.

The opening credits of *It's Always Sunny in Philadelphia*, a compilation of scenes filmed from a car window, established Philadelphia and the surrounding area as the primary setting for every episode. Shot by Day on a digital camera while he drove through Philadelphia one night, the opening credits featured the Benjamin Franklin Bridge, Penn's Landing, Lincoln Financial Field, Swann Memorial Fountain in Logan Circle, Boathouse Row, Thirtieth Street Station, and South Street. In the life of the series, many other notable landmarks were mentioned, including the Strawberry Mansion Bridge, Citizens Bank Park, Independence Hall, the Italian Market, the Historical Society of Pennsylvania, Penn State, Atlantic City, and the Jersey Shore. The show depicted its characters as avid fans of the Phillies, Eagles, and Flyers.

By including frequent mentions of Wawa convenience stores and homages to movies like *Rocky* and *Invincible*, *It's Always Sunny in Philadelphia* brought the culture of Greater Philadelphia to national audiences. In doing so, the show engrained itself in the culture of the region.

Sports Teams (Major Leagues)

Roger D. Simon

Professional sports teams are part of the glue that holds the Greater Philadelphia region together. They are an extension of the community and carry the region's reputation and honor in intracity rivalries. To attend a great game is to participate in something larger than oneself; it might be remembered for a lifetime.

FIGURE 99. Mike Schmidt playing at Veterans Stadium, undated. With the Phillies from 1972 to 1989, Schmidt set home run records and earned admission to the Baseball Hall of Fame, which lauded him as "one of the best all-around third basemen in baseball history." SPECIAL COLLECTIONS RESEARCH CENTER, TEMPLE UNIVERSITY LIBRARIES.

BASEBALL

Until the middle of the twentieth century baseball truly was "America's pastime." Philadelphia joined in the nation's enthusiasm for the game as it evolved in the nineteenth century among amateur and semiprofessional clubs. In 1876, eight of the stronger teams, including the Philadelphia Athletics (A's), formed the National League (NL). The Athletics disappeared after one season, but in 1883 the league organized a new team, nicknamed the Phillies. Although competitive at times, the hapless Phillies suffered decades of mediocrity. Through the 2022 season they ranked third from the bottom among all teams in percentage of games won.

In 1901 the new American League included a Philadelphia franchise, reviving the name Athletics, with Connie Mack as manager. Because Mack also owned a stake in the club he was never fired and managed the team for an astonishing fifty years, although not always well. The A's were an immediate success, winning seven league championships (pennants) and three World Series between 1902 and 1914. In 1915 the Phillies, with pitching great Grover Cleveland Alexander, won their first pennant.

In the six seasons between 1910 and 1915, five World Series were played in Philadelphia, creating an enthusiastic base of fans. In 1910, when the A's won the World Series in Chicago, fifty thousand people turned out to welcome them home. Fans could walk to the ballparks then located in dense working-class neighborhoods. Beginning in 1909 the A's played in Shibe Park at Twenty-First Street and Lehigh Avenue (after 1953, Connie Mack Stadium), a concrete and steel facility that, when enlarged, seated about forty thousand. Until 1938 the Phillies played in Baker Bowl at Broad and Lehigh.

Another great A's team emerged between 1929 and 1932. Led by Jimmy Foxx, Al Simmons, Mickey Cochran, and pitcher "Lefty" Grove, the team captured three pennants and two more World Series titles. The 1929 World Series, in which the A's defeated the Chicago Cubs in five games, generated tremendous excitement. Yet, after 1915 and again in the mid-1930s Connie Mack sold his best players and broke the fans' hearts. The all-time nadir of baseball in Philadelphia came between 1936 and 1942 when, in five different seasons, both the A's and the Phillies finished in last place.

In 1950 the Phillies, playing in Shibe Park with young players nicknamed the "Whiz Kids," led by Robin Roberts, Richie Ashburn, and Jim Kostanty, won their second pennant but lost the World Series to the New York Yankees. While remaining competitive for the next few seasons the team did not come close to first place. In 1964 they appeared headed for another pennant, but shockingly collapsed at the end of the season, demoralizing fans. Meanwhile, following a national trend of teams relocating to growing cities in the South and West, the A's moved to Kansas City, Missouri, in 1954.

African Americans, excluded from the major leagues, formed their own clubs. The Hilldale Daisies, a professional team after 1917, played primarily in Darby. They won the pennant in the Easton Colored League in 1923 and 1924; in 1925 they won the Colored World Series. Their greatest player was William "Judy" Johnson of Wilmington. The Daisies folded after 1931, but a new team, the Philadelphia Stars, joined the eastern-based Negro National League in 1932, winning the league championship in 1934. Integration of the major leagues began in 1947, but both the A's and Phillies owners were deeply hostile to integration; consequently, both teams missed opportunities to sign great Negro League players. The A's rostered a Black player in 1953. The Phillies resisted until 1957 and did not field a star Black player until Richie "Dick" Allen in 1964. Both fans and even some teammates subjected Allen to racial abuse.

In 1971 the Phillies moved to the new Veterans Stadium (the Vet) at the south end of Broad Street, a multipurpose facility never satisfactory for baseball or football because it placed the fans far from the playing field. In the late 1970s, the Phillies finished first in the NL East three years in a row, and, in 1980, led by slugger Mike Schmidt and pitchers Steve Carlton and Tug McGraw, they finally won the World Series. They won the pennant again in 1983. In 1993 they surprised fans with a scrappy, rather disheveled team led by Darren Daulton, John Kruk, and Lenny Dykstra that went from last to first place in one season and almost won the World Series. In 2004 they moved across the parking lot to Citizens Bank Park, a baseball-only stadium with natural grass, where another strong team won five consecutive NL East titles and played in the 2008 and 2009 World Series, with Chase Utley and Cole Hamels, winning in 2008. In 2022 they shocked everyone, including their fans, by winning the pennant, but they lost the World Series to the Houston Astros.

FOOTBALL

Football was already deeply entrenched in American culture when a number of amateur and semipro clubs formed the professional National Football League (NFL) in 1920. Locally, two franchises played in the twenties, the neighborhood-based Frankford Yellow Jackets and the Pottsville Maroons. In 1925 the Maroons had the best record in the league, and the Yellow Jackets won the 1926 NFL championship. But declining attendance led to the Maroons moving to Boston after the 1929 season and the Yellow Jackets folding in 1931.

Philadelphia acquired a new NFL franchise in 1933, taking the nickname Eagles, the symbol of the New Deal economic recovery program. Until the late 1940s the Eagles compiled a dismal record, attracted few fans, and lost money, but then, in 1948 and 1949, a strong team won the NFL championships. In 1960, in the pre–Super Bowl era, under quarterback Norm Van Brocklin and Chuck Bednarik, the last man to play both offense and defense, the Eagles defeated the Green Bay Packers for the NFL championship before seventy-eight thousand fans at Franklin Field; they had won the hearts of the city.

In the 1950s, the public's interest in professional football increased dramatically, particularly when television greatly widened the national audience. Football, with its tightly concentrated play, was more suited to television than baseball. In the 1960s and 1970s football replaced baseball as the country's most popular professional sport. Even though the Eagles sank into mediocrity with only one winning season between 1962 and 1977, they nevertheless built an enormously loyal, sometimes fanatical base of supporters and regularly played before sell-out crowds. In the late 1970s they twice made the playoffs, and, in 1981, led by quarterback Ron Jaworski, played in their first Super Bowl, losing to Oakland. From 1971 until 2002 the Eagles played at the Vet on artificial turf considered the worst in the league and lost about as many games as they won. In 2003 they moved to Lincoln Financial Field (the Linc), a dedicated football stadium with real grass. A revitalized team played in the 2005 Super Bowl, losing to New England. In 2018, led by quarterbacks Carson Wentz and then Nick Foles, the Eagles finally won their first Super Bowl. In 2025, led by quarterback Jalen Hurts, the Eagles achieved a second Super Bowl victory by dominating Kansas City.

Attempting to cash in on the support for football, on two occasions, upstart leagues fielded short-lived local teams: the Bell (1974–75) and the Stars (1983–84), which won the 1984 U.S. Football League championship. The Soul played in the Arena Football League from 2004 to 2008 and 2011 to 2019.

BASKETBALL

Basketball, invented in 1891, spread quickly, with YMCAs, fraternal organizations, independent clubs, and local schools forming teams. The semipro American Basketball League, founded in the midtwenties, flourished in the region. The most prominent local club was the SPHAS (South Philadelphia Hebrew Association). Playing in several different leagues, the SPHAS won eleven championships between 1924 and 1945.

In 1946 a genuinely professional club, the Warriors, joined a new league soon named the National Basketball Association (NBA). The Warriors won the NBA championship in 1947 and again in 1956. In 1959 the Warriors acquired their greatest player, Philadelphia native seven-foot-one Wilt Chamberlain. But the team's association in Philadelphia ended in 1962, when the franchise was sold and moved to San Francisco.

Local investors filled the city's basketball void in 1963 by purchasing the Syracuse Nationals, moving the team to Philadelphia, and renaming it the 76ers (the Sixers), a nod to Philadelphia's fame as the nation's birthplace. The Sixers brought back Chamberlain, who in 1967 led the way to the NBA championship with arguably their finest team ever. But the Sixers traded Chamberlain in 1968, and the team went into a decline. After Julius Erving joined the club, it made the NBA playoffs in 1977, 1980, and 1982. In 1983, with the addition of Moses Malone the Sixers again won the NBA championship. Over the next forty years, with such stars as Charles Barkley and Allen Iverson they often made the playoffs but only played in the championship series in 2001.

Together with Philadelphia's pro teams for baseball and football, the Sixers drew fans to South Philadelphia, where they played from 1967 to 1996 at the Spectrum, S. Broad Street and Pattison Avenue, and then the larger Wells Fargo (formerly CoreStates) Center. Expanding its regional footprint, the team also built a training facility in Camden, New Jersey. In 2022 the owners proposed building a new arena in Center City at Eleventh and Market Streets, but residents and allies of nearby Chinatown protested vociferously that it would destroy the neighborhood.

Professional women's basketball came to the region in 1997 when the American Basketball League (ABL) relocated the Rage to the city. The Women's National Basketball Association (WNBA) began play the same year, but the new league did not have a Philadelphia team because the city already had the Rage. This left Philadelphia without a women's pro team after the bankruptcy of the ABL in December 1998. Prospects for

FIGURE 100. Wilt Chamberlain, 1967. Playing for the Sixers, Chamberlain reached for the net over Bill Russell in this matchup against the Boston Celtics. SPECIAL COLLECTIONS RESEARCH CENTER, TEMPLE UNIVERSITY LIBRARIES.

a local WNBA team club revived later with Philadelphia on a short list for an expansion club in 2025.

HOCKEY

Professional hockey arrived in Philadelphia in 1930–31, when the National Hockey League (NHL) had a local team, the Quakers, which folded after one season. In 1967 the NHL added an expansion team in Philadelphia, the Flyers. The team initially met with skepticism and few fans, but interest grew even though they did not have a winning season until 1972–73.

The Flyers earned the nickname "Broad Street Bullies" for their aggressive and intimidating play. Hockey purists were appalled; Philadelphians loved it. In 1974, led by Bobby Clarke and Bernie Parent under coach Fred Shero, they won the NHL championship, the Stanley Cup. The next day, starved for a genuine winner, two million euphoric fans turned out for the Flyers victory parade, a crowd only exceeded by the 2.5 million who cheered on the championship team the following year. In the 1979–80 season they compiled a streak of thirty-five wins and ten ties without a loss and won the conference championship. Over the next forty years they won their conference four more times, but the Stanley Cup continued to elude them. Nevertheless, the Flyers acquired an intensely loyal and dedicated fan base.

SOCCER AND LACROSSE

Philadelphia did not gain a professional soccer team until the twenty-first century, but the sport had a long local tradition of amateur play dating to British immigrants in late nineteenth century. Amateur teams, often associated with companies or ethnic clubs, formed leagues, and the region acquired a reputation as a major center of the sport. Throughout the twentieth century a number of semipro soccer teams played in Philadelphia, notably the American Soccer League Ukrainians, Nationals, and Spartans. In 1973 the Atoms joined the North American Soccer League, winning the championship in its first year but folding after four seasons. The Philadelphia Fury played in the league from 1978 to 1980. Another team with the same name played in a minor league in the 2019–20 season.

The country's first truly professional men's soccer league, Major League Soccer, began in 1996, but the Philadelphia region did not have a team until 2010 with the arrival of the Philadelphia Union, playing in Chester at Subaru (originally PPL) Park. In 2022, for the first time, the Union played in the championship series, but lost to Los Angeles.

Professional lacrosse first made an entry in the region with the Philadelphia Barrage of Major League Lacrosse. They played from 2004 through 2007, winning three league championships. The franchise

FIGURE 101. Bobby Clarke with Stanley Cup, 1975. The Flyers captured their second straight Stanley Cup championship in game six against the Buffalo Sabres. PHOTOGRAPH BY SALVATORE C. DIMARCO, SPECIAL COLLECTIONS RESEARCH CENTER, TEMPLE UNIVERSITY LIBRARIES.

FIGURE 102. Billie Jean King at the Palestra, 1978. Shown playing in the Virginia Slims tennis circuit, during the 1970s King also served as player-coach of the Philadelphia Freedoms of WorldTeam Tennis. PHOTOGRAPH BY MICHAEL J. MAICHER, SPECIAL COLLECTIONS RESEARCH CENTER, TEMPLE UNIVERSITY LIBRARIES.

folded after 2008 but was resurrected briefly in 2020. The Philadelphia Wings played professional indoor or box lacrosse from 1987 to 2014 at the Spectrum and later Wells Fargo Center. A new franchise with the same name began play in 2020.

UNDYING LOYALTIES

Nationally, team loyalty has often taken on the dimensions of a secular religion, and that has been especially the case in Philadelphia. In fact, by the early twenty-first century the Eagles fight song, "Fly, Eagles Fly," seemed to be the city's unofficial anthem. But fan loyalty also has a dark side. As early as the 1910s Philadelphia fans acquired a reputation for being unruly, and by the 1950s, raucous and rowdy behavior had become legendary. There were notorious incidents of fans tossing snowballs at referees and at Santa Claus, fighting in the stands, cheering when an opponent player was injured, and throwing objects on the playing field. Eagles fans may have been the country's most fanatical, with fights in the parking lots and vandalism to cars bearing stickers of opposing teams. For several years, the city maintained a temporary jail and courtroom at the Vet to swiftly adjudicate misbehavior. Some local commentators regarded this characterization as unfair, but fans were still known to boo their own teams. In popular culture this unbridled fanaticism was depicted in the 2012 film *Silver Linings Playbook*, in which the character played by Robert DeNiro is banned from Eagle games for fighting.

Between 1974 and 1983, when the region faced deindustrialization, labor unrest, racial tension, and a declining population, the sports teams gave people something to be proud of. The Flyers and the 76ers each played in four championship series, the Phillies finally won the World Series, and the Eagles played in the Super Bowl. The 1976 film *Rocky* depicted that difficult era and provided Philadelphia's most iconic sports hero. It tells the story of a socially marginal boxer, Rocky Balboa, who, improbably, gets an opportunity to fight the heavyweight champion. The film shows Rocky training through the gritty city streets. When he dashes up the steps of the Philadelphia Museum of Art (the "Rocky Steps") and throws his arms in the air, it reflects the city's struggle for respect.

Sports Mascots

Ed Moorhouse

The origins of the word "mascot" can be traced to France, where it was once used to describe anything that brought luck. But in the sports world, mascots are much more than good-luck charms. They are larger-than-life cheerleaders who encourage fans to root for the home team, laugh, and even have some fun at the expense of opponents. In Philadelphia, mascots have become as much a part of the fabric of sports culture as the city's teams.

Chief among all mascots in the sports-crazed City of Brotherly Love, the Phillie Phanatic became a nationally recognized symbol of Philly fandom. The Phanatic started entertaining baseball fans at Veterans Stadium in April 1978, replacing Philadelphia Phil and Phyllis, a short-lived, colonial inspired mascot duo unveiled in 1971.

Bill Giles, then chairman and part owner of the Phillies, believed entertaining the fans was as important as the game itself. Giles tasked *Sesame Street* puppet creators Bonnie Erickson and Wayde Harrison to design a "fat, green, indefinable, and lovable" mascot to represent the "fanatical" fans of Philadelphia. Famously, Giles did not think the Phanatic would catch on, and he initially refused to purchase the copyright for the new mascot. His hunch was wrong, and he later bought the copyright for $200,000. (In 2020 a legal dispute over the copyright led the Phillies to introduce a slightly altered version of the mascot, but the original Phanatic returned in 2021 after a settlement.) The Phanatic, wildly popular with the fans at Phillies home games, charity functions, and parties, became recognizable all over the world. In 2002, he was enshrined in the National Baseball Hall of Fame and Museum in Cooperstown, New York.

Other pro sports teams in Philadelphia have used mascots to lead fans in cheering as well. The National Football League's Eagles employed Swoop, a bald eagle, beginning in 1995, and used two live eagle mascots from the Elmwood Park Zoo to greet fans and provide educational opportunities on the Lincoln Financial Field concourse. The National Basketball Association's 76ers first had a large, blue, orange-haired, sunglasses-wearing monster named Big Shot, which gave way to a basketball-dunking rabbit named Hip Hop. Neither was popular with fans, and both were benched in favor of Franklin, a family-friendly blue dog with a Philadelphia founding father namesake. Franklin debuted in 2016 and was designed to represent a sense of fun and excitement at home basketball games. In Major League Soccer, the Philadelphia Union adopted Fang, a snake, as its mascot inspired by the "Join or Die" political cartoon attributed to Benjamin Franklin.

The National Hockey League's Flyers' Gritty, a furry orange creature with googly eyes, burst onto the scene in 2018 complete with a backstory that he had emerged from the Wells Fargo Center after construction disturbed his secret hideout. Although bewildering at first, Gritty was quickly embraced by the Flyers faithful, amassing two hundred thousand social media followers on Twitter within two months and attracting national media attention. The Flyers had a mascot named Slapshot in 1976, but it was discontinued, never coming close to Gritty's cult following.

Among Philadelphia's higher education institutions, mascots have been inspired by university roots, standards, and defining characteristics. Temple University's Owl has been a symbol of the school since its founding in 1884. The nocturnal bird of prey was considered ideal for a college where most students then attended classes at night. University founder Russell Conwell encouragingly advised the evening scholars

FIGURE 103. Phillie Phanatic, undated. Introduced in 1978, the Phillies' mascot entertained players and fans on and off the field. PHOTOGRAPH BY TERRY FOOTE, WIKIMEDIA COMMONS.

FIGURE 104. Gritty with his fans, 2018. The Flyers' mascot became a viral sensation. PHOTOGRAPH BY J. FUSCO FOR VISIT PHILADELPHIA.

that "the owl of the night makes the eagle of the day." Another winged mascot, Saint Joseph's Hawk, first appeared in 1956 during a basketball game at the famed Palestra. The Hawk represented Saint Joseph's motto, "The Hawk Will Never Die," as it flapped its wings throughout every basketball game.

Some mascots lacked historical accuracy but became part of university identity nonetheless. Although the Penn Quaker became the mascot of the University of Pennsylvania, the school had no religious ties to Quakerism. According to university archivists, sportswriters in the late 1800s referred to Penn athletic teams as Quakers because Philadelphia was known as the Quaker City. The Dragons nickname for Drexel University also came from the press, first appearing in a 1928 football headline. LaSalle University students' selection of the nickname Explorers in 1932 may or may not have been influenced by the error of a Baltimore sportswriter who mistakenly wrote that LaSalle was named for the famous French explorer (René-Robert Cavelier, sieur de La Salle) instead of St. John the Baptist de la Salle.

At Villanova, a campus-wide naming contest in 1926 led the university to adopt the Wildcat, meant to convey ferocious attitude, speed, agility, and alertness. Birds dominated as the mascots of choice for neighboring institutions like Rowan University (an owl, for the college's emphasis on education), the University of Delaware (a blue hen, a fighting breed popular with area soldiers during the American Revolution), and Rutgers–Camden, whose teams became known as Scarlet Raptors in 2001.

For colleges and the pros, mascots embodied team pride and good luck. In Philadelphia, where they could be seen roaming the stands at any sporting event, they became as synonymous with the city as its passionate fans.

Rocky

Laura M. Holzman

More than just a popular series of Hollywood films or the fictional prizefighter whose life and career they chronicle, Rocky became a late twentieth-century cultural phenomenon that reframed Philadelphia for local, national, and international audiences.

The movie *Rocky* premiered in 1976. Written by and starring Sylvester Stallone, the film introduced audiences to Rocky Balboa: a down-and-out boxer and debt collector from Philadelphia who gained confidence as he trained to fight Apollo Creed, the reigning heavyweight champion. Although nearly everyone in Rocky's world recognized that he was outmatched and expected him to lose badly, he held his own in a fight that lasted fifteen long rounds.

Fictional heavyweight Rocky Balboa had analogues in several actual boxers who fought during the twentieth century. Balboa shared his first name with Rocky Marciano, the undefeated heavyweight champion from the 1950s. Chuck Wepner, who famously endured fifteen rounds in a 1975 match against heavyweight champion Muhammad Ali, was later dubbed "the real Rocky." Also like Rocky, Philadelphia-based heavyweight champion Joe Frazier was hailed as a hardworking blue-collar counterpart to his rival Ali in the early 1970s.

Rocky, a low-budget production, won Academy Awards for best picture, directing, and film editing. A franchise emerged. *Rocky II* (1979), *Rocky III* (1982), *Rocky IV* (1985), *Rocky V* (1990), and *Rocky Balboa* (2006) tracked the eponymous protagonist as he persevered in the face of professional and personal challenges. The world of Rocky later expanded further, with a musical adaptation opening on Broadway in 2014 and a new series of *Creed* films (2015, 2018, 2023) focused on Apollo Creed's son.

Primarily set in Philadelphia, with many scenes filmed around the city, *Rocky* and several of the subsequent movies offered viewers both an imagined and an actual image of Philadelphia. Local viewers could take pride in seeing their city on screen, while audiences elsewhere could survey Philadelphia as they watched Rocky run past the Navy Yard, along the Schuylkill River, through the Italian Market, and up the Benjamin Franklin Parkway. Other sites that appeared throughout the films, including Laurel Hill Cemetery, Rittenhouse Square, and Broad Street near city hall, marked the setting as Philadelphia. Row houses and shops in Rocky's urban neighborhoods of Kensington and, later, South Philadelphia, represented the residential city. As the cityscape changed over the course of four decades of films, the movies documented that transformation.

In addition to their role as a backdrop to the film, some sites, like the steps in front of the Philadelphia Museum of Art, actively contributed to Rocky's story. The climax of *Rocky* occurred during a training montage when Rocky triumphantly bolted up the seventy-two steps that lead from the Benjamin Franklin Parkway to the neoclassical façade of the museum. Rocky's physical ascent demonstrated how his self-esteem had grown throughout the film. When he arrived at the top, he gazed out at the Philadelphia skyline; on his way to becoming a nationally recognized boxing star, Rocky appeared to hold the entire city in his vision. The scene's symbolism depended, too, on the museum's cultural significance. Rocky's journey from working-class Kensington to a recognizable bastion of high culture foreshadowed the wealth and cultural clout that the boxer earned as his career progressed.

The narrative of *Rocky* also overlapped with narratives about Philadelphia, its spirit, and its reputation. Rocky's ability to beat the odds and transform from an average "bum from the neighborhood" into a nationally and internationally successful boxer corresponded to Philadelphia's arc during the late twentieth century. No longer the manufacturing power of decades earlier and suffering from woes related to crime and political corruption, 1970s Philadelphia, like Rocky, was down and out. Rocky's gritty perseverance became symbolic of the spirit of the city, suggesting that Philadelphians could similarly succeed in the face of seemingly overwhelming challenges. Nationally published newspaper articles and locally generated publicity promoted this belief. As policy changes, economic shifts, and tourism initiatives began to revive Philadelphia in the 1990s, the city demonstrated that, like Rocky, it could improve its condition and reassert its national and international significance.

Rocky and Philadelphia developed a symbiotic relationship that blurred the lines between the world of the films and actual Philadelphia. Some critics expressed concern that the films' version of Philadelphia framed the city through the eyes of a white working-class protagonist at a time when racial tensions in the city ran particularly high. Critics also pointed to racism when noting that Rocky's prominence overshadowed Joe Frazier. Even so, Rocky's fictional experiences and the image of the city that grew out of the early films resonated across diverse audiences.

Running up the steps of the Museum of Art became a popular tourist activity and a recurring trope in each *Rocky* movie. By the 1990s, the museum's steps acquired a widespread vernacular title, "the Rocky Steps." In addition to reenacting the popular scene from the film, runners understood their behavior as a performance that allowed them to channel Rocky's perseverance.

In 1980, Stallone commissioned sculptor A. Thomas Schomberg to create a bronze statue of Rocky. The eight-foot, six-inch piece appeared in *Rocky III* as the city of Philadelphia's tribute to its by-then-famous hometown hero. Stallone donated the sculpture to the city and proposed installing it in the same location where it appeared in the film. While critics rejected the sculpture as not worthy of display at the museum, supporters argued that embracing the statue would give deserved recognition to the Hollywood hit that generated valuable publicity and tourism. The sculpture was moved several times over the next twenty-five years, but it spent much of that period on view outside the Spectrum arena in South Philadelphia. In 2006, the statue was permanently installed just north of the base of the Rocky Steps. There, it commemorates the character, the films, and their important reciprocal relationship with Philadelphia.

FIGURE 105. Rocky's footsteps, 2017. At the top of the "Rocky Steps" of the Philadelphia Museum of Art, a view toward Philadelphia City Hall rewards runners following in the footsteps of fictional Rocky Balboa. PHOTOGRAPH BY M. FISCHETTI FOR VISIT PHILADELPHIA.

ROCKY

EXPLORE MORE

The best way to explore Philadelphia's popular culture is to become a participant or join the audience. Digital archives and streaming services provide abundant access to movies, television, and music. To place locally set creations in national context, see works such as Robert Sklar, *Movie-Made America: A Cultural History of American Movies* (Vintage, revised and updated 1994) and Erik Barnouw, *Tube of Plenty: The Evolution of American Television* (Oxford University Press, 2nd revised edition, 1990). The image of Philadelphia, not limited to popular culture, is explored in Philip Stevick, *Imagining Philadelphia: Travelers' Views of the City from 1800 to the Present* (University of Pennsylvania Press, 1996), and Steven Conn, *Metropolitan Philadelphia: Living with the Presence of the Past* (University of Pennsylvania Press, 2006). For three examples of Philadelphia's image through controversies surrounding public art, including the Rocky statue, see Laura M. Holzman, *Contested Image: Defining Philadelphia for the Twenty-First Century* (Temple University Press, 2019).

The deep vein of deprecating humor tapped by W. C. Fields is traced by Edwin Wolf II in "The Origins of Philadelphia's Self-Depreciation, 1820–1920," *Pennsylvania Magazine of History and Biography* 104, no. 1 (January 1980): 58–73. Fields is acknowledged by a historical marker at Eighth and Market Streets, near the location of one of his boyhood jobs with the Strawbridge & Clothier department store. His early years in Philadelphia and adjacent counties are covered in Arthur Frank Wertheim, *W. C. Fields from Burlesque and Vaudeville to Broadway: Becoming a Comedian* (Palgrave Macmillan, 2014).

Philadelphia's popular music can be traced across time beginning with Oscar Sonneck, *Francis Hopkinson: The First American Poet-Composer (1737–1791) and James Lyon, Patriot, Preacher, Psalmodist, (1735–1794)* (Da Capo Press, reprint edition, 1967); Dorothy T. Potter, *"Food for Apollo": Cultivated Music in Antebellum Philadelphia* (Lehigh University Press, 2011); and Charles K. Jones, *Charles K. Francis Johnson (1792–1844): Chronicle of a Black Musician in Early Nineteenth-Century Philadelphia* (Lehigh University Press, 2006). On minstrelsy, see William J. Mahar, *Behind the Burnt Cork Mask: Early Blackface Minstrelsy and Antebellum American Popular Culture* (University of Illinois Press, 1999). Moving forward through the twentieth century, James Rosin offers an overview in *Philly Pop, Rock, Rhythm & Blues: A Look Back at the Musical History of Philadelphia* (Autumn Road, 2013), and the impact of Philly Soul is examined in John A. Jackson, *A House on Fire: The Rise and Fall of Philadelphia Soul* (Oxford University Press, 2004).

Philadelphia's early role in moviemaking is the subject of Joseph P. Eckhardt, *The King of the Movies: Film Pioneer Siegmund Lubin* (Fairleigh Dickinson University Press, 1997), and the Lubin Manufacturing Company records are in the collections of the Free Library of Philadelphia. The Greater Philadelphia Film Office (https://film.org/) maintains an online list of movies and television shows filmed in Philadelphia from 1975 to the present as well as resources for production companies and information about the industry's economic impact. On *The Philadelphia Story*, see Donald R. Anderson, *Shadowed Cocktails: The Plays of Philip Barry from* Paris Bound *to* The Philadelphia Story (Southern Illinois University Press, 2010). *Silver Linings Playbook* is based on the novel of the same title by Collingswood, New Jersey, native Matthew Quick (Farrar, Straus and Giroux, 2008). Filmmaker M. Night Shyamalan is the subject of Adrian Gmelch, ed., *M. Night Shyamalan: Interviews* (University Press of Mississippi, 2023), and Michael Bamberger, *The Man Who Heard Voices: Or, How M. Night Shyamalan Risked His Career on a Fairy Tale* (Gotham Books, 2006). On the enduring appeal of Rocky, see Michael Vitez and Tom Gralish, *Rocky Stories: Tales of Love, Hope, and Happiness at America's Most Famous Steps* (Paul Dry Books, 2006).

The iconic television show *American Bandstand* rates a historical marker at the site of its former studio, Forty-Sixth and Market Streets, and its impact and reflection of 1950s Philadelphia are examined by Matthew F. Delmont in *The Nicest Kids in Town: American Bandstand, Rock 'n' Roll, and the Struggle for Civil Rights in 1950s Philadelphia* (University of California Press, 2012). The program's influence in popular music is the subject of

John A. Jackson's *American Bandstand: Dick Clark and the Making of a Rock 'n' Roll Empire* (Oxford University Press, 1997). Host Dick Clark coauthored two accounts of the show: with Richard Robinson, *Rock, Roll & Remember* (Popular Library, 1976), and with Michael Shore, *The History of American Bandstand: It's Got a Great Beat and You Can Dance to It* (Ballantine Books, 1985). The papers of *American Bandstand* producer Lew Klein are preserved at the Special Collections Research Center, Temple University Libraries.

A membership organization, Broadcast Pioneers of Philadelphia, collects memorabilia of local programs and personalities and makes selections available online (https://broadcastpioneers.com/). Long-running *It's Always Sunny in Philadelphia* inspired character analysis in a volume edited by Roger Hunt and Robert Arp, *It's Always Sunny and Philosophy: The Gang Gets Analyzed* (Open Court Publishing Company, 2015), and popular culture scholarship by Kenneth Ladenburg in "Illuminating Whiteness and Racial Prejudice through Humor in *It's Always Sunny in Philadelphia*'s 'The Gang Gets Racist,'" *Journal of Popular Culture* 48, no. 5 (October 2015): 859–77. Paddy's Pub, the bar that inspired the show, draws tourists to 228 Race Street in the city's Old City section.

Exploring Philadelphia sports culture should begin at the complex of stadiums and arenas in South Philadelphia, where monuments to iconic athletes and moments include *Philly Special*, which casts in bronze the pivotal play call that helped the Eagles win the 2018 Super Bowl. To delve into the ways that stadiums can shape and reflect urban life, see Bruce Kuklick, *To Every Thing a Season: Shibe Park and Urban Philadelphia, 1909–1976* (Princeton University Press, 1991). Overviews of Philadelphia sports history include Rich Westcott, *A Century of Philadelphia Sports* (Temple University Press, 2001); for statewide scope, see Karen Guenther, *Sports in Pennsylvania* (Pennsylvania Historical Association, 2007). Major league baseball is the subject of Morris Levin, ed., *The National Pastime: From Swampoodle to South Philly: Baseball in Philadelphia & the Delaware Valley* (Society for American Baseball Research, 2013); for the Negro leagues, see works by Neil Lanctot, including *Negro League Baseball: The Rise and Ruin of a Black Institution* (University of Pennsylvania Press, 2004). A memorial park dedicated to the Philadelphia Stars of the National Negro League includes a marker, mural, and monument at Parkside and Belmont Avenues adjacent to Fairmount Park.

Books about the Philadelphia Eagles include Ray Didinger with Robert Lyons, *The New Eagles Encyclopedia* (Temple University Press, 2014) and Phil Anastasia, *Broken Wing, Broken Promise: A Season Inside the Philadelphia Eagles* (Camino Books, 1993). For hockey, see Jack Chevalier, *Broad Street Bullies: The Incredible Story of the Philadelphia Flyers* (Collier Books, 1974), and Jay Greenberg, *Full Spectrum: A Complete History of the Philadelphia Flyers Hockey Club* (Triumph Books, 1996). The prowess of Philadelphia-area boxers is traced by several works, among them: Gabe Oppenheim, *Boxing in Philadelphia: Tales of Struggle and Survival* (Rowman & Littlefield, 2015); Tracy Callis, Chuck Hasson, and Mike DeLisa, *Philadelphia's Boxing Heritage: 1876–1976* (Arcadia, 2002); John Desanto and Matt Ward, *Boxing in Atlantic City* (Arcadia, 2021); and James Curl, *Jersey Joe Walcott: A Boxing Biography* (McFarland, 2012). Walcott, a South Jersey native, is memorialized with an eight-foot statue on the Camden waterfront, a real-life counterpart for Philadelphia's statue of the iconic but fictional boxer Rocky Balboa.

Contributors

Stanley Arnold is an associate professor of history at Northern Illinois University and author of *Building the Beloved Community: Philadelphia's Interracial Civil Rights Organizations, 1930–1970* (2014).

William V. Bartleson is a professor of history at Moore College and Delval University. His areas of concentration are nineteenth-century American history and historical methodology.

Jacqueline Beatty is an assistant professor of history at York College of Pennsylvania and author of *In Dependence: Women and the Patriarchal State in Revolutionary America* (2023).

Jean-Pierre Beugoms is a military historian and superforecaster who holds a Ph.D. in history from Temple University.

Kelli Billings holds a master's degree in history from West Chester University, where she works in special collections. Her research centers on early printed books.

Jake Blumgart is a reporter for the *Philadelphia Inquirer.*

Seth C. Bruggeman is a professor of history at Temple University and author of *Lost on the Freedom Trail: The National Park Service and Urban Renewal in Postwar Boston* (2022).

Stephen Burciaga is a Ph.D. candidate in history at the University of Buffalo.

Will Caverly is an author living in southeastern Pennsylvania, writing about history and the outdoors. His work can be found on his website, https://willcaverly.com/.

Nathaniel Conley is a lecturer in the African and African American Studies Department at the University of Arkansas.

Vibiana Bowman Cvetkovic (Ph.D., childhood studies) is a librarian emerita of Rutgers University. She specializes in popular culture, critical-thinking skills, and intellectual honesty.

Lucy Davis is a research and digital publishing assistant for *The Encyclopedia of Greater Philadelphia.*

Michael DiCamillo has worked for the University of Pennsylvania, the Historical Society of Pennsylvania, and the Hagley Museum and Library as an archivist and librarian.

Andrew Diemer is an associate professor of history at Towson University and author of *Vigilance: The Life of William Still, Father of the Underground Railroad* (2022).

Jeffery M. Dorwart is Professor Emeritus of History at Rutgers University. He has written extensively on the community and military histories of Greater Philadelphia.

Shannon E. Duffy, Ph.D., is senior lecturer at Texas State University. Her book manuscript is titled "Defiantly Neutral: The Deep Roots of Quaker Pacifism in Pennsylvania."

Madison Eggert-Crowe has her master's in public administration from the University of Pennsylvania and is vice president of political affairs for Comcast.

Jordan AP Fansler is a professor at Great Bay Community College in Portsmouth, New Hampshire, where he uses history and archaeology to study the Atlantic world at its local levels.

Hannah Farber, an assistant professor of history at Columbia University, is the author of *Underwriters of the United States: How Insurance Shaped the American Founding* (2021).

Siobhan Fitzpatrick has worked with history organizations in New Jersey and at Valley Forge National Historical Park.

Gwendolyn Fowler is a Ph.D. student at Rutgers University, where she studies African American history. Her dissertation focuses on welfare rights in Detroit.

Tamara Gaskell is an editor of *The Selected Papers of Elizabeth Cady Stanton and Susan B. Anthony* (vols. 1 and 2, 1997 and 2000) and of *Women Making History: The 19th Amendment* (2020).

Holly Genovese is a Ph.D. candidate in American studies at the University of Texas and studies southern Black art forms as a resistance to incarceration.

James Gigantino is a professor of history at the University of Arkansas whose books include *The Ragged Road to Abolition: Slavery and Freedom in New Jersey, 1775–1865* (2014).

Patrick Grubbs is the associate dean of arts, humanities, and social sciences and professor of history at Northampton Community College in Bethlehem, Pennsylvania.

Brian Hendricks holds a master's degree in political science and is a doctoral candidate in history (early American emphasis) from Southern Illinois University.

John Hepp is Emeritus Professor of History at Wilkes University, and he writes on social, economic, and technological change in urban settings since 1700.

Lucien Holness is an assistant professor of history at Virginia Tech.

Laura M. Holzman is a professor of art history and museum studies and public scholar of curatorial practices and visual art at Indiana University Indianapolis.

Ricardo Howell works in academic affairs in arts and sciences at the University of Pennsylvania. He researches African American history, culture, and community formation.

Jennifer Lawrence Janofsky is the Megan Giordano Fellow in Public History at Rowan University and the director of Red Bank Battlefield Park.

Ann K. Johnson is Associate University Librarian for Publishing, Preservation, Research, and Digital Access at the University of Delaware.

Elise Kammerer received her Ph.D. in American history from the University of Cologne. Her interests include free Black education and the early national antislavery movement.

Michael Karpyn, Ph.D., teaches government and economics at Marple Newtown Senior High School and is editor of *Teaching the Causes of the American Civil War, 1850–1861* (2020).

Hillary S. Kativa is an archivist in the Greater Philadelphia region and holds graduate degrees in history and library science from Villanova and Rutgers University.

Daniel T. Kirsch received his Ph.D. from the University of Massachusetts Amherst and is a professor of political science at Northern Virginia Community College.

Scott Gabriel Knowles is a professor in the Graduate School of Science and Technology Policy at the Korea Advanced Institute of Science and Technology (KAIST) and author/editor of six books.

Robert J. Kodosky, Ph.D., is a history professor at West Chester University and author of *Tuskegee in Philadelphia: Rising to the Challenge* (2020).

Joanna Kolendo is an associate professor of library and information services at Chicago State University and works as a research, instruction, and electronic resources librarian.

James Kopaczewski received his Ph.D. in United States history from Temple University in 2022.

Emily Krichbaum is an Ohio-based historian who has published work on the Gray Panthers, Frederick Douglass, Elizabeth Cady Stanton, and the Older Women's League.

Stuart Leibiger, a specialist in Revolutionary, early national, and Civil War history, is a professor and history department chair at La Salle University.

Michael A. Martorelli is Director Emeritus at the investment banking firm Fairmount Partners in Radnor and a frequent contributor to *Financial History* magazine.

Jack McCarthy is an archivist and historian who specializes in three areas of Philadelphia history: music, business and industry, and Northeast Philadelphia.

Amanda McClain is an associate professor of communications at American Public University. Her research interests include reality TV, social media, and celebrities.

Jordan McClain, Ph.D. (Temple University, mass media and communication), is an independent scholar and former president of the Mid-Atlantic Popular and American Culture Association.

Steven McGrail holds graduate degrees in history and is a managing editor at Wiley. He lives with his wife and son in North Carolina.

Laura Michel holds a Ph.D. in history from Rutgers University. Her work considers the intersection of philanthropy, reform, and identity in the early American republic.

Charlene Mires is a professor of history at Rutgers University–Camden and editor-in-chief of *The Encyclopedia of Greater Philadelphia.*

Ed Moorhouse is Director of Media and Communications at Ursinus College and is responsible for a team that oversees the office's communications responsibilities.

Virginia Mulligan is a graduate of Longwood University (2019) and West Chester University (2021). She is a history graduate student at Rutgers University–Camden.

Gary B. Nash was Professor of History Emeritus at UCLA and author of many books, including *First City: Philadelphia and the Forging of Historical Memory* (2002).

Richard S. Newman is a professor of history at Rochester Institute of Technology. His current book project is "American Emancipations: The Making and Unmaking of Black Freedom, 1619–Present."

Toni Pitock is an assistant teaching professor of history and Jewish studies at Drexel University.

David Reader is a history teacher at Haddonfield Memorial High School and volunteers at the Historical Society of Pennsylvania and the Historical Society of Haddonfield.

Sarah E. Robey is an associate professor of history at Idaho State University. Robey's research focuses on the history of nuclear science and civic participation.

Martha K. Robinson, Ph.D., is an associate professor of history at PennWest Clarion University, where she teaches classes on early America and the American Revolution.

Mabel Rosenheck is the director of education and exhibition planning at LancasterHistory.

Dan Royles is an associate professor of history at Florida International University. He authored *To Make the Wounded Whole: The African American Struggle Against HIV/AIDS* (2020).

John Saillant is a professor of English and history at Western Michigan University. His work has appeared as essays, books, and edited documents since 1992.

Jim Saksa is a journalist who considers Philadelphia home no matter where life takes him.

Cody Schreck serves as Executive Director of the Ephraim Historical Foundation in Wisconsin and is a descendant of a long line of Greater Philadelphians.

Roger D. Simon is Emeritus Professor of History at Lehigh University. He is the author of *Philadelphia: A Brief History* (2003, revised edition, 2017) and has also written on Milwaukee and Pittsburgh.

John E. Smith III is a 2018 graduate from Temple University's Center for Public History. He is the archivist at the Chester County Archives.

Robert F. Smith is Provost at Valley Forge Military College and author of the book *Manufacturing Independence: Industrial Innovation in the American Revolution* (2016).

Matthew J. Soderblom is a Ph.D. student at Temple University, where he specializes in nineteenth-century American literature and frontier literature.

Jean R. Soderlund is Professor of History Emeritus at Lehigh University. Her books include *Lenape Country: Delaware Valley Society Before William Penn* (2015).

Alexandra Jordan Thelin is a fashion historian whose work combines fashion, popular culture, and art history. She works in digital marketing and communications.

Beverly C. Tomek is the author of *Slavery and Abolition in Pennsylvania* (2021).

Coxey Toogood is a historian, formerly in the Cultural Resources Management Division of Independence National Historical Park.

Andrew T. Tremel is an independent researcher and public historian at the U.S. Capitol Visitor Center.

Martin W. Wilson is Emeritus Professor of History at East Stroudsburg University. He taught United States, Pennsylvania, urban, and Latin American history before retiring after twenty-two years of teaching.

Stephanie Grauman Wolf, retired professor of history, was director of the Winterthur Program and the McNeil Center for Early American Studies.

James Wolfinger is Dean of the School of Education at St. John's University. He is the author of *Philadelphia Divided: Race & Politics in the City of Brotherly Love* (2007) and *Running the Rails: Capital and Labor in the Philadelphia Transit Industry* (2016).

James J. Wyatt, Ph.D., is Director of Programs and Research at the Robert C. Byrd Center for Legislative Studies.

Megan C. McGee Yinger earned her American studies degrees from La Salle University (B.A.) and Penn State Harrisburg (M.A., Ph.D.).

Theodore Zeman is an adjunct professor of history at Saint Joseph's University and at Penn State University Abington and author of various Civil War era studies.

Melissa Ziobro is the specialist professor of public history at Monmouth University. She served as a command historian at Fort Monmouth from 2004 to 2011.

Subject Index

B

C

F

G

H

I

J

K

L

M

N

O

P

Q

R

S

T

U

V

W

Y

Place Index

G

H

I

J

K

L

M

N

O

P

R

S

T

U

V

W

Y

Z

Biographical Index

A

B

C

D

E

F

G

H

M

N

O

P

R

S

T

U

V

W

Y

Z

Acknowledgments

This book would not be possible without the many years of effort by individuals, associations, and funders associated with *The Encyclopedia of Greater Philadelphia* project. Preliminary plans for an encyclopedia of Philadelphia were discussed at the University of Pennsylvania Press as early as 2000. Then conceived as a print volume, the idea revived during 2007 among individuals involved in commemorating the twenty-fifth anniversary of *Philadelphia: A 300-Year History* with a special issue of the *Pennsylvania Magazine of History and Biography* (October 2007) and an event at the Historical Society of Pennsylvania (HSP). *PMHB* editor Tamara Gaskell and the special issue guest editor, Charlene Mires, worked together to initiate these projects, with the cooperation of the Barra Foundation and HSP. Mires encouraged historian Gary Nash to mention the prospect of an encyclopedia as a new initiative for Philadelphia history in his historiographical essay in the special issue, a call he amplified in his featured address at the HSP event.

The University of Pennsylvania Press subsequently enlisted three Philadelphia-area scholars to serve as general editors and leaders of the project: Charlene Mires, then of Villanova University; Howard Gillette of Rutgers University–Camden, then the director of the Mid-Atlantic Regional Center for the Humanities (MARCH); and Randall Miller of Saint Joseph's University. Gillette's influence broadened the project's focus from the city of Philadelphia to the region at large. The project began in earnest in April 2009 with a two-day Civic Partnership and Planning Workshop, and public engagement continued through a series of Greater Philadelphia Roundtable discussion programs, thematic essays copublished with WHYY and the *Philadelphia Inquirer*, teachers' workshops in collaboration with public history partners, and an online invitation for nomination of topics.

In 2010, the Mid-Atlantic Regional Center for the Humanities at Rutgers–Camden became the project's home after Mires succeeded Gillette as the center's director. Guided by public input and advice from potential funders, the project evolved from the concept of a book with companion website (the model of *The Encyclopedia of Chicago*, 2004) to a digital platform envisioned as aggregating and disseminating knowledge in a variety of ways. The project grew topic by topic online, making possible the set of thematic books now published with the University of Pennsylvania Press. Readers are encouraged to visit the digital encyclopedia, https://philadelphiaencyclopedia.org/, to explore topics beyond the scope of the present volume and to read new topics as they appear.

The Encyclopedia of Greater Philadelphia TEAM, 2009–23 (CUMULATIVE LIST)

EDITOR-IN-CHIEF: Charlene Mires.

CO-EDITORS:
Howard Gillette, Randall Miller, Tamara Gaskell.

CONSULTING EDITORS:
Gary Nash, Emma Lapsansky-Werner.

ASSOCIATE EDITORS:
Carolyn Adams, William W. Cutler III, Andrew Heath, Tyler Hoffman, Hillary Kativa, Cyril Reade, Nancy Rosoff, Philip Scranton, Jean R. Soderlund, Domenic Vitiello, Stephanie Grauman Wolf.

EDITORIAL, TECHNICAL, AND EDUCATIONAL ADVISERS:
Eugenie Birch, Vibiana Bowman Cvetkovic, Richardson Dilworth, Travis DuBose, Charles Hardy, Amy Hillier, Ken Hohing, Guian McKee, Alexis Moore, Elizabeth Nash, Richard Newman, Daniel Richter, Mary Rizzo, Lori Shorr, George Thomas, Zara Wilkinson, Kathryn Wilson, Rebecca Yamin.

MANAGING EDITORS:
Donald D. Groff, Hillary Kativa (books).

PRODUCTION EDITORS:
Lucy Davis, Luther Hoheisel.

EDITORIAL ASSISTANTS:
Tia Antonelli, Lucy Davis, Joshua DiPrima, Luther Hoheisel, Hannah Lee, Mikaela Maria, Gina Torres.

COPY EDITORS:
Donald D. Groff, Lauren Cooper, Lucy Davis.

DIGITAL MEDIA COORDINATORS:
Sharece Blakney, McKenna Britton, Audrey Johnson, Scott Hearn, Jennifer Long Levy, Amy Osterhout.

ADMINISTRATIVE COORDINATOR: Sharon Smith.

RESEARCH, DIGITAL PUBLISHING, AND FACT-CHECKING ASSISTANTS:
Tia Antonelli, Kelly Banks, William Bartleson, Sharece Blakney, Brandon Borrelli, McKenna Britton, Melissa Bryson, Melissa Callahan, Vincent Cammarota, Kimberly Coulter, Amanda Cross, Lucy Davis, Joshua DiPrima, Elizabeth Eimer, Olivia Errico, Sabrina Gonzalez-Morabito, Scott Hearn, Luther Hoheisel, Fatima Ijaz, Audrey Johnson, William Krakower, Sebastian LaVergne, Hannah Lee, Joshua Lisowski, Mandi Magnuson-Hung, Mikaela Maria, Daniel Marren, Thomas McPherson, Maggie Montalto, Arthur Murphy, Andin Ncho, Darragh Nolan, Alaina Noland, Miriam Parrotto, Victoria Scannella, Nicole Skalenko, Benjamin Thompson, Gina Torres, Kevin Wakefield, Quincy Wansel, Mariam Williams, Emily Winters, Victoria Wroblewski, and additional students in publishing and editing seminars taught by Carol Singley at Rutgers–Camden.

WEBSITE DEVELOPMENT:
Azavea (Brian T. Jacobs), Roy Rosenzweig Center for History and New Media (Ken Albers), Rutgers Web Consulting Services (Ivanok Tavarez, Bart Grebowiec).

CIVIC AND ARCHIVAL PARTNERS:
African American Museum in Philadelphia, American Philosophical Society, Association of Philadelphia Tour Guides, Athenaeum of Philadelphia, Avenging the Ancestors Coalition, Camden County Historical Society, City of Philadelphia Department of Records, City of Philadelphia Mural Arts Program, Eastern State Penitentiary Historic Site, Economy League of Greater Philadelphia, Fels Institute of Government, Foundations of the Union League, Free Library of Philadelphia, Friends of Laurel Hill Cemetery, Global Philadelphia Association, Greater Philadelphia Tourism Marketing Corporation (Visit Philadelphia), Historic Germantown, Historical Society of Pennsylvania, Independence Hall Association, Independence National Historical Park, Independence Seaport Museum, International Visitors Council, Library Company of Philadelphia, National Archives–Mid-Atlantic Region, National Constitution Center, National Museum of American Jewish History, Philadelphia Consortium of Special Collections Libraries, Philadelphia History Museum, Philadelphia Museum of Art, Preservation Alliance for Greater Philadelphia, Temple University Libraries, WHYY, Young Involved Philadelphia.

FUNDERS:
Barra Foundation, Mayor's Fund for Philadelphia, Mid-Atlantic Regional Center for the Humanities, National Endowment for the Humanities, Pennsylvania Humanities Council, Pew Center for Arts and Heritage, Poor Richard's Charitable Trust, Rutgers–Camden Dean of Arts and Sciences, Rutgers–Camden Digital Studies Center, Rutgers Research Council, William Penn Foundation, University of Pennsylvania Press, and generous individual donors.